Springer Series on Behavior Therapy and Behavioral Medicine

Series Editors: Cyril M. Franks, Ph.D., and Frederick J. Evans, Ph.D.
Advisory Board: John Paul Brady, M.D., Robert P. Liberman, M.D., Neal E. Miller, Ph.D., and Stanley Rachman, Ph.D.

Michel Hersen, Ph.D., received his doctoral degree in 1966 from the State University of New York at Buffalo, and is Professor of Psychiatry and Psychology at the University of Pittsburgh. He is the Past President of the Association for the Advancement of Behavior Therapy. He has co-authored and co-edited 40 books, including: *Single-Case Experimental Designs: Strategies for Studying Behavior Change (1st edition), Behavior Therapy in the Psychiatric Setting, Behavior Modification: An Introductory Textbook, Introduction to Clinical Psychology, International Handbook of Behavior Modification and Therapy, Outpatient Behavior Therapy: A Clinical Guide, Issues in Psychotherapy Research, Handbook of Child Psychopathology, The Clinical Psychology Handbook, Adult Psychopathology and Diagnosis*, and *Handbook of Psychological Assessment*. With Alan S. Bellack, he is editor and founder of *Behavior Modification* and *Clinical Psychology Review*. He is Associate Editor of *Addictive Behaviors* and Editor of *Progress in Behavior Modification*. Dr. Hersen is the recipient of several grants from the National Institute of Mental Health, the National Institute of Handicapped Research, and the March of Dimes Birth Defects Foundation.

Cynthia G. Last, Ph.D., received her doctoral degree in 1983 from the State University of New York at Albany. Currently, she is an Assistant Professor of Child Psychiatry in the Department of Psychiatry at the University of Pittsburgh School of Medicine. Dr. Last's research interests include the assessment and treatment of anxiety disorders in children and adolescents.

Behavior Therapy Casebook

Michel Hersen, Ph.D.
Cynthia G. Last, Ph.D.
Editors

Springer Publishing Company
New York

To Victoria Hersen and Sally Mailman

Springer Publishing Company, Inc.
536 Broadway
New York, New York 10012

92 93 94 95 96 / 6 5 4 3 2

Library of Congress Cataloging in Publication Data

Main entry under title:
Behavior therapy casebook.

   (Springer series on behavior therapy and behavioral
medicine ; vol. 16)
   Includes bibliographies and index.
   1. Behavior therapy—Case studies. 2. Psychotherapy—Case studies. 3. Child
psychotherapy—Case studies. I. Hersen, Michel. II. Last, Cynthia G. III. Series:
Springer series on behavior therapy and behavioral medicine ; v. 16. [DNLM: 1. Behavior Therapy—case studies. W1 SP685NB v.16 / WM 425 B41953]
RC489.B4B43514 1985   616.89′142   85-7932
ISBN 0-8261-4670-8

Printed in the United States of America

Contents

v

Preface

The old adage "A picture is worth a thousand words" when applied to the behavior therapy enterprise now might read: "A good clinical case description is worth a dozen theoretical descriptions." We most certainly believe that this holds true for the students of behavior therapy, who grapple on a daily basis with the issues of how to conceptualize, assess, and treat their clients. We do not imply at all that a full understanding of the theoretical basis of behavior therapy is of little value. Quite to the contrary, we argue that an understanding of the foundations is requisite to performing treatment. But unfortunately, even for those of us who are steeped in the behavioral tradition, the mysteries and ambiguities of what transpires between therapist and client in the consulting room still abound. Indeed, we are struck that the academic descriptions of behavior therapy far outnumber those texts designed to give the student the real "how-to" flavor. The objective of our present *Casebook*, therefore, is to clarify for the student and fellow professional alike the what, how, and when aspects of behavior therapy.

In spite of the enormous behavioral literature, there are very few casebooks. Other than Ullmann and Krasner's *Case Studies in Behavior Modification*, published in 1965, and Wolpe's *Theme and Variations*, published in 1976, there is none more recently published that fits the description very well. However, at this time, Ullmann and Krasner's work is two decades old, and Wolpe's follows his unique theoretical perspective.

In the *Behavior Therapy Casebook* we have endeavored to be as ecumenical as possible and have invited contributors who represent a variety of operant, classical conditioning, and cognitive perspectives. The book is divided into three parts. In the first part, the editors present an overview of the clinical considerations involved in the practice of behavior therapy. Part II includes case descriptions for a variety of simple and complex adult disorders. Finally, in Part III, child and adolescent cases typically encountered are described. Throughout, references have been kept to a minimum.

In order to have a unified structure for the book, each of the case histories follows a standard format: (1) description of the disorder, (2) case identification, (3) presenting complaints, (4) history, (5) assessment, (6) selection of treatment, including the therapist rationale, (7) course of treatment, (8) termination, (9) follow-up, and (10) overall evaluation.

We first wish to thank our eminent contributors for carrying out our rather rigid instructions to the best of their abilities. Next, we extend our appreciation to Mary Newell, Kim Sterner, and Janet Twomey for their technical assistance. Finally, but hardly least of all, we thank Cyril Franks for giving us the green light on the project, and Barbara Watkins, our editor at Springer Publishing Company.

Contributors

Angelynne E. Amick, M.S., is currently completing work on her Ph.D. degree in clinical psychology at the University of Georgia at Athens. She received her master's degree in psychology in 1983 from the University of Georgia. She served her psychology internship in the Department of Psychiatry and Behavioral Sciences at the Medical University of South Carolina at Charleston in 1983–84 and has been awarded a postdoctoral fellowship within the department, beginning the summer of 1985.

Frank Andrasik, Ph.D., received his doctoral degree from Ohio University in 1979. Presently he is an Associate Professor in the Department of Psychology and Associate Director of the Center for Stress and Anxiety Disorders, both at the State University of New York at Albany. His teaching and research interests center on behavioral medicine, with a special focus on stress-related disorders and pain management.

J. Gayle Beck, Ph.D., received her doctoral degree in 1984 from the State University of New York at Albany. She joined the faculty at the University of Houston in 1984 and is currently an Assistant Professor in the Department of Psychology. Her research interests include sexual psychophysiology and clinically relevant factors in the anxiety disorders.

Gary R. Birchler, Ph.D., received his doctoral degree in clinical psychology in 1972 from the University of Oregon in Eugene. That same year, he joined the Department of Psychiatry at the University of California at San Diego and the San Diego VA Medical Center. Currently as Clinical Professor of Psychiatry and Associate Chief, VA Psychology Service, Dr. Birchler is active in clinical care, teaching, and research as Director, Family Mental Health Program, San Diego VA Medical Center.

Mary Jane Black, Ph.D., received her doctoral degree in clinical psychology from Kent State University in 1981. Since 1978, she has served in a variety of clinical capacities at St. Luke's Hospital, Cleveland, Ohio, where her particular interest is behavioral medicine. She also maintains a private practice in which communication skills and interpersonal effectiveness are special areas of concentration.

Richard R. Bootzin, Ph.D., received his doctoral degree in 1968 from Purdue University. He joined the faculty at Northwestern University in 1968 and currently is Professor and Chairman of the Department of Psychology. His research interests include sleep and sleep disorders and the role of expectancy in behavior change.

Glenn R. Caddy, Ph.D., received his doctorate from the University of New South Wales, Australia, in 1973. He holds Diplomates in Clinical Psychology and in Behavioral Medicine and presently is Professor and Director of Clinical Training at Nova University. Dr. Caddy also is Clinical Director of the Clinical Psychology Institute in Fort Lauderdale, Florida. He has practiced and published widely in the areas of cognitive behavior therapy, addictive behavior, and forensic psychology.

Joseph R. Cautela, Ph.D., is Professor of Psychology at Boston College and Director of the Behavior Modification Program. He is Past-President of the Association for Advancement of Behavior Therapy. He has published four books and over 80 articles.

Edward Dengrove, M.D., is a Diplomate of the American Board of Psychiatry and Neurology. He received his doctoral degree from the Medical School of the Royal Colleges, Edinburgh, Scotland, in 1939, and is in the private practice of psychiatry. His interests lie in behavior therapy, hypnosis, sexual disorders, medicolegal problems, and veteran psychiatry. He has written and published extensively.

Paul M. G. Emmelkamp, Ph.D., is Professor in the Department of Clinical Psychology, Academic Hospital, Groningen, The Netherlands. His research interests are the assessment and treatment of anxiety-based disorders. He is the author of *Phobic and Obsessive-Compulsive Disorders: Theory, Research, and Practice.*

Edna B. Foa, Ph.D., is currently Professor in the Department of Psychiatry at the Temple University Medical School. She received her doctorate in clinical psychology from the University of Missouri in 1970. She has written numerous articles on behavioral treatment and co-authored or co-edited three books, most recently *Failures in Behavior Therapy* (with P. M. G. Emmelkamp). She is a recipient of an ongoing National Institute of Mental Health grant to study obsessive-compulsive disorders. Her research interests include behavioral and cognitive models for treatment of anxiety disorders.

Cynthia L. Frame, Ph.D., received her doctoral degree in clinical psychology from Indiana University in Bloomington and served her clinical psychology internship at Western Psychiatric Institute and Clinic in Pittsburgh. She joined the faculty of the University of Georgia in 1982, where she is currently an Assistant Professor in the Department of Psychology. Dr. Frame's primary research interests involve behavioral approaches to child and adult psychopathology.

Alan M. Gross, Ph.D., received his doctoral degree from Washington State University in 1979. He joined the faculty of Emory University in 1979 and is currently an Assistant Professor of Psychology. His research interests are in the area of behavioral medicine and child behavior therapy.

Francis C. Harris, Ph.D., obtained his doctoral degree in clinical psychology from the University of Georgia in 1980. He has been a member of the faculty at the University of Pittsburgh, School of Medicine, Department of Psychiatry, since 1981. His research and clinical interests include the behavioral assessment and treatment of eating disorders and conduct disorders.

Joan L. Jackson, Ph.D., received her doctoral degree from the University of Georgia in 1977. She was an Assistant Professor of Psychology at Eastern Kentucky University before returning in 1979 to the University of Georgia, where she is currently an Assistant Professor. Her research interests include various topics related to pediatric psychology and the long-term effects of childhood sexual abuse.

Mary Margaret Kerr, Ed.D., obtained her doctoral degree in Special Education from The American University in 1977. For the past four years, she has served as Co-Director of the Mellon Evaluation Center for Children and Adolescents. She is actively involved in research and consultation on adolescents' school problems.

Dean G. Kilpatrick, Ph.D., received his doctoral degree in clinical psychology from the University of Georgia at Athens in 1970 and has been with the Medical University of South Carolina at Charleston since that time. He is a Professor and Director of the Laboratory for the Study of Violent Behavior in the Department of Psychiatry and Behavioral Sciences. He has been Principal Investigator on two NIMH grants and one National Institute of Justice grant studying assessment and treatment of female crime victims. He is a founding member of People Against Rape, a 10-year-old rape crisis center in Charleston.

Robert K. Klepac, Ph.D., received his doctorate from Kent State University in 1969. After three years as an Assistant Professor at Western Washington University, he joined the faculty at North Dakota State University, where he served as Associate Professor, Director of Programs in Health and Behavior, and Chairman of the Psychology Department. Since 1982 Dr. Klepac has been Associate Professor, Director of The Dental Behavior Research Clinic, and Director of Clinical Training in the Department of Psychology at Florida State University, where he continues his research into fear and avoidance of dental/medical procedures, pain, and the application of microcomputer technology to psychological research and practice.

Benjamin B. Lahey, Ph.D., received his doctoral degree from the University of Tennessee in 1970. After teaching at the University of Central Florida and the University of South Carolina, he joined the faculty of the University of Georgia in 1975, where he is now Professor of Psychology and Director of the Georgia Children's Center. His research interests include diagnostic classification, the etiology of children's learning and behavior disorders, and child abuse.

Barry M. Maletzky, M.D., received his bachelor and doctoral degrees from Columbia University in 1963 and 1967, respectively. He took his internship in psychiatry at the Albany Medical Center in Albany, New York, and took a residency in Psychiatry at the Oregon

Health Sciences University in Portland. Following a two-year commitment to the military, he entered the private practice of psychiatry for 11 years. Presently, Dr. Maletzky is Associate Clinical Professor of Psychiatry at the Oregon Health Sciences University. In 1978, he founded and currently serves as Director of the Sexual Abuse Clinic, with five laboratories and offices in the Northwest. In addition to active involvement in research on the treatment of sexual offenders, he conducts research on the biological approaches to affective illnesses.

Ronald A. Mann, Ph.D., received his doctoral degree in developmental and child psychology from the University of Kansas in 1971. He then served as Associate Chief of the Behavior Therapy Unit at Brentwood VA Hospital in Los Angeles where he designed an effective token-economy treatment program and conducted behavior therapy research. During this same period, Dr. Mann served on the faculties of the Departments of Psychology and Psychiatry at UCLA, where he taught graduate seminars in applied behavior analysis. Later, Dr. Mann joined the faculty of the Division of Child and Adolescent Psychiatry at the University of Texas Medical Branch in Galveston as Assistant Professor. He later returned to California, where he accepted a position as the Adolescent Program Director of a small psychiatric hospital and served as Assistant Clinical Professor of Psychiatry at UCLA. He has conducted research in the areas of adolescent inpatient treatment and contingency contracting. Currently, Dr. Mann is in private practice and specializes in the treatment of child and adolescent problems with an emphasis on parent education.

Marsha D. Marcus, Ph.D., received her doctoral degree from the University of Pittsburgh in 1984. She is currently an instructor at the University of Pittsburgh and is actively involved in ongoing research in bulimia and obesity.

Debra L. Mills, M.A., received her master's degree in educational psychology from the University of California, Santa Barbara, in 1981. She is currently obtaining a doctoral degree in psychology from the University of California, San Diego. Her research interests are in cognitive development and language acquisition in autistic children.

Gerald T. O'Brien, Ph.D., received his doctoral degree in clinical psychology in 1978 from the University of Iowa. He was an assistant professor in the Department of Psychology at the State University of New York at Albany from 1978 through 1983. While at Albany, Dr. O'Brien also was the Associate Director of the University's Phobia and Anxiety Disorders Clinic, and he conducted research on agoraphobia, other anxiety disorders, and anger. Since August 1983, Dr. O'Brien has been a staff psychologist at Temple University's Agoraphobia and Anxiety Program.

Pamela G. Osnes, M.A., received her master's degree in 1981 from West Virginia University. For the past three years, she has been the director of Carousel Services for Children and Families, a preschool located in Morgantown, West Virginia, which also offers consultation services. In addition to her interests in the application of contingency management skills in educational and home settings, her research interests include the development of generalized verbal control, maintenance of behavior changes, and staff training.

John C. Piacentini, M.S., is a doctoral candidate in clinical psychology at the University of Georgia. He is currently completing his clinical internship at the Neuropsychiatric Institute, UCLA Center for the Health Sciences, in Los Angeles. Research interests include conduct disorders and socialization in children and the etiology of child behavior problems.

Elizabeth A. Schaughency, M.S., is a doctoral candidate in clinical psychology at the University of Georgia. She is currently interning at the University of Oregon Medical School. Research interests include etiology of childhood psychopathology and child behavior therapy.

Laura Schreibman, Ph.D., received her doctoral degree from the University of California, Los Angeles, in 1972. She joined the faculty at Claremont McKenna College, where she remained until 1983. She is now Professor in the Department of Psychology at the University of California, San Diego. Her research interests include childhood autism, applied behavior analysis, and parent training.

Harold E. Schroeder, Ph.D., received his doctoral degree in clinical psychology from the Pennsylvania State University in 1967. He is currently Professor of Psychology at Kent State University. His research interests include applications of behavioral procedures to medical problems and emotional contributions to information processing in addition to social skills training. Dr. Schroeder is also an active therapist, dealing with a wide range of clinical problems.

Alison E. Stanley, M.A., received her master's degree in general psychology from California State University, Los Angeles, in 1981. She will soon be receiving her doctoral degree in psychology from Claremont Graduate School. Her research interests include childhood autism, stereotyped behavior, and pediatric feeding disorders.

Gail S. Steketee, M.S.S., received her master's degree in 1973 from Bryn Mawr Graduate School of Social Work and Social Research, where she is presently a doctoral student, expecting her Ph.D. in 1985. As research associate at the Department of Psychiatry, Temple University Medical School since 1977, she is presently engaged in clinical research, teaching, and treatment of anxiety disorders. Her research interests include social support networks and cognitive behavioral treatments for anxiety disordered patients.

Trevor F. Stokes, Ph.D., received his doctoral degree in 1977 from the University of Kansas. He joined the faculty at West Virginia University in 1978 and is currently an Associate Professor in the Department of Psychology and a Clinical Associate Professor in the Department of Behavioral Medicine and Psychiatry. His research interests include generalization of behavior, self-control, and verbal mediation of behavior changes.

Michael E. Thase, M.D., graduated from Ohio State University College of Medicine in 1979 and completed residency training at the Western Psychiatric Institute and Clinic of the University of Pittsburgh School of Medicine. He was chief resident from 1982 to 1983 and completed a two-year NIMH-sponsored clinical research fellowship in 1984. Dr. Thase currently is an Assistant Professor in the Department of Psychiatry at the University of Pittsburgh. His research interests center on biological and cognitive behavioral approaches to assessment and treatment of depression.

I
Introduction

1

Clinical Practice of Behavior Therapy

Cynthia G. Last
Michel Hersen

Introduction

During the past two decades, numerous textbooks on behavior therapy have appeared. Typically, the content of these books has focused
on the methods used for treating a variety of specific problems (e.g.,
systematic desensitization for phobias, social skills training for depression). Case vignettes often are utilized (to give the text a clinical
flavor), in which clients are described as having single, well-circum-
scribed disturbances that respond to treatment in a relatively brief
period of time (i.e., 12–15 sessions). Collateral or coexisting problems
are not discussed, nor are therapeutic obstacles commonly encountered
in clinical practice. The reader is led to believe that most clients are
compliant and responsible: they fill out self-report measures, follow
the therapist's directives, complete homework assignments, arrive
on time for sessions, and pay for treatment on a regular basis. Crisis
intervention is rarely, if ever, required.

  Similarly, the empirical literature on behavior therapy leads one
to believe that application of behavioral techniques is a rather simple
and straightforward task. Because journals tend to favor publishing
investigations that yield positive findings, treatment failures are un-
derreported. Moreover, since brevity is highly valued in scientific

writings (largely because of the limited space available), most researchers omit or limit discussion of problems confronted during the course of their clinical trials.

Thus, the majority of writings on behavior therapy do not convey the complexities of conducting this type of treatment in actual clinical settings (e.g., hospitals, outpatient clinics, private practice). For those of us who deliver services in one or more of these settings, it is painfully clear that clients usually present with ill-defined and multiple difficulties. Only after a relatively detailed assessment period (which often can last for weeks or even months) can the therapist begin to "translate" the original complaints into clearly defined target behaviors. Selection of an intervention also often poses a considerable challenge to the behavior therapist. Based on pretreatment assessment findings, client expectancies, historical data, and time and financial considerations, the therapist must choose the most appropriate treatment (or treatments) from a wide range of available, and demonstrably effective, procedures. During the course of treatment, crisis events, client disclosures, resistance to treatment, and/or lack of clinical response may indicate that the treatment plan needs to be changed or modified in some way. Even after termination (arriving at which usually requires many more than 12–15 sessions), clients may show complete or partial relapse and need to return for periodic "booster sessions."

The aim of this *Casebook* is to engender an understanding of the decisions and complexities involved in the clinical practice of behavior therapy. In this regard, cases detailing the treatment of a variety of different clinical problems have been included, in order to acquaint the reader with the particular issues pertinent to each. In the remainder of the present chapter, more global clinical considerations, briefly mentioned above, and current issues facing the behavior therapist will be discussed at length.

Clinical Considerations

If this chapter had been written some 20 years ago, our approach to clinical issues would be vastly different. In the earlier part of the behavior therapy movement, in the mid-1960s, the major thrust was on showing the therapeutic world how vastly superior and different behavioral approaches were in contrast to other contemporary psychotherapies. Elsewhere we have referred to this as the inevitable "breast beating" that takes place when a challenge is being posed to the reigning orthodoxy (Hersen, 1981). Even when we look at this phenomenon in its historical perspective (see Kazdin, 1978), some of the assertions of yesteryear most certainly have a comical ring.

Without belaboring this issue, let us very briefly consider some of the statements that were being made then in press about behavior therapy: (1) Behavior therapy is short-term, ranging from 10–15 sessions. (2) Removal of symptoms leads to cure of the neurosis. (3) Psychiatric diagnosis is not relevant to implementation of behavior therapy. (4) Cognitions of the client are unimportant; motor behavior is the focus of treatment. (5) The therapist–client relationship is of secondary importance; it is the technical strategy that brings about behavioral change. (6) Symptom substitution is a myth perpetrated by psychoanalysts. (7) There is no such thing as patient resistance. (8) Most behavioral techniques can be automated and implemented without the presence of a therapist.

In contrast to the above, note how two well-known behavioral clinicians (Fishman & Lubetkin, 1983) recently described changes in how they have conceptualized client problems over the 10 years of their practice:

> As clients' problems have become less circumscribed and multifaceted (this distinction may be more apparent than real—the change may be due to the way problems are currently assessed) over the decade of our practice, our own emphasis has shifted from a problem-centered, technique-oriented approach to strategies that provide our patients with more general coping capabilities. Our goals for therapy are to provide the patient with skills for exercising greater control over their (sic) presenting problems and further, to provide them with the means for both assessing and remediating problems that may arise in their (sic) future functioning. This shift in emphasis in our own treatment planning is reflected in the fact that our mean number of sessions from intake to termination has increased from approximately 22 sessions, 10 years ago, to about 50 sessions per patient currently. By way of summary, this change in the actual number of contact hours per patient can be attributed to a number of or combination of factors alluded to above: (1) the field has been modified in general, which has led practitioners to being sought out for and addressing more global problems; (2) with increased procedural sophistication in methods of assessment, practitioners are now focusing on more aspects of patients' problems and not targeting only the manifest problem; and (3) practitioners are functioning in a much more holistic way in the application of the various cognitive-behavioral approaches in a "coping skills" paradigm. . . . (pp. 23–24)

Indeed, the views espoused by Fishman and Lubetkin are akin to our own and definitely reflect the shifts in how clinical behavior therapy is carried out today. With this in mind, then, let us consider the important features of contemporary behavior therapy and the context in which they are practiced.

Assessment and Diagnosis

Throughout its relatively brief history, a major strength of behavior therapy has been the extremely close relationship between assessment and treatment (Hersen & Bellack, 1976, 1981). In controlled single-case applications in particular (Hersen & Barlow, 1976), the repeated monitoring of targeted behaviors during baseline and treatment phases has allowed clinical researchers to determine the specific impact of a given strategy. That is, the controlling effects of the treatment over the targeted behavior could be determined. This frequently has been termed the "functional relationship" by those of operant persuasion. Such precise study, of course, has led to the refinements of our technical applications for a large variety of problems presented by our clients.

In implementing the aforementioned objectives, however, behavioral clinicians have, at times, pursued very narrow objectives. In so doing, some of the broader clinical implications may have been overlooked. This especially is the case with regard to the question of psychiatric diagnosis. Earlier, behavior therapists eschewed the value of the psychiatric scheme for diagnosis, pointing to its unreliability and validity (see Hersen, 1976). However, with the advent of *DSM-III* (APA, 1980) and the inclusion of the multi-axial system, many of the original criticisms no longer held. Indeed, from a variety of perspectives, it now behooves behavioral clinicians to classify their clients according to *DSM-III* in addition to conducting behavioral analyses (see Hersen & Turner, 1984; Kazdin, 1983). This point has been reinforced in Kazdin's (1983) excellent paper entitled "Psychiatric Diagnosis, Dimensions of Dysfunction, and Child Behavior Therapy." However, the points at issue apply equally well to behavior therapy conducted with adults. Kazdin argues that

> Child behavior therapy has tended to focus on target behaviors or presenting areas of dysfunction that are often defined narrowly. Within behavior therapy there is increased recognition that narrowly defined, isolated behaviors do not reflect the breadth of therapeutic change and do not do justice to the organization of behavior . . . Within child and adult psychiatry, epidemiological research has shown that the prognosis for a given behavior or symptom may vary greatly as a function of vari-

ables that are not currently observed in immediate behavior. The data already argue for expanded assessment to elaborate dimensions of behavior and to make discriminations among children and behaviors based on other dimensions than the presenting problem. Expanded assessment and conceptualization of childhood disorders can be pursued without sacrificing the methodological approaches of behavior therapy. Proponents of behavior modification need not retreat from what might be viewed as territorial gains in the conceptual war on intrapsychic-disease versus social-learning based models of psychopathology. . . . In fact, consolidation of existing gains may only be guaranteed by expanding assessment in acknowledgement of variables empirically shown to relate to childhood problems and their treatment. (pp. 95–96)

Another important diagnostic issue is to rule out the possible contribution of a medical etiology (see Ganguli, 1983). Many psychological practitioners are painfully unaware that there are medical conditions that either mimic or lead to the production of symptoms of anxiety and depression. For example, cardiovascular disorders (e.g., mitral valve prolapse), endocrine conditions, neurological problems, and other miscellaneous conditions (e.g., collagen diseases) are all implicated in producing anxiety. Similarly, endocrine and neurological disorders, malignancies, drug-induced syndromes, and other miscellaneous conditions (e.g., electrolyte imbalance) can result in classic depressive symptoms. Finally, infections of the nervous system, tumors of the brain, epilepsy, endocrine disorders, porphyria, and drugs can induce psychotic behavior. As noted by Ganguli (1983), such " . . . patients do present themselves for psychological or psychiatric services. In order to avoid dangerous mistakes and delay in applying the appropriate remedies, a medical assessment of all clients with mental symptoms is advisable. Since the illnesses that cause these symptoms are often atypical or rare diseases, the assessment requires an expert and experienced clinician" (p. 463).

A third consideration when assessing and diagnosing clients is to determine which system or systems are to be monitored during baseline, treatment, and follow-up. Although ideally the tripartite division of the motoric, physiological, and self-report systems should be followed (e.g., as in Van Hasselt, Hersen, Bellack, Rosenblum, & Lamparski, 1979), in practice this is not always the case. As Bellack and Hersen (1985) recently pointed out, there tends to be somewhat of a discrepancy, at times, between the theory and practice of behavior therapy. However, this theory–practice distinction is less pronounced than in some of the other schools of treatment.

Depending on the setting where a given client is seen for treatment, either one of all three systems will be evaluated. In instances when greater control over the client is exerted (e.g., the inpatient setting) or when research personnel are plentiful (during the course of single-case experimental analyses), more elaborate evaluations involving expensive physiological equipment and multiple observers of overt behavior are possible. This is not the case, however, in outpatient settings such as clinics and office practices. Indeed, in the outpatient practice of behavior therapy there is extensive reliance on the client's verbal report of his or her activity (see Hersen, 1978, 1983). Furthermore, the renewal of interest in the cognitive activity of clients (Meichenbaum, 1976) once again has relegitimized the value of the self-report.

Of course, even in the outpatient setting, sources of information other than the self-report are available. Astute clinicians, irrespective of their theoretical allegiance, generally are very keen observers of the subtle nuances of change in their clients' overt responses. A grimace, nod, hostile expression, or a given gesture *all* can add tremendously to a proper assessment when placed in their appropriate context of historical issues and ongoing problems. And finally, behavioral clinicians do bolster diagnostic impressions by obtaining confirming or disconfirming information from the significant others in their clients' lives. Such information can have remarkable impact on assessment and diagnosis. We know of instances in which, despite the client's report of no progress, information from collateral informants proved to be contradictory, indicating good progress after all. And at times both the self-report and collateral sources seem to be in concert. At yet other times the client's self-report of progress fails to be confirmed by the outside observer. In each of the three possibilities, it is advantageous for the clinicians to have maximum amounts of data at their disposal. Behavioral therapy proceeds most smoothly when therapists are fully informed, thus enabling them to maximize their technical expertise.

Therapist–Client Relationship

Graduate level students (in clinical psychology and psychiatry) learning how to apply behavioral strategies unfortunately are still entering the clinical setting with a good number of misconceptions as to how senior behavior therapists operate. Some of these misperceptions, of course, can be traced to the earlier writings of behavior therapists, who underscored the technical aspects of treatment at the expense of important clinical considerations that apply to clinicians irrespective of their theoretical stance. These notions were further bolstered by the claims that under certain circumstances clinical procedures such as systematic desensitization could be applied mechanically in the absence of a therapist (e.g., Krapfl & Newas, 1969; Lang, 1969).

In our comments here, we certainly do not underestimate the critical technical innovations of behavior therapists over the years. But contrary to these earlier arguments (highlighting the techniques), experience has shown us that a "warm" therapeutic relationship with the client is mandatory for the successful application of the many facets of a given behavioral strategy. That we should be writing this at the present time is somewhat paradoxical, especially when we consider the fact that behavior therapists, in controlled clinical trials, have been rated as significantly more empathic, congruent, and supportive than their nonbehavioral counterparts (Greenwald, Kornblith, Hersen, Bellack, & Himmelhoch, 1981; Sloane, Staples, Cristol, Yorkston, & Whipple, 1975). Thus, both in research trials and in clinical practice, the myth of the cold, calculating, and mechanistic behavioral clinician should finally be dispelled.

Of the vast variety of psychotherapeutic approaches currently in practice, there is none where the full cooperation of the client is as important as in behavior therapy. In the absence of a warm and empathic therapeutic relationship, clients simply will resist carrying out all of the extratherapeutic assignments demanded of them that are dictated by the particular therapy (see DeVoge & Beck, 1978; Hersen, 1971, 1983; Martin & Worthington, 1982). Is it conceivable that without a warm therapist–client relationship that clients will (1) keep detailed records and diaries, (2) self-monitor, self-evaluate, and self-reinforce, (3) practice relaxation exercises, (4) carry out *in vivo* assertion exercises, (5) maintain behavioral contracts with family members, (6) gradually and systematically decrease addictive approach behaviors, (7) gradually and systematically decrease deviant sexually arousing approach behaviors, and (8) practice incompatible responses? The answer obviously is no! As the old song goes: "You can't have one without the other!"

But even in the most ideal therapist–client relationships the road to therapeutic success is paved with resistance (cf. DeVoge & Beck, 1978; Hersen, 1971; Martin & Worthington, 1982). There are many reasons for this phenomenon, and the astute and experienced clinician usually is able to identify the specific source of resistance. *First*, some clients (often those who have had previous therapy with nonbehaviorists) have inaccurate expectations of their role in the behavioral scheme. This, of course, requires some relearning on the part of the client and careful structuring and feedback on the part of the therapist. *Second*, a different group of clients, albeit uncomfortable with their symptoms and status, are yet more apprehensive of changing the very delicate balance (at times dysfunctional, however) that they have achieved in their lives. Paradoxically, they feel "comfortable" with their symptoms and are resistive to implementing the required behavioral changes. And when the issue primarily is interpersonal, the family or social environment may be reinforcing such intransigence. Here the therapist is faced with the most difficult task of modifying the client's erroneous cognitions in addition to altering the reinforcing consequences of the environment. The *third* group of clients who resist are the most difficult to motivate properly. In many instances, in spite of the best therapeutic alliance and technical maneuvers, these clients simply are not ready for therapy, behavioral or otherwise. They have not yet made the necessary commitment that is required to bring about behavioral change. Under these circumstances it has been tempting, in the past, to blame the therapist as an inadequate teacher. But this certainly cannot always be the case. Even if tasks are presented in the most graduated manner and the therapeutic alliance is close, we still see some failures. Experience here dictates that in some cases a postponement or holiday from therapy may be warranted. The option is always available for clients to return when they are ready or if symptoms worsen. The second attempt at behavioral intervention, then, may prove to be more fruitful.

Therapeutic Flexibility

Over the last few decades, as behavior therapy has matured out of its adolescence, behavioral practitioners have evinced greater technical flexibility and broadness in their approach to the multitude of clinical problems presented by clients (see Hersen, 1981, 1983). Such flexibility and broadness now has become apparent in a number of ways: (1) markedly increased treatment time acknowledged to achieve success, (2) greater willingness to shift therapeutic gears during the course of treatment when warranted, (3) recognition of the value of nonbehavioral considerations (e.g., the therapeutic use of catharsis), (4) judicious application of pharmacological and behavioral strategies, both sequentially and concurrently, and (5) use of paradoxical intention as a manipulative strategy when client resistance cannot be dealt with through feedback or even mild confrontation.

Let us briefly comment on each of the five issues raised above. We will not belabor the point about the need for longer term treatment for the more difficult cases that have become integral to our practices. However, we do wish to underscore how in many of these cases, not only is the treatment lengthy, but so is the follow-up period. It is not uncommon for behavioral practitioners to follow up and provide booster treatment for increasingly extended time intervals over a several-year period (see Hersen, 1981).

With regard to therapeutic change of gears, only the most unsophisticated behavior therapist would continue planned desensitization in the face of an acute interpersonal crisis reported by a client. As we have argued elsewhere, behavioral crisis intervention is quite feasible (Eisler & Hersen, 1973). In this connection, we teach our students to deal with the specific crisis when it occurs. If the therapist feels that application of the particular behavioral strategy is critical as well, it is perfectly legitimate to divide the therapeutic hour in two: one half to deal with crisis material, the other half to deal with the originally planned intervention.

Very similar to the above point is the use of catharsis. There may be times during the course of treatment when the client, as the saying goes, needs to "get something off his/her chest." Such a need may occur while the therapist is in the process of doing systematic desensitization, flooding, assertion training, or behavioral contracting. Once again, however, the therapist is well advised to stop the specifics and allow the client some free rein. Otherwise, the client will feel frustrated and may resist continuation of behavioral treatment in a passive-aggressive fashion. The issue here obviously is one of therapeutic sensitivity and timing. The correct approach at the wrong time is as useless as an incorrect approach at the right time.

The next issue concerns the use of pharmacological agents in conjunction with behavioral strategies. This should not prove to be a threat to nonmedical behavioral practitioners. We say this primarily because no medical treatment will ever be able to supplant the teaching of new skills and repertoires. But there are many instances in which use of drugs will pave the way for subsequent application of behavior therapy, such as in the case of psychotic patients whose symptomatology interferes with carrying out behavioral tasks. Also, in some instances medication will bring about more rapid symptomatic relief than behavioral treatment (such as tricyclics for depression). Here, for the client who is unable to tolerate delay, the sequential use of drugs first and behavior therapy second is recommended.

Finally, we already have documented the existence of recalcitrant clients who seem most delighted in frustrating the best efforts of their therapists. Despite all the behavioral tricks at hand, they tend to be noncompliant, failing to perform required extratherapeutic behavioral tasks. Given their resistant characterological structure, at times the careful use of paradoxical intention will serve to bring about therapeutic movement.

Current Issues

Over the years, the practice of behavior therapy has changed radically. At the very beginning of the behavioral movement, directly observable behaviors were considered to be the focus of intervention. This view stemmed in large part from the operant or instrumental conditioning model, whose principles and methodology played a profound role in the development of applied behavior analysis. More recently, however, "private events" (i.e., those that are not directly observable), including cognitions and physiological responses, have achieved comparable status and are seen as falling within the realm of behavior therapy.

Cognitive behavior modification (e.g., Mahoney, 1974; Meichenbaum, 1977) represents a major shift from traditional behavior therapy in that the focus is on modifying thoughts, rather than overt behavior. Here, specific thoughts are believed to mediate maladaptive emotional and behavioral responses. For example, anxiety reactions (as in the case of a phobic disorder) may arise from catastrophic ideation, which serves to escalate arousal and elicit avoidance behavior. Depressed affect, on the other hand, may develop as a result of negative cognition distortions about one's self and one's environment. In either case, treatment is aimed at changing dysfunctional cognitions by substituting more adaptive self-statements. Also of importance is the incorporation of behavioral experience into treatment (via *in vivo* homework assignments), since such experience may be critical to engendering cognitive change.

Similarly, physiological responses may be targeted for intervention using behavioral techniques. For sexual deviations, arousal patterns may be modified directly by decreasing or eliminating arousal to inappropriate situations or objects through the use of aversive techniques or counterconditioning procedures. In the treatment of generalized anxiety, high levels of chronic anxiety (which do not appear to be linked to any particular stimulus or set of stimuli) may be alleviated with relaxation training and/or cognitive behavior modification. In both of these instances, the focus is on modifying a maladaptive arousal pattern, rather than on the behavioral ramifications of that arousal. On many occasions, however, successful intervention in the physiological response component will have far-reaching effects, in that changes in behavior (and/or cognitions) will follow.

Even when cognitions or physiological reactions are not the primary focus of treatment, behavior therapists may monitor changes in these response systems so as to determine their relationship to behavior change. For example, Last, Barlow, and O'Brien (1984) recently examined cognitive and physiological changes during the behavioral treatment of agoraphobia. The authors found that changes in the three response components were not always synchronous. More specifically, in many cases behavioral improvement evident following treatment was not accompanied by cognitive and/or physiological improvement. That is, while clients displayed a greater ability to confront feared situations, their thoughts and heart rate revealed that they still were quite frightened.

Another way in which the practice of behavior therapy has changed concerns the number of clinicians who administer behavioral interventions in conjunction with psychoactive medication. Such a combined treatment approach may be chosen because (1) severe or life-threatening symptomatology may preclude the use of a behavioral technique alone (as in the case of a suicidal depressive or chronic schizophrenic), or (2) a combination of the two treatments may yield a better outcome than use of either alone (as in the case of an agoraphobic with spontaneous panic attacks). For these reasons, behavioral practitioners often select combined interventions for their schizophrenic, depressed, and anxious clients, among others.

Finally, we would like to point out that behavior therapy no longer is practiced exclusively on the individual level. That is, the relationship between or among individuals often is the object of attention and focus of intervention. As a result, new treatment techniques, such as behavioral marital therapy and behavioral family therapy, have arisen. Even when maladaptive interactions are not targeted directly for intervention, significant others may be incorporated into a treatment program to increase its efficacy. Inclusion of a spouse or other family member has been found to be helpful in eliminating a wide variety of adult and childhood problems, some of which include obesity, sexual dysfunction, agoraphobia, histrionic personality, separation anxiety, and oppositional behavior.

References

American Psychiatric Association (1980). *Diagnostic and statistical manual of mental disorders* (3rd ed.). Washington, DC: Author.
Bellack, A. S., & Hersen, M. (1985). General considerations. In M. Hersen

& A. S. Bellack (Eds.), *Handbook of clinical behavior therapy with adults*. New York: Plenum.

DeVoge, J. T., & Beck, S. (1978). The therapist-client relationship in behavior therapy. In M. Hersen, R. M. Eisler, & P. M. Miller (Eds.), *Progress in behavior modification* (Vol. 6). New York: Academic Press.

Eisler, R. M., & Hersen, M. (1973). Behavioral techniques in family oriented crisis intervention. *Archives of General Psychiatry, 28*, 111–116.

Fishman, S. T., & Lubetkin, B. S. (1983). Office practice of behavior therapy. In M. Hersen (Ed.), *Outpatient behavior therapy: A clinical guide*. New York: Grune & Stratton.

Ganguli, R. (1983). Medical assessment. In M. Hersen, A. E. Kazdin, & A. S. Bellack (Eds.), *The clinical psychology handbook*. New York: Pergamon.

Greenwald, D. P., Kornblith, S. J., Hersen, M., Bellack, A. S., & Himmelhoch, J. M. (1981). Differences between social skills therapists and psychotherapist in treating depression. *Journal of Consulting and Clinical Psychology, 49*, 757–759.

Hersen, M. (1971). Resistance to direction in behavior therapy: Some comments. *Journal of Clinical Psychology, 27*, 375–378.

Hersen, M. (1976). Historical prospectives in behavioral assessment. In M. Hersen & A. S. Bellack (Eds.), *Behavioral assessment: A practical handbook*. New York: Pergamon.

Hersen, M. (1978). Do behavior therapists use self-reports as major criteria? *Behavioral Analysis and Modification, 2*, 328–334.

Hersen, M. (1981). Complex problems require complex solutions. *Behavior Therapy, 12*, 15–29.

Hersen, M. (Ed.). (1983). *Outpatient behavior therapy: A clinical guide*. New York: Grune & Stratton.

Hersen, M., & Barlow, D. H. (1976). *Single case experimental designs: Strategies for studying behavior change*. New York: Pergamon.

Hersen, M., & Bellack, A. S. (1976). Multiple-baseline analysis of social-skills training in chronic schizophrenics. *Journal of Applied Behavior Analysis, 9*, 239–245.

Hersen, M., & Bellack, A. S. (Eds.). (1981). *Behavioral assessment: A practical handbook* (2nd ed.). New York: Pergamon.

Hersen, M., & Turner, S. M. (1984). DSM III and behavior therapy. In S. M. Turner & M. Hersen (Eds.), *Adult psychopathology and diagnosis*. New York: Wiley.

Kazdin, A. E. (1978). *History of behavior modification: Experimental foundations of contemporary research*. Baltimore: University Park Press.

Kazdin, A. E. (1983). Psychiatric diagnosis, dimensions of dysfunction, and child behavior therapy. *Behavior Therapy, 14*, 73–99.

Krapfl, J. E., & Newas, M. M. (1969). Client-therapist relationship factors in systematic desensitization. *Journal of Consulting and Clinical Psychology, 33*, 435–439.

Lang, P. J. (1969). The mechanics of desensitization and the laboratory study of human fear. In C. M. Franks (Ed.), *Behavior therapy: Appraisal and status*. New York: McGraw-Hill.

Last, C. G., Barlow, D. H., & O'Brien, G. T. (1984). Cognitive change during treatment of agoraphobia: Behavioral and cognitive-behavioral approaches. *Behavior Modification, 8*, 181–210.

Mahoney, M. J. (1974). *Cognition and behavior modification*. Cambridge, MA: Ballinger.

Martin, G. A., & Worthington, E. L. (1982). Behavioral homework. In M. Hersen, R. M. Eisler, & P. M. Miller (Eds.), *Progress in behavior modification* (Vol. 13). New York: Academic Press.

Meichenbaum, D. H. (1976). A cognitive-behavior modification approach to assessment. In M. Hersen & A. S. Bellack (Eds.), *Behavioral assessment: A practical handbook*. New York: Pergamon.

Meichenbaum, D. H. (1977). *Cognitive behavior modification*. New York: Plenum.

Sloane, R. B., Staples, F. R., Cristol, A. H., Yorkston, N. J., & Whipple, K. (1975). *Psychotherapy versus behavior therapy*. Cambridge: Harvard University Press.

Van Hasselt, V. B., Hersen, M., Bellack, A. S., Rosenblum, N. D., & Lamparski, D. (1979). Tripartite assessment of the effects of systematic desensitization in a multiphobic child. An experimental analysis. *Journal of Behavior Therapy and Experimental Psychiatry, 10*, 51–55.

II

Adult Cases

2

Simple Phobia

Gerald T. O'Brien

Defining Simple Phobia

A simple (or specific) phobia involves an unrealistic fear of a specific stimulus accompanied by a strong tendency to avoid the stimulus. Simple phobias are quite common in the general population, but they are seen relatively infrequently by clinicians. For the majority of simple phobics, the problem does not seem to be sufficiently severe or bothersome to warrant the time, energy, and expense of professional treatment. However, some simple phobics do experience sufficient discomfort, inconvenience, and disruption in functioning as a result of their fears to motivate them to seek treatment. Fortunately for them, a wide variety of behavioral interventions have been demonstrated to be both effective and efficient in the treatment of simple phobias. In the present chapter, the behavioral treatment of a woman with a driving phobia will be described.

Case Identification

Jodi P. was a 37-year-old married mother of two young children who had lived in the Philadelphia area all of her life. She had a Master's degree in education and was a teacher in an inner-city elementary school. Her husband was a successful businessman.

Jodi was a pleasant, intelligent, and highly verbal woman who generally appeared cheerful and bubbly. Jodi was an ideal client in that she was highly motivated to change and extremely cooperative throughout assessment and treatment.

Presenting Complaints

The client presented with a 15-year history of fears of driving, particularly when alone or with her children. At the time of the initial evaluation, Jodi drove alone only within an approximately 2.5-mile radius of her home. For example, Jodi's school was about 7 miles from her house, and she had not driven to work in more than 5 years. Instead, Jodi relied on mass transit to travel to and from work, even though this was quite inconvenient at times.

Even within her "safety zone" close to home, Jodi commonly experienced anxiety when driving alone. She avoided driving alone in heavy rain or the slightest snowfall, in traffic jams, on steep hills, and over bridges. She was frightened by any unusual engine sounds, which might be a sign of mechanical problems.

When accompanied by her husband or another licensed adult driver, Jodi was able to drive longer distances and with greater comfort. However, she typically requested her travel companion to drive if she encountered bad weather, bridges, steep hills, traffic congestion, or expressways. Jodi did not avoid riding as a passenger in a car, although she experienced mild to moderate anxiety in any of the fear-eliciting situations just mentioned. When traveling by bus, train, or taxi, Jodi always distracted herself by working, reading, or talking to avoid looking out the window.

The principal anxiety symptoms experienced by Jodi in phobic driving situations included sweaty palms, blurred vision, dizziness, loss of balance, and muscle tension, especially in her neck. When driving, Jodi frequently had catastrophic thoughts of having an accident as a result of fainting, temporary blindness (because of blurred vision), or "freezing" with fear.

Jodi did not report any other significant areas of difficulty. Her parents were divorced and her relationship with her father was strained. Her relationship with her husband was generally good. He usually was supportive and compassionate, although at times he became impatient with her driving fears.

History

Jodi had experienced several traumas associated with driving. When Jodi was young, her mother hit and injured a child while driving. Her mother never drove again. At the age of 12, Jodi was in an accident in a car driven by her father. Upon impact, Jodi went through the windshield. She went into shock and did not speak for three days. When she was 22, Jodi was a passenger in a car that was involved in a 10-car accident on an interstate highway. Jodi suffered severe injuries. She required months of physical therapy and had to wear a traction brace for her back for years.

This last accident occurred in heavy traffic near a bridge. For months after the accident, Jodi experienced nightmares of driving off or being pushed off a bridge and falling to her death. Jodi began to avoid driving alone over major bridges. Gradually, over a period of years, her fears increased and she began to avoid driving alone in more and more situations.

Within a one-year period when Jodi was 28, four members of her family died, including her maternal grandmother and two uncles. Although none of these deaths involved automobile accidents, they increased Jodi's concerns about mortality and about her own safety and that of her family. During this year, Jodi's driving phobias worsened further.

When Jodi was about 30, she was diagnosed as having hypoglycemia, based on a glucose tolerance test. One of the symptoms of her hypoglycemia was feeling faint. When Jodi had her first child several months later, she began to fear that she might pass out while driving with him in the car. Even though her hypoglycemia became largely controlled through diet, Jodi's fears of fainting while driving persisted. She continued to restrict her driving until her "safety range" was approximately 2.5 miles from home, which remained relatively stable for several years until she presented for treatment.

Assessment

Jodi's pretreatment status and the course of her phobia during and following treatment were assessed by means of clinical interviews, self-report questionnaires, and self-monitoring.

Clinical Interviews

Clinical interviews were conducted for the initial evaluation and again for follow-up assessment five months posttreatment. Although the interviews did not provide quantitative data, they did provide detailed information about the development, nature, and course of Jodi's driving phobia. Most of the information in the preceding two sections was obtained from interviews conducted during the initial evaluation and the first treatment session.

Self-report Questionnaires

Prior to the beginning of treatment at our clinic, all clients complete a battery of self-report questionnaires for both clinical and research purposes. Most of these were readministered to Jodi at a five-month follow-up assessment. Only those measures that are relevant for the present case will be described. Data from these measures will be presented in Table 2.1.

Mobility Inventory. On this inventory, clients rate on a 1–5 scale the extent to which they avoid a wide variety of situations. A rating of "1" indicates "never avoid," "3" indicates "avoid about half the time," and "5" indicates the individual "always avoids" the situation. Only the four items specifically related to driving (see Table 2.1) will be reported. Jodi's pretreatment score on virtually all other items was "1."

Fear Questionnaire. The Fear Questionnaire is a widely used, brief fear survey schedule that provides subscale scores for the client's "main fear" (for Jodi: "driving alone"), agoraphobic fears, social

Table 2.1. Pretreatment and Follow-up Questionnaire Data

Dependent Measure[a]	Pretreatment	Five-month Follow-up
Mobility Inventory Avoidance Ratings:		
Driving alone in a car at any time	4	2
Driving in a car at any time when accompanied	4	1
Driving alone on expressways	5	3
Driving on expressways when accompanied	3	1
Fear Questionnaire:		
Main fear ("driving alone"; range: 0–8)	8	1
Agoraphobia (range: 0–40)	8	2
Social fears (range: 0–40)	6	2
Blood and injury fears (range: 0–40)	5	4
Body Sensations Questionnaire (range: 1–5)	2.9	1.2

[a]On all measures, higher scores are indicative of greater avoidance or anxiety.

fears, and fears related to blood and injuries (scoring range for main fear is 0–8 and for the other subscales it is 0–40).

Body Sensations Questionnaire. This is an inventory of 17 specific bodily sensations that may be associated with fear (e.g., heart palpitations, dizziness). Respondents rate how fearful they are of each of the sensations on a scale of 1 to 5. A mean score is computed, with higher scores indicating greater fear of internal sensations.

Self-monitoring

Self-monitoring provided the most sensitive and continuous measure of change over time in Jodi's driving behavior and subjective anxiety experienced while driving. On printed self-monitoring sheets, Jodi recorded the following information about all driving she did: day of the week, date, destination and/or activity, total driving time, amount of time driven alone, maximum level of anxiety while driving (on a 0–10 scale), and total miles driven. Data derived from self-monitoring are presented in Table 2.2 under "Follow-up."

Unfortunately, Jodi did not receive the formal self-monitoring sheets until the third week of therapy. She did, however, keep some less complete driving records during the first three weeks of treatment. Jodi kept two weeks of self-monitoring data for follow-up assessment beginning 4¼ months following the final treatment session.

Selection of Treatment

The behavior therapist can select from a wide variety of intervention strategies of demonstrated effectiveness for the treatment of simple phobias, including systematic desensitization, imaginal flooding, reinforced practice, modeling, and prolonged *in vivo* exposure (O'Brien, 1981). All of these interventions share one common feature: namely, providing repeated exposure to anxiety-provoking stimuli. Such repeated exposure is presumed by most behavior therapists to be a necessary and perhaps sufficient condition for the reduction of phobias.

I took into consideration a number of factors in designing a treatment program for Jodi. First, some empirical evidence suggests that *in vivo* exposure is more effective and efficient than imaginal exposure for fear reduction (Marks, 1978). Another consideration was that Jodi was highly motivated for treatment. She expressed a willingness "to do whatever it takes" to overcome her driving phobia. At the same time, Jodi was impatient for improvement to occur. An im-

Table 2.2. Summary Data From Self-Monitoring Records

| | Assessment Period | | | | |
Dependent Measure	Treatment Week 1	Treatment Week 3	Treatment Week 6	One-Week Posttreatment	Four-Month Follow-up
Total trips driven, alone or accompanied	17	30[a]	14	18	21[b]
Total trips driven, alone	11	11	8	14	13[b]
Percentage of total trips driven alone (# of total trips/# of trips alone)	65%	37%	57%	78%	62%
Mean distance driven per trip, in miles	1.6	6.3	9.1	7.2	8.1
Mean distance driven per trip when alone, in miles	1.3	2.6	7.4	8.2	7.5
Mean maximum anxiety rating per trip (range: 0–10)	no data[c]	1.2	.4	.2	.3
Mean maximum anxiety rating per trip when alone	no data[c]	1.6	.8	.2	1.1[d]
Number of trips in which maximum anxiety > 3	no data[c]	5	1	0	1

[a]High total number of trips is partly due to five-day vacation, with frequent short trips to beach, etc.
[b]Mean number of trips per week during the two-week follow-up period.
[c]Client did not record anxiety ratings during this week.
[d]Anxiety level was inflated by one entry of "9," following near accident when another car drove through a light.

portant practical consideration was that Jodi had a car available for driving practice both during and between treatment sessions. Also, the clinic was on the outskirts of Jodi's initial "safety zone" and within close proximity were numerous driving situations (e.g., bridges, steep hills, expressways) relevant for practice during treatment sessions.

The program that I designed for Jodi included weekly treatment sessions, self-monitoring of all driving activities, training in anxiety-coping strategies, and *in vivo* exposure to feared driving situations. *In vivo* exposure involved a combination of therapist-assisted driving practice during sessions and homework assignments for driving practice between sessions. The goal of this program was to encourage Jodi to obtain as much driving experience as possible as quickly as possible and for her to be able to begin to observe improvement early in treatment.

Course of Treatment

Jodi received 10 treatment sessions. Session 1 was an extension of the initial evaluation begun previously by the clinical director and session 10 was a treatment termination session. In this section, I will summarize the course of treatment during sessions 2 through 9, during which the majority of treatment work was conducted.

Session 2

Session 2 involved the presentation of the treatment rationale, initial training in coping skills, and our first driving practice. In the treatment rationale, I emphasized the importance of learning in both the development and modification of phobias. Jodi's history exemplified how direct traumatic conditioning (being injured in two accidents), modeling (her mother's avoidance of driving following an accident), and generalization contributed to the development and exacerbation of her driving phobia. I explained that repeated, prolonged exposure to feared driving situations, with the aid of coping skills and therapeutic support, would result in the gradual decrease of her learned fears of driving. I expressed confidence in the effectiveness of treatment and encouraged Jodi to push herself as much as possible during treatment, though I assured her that I would never force her to do anything. Jodi indicated that she understood the treatment rationale and that she was willing to follow my treatment recommendations.

The anxiety-coping skills that I presented included identifying and modifying catastrophic thoughts, focusing on the present, the "rubber band" technique, and diaphragmatic breathing. Although the incremental effectiveness of such coping skills has not been established empirically, I have found that phobic clients are more willing to carry out exposure instructions if they have available to them coping skills for dealing with anxiety.

I instructed Jodi to pay attention to her thoughts associated with driving and to recognize that catastrophic thoughts (e.g., "What if I become lightheaded, pass out, and have an accident?") maintained and increased her driving fears. Jodi was encouraged to recognize that such catastrophic thoughts were unrealistic overreactions to normal physical fear symptoms that were unpleasant and frightening but not dangerous. Another technique for dealing with catastrophic thoughts and fear reactions is to focus on the present, as opposed to anticipating dreaded consequences in the future. Jodi was encouraged to use all of her senses to become increasingly aware of her moment-to-moment experience. For example, while driving Jodi learned to focus, not only on what she could see, but also on things that she experienced through touch (e.g., the steering wheel, the car seat) and through hearing (e.g., the sounds of traffic). If Jodi noted symptoms such as sweaty palms or increased heart rate, she was to recognize that they were normal bodily reactions to fear and to observe what the experience felt like *at the present moment*, rather than to catastrophize about what might happen as a result of them in the future. Jodi also was instructed to wear a thin rubber band around her wrist at all times. Whenever she identified catastrophic thoughts, she was to immediately snap her rubber band to disrupt the negative thoughts and remind herself to focus back on the present.

I also instructed Jodi in diaphragmatic breathing techniques as an additional method for coping with fear. This seemed particularly important to her, since some of the presenting symptoms (e.g., dizziness, blurred vision) could be caused by hyperventilation. Diaphragmatic breathing involves breathing through the nostrils, taking slow and regular breaths, and expanding the abdomen during inhalation without using the upper chest muscles.

Following presentation of the coping skills, we were ready to begin *in vivo* driving practice. With driving phobics, I usually begin with relatively easy driving situations and assess the client's basic driving skills as well as anxiety and avoidance. I generally instruct the client which roads to take, with the understanding that the client can refuse to follow my directions if she feels too anxious to attempt a particular driving situation. In such cases, I attempt to arrange for practice in an easier, though similar situation, so that the client can gain sufficient confidence to try the more difficult situation.

During our first driving practice, Jodi drove with me in the car first on a relatively heavily traveled state highway with numerous stop lights and a speed limit of 35 miles per hour and then on drives through a major urban park. Her reported anxiety level fluctuated from 1 to 3 on a 0–10 scale, indicating only mild anxiety. Jodi reported that my being with her in the car helped her feel more comfortable. Jodi demonstrated that she was a competent and careful driver.

Jodi's homework assignment was to practice driving alone both within and outside of her normal safety zone and to make a list of her driving goals: that is, places to which she wanted to be able to drive by herself or with her children.

Session 3

Beginning with session 3, we adopted a fairly routine format for our treatment sessions. First we briefly reviewed the previous week, with a particular focus on Jodi's self-monitoring records, and then we began *in vivo* driving practice. During sessions 3 through 6, I accompanied Jodi while she drove in her car. During sessions 7 through 9, I followed Jodi in my car while she drove ahead. I usually gave Jodi a homework assignment following driving practice.

Jodi had completed her assignment to make a list of specific driving goals (e.g., "to be able to drive into Center City, Philadelphia, via any route," "to drive to King of Prussia"). Some of these goals were used to plan subsequent treatment sessions and homework assignments.

During our *in vivo* travel work, Jodi first drove with me in the car through residential city streets to her school – the first time that she had driven there in seven years! Following the return trip via a more difficult route, I asked Jodi to drop me off in a parking lot so that we could include work on her driving alone during treatment sessions. Jodi then took a five-mile round trip alone on the state highway where we had driven together in the preceding session. This was the first time in years that Jodi had driven alone on this highway. Jodi was delighted with her accomplishments during this session and I congratulated her enthusiastically. Interestingly, despite Jodi's anticipation of much higher anxiety, the maximum level she reported during the entire session was 2. Anticipation of high anxiety and the actual experience of only mild to moderate anxiety was a trend that occurred during most of our driving practice sessions.

Jodi's homework assignment was to attempt to drive alone to school once during the week.

Session 4

Jodi had obtained a great deal of practice driving with others as well as alone during the previous week. She practiced driving alone to school once. During the trip to school, she reported a peak anxiety level of 8, with symptoms such as blurred vision, tension in her legs, and shakiness throughout her body. However, she discovered that she was able to cope adequately with this anxiety. During the return trip, her maximum anxiety was 3. Jodi was very excited about her success at driving alone to school for the first time in seven years.

During our travel work today, Jodi drove a total of 30 miles and practiced driving on two expressways and on steep hills. Her maximum anxiety level was 5, when she first drove down a steep hill with me in the car, but she used her coping skills and quickly reduced her level to 1. She then practiced driving alone up and down this hill, with no problem.

Jodi's assignment was to again practice driving alone to school and to make a list of driving situations that still were difficult for her.

Sessions 5 and 6

Jodi continued to make excellent progress during these weeks. She practiced driving frequently, including six round trips alone to school. She experienced significant anxiety during only one of these trips to school, when she briefly reached a level of 5 when her car stalled in the middle of a busy intersection. Toward the end of the last week, Jodi began to have difficulty finding time to practice driving alone due to her busy schedule involving work, caring for her children, and other commitments. This continued to be a problem periodically during the remainder of treatment.

In our travel work together, Jodi practiced driving on hills, through various Philadelphia neighborhoods, to Center City, on the Wissahickon Drive (a very winding, heavily traveled drive through Fairmount Park), and on the Benjamin Franklin Bridge (a major toll bridge connecting Philadelphia with New Jersey). Only the latter two situations evoked any anxiety for Jodi, and this anxiety was generally brief and mild (maximum of 3).

Jodi's homework assignments were to continue to practice driving alone and to arrange her schedule so that she would have time available to practice.

Session 7

For the first time, Jodi had a bad week at home with regard to driving. She experienced high anxiety (exact levels are not available; Jodi misplaced self-monitoring records) on two days driving to and from school. During the second return trip, Jodi drove in a severe thunderstorm, which was the first time since treatment began that Jodi encountered heavy rain while driving. For the remainder of the week, Jodi experienced moderate anxiety while driving, though she nevertheless continued to drive to work.

Not coincidentally, Jodi also reported experiencing stress and fatigue as a result of her husband's new business ventures, which kept him extremely busy. This meant that Jodi saw him less and had to spend time doing more chores and errands that he usually did. It is not unusual for phobias to worsen temporarily during times of external stress. I pointed out to Jodi the probable relationship between her stress at home and her increased anxiety while driving, and I reassured her that she was not having a major setback. We discussed possible ways of dealing with the added stress at home, and I encouraged her to continue to practice driving as much as her busy schedule would allow. Jodi appeared to be relieved after our discussion.

Despite Jodi's bad week, I decided to follow through on my original plan to have Jodi drive alone in her car today while I followed close behind her in my car. We drove approximately 20 miles on the local state highway. In contrast to her experience during the preceding week, Jodi experienced generally minimal anxiety during our practice, with a maximum level of 3. Jodi was quite encouraged by the success of today's driving practice.

Sessions 8 and 9

Following the previous difficult week, Jodi rebounded with two weeks of excellent progress. Jodi continued to drive to work regularly with minimal anxiety, and she obtained experience driving in other new situations. On one evening, for example, Jodi drove her entire family on a 50-mile round trip on the expressway and local roads in fog and rain. Her maximum anxiety was 3.5 for a brief period in heavy fog. Jodi marked this as a "banner day" on her self-monitoring record!

For our travel work in both sessions, Jodi practiced driving alone with me following on the Schuylkill Expressway, a heavily traveled limited access highway that Jodi freely admitted that she detested (a feeling that is shared by many local residents!). During the first session, when Jodi drove about 7.5 miles on the expressway, her anxiety level reached a maximum of 5. The following week Jodi drove 14.8 miles on the expressway and her anxiety reached 2.5 briefly when she entered the expressway. When driving alone on other local roads, Jodi experienced very little anxiety.

Termination

Jodi made rapid progress during treatment. It was no surprise, therefore, during the ninth treatment session, that Jodi requested that we taper off our sessions. Jodi felt that she had accomplished most of her original treatment goals and that she could continue to make progress by practicing regularly on her own. We agreed to meet thereafter every four to six weeks.

When we next met one month later, however, Jodi announced that she did not believe that she needed any additional treatment. She had made further progress during the preceding month and felt confident that she could continue to make progress on her own, with the assistance of her husband.

Although I felt that Jodi would benefit from three to six additional monthly treatment sessions, Jodi's mind seemed to have been made up with regard to terminating treatment at the present time. In addition, Jodi's excellent motivation and progress during treatment suggested that she would be likely to continue to work faithfully on her driving "program" on her own. For these reasons, I did not pressure Jodi to continue in treatment. I did encourage her to contact me at any time if any problems developed or if she were having difficulties working on her driving fears on her own.

Follow-Up

Follow-up assessment consisted of 2 weeks of daily self-monitoring, beginning 4.5 months after treatment ended, and administration of self-report questionnaires and a follow-up interview at 5 months posttreatment. Quantitative data obtained from questionnaires and self-monitoring are presented in Tables 2.1 and 2.2, respectively. All self-report questionnaires display improvement at follow-up in Jodi's driving fears. Self-monitoring data reveal improvement in length of driving trips and in subjective anxiety from early to mid-treatment and from that point a generally stable pattern through the end of treatment and the 4-month follow-up.

Jodi reported in the follow-up interview that she felt that she had maintained all of the progress she accomplished during treatment and that in some areas she had made some further progress. She reported no limitations in her ability to drive when accompanied, including when driving long distances, on expressways, and over major bridges. "Even if I have . . . anxiety," she stated, "it never goes above a 2.5 or 3. It's only momentary. Once I get in [the car] and driving, I'm okay."

Jodi felt that she had made some further progress in driving alone in rain and snow. Currently, Jodi had no difficulties driving in rain unless she were in a severe downpour in heavy traffic or visibility was significantly impaired. Jodi was able to drive in light, falling snow, though she avoided driving in any accumulation before plows cleared the streets and any time the roads were icy.

Although Jodi had driven alone to some previously avoided places since treatment ended, she still was restricted in her ability to drive alone. She had not traveled much more than 10 miles from her home alone, nor had she been alone on expressways or across any major bridges. Jodi had not yet accomplished a number of goals for driving alone and with her children that she had set for herself toward the end of therapy, but she blamed this more on lack of time and opportunity than on avoidance due to fear.

Indeed, Jodi reported being extremely pleased with her accomplishments made during treatment and with her ability to maintain and partially extend her progress following the end of treatment. Jodi also found that her coping skills generalized to other specific situations that were difficult for her in the past, such as parent–teacher conferences and faculty meetings. This was an unexpected, added benefit of treatment to Jodi.

Overall Evaluation

Overall, the treatment program was a big success. Over a relatively short period of time and in only 10 treatment sessions, Jodi made tremendous progress in overcoming her driving phobia. Treatment reduced Jodi's subjective anxiety and avoidance of driving and markedly increased her mobility.

One of the most surprising aspects of treatment was Jodi's generally low level of subjective anxiety during driving practice. Prior to treatment, Jodi had avoided for years driving alone outside of her narrow safety zone, for fear of experiencing panic attacks and even worse catastrophes. However, as soon as Jodi started to venture beyond her safety zone, she discovered that generally she was much less anxious in various driving situations than she had anticipated. Even when Jodi did experience anxiety while driving, she was able to remain in the situation and manage her anxiety by using the coping skills, which she had learned well.

Undoubtedly, Jodi's rapid progress was greatly facilitated by her driving practice between sessions, which greatly increased the amount of exposure to driving stimuli that Jodi obtained. Indeed, Jodi's progress in treatment began to level off at about the time that she began to have difficulty finding time to practice driving alone.

Treatment was not an unqualified success. Even though Jodi expressed great satisfaction with her progress and accomplishments, there was considerable room for further improvement in Jodi's ability to drive alone. This was a case in which the therapist's expectations appeared to be higher than the client's! Jodi planned to continue working on her phobia on her own following treatment termination. However, the progress that Jodi did make during the follow-up period was small and was accomplished in an unstructured fashion, depending upon driving situations that happened to come up. Continued supervised and structured practice almost certainly would have enabled Jodi to make even further progress.

References

Marks, I. M. (1978). Behavioral psychotherapy of adult neurosis. In A. E. Bergin & S. Garfield (Eds.), *Handbook of psychotherapy and behavior change*. New York: Wiley.

O'Brien, G. T. (1981). Clinical treatment of specific phobias. In M. Mavissakalian & D. H. Barlow (Eds.), *Phobia: Psychological and pharmacological treatment*. New York: Guilford Press.

3

Agoraphobia

Gail S. Steketee
Edna B. Foa

Description of the Syndrome

Agoraphobia is characterized by a predominant fear of being alone or in public places in which the afflicted individual feels that escape to safety will be difficult. Commonly feared external situations include crowds, enclosed spaces such as elevators or tunnels, theaters, restaurants, shopping malls, department stores and churches, traveling on public transport such as buses and trains, driving on expressways or one-way streets, standing in lines, and sitting in the dentist's or hairdresser's chair. Anxiety in these circumstances tends to be lower in the presence of a trusted companion and higher when alone, far from home, in unfamiliar situations, and when the anticipated stay is lengthy.

Commonly, such situations are feared and avoided because of their association with the possibility of a panic attack. Panic typically involves rapid heart beat, shortness of breath, hyperventilation, dizziness, feelings of faintness, tingling sensations, weakness in the legs, waves of warmth, and feelings of unreality or depersonalization. The agoraphobic fears that such internal bodily sensations will precipitate physical and/or psychological catastrophes. These may include loss of control of bodily functions (e.g., urination), fainting, having a heart

Preparation of this chapter was supported in part by NIMH grant #31634 awarded to the second author.

attack or stroke which leads to debilitation or death, as well as insanity or lesser variants such as screaming or creating a public scene which engenders ridicule or loss of others' respect.

Another feature of agoraphobia is extensive avoidance of external situations in an effort to minimize the likelihood that a panic attack will occur. Avoidance can range from complete refusal to leave home to participation in all normal activities in the company of a "safe" person or under special restrictions, such as grocery shopping at uncrowded times or going to movies but sitting near the exit.

The sources of fear and avoidance may be internal physical cues with thoughts of future catastrophes or external situations that the agoraphobic construes as likely to provoke a panic attack. The spiral effect of fear of fear is depicted in Figure 3.1. As can be seen, external situations (e.g., crowded supermarkets) lead to sensations of anxiety with accompanying anticipations of future harm (e.g., heart attack), which further increases anxiety and the physiological sensations that characterize it (e.g., heart palpitations), leading to greater fears of harm, and ultimately to a panic attack.

The following case history is illustrative of the symptoms of agoraphobia. Methods for assessment of symptoms, selection and implementation of appropriate treatment, and follow-up evaluation for the individual are described below.

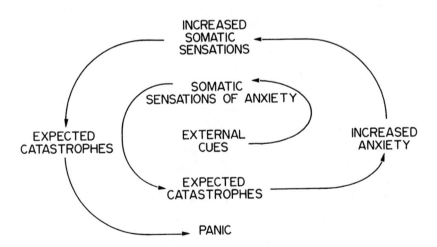

Figure 3.1. Spiral effect of fear of fear.

Case Identification

Margaret was a 52-year-old Irish Catholic housewife who sought treatment for debilitating fears of driving and of leaving home alone, and increasing restriction of daily activities and social contacts. Quite embarrassed by her "ridiculous" fears, she came to treatment at the urging of her youngest son, age 25, then a first-year graduate student, who was receiving behavioral therapy for moderately severe but not incapacitating compulsive ordering and checking rituals. He was pleased with the outcome of his own treatment and convinced his mother to apply to the outpatient clinic. She had not sought help previously except to obtain medication for "nerves" from her family doctor. Although patients with this disorder typically delay their search for treatment many years beyond its disabling effects, with her 20-year symptom history, Margaret had waited longer than most.

Presenting Complaints

Margaret reported that she was able to walk to the stores in her neighborhood two blocks away but preferred to go in the company of her husband or two sons. She was unable to drive under any circumstances. The fear of driving had begun with the onset of agoraphobic symptoms. It initially led to only partial restrictions; she could travel local roads but was unable to drive on expressways. This fear had become exacerbated 15 years later after her son Tom had a serious car accident in which his fiancée was killed and he suffered brain damage which impaired his memory and reduced his intellectual capacity from above average to mildly retarded. Following the accident, Margaret became unable to drive at all and also was fearful sitting in the passenger's seat, although she tolerated this discomfort.

In addition to the restrictions in mobility, Margaret also avoided theaters and potentially crowded locations, such as local stores on Saturday and shopping malls. Although she continued to go to mass regularly, she sat in the last row near the aisle closest to the exit. Margaret had taken public transportation infrequently (e.g., to get to doctor's appointments), but avoided it when possible. Surprisingly, in a recent trip to New York City with her husband and two close friends, she toured the city alone with little anxiety. She attributed this ability to a general feeling of confidence and enjoyment of a rare vacation. By contrast, she had avoided going to the New Jersey shore with her family for vacations. Such inconsistencies are typical of many agoraphobics, who report that on "good" days they are able to move about with little or no fear, whereas on "bad" days their general apprehension prohibits them from leaving home altogether.

Margaret attributed her travel limitations to fears of becoming panicky. These fears were accompanied by panting, severe dizziness and lightheadedness, weakness in her legs, feelings of faintness accompanied by a pressure in her head like a headache, and concomitant confusion and disorientation. She also feared an inability to breathe and was concerned that she might pass out in public and that others would notice her difficulty and would think she was having a "nervous breakdown."

History

Margaret's fears had begun 20 years earlier following two distinct experiences. The first occurred while driving alone; she felt extremely dizzy, pulled over, and after a delay of a few minutes, during which she worried about the possibility of an accident, she drove home resolving that she should see her doctor for a checkup. A medical examination yielded no evidence of a physical problem. Nevertheless, Margaret started to drive more cautiously and less often than before. The second experience occurred a few weeks later, when she had her first panic attack in a large department store. The predominant feeling was of dizziness and shortness of breath. She returned home immediately and again sought help from her family physician, who prescribed a tricyclic antidepressant drug and butisol, a barbiturate that he suggested would be helpful for her dizziness.

An inquiry by the therapist regarding other important events at the time of onset led Margaret to wonder about a possible relationship between her heightened anxiety and the birth of the last of her seven children. In previous pregnancies she had experienced periodic brief dizzy spells, which on one occasion led to a one-week hospitalization for observation. She also suffered postpartum depression for a period of a few weeks after two of her deliveries. During one of these episodes Margaret recalled being left alone in the hospital room at the end of visiting hours and feeling a strong fear that the hospital room would cave in on her. She did not discuss this with anyone at the time. Although she speculated during the first interview that she may have felt trapped by the prospect of taking care of so many children, Margaret was uncertain that she actually felt this at the time of onset of her symptoms. Her experience, like that of many agoraphobics, was that the sensations "came out of the blue."

Margaret's present household consisted of her husband, John, 55, and two sons, Pat, 19, and Tom, 28, who had suffered brain damage from the auto accident. She described the relationships in the household as functioning smoothly with only minor tensions (for example, over scheduling of car use) occurring once every week or two. She felt emotionally close to all of her seven children who ranged in age from 19 to 33, although only two lived in the same city. She enjoyed them despite the restrictions imposed by her agoraphobia and wondered whether having such a large family hadn't made it easier for her to avoid coping with nonfamily social settings.

With her husband John, Margaret experienced greater tension than with her children. The manager of a business office for the past 20 years, John "loved the children" and was "a good father." While direct conflict with John was rare, Margaret was unhappy about the absence of any sexual relationship with him for the past seven years due to his inability to maintain an erection. Sexual difficulties had begun early in their marriage. Periodic performance problems had gradually increased until John became more uncomfortable and avoided sex more frequently; their last effort at intercourse had taken place seven years earlier. The affection that John had continued to demonstrate with hugs and kisses had decreased in recent years. Margaret attributed this to the agitation and depression they both felt after Tom's auto accident and lengthy hospitalization five years earlier. While Margaret felt frustrated by the lack of affection and expressed some interest in sex therapy, she saw no connection between the onset of the sexual problem, its psychological effects on her, and the agoraphobia symptoms.

Margaret had suffered from an ulcer of some 20 years' duration which produced mild discomfort or pain once or twice a year. Previous medical problems included a hiatal hernia two years earlier, appendicitis at age 15, and a tubal pregnancy at age 33, all of which had necessitated surgical interventions which had proceeded without complications. A recent test for glucose tolerance was negative.

Assessment

Margaret's presenting fears were assessed in two ways: (1) subjective report of fear and avoidance via interview and standardized questionnaires, and (2) behavioral recordings of travel restrictions.

Subjective Report

During the first interview, Margaret was taught the use of the SUDs (Subjective Units of Disturbance scale) (Wolpe, 1958) and was asked to apply this to her feared situations. On this scale, zero was designated "no discomfort, completely at ease" and 100 represented "the most anxious you have ever felt." To the therapist's question "What would be the most difficult situation for you and how upset would it make you?", Margaret responded with the following list: driving alone on expressways, 100; driving alone on city streets, 90; sitting unaccompanied in church midway up the aisle, 90; standing in line at the supermarket or at the bank, 75; traveling alone by city bus, 80; shopping alone in a department store on the first floor, 50; shopping alone in a department store on upper floors, 70; eating in a restaurant accompanied, 30; attending a party at her children's or friend's house, 20. This list provided the basis for the treatment program.

Margaret also was asked to complete a modified version of the Avoidance Behavior Inventory (Chambless, 1982a) which lists 26 situations (e.g., riding in trains, staying home alone) and requests ratings of the degree of avoidance when accompanied and when alone on a zero to four scale. Out of a possible score of 104, Margaret's total avoidance score was 58 when accompanied and 82 when alone.

In addition to this measure, Margaret also completed the Bodily Sensations Questionnaire (Chambless, 1982b), which measures the degree of breath, wobbly legs), rated from 1 ("not frightened or worried by this sensation") to 5 ("extremely frightened by the sensation"). Her score was 37 out of a possible 85.

Four behavioral target goals for treatment were delineated by the client and each was rated separately by her for fear (0–10) and avoidance when alone (0–4). These were:

	Fear	Avoidance
Driving	10	4
Attending church	8	3
Going to Gimbels department store	4	2
Going to the bank	4	1

Behavioral Recordings

In order to assess her actual behavior, we asked Margaret to record travel from home on a Travel Diary (see Appendix A, p. 47) provided for this purpose. She noted the departure and return times, whether she was alone or accompanied, her destinations and durations of stay in each, and the mode of travel (e.g., auto, foot). On a separate Panic and Anticipatory Anxiety Diary (see Appendix B, p. 48), she recorded the circumstances of any anticipated or unexpected panic attacks and checked off the sensations experienced on each occasion. The first two weeks of recordings indicated that Margaret ventured out alone only once to the neighborhood grocery and was accompanied six times to area locations including the bank, supermarket, and a friend's house. Although she felt anticipatory anxiety lasting from 5 to 90 minutes on five occasions, no panic attacks were reported. That Margaret's sensations associated with anticipatory anxiety did not lead to panic appeared to be due to her attribution of relative safety to the settings in which these occurred; that is, she experienced some fear when she was either accompanied by a safe person or when at home contemplating a future excursion.

Selection of Treatment

Margaret's fears focused on three sources: external situations, internal physical sensations thought to signal panic, and anticipation of possible unfortunate consequences of intense anxiety, including fainting and criticism from others. In response to these fears, she had developed extensive avoidance patterns which virtually confined her to the home if unaccompanied. Additional concerns centered around comfort in social situations and the inadequacy of her sexual relationship with her husband. Because of the primacy of the agoraphobic symptoms, these were addressed first. The available treatments for agoraphobic symptoms were then discussed. Despite continued controversy regarding the utility of drugs for the treatment of agoraphobia, at least two, imipramine and phenelzine, appear to reduce panic attacks. However, in Margaret's case, the relative rarity of panic attacks argued against the use of drugs.

Exposure procedures, both imaginal and *in vivo*, have proven highly successful in the treatment of this disorder. It has been proposed that imaginal procedures may prove most useful when the patient's fear complex includes situations not readily presentable in reality. If, however, the fears can be fully evoked with direct exposure to actual situations, this method is preferred since any difficulty with generalization of effects from the imagined to the real circumstance is obviated.

Although Margaret was concerned with the social consequences of a panic attack, a direct fear of the unpleasant physical sensations

associated with panic prevailed. In order to habituate anxiety aroused
by such fear responses, these sensations should be repeatedly evoked.
Exposure *in vivo* to the feared situation was employed to this end.
Treatment was conducted in natural settings which aroused moderate anxiety, each exposure lasting one to two hours. Although exposure in a group setting might have provided the additional benefit
of observing other fearful individuals struggle with similar anxieties,
this option was not available in our clinic at the time Margaret sought
treatment. On questioning, Margaret felt that her husband might be
able to assist with exposure homework. Since spouse-assisted treatment has proven quite effective for agoraphobics (e.g., Barlow, O'Brien,
& Last, 1984), John's assistance was enlisted.

Course of Treatment

For Margaret, the collection of information about her presenting
problem, its history, and the assessment of her functioning required
three interviews lasting two and a half hours. During the latter half
of the third session, the therapist planned the treatment program
with her. First, the need for lengthy exposure to feared situations was
emphasized. The following dialogue ensued:

> *T*: In the past, you have coped with your fears by avoiding the
> situations that might bother you. In doing so unfortunately you've
> been making your fear worse. Let's take the last time you went
> to mass as an example. You were sitting about a quarter of the
> way up on the aisle, right?
>
> *P*: That's about right.
>
> *T*: Then you started to feel upset and you began to worry about
> having a panic attack. You got up and went to the back of the
> church. As soon as you got to the rear, you started to feel better.
>
> *P*: Within a few minutes I sort of calmed down a bit.
>
> *T*: Right. Then you made the connection that if you leave, you'll
> feel better and so now you are even more likely to leave or avoid
> going altogether. But if you had just sat there and allowed your-
> self to experience the anxiety feelings instead of trying to avoid
> them, eventually you would have felt better anyway.
>
> *P*: Actually, I did that once, when I didn't have a choice. I was
> at my daughter's wedding and I couldn't just walk out, you know.
> I did feel better after about 20 minutes, but it was hell for the
> 20 minutes.

T: That's a good example. Our task in treatment is to keep you in the church pew or any other situation that upsets you, until you learn that your fear decreases if you just stick it out. You eventually learn that, in fact, there's nothing to fear and you can handle the sensations.

After agreeing to subject herself to exposure treatment, Margaret and the therapist began to plan the order of exposure situations. The final list is given below:

Shopping at Gimbels on the first floor	50 SUDs
Eating lunch at the Bagel Nosh	55 SUDs
Riding a bus downtown and back	60 SUDs
Going to the St. Patrick's Day party at Mary and Mike's house	65 SUDs
Shopping on the upper floors of Gimbels	70 SUDs
Going to the Pathmark on Wednesday afternoon (a crowded time)	75 SUDs
Going to the bank on Friday	75 SUDs
Sitting halfway up in church, three or four seats from the aisle	90 SUDs
Driving on city streets	90 SUDs
Driving on four-lane highways	95 SUDs
Driving on expressways	100 SUDs

The therapist requested that Margaret invite her husband to the next session to discuss his participation in assisting her with exposure homework practice. As mentioned above, Margaret felt that he would be willing to help and agreed that their relationship would be likely to benefit from his involvement in her treatment program. Additionally, for the first few weeks the frequency of sessions was increased to twice a week (90 minutes each) in order to provide more frequent exposures to feared situations under the therapist's direction.

In the fourth session, Margaret arrived at the office with her husband. During a joint interview, John's observations and reactions to his wife's longstanding avoidance behavior were discussed. Their interaction evidenced mutual respect and liking. However, some emotional distance was apparent as reflected in their physical posturing, infrequent communication at home, and in John's unawareness of the degree of fear that Margaret experienced in the situations discussed above. The sessions ended with John expressing a willingness to assist in exposure homework and to attend therapy sessions as often as needed. He was instructed to help Margaret over the weekend to expose herself to situations identical to those practiced with the therapist in the next session, which was scheduled two days hence. With the therapist's aid, the couple worked out a scheme for communicating Margaret's level of fear and her ability to employ the suggested coping strategies during exposure practice. The therapist elected to delay discussion about the sexual problem until progress had been made with respect to the agoraphobia.

In the following session, Margaret indicated that she had experienced a panic attack in the dentist's waiting area. She left the office briefly but returned since she had waited for two months to get the appointment and felt it was important to stay. Anxiety was reduced by self-reassurance that the dentist was a trustworthy person and would probably be able to help her if needed. Essentially, she designated the setting as a "safe place." The therapist used this opportunity to reiterate the purpose of treatment and to emphasize the importance of remaining in feared settings despite the initial discomfort.

During the first treatment session, the therapist accompanied the patient to the first floor of Gimbels where they parted, having arranged to meet 15 minutes later. Margaret was instructed to allow herself to experience sensations of anxiety when they occurred and to remain in the store without seeking safety, since this was precisely the type of situation to which she needed to become accustomed when alone. She was asked not to struggle with the anxious feelings but instead to observe them and to note her anxiety level every five minutes on a record form provided by the therapist. Fifteen minutes later Margaret returned to a prearranged rendezvous, where the therapist asked her about her experience. She had felt only minor discomfort (35 SUDs) immediately after separating from the therapist and was only 15 SUDs (her usual resting rate) when they met again. A separation of 30 minutes then followed, again producing an initial rise and rapid decline in discomfort. Margaret had completed her shopping quite comfortably. The session was terminated with the homework assignment to repeat that exposure before the next appointment, with her husband driving her downtown.

The next treatment session took place the following week. After verifying that her homework assignment had been successfully completed, Margaret boarded a bus heading downtown where she was to meet the therapist 25 minutes later. She was instructed again to observe her bodily sensations and thoughts. Margaret was apprehensive before and during the first 10 minutes of the ride (maximum level 50 SUDs) but remained relatively calm (20 SUDs) for the last half.

After reporting to the therapist, she was asked to eat alone at a nearby cafeteria, again recording her anxiety. She returned home by bus. The therapist applauded, not her low anxiety, but rather her *ability to tolerate discomfort* and to remain alone in the cafeteria *in spite of it* until it subsided.

In this fashion, Margaret progressed relatively smoothly through most situations on the hierarchy. Homework on weekends continued with her husband, who attended the first part of the sessions once weekly to clarify difficulties and plan strategies. Symptoms of a panic attack occurred only once. Margaret was alone in church and the entrance of other parishioners necessitated her moving into the center of the pew, where she began to feel trapped and to worry about the disturbance she would cause if she had to leave. She became dizzy, faint, and weak-kneed so that she was barely able to stand during the portion of the service where this was required. Nonetheless, Margaret did not try to flee and felt better 10 minutes later. She remained mildly apprehensive for an additional 30 minutes but was pleased at her ability to tolerate the discomfort.

Greater difficulty was encountered with the driving fear; Margaret was unable to drive alone as requested for homework after doing so briefly during a session. Fears of losing control of the car intruded and she returned home after driving only one block. During a joint session with John, the therapist suggested that driving homework be broken down into steps. Margaret was to drive first with her husband in the car while he read a magazine and did not watch the road or the execution of driving maneuvers. After driving in this manner on a four-lane highway and on an expressway for 30 minutes with little discomfort, she would drive alone, first on local streets and then in more difficult settings. This plan facilitated progress, and Margaret began driving alone within two weeks.

Because of the increasing ease with which the couple was able to carry out homework assignments, after a four-week period the therapist reduced the frequency of sessions to once weekly, leaving the majority of exposure exercises to be conducted outside of the office. Margaret's diaries showed an increasing number of journeys alone with relatively little discomfort. For example, she could stop in the supermarket for an hour on a crowded day with an anxiety level of 20. Driving alone to the market 15 minutes from her home produced 30 SUDs. After 12 sessions of exposure over a period of 10 weeks, all further assignments were carried out alone or with the husband's assistance. A check of the daily diaries indicated no panic attacks in the past month and a maximum level of 25 SUDs in the previous two-week period, despite an increase in unaccompanied journeys from home (averaging once to twice a day). Also, the diary indicated no apparent restrictions in local driving; Margaret was able to drive alone to perform all needed errands, although she preferred that John drive whenever they were traveling together. In order to prevent future difficulties, the therapist warned Margaret that in the next few months some panicky feelings were to be expected. Such expectations are likely to assist patients in coping with inevitable occasional occurrences of anxiety, so that such experiences are not interpreted as failures.

The therapist then raised two remaining issues of concern: Margaret's sensitivity to criticism and consequent avoidance of certain social contexts, and her unhappiness with her husband's sexual response. She felt that the former issue had abated somewhat as she had regained confidence from the exposure practice and now felt less inadequate in relation to her peers. An example was a shower for a friend's daughter that she had not avoided and at which she had in fact felt quite comfortable conversing with two women she had not known previously. While she still felt somewhat sensitive to criticism, Margaret did not elect to work on this problem.

The sexual concerns were more disturbing to her. She noted that in the past few weeks her husband had become more affectionate during the evenings and on weekends; this, however, seemed to increase the tension at night because he was afraid to initiate sexual activity. This issue was raised in the next joint meeting. The couple did enter into sex therapy and after several additional sessions over the next few months, these difficulties were resolved. Since this treatment is not the focus of the present chapter, details will not be discussed here.

During the course of the sex therapy, the therapist enquired regularly about Margaret's progress regarding her agoraphobic symptoms; it remained essentially stable throughout this period. A minor setback followed an experience of dizziness while driving and consequent avoidance of executing the errands planned that day. The therapist reminded her that occasional anxiety was to be expected and pointed out the need to reexpose herself to prevent avoidance patterns from developing. She agreed to do so and deliberately drove several times in the next few days.

An interview five months after the initial contact with the clinic provided the following information: On the Avoidance Behavior Inventory, the avoidance score when alone decreased by 20 points to 38. The Bodily Sensations Questionnaire score was reduced from 37 to 23. Progress was evident on all four target goals, particularly on driving alone, which she now rated as 2 of 10 on fear and 2 of 5 on avoidance. The Panic and Travel Diaries showed approximately the same absence of panic symptoms and frequent travel alone (usually for household errands) on a virtually daily basis as had been apparent prior to the sex therapy. Margaret and her husband reported an improvement in their own relationship, which had begun prior to the sex therapy and had continued thereafter.

Termination and Follow-up

Treatment terminated when Margaret and John indicated satisfaction with the outcome. Margaret suggested that she come in after one month and, if all was proceeding well, John would not join her. At that appointment Margaret expressed satisfaction with her gains. A brief experience of panic, triggered following a near-miss accident while driving, did not prevent her driving again the next day, although her anxiety level increased initially but decreased during the driving. She felt able to cope with temporary increases in anxiety and was determined not to avoid situations in which such increases occurred. A telephone interview with her husband revealed satisfaction with Margaret's functioning, as well as with their personal and sexual interaction.

A telephone conversation three months later indicated that the gains achieved in treatment were maintained. Margaret and John were planning a driving trip to the West Coast to visit relatives and go sightseeing, a trip that they had discussed many times before but that Margaret had never been able to consider seriously. She reported continued progress and satisfaction and agreed to keep the diary for two weeks and to fill out forms after their return. These measures, completed four months after termination of treatment, showed essentially the same positive outcome as had been apparent previously.

Overall Evaluation

The case described in this chapter is relatively typical of agoraphobia. Margaret developed agoraphobia in her middle 30s following an episode of physical stress (childbirth and two experiences of dizziness). The course of treatment also is typical for successful therapy (65% respond to exposure treatment). What is unusual is the relative absence of obstacles throughout the therapy process. Margaret was much above average in compliance. Her relatively good relationship with her husband no doubt facilitated her ability to utilize his aid, thereby hastening her progress. Indeed, the quality of the marriage has been found related to treatment outcome by several authors (Bland & Hallam, 1981; Milton & Hafner, 1979). Also representative is the fact that treatment did not result in complete removal of the agoraphobic symptoms. Most agoraphobics continue to experience occasional anxiety in situations they previously avoided and some residual travel restrictions. Like other agoraphobics, Margaret was comfortable with the degree of improvement she achieved at the end of treatment and did not aspire to expand her horizons beyond a comfortable daily existence, which she maintained over time.

References

Barlow, D. H., O'Brien, G. T., & Last, C. L. (1984). Couples treatment of agoraphobia. *Behavior Therapy, 15,* 41–58.

Bland, K., & Hallam, R. S. (1981). Relationship between response to graded exposure and marital satisfaction in agoraphobics. *Behaviour Research and Therapy, 19,* 335–338.

Chambless, D. L. (1982a). *A self report instrument for agoraphobic avoidance behavior.* Paper presented at the Association for the Advancement of Behavior Therapy, Los Angeles, CA.

Chambless, D. L. (1982b). *The measurement of fear in agoraphobics, part II.: The revised agoraphobic cognitions questionnaire.* Paper presented at the Association for the Advancement of Behavior Therapy, Los Angeles, CA.

Milton, F., & Hafner, J. (1979). The outcome of behavior therapy for agoraphobia in relation to marital adjustment. *Archives of General Psychiatry, 36,* 807–811.

Wolpe, J. (1958). *Psychotherapy by reciprocal inhibition.* Stanford: Stanford University Press.

APPENDIX A
TRAVEL DIARY

NAME: _____

DATE	TIME		Alone	Anxiety 0–100	BRIEF DESCRIPTION OF ACTIVITY	TIME SPENT AT DESTINATION					TRAVELING TIME			
	Out	In				Work	Visit	Shop-ping	Enter-tainment	Other	Foot	Car	Public trans-port	Other

PANIC & ANTICIPATORY ANXIETY DIARY

NAME: _____

Date	Time Started	Time Ended	Place & Circumstances of Panic Attacks	SYMPTOMS EXPERIENCED (✓)														TYPE OF ATTACK		Amount of time spent in anxious worrying about entering a feared situation or having a panic attack (in minutes or hours)
				Short of breath	Choking sensation	Heart racing	Chest pain	Sweating	Faintness	Dizziness	Unreality	Numbness/tingling	Hot & cold flushes	Shaking	Nausea	Fear of dying	Fear of going crazy	Unexpected spontaneous panic attack	Situational panic attack	
Mon.																				
Tues.																				
Wed.																				
Thurs.																				
Fri.																				
Sat.																				
Sun.																				

4

Obsessional Thinking

Edward Dengrove

Description of the Syndrome

According to *DSM-III*, obsessions are recurrent, persistent ideas, thoughts, images, or impulses that are ego-dystonic; that is, they are not voluntarily produced. On the contrary, they are thoughts that invade consciousness and are experienced as senseless or repugnant. Obsessions are a significant source of distress to the individual and interfere with social or role functioning. Attempts are made to ignore or suppress them. The most common obsessions are repetitive thoughts of violence (e.g., killing one's child), contamination (e.g., becoming infected by shaking hands), and doubt (e.g., repeatedly wondering whether one has performed some action, such as having hurt someone in a traffic accident). Depression and anxiety are common. Frequently, there is compulsive behavior and phobic avoidance of situations that involve the content of the obsession, such as dirt or contamination. Although the disorder usually begins in adolescence or early adulthood, it may begin in childhood. The course is usually chronic, with waxing and waning of symptoms. Impairment is generally moderate to severe.

Case Identification

When first seen, Lisa B. was a 34-year-old accounting secretary, intelligent, attractive, single by choice, living with her parents. She had graduated from a four-year college and had taught school but hated it and took her present job instead.

Presenting Complaints

She complained of being depressed and tearful, obsessed by thoughts of cancer for the previous two years, and fearful of being around people with it. She complained: "I'm afraid to go out and I'm afraid I'll meet people who have it in the family. I wash my hands 20 times a day and I take a lot of showers but I can't get rid of it. I'm afraid to shake hands with people. I am not very good at all. I stayed home from work for the past week and a half. I get so tense I throw up. I've lost five pounds. I keep thinking I'm contaminated. I've not douched. I take soap and wash outside and up inside. I do it when I take a shower at night. I do it once a day for a few minutes." She feared contamination from, of all things, antiseptics; also household ammonia, Clorox, medicines – she did not know what was in them – medicated soaps, rubbing alcohol, detergents, peroxide, perfumes, Lysol, gasoline, ear drops, iodine and mercurochrome, spot cleaners, scouring powders, and Drano. She was afraid she would get a staph bladder infection if she used her bathroom and was particularly careful of contamination there. She feared going out among people for fear of the cancer contact. She would walk with her head down to see if someone had spit on the sidewalk. She was afraid to be alone, for then her fears would be more intense. She avoided visiting friends and even members of her own family in hospital. If she bought something under five dollars, she thought it would bring bad luck. Following a urethral dilatation for a urethritis, she washed her vagina for fear of contamination. She could not walk on part of the living room rug and part of the bathroom floor for these areas were likewise contaminated. For similar reasons, she washed her hair frequently.

History

Lisa had always been a perfectionist, a worrier. Whenever she got upset she could not eat and would throw up. She used to go out with boys a lot (she was a very attractive girl) but gradually this began to bother her. She would be most upset by boys who wanted to be serious. She said: "I don't trust serious men. They can hurt me by getting me involved. I was never hurt by a boy before because I dropped him before he dropped me. I did it before they did it to me." She feared rejection and loss of control. To continue, "When I was a little girl I'd be afraid to say hello to people for fear they'd not say hello back to me." She learned early to avoid situations which she did not control and to defend herself by avoiding any serious involvement with others.

For the previous seven years she had gone out with Jack. He was separated from his wife and she therefore felt safe going with him since he was otherwise involved. He would go out with other women and this ensured that he would not get serious with her. However, two years before she came to me, "He was going with another woman and stopped going out with her. I wanted him to get a divorce. Ten days after I spoke about it, I visited a girl friend and she told me her father had cancer. That's when it started. He said he'd get a divorce and he did. Then he decided he really didn't want to get married. Last summer I went out with others but it didn't help. I feel better when I stay home. I had trouble sleeping." She felt she had to continue seeing Jack, with whom she was also sexually intimate, for while she was repelled by any serious advance she felt very much more attracted to him. However, it cost her heavily by the fact that her condition became worse. Trivial things would upset her; she felt tense and could not function. She developed an odd compulsion to drink soapy water (Ivory). She noted, "I'm afraid to stop, for when I used to douche I got the infection. I'll get this infection." She was afraid to eat chicken and eggs, feeling that they were in some way involved in her problems. Asked what she needed to clean out of herself, she answered, "Jack. He popped up a week ago Friday. I had two drinks with him. He told me six times he loved me. It does me no good." At this point she cried. She described ambivalent feelings for Jack. On the one hand she wanted him to leave her alone, but underneath it all she really liked to be with him. "Maybe it was the sex. It was very good and very nice. But it didn't get me what I wanted. So scratch that. So don't bother with sex because I always end up getting the raw end of the deal. I take it too seriously. I couldn't be promiscuous. When I care for someone, I care all the way. As a kid I was afraid of getting mumps and if I was near someone who had it, I'd back away." She continued dating other men, preferring those who were married or older and therefore not available as serious contenders. For a while she developed a vaginal infection which was resistant to treatment, and this complicated her progress.

Assessment

Following a general history taking, attention was directed toward the target behaviors to be changed. A list was made of the stimulus conditions under which the obsessive-compulsive disorder originally developed (e.g., the numerous contaminants she avoided), together with the secondary or generalizing stimuli which were maintaining her problem (e.g., rugs and floors she would not walk upon). Consideration was given to the avoidance behaviors she practiced, the social fears she experienced, her perfectionistic personality, which had become burdensome to her and had then broken down into symptomatic behaviors, and the problems against which she needed to defend herself.

Selection of Treatment

A broad-spectrum multifaceted program was instituted. Specific target behaviors were selected for modification, such as avoidance of contaminants, by systematic desensitization, both in imagery, with and without hypnotic techniques, and *in vivo*. Thought-blocking procedures were utilized for the obsessive thinking (see below). Response prevention was used for compulsive and ritualistic behaviors. Perfectionism was treated through cognitive restructuring and assertive learning. All these were tied together with homework assignments, and, additionally, medication was offered for symptomatic relief.

Course of Treatment

This followed the above delineated selection. Obsessive and worrisome thinking was treated through a thought-block technique which worked well for her (Dengrove, 1974). My approach is a little more sophisticated than the shouting STOP technique or the heavy-gauge elastic band upon the wrist.

It is usual for a patient with chronic, obsessional thinking to report that she cannot shut out the stream of ideas that run through her head. It therefore becomes important to demonstrate, through practice, that she does have the necessary self-control. To do this, I use a modification of a method introduced by Wolpe, using an aversive device. However, the aversive element is not a prominent part of treatment. There is no intent to punish the individual for having obsessive thoughts but to teach her how not to have them.

I use an electrical impulse box with wrist electrodes which also produces a loud buzzing sound when the button is pressed. The box was manufactured by State Hospital, Carstairs Junction, Lanarkshire, Scotland. It costs about $10. However, a number of American manufacturers produce a similar, though more expensive instrument.

The patient lies on a couch, or sits in a chair, with the electrode from the impulse box placed upon a wrist or forearm. The current is adjusted until it produces a painful response that is intense but not unbearable. At this point the patient is instructed to close her eyes and to think, first, of a bad thought, then of a good one. A bad thought is a repetitive idea that she cannot dismiss; a good thought is any constructive or pleasant idea or scene. These may be worked out and listed beforehand.

She is asked, first, to think of a bad thought and to signal to me by raising her free forearm at the elbow. She is to be aware that, whenever the free forearm is raised, she is thinking a bad thought and is "fair game" for a painful shock. Whenever she is thinking a good thought, her forearm must be down, and she is reassured that, when the forearm is down, at no time will she suffer a painful stimulus.

Further, whenever the forearm is up, she may or may not get a shock and, if she does, it may come earlier or later in a random manner. She has the option of avoiding a shock if she will change the thought herself to a good one and bring down the forearm. However, she must not cheat! She cannot bring down the forearm until she has changed her thought to a good one. Sometimes a patient will bring down the forearm in an effort to avoid the painful shock without changing her thought pattern; this is not permitted. The thought must be changed before she signals with the lowering of the forearm. It is desirable to check with the patient to be certain that she is doing this correctly by discussing, after each completed signal event, what her bad and good thoughts were. This should be done at least at the onset. Sometimes the patient is able to block off the bad thought but can think of no replacement, stating, "My mind is blank." If she can reassure herself that everything will be all right, then this response is acceptable. If she persists in a bad thought, the shock is continued until she desists, or the current is turned up a little until its intensity prevents such persistence. Sometimes a patient is unable to summon up a bad thought at all; this is what we are seeking.

The presentation of the pain precludes any other thinking. It is not possible to think of anything but the pain, so that the bad thought is blocked out immediately. A good thought must substitute for a bad one.

Our goal is to change an aversive response to an avoidance one. The patient learns rapidly to anticipate the change before a painful shock is given. At this point, the patient becomes aware that she has control of her thought processes, that on her own command she can dismiss an unwanted idea. This is self-control.

It is not sufficient, however, to depend solely upon such training at therapeutic sessions once or twice a week. Homework is essential, with constant attempts made to dismiss unwanted thoughts. For this purpose, the patient wears the heavy-gauge rubber band around the wrist. It is stretched and allowed to snap back to disrupt thought sequences. Just the thought of its availability may be sufficient to block off the bad thought. Whenever she has difficulty switching away from her bad thoughts, she gives herself a "shock" with the rubber band. It effectively distracts her so that she thinks of the pain she feels, even if only for a fraction of a second. Should the bad thought return, she repeats the "shock" time and again, till the thinking is running in other channels. It does not take long for her to decide to change her thinking in lieu of giving herself another "shock." Aversion again becomes avoidance, and the patient has learned ideational self-control. In my experience, the method is effective, providing the patient uses it as instructed. Since patients with obsessional thinking tend to follow instructions, it works out.

Sometimes a patient will complain that the thoughts recur in the presence of others and she is ashamed to pull on the elastic device in such circumstances. She is told that she has the choice either of ridding herself of the obsessional thinking or excusing herself to find a spot where she can shock herself.

The patient quickly learns to control her obsessive thinking, avoidance becomes established as the primary means of control, and she feels more comfortable with herself. The method works by means of distraction rather than aversion, the pain acting only to distract her from inner thoughts, much as the word STOP does when yelled loudly enough. The attention-scanning mechanism of the brain is steered away from repetitive thinking, which appears to differ from the preservation seen in organic states. "The good thought" substituting for the "bad thought" does not have the same fixed quality and can be easily dissipated. It substitutes a pleasureful thought for an unpleasant or painful one.

With this thought block technique, Lisa quickly learned to substitute her bad thoughts with the good ones, and I was able to apply other broad-spectrum techniques as listed in Selection of Treatment above.

Pharmacologically, I saw Lisa in the early days of the benzodiazepine tranquilizers. However, she was treated initially with Meprobamate (a nonbenzodiazepine) and then transferred to Valium 5 mg as needed. She had complaints of nausea and vomiting as a result of her anxiety when first seen and this was controlled with Combid (a Compazine combination). Because of a tendency toward insomnia which interfered with treatment, she was also placed on a barbiturate. There is still an infrequent need for Valium 5 mg and/or an hypnotic. They make her more comfortable in stressful situations and she uses them judiciously. They are a crutch that make her life more comfortable.

There are other methods for treating obsessional thinking that I did not use: (1) flooding, (2) the worry chair, and (3) antidepressant medication. In flooding, the patient is strongly encouraged and cajoled to continue exposure to the worrisome ideas until a significant diminution occurs, the therapist providing reassurance and calming encouragement throughout the session. In the worry chair technique, the patient devotes her full attention to the obsessive thoughts, worrying out loud and tape-recording the session for at least 30 minutes. All obsessing is done in the worry chair. This is followed by a circumscribed period of time spent in listening to repeated playbacks of the dictated and recorded obsessive thoughts. Antidepressants, such as the tricyclic clomipramine hydrochloride, have been found to be associated with significant improvement. Antiobsessional responses to clomipramine do not depend on the presence of depression.

Termination and Follow-up

Treatment at first was on a weekly basis, then every other week, followed by monthly visits, and now every other month. At present she is 48 years old and has been in treatment for 14 years. However, treatment of her various symptoms has long since ceased for her phobic, obsessive, and compulsive symptoms. Obsessional patients tend to hang onto therapy for long periods of time, mostly for reassurance and reinforcement, rather than for therapy per se. Actually, she is the only obsessional patient to remain in regular contact with me for so long a period. Sessions are only for counseling. She remains single by choice, her decision to remain so reinforced by her sister's unhappy marriage and divorce. Jack died, but she had not been seeing him for long periods of time anyway. She continues dating married men who present no threat to her. She is not promiscuous. She changed her job several times but only to better her financial position. Overall, she appears to be happy and satisfied with her life.

With other obsessional patients, termination of therapy takes place gradually over lengthening periods of time, until a point is reached where we mutually agree to terminate, with the provision that I will be available should they require me for further reinforcing sessions. These are infrequent and then cease. Lisa prefers to continue our therapeutic relationship, though on an attenuated basis.

Overall Evaluation

Obsessional thinking used to present an impossible therapeutic situation, prior to the advent of behavior therapy. These new approaches have produced satisfactory amelioration of "bad" thoughts and their repetitive, worrisome concomitants, and aid in the amelioration of habitual and poor thought patterns and the learning of good ones through self-control and homework.

Reference

Dengrove, E. (1974). Thought block in behavior therapy. *Journal of the American Society of Psychosomatic Dentistry and Medicine, 21*, 19–24.

5

Compulsive Rituals

Paul M. G. Emmelkamp

Description of Compulsive Rituals

Compulsive rituals and obsessive thoughts (obsessions) are usually distinguished, although most obsessional patients have obsessions as well as compulsions. Obsessions are often accompanied by urges and rituals. Pure rituals without accompanying obsessive thoughts are rare. Rituals or compulsions are repetitive actions, which usually serve to reduce anxiety and discomfort. The most common compulsive behaviors involve "cleaning" and "checking."

The rituals (e.g., washing, cleaning, checking, repetition) have discomfort- and anxiety-reducing effects. There is now considerable evidence that urges to perform rituals are provoked by exposure to distressing situations (e.g., washing after contamination with dirt) and that the performance of rituals leads to relief of anxiety and discomfort. A number of studies have shown that prolonged exposure to distressing stimuli plus prevention of the performance of rituals (response prevention) is effective in dealing with the obsessive-compulsive behavior (Emmelkamp, 1982).

Case Identification

The present case was chosen because of its complexity. Research articles seldom provide information with respect to treatment strategies in individual cases. What occurs in clinical behavior therapy is not quite the same as what is frequently depicted in research papers. Most research studies in the area of obsessive-compulsive disorders have evaluated the effectiveness of *in vivo* exposure techniques, but reports on the treatment of associated problems of these patients are almost nonexistent. The goal of the present chapter is to provide a description of the assessment and treatment of an obsessive-compulsive ritualizer, and to give the reader some idea of the complexities often involved in the clinical treatment of such cases. The first part of the treatment was carried out in the context of a research study.

Presenting Complaints

The presenting client is a 26-year-old woman named Sarah who has lived with her boyfriend for about four years. She works as a librarian. The main complaint is that she feels compelled to clean things and to be excessively neat. Every day she must clean the doors, mop the floors, vacuum the house, and clean the couch, underneath as well. These activities sometimes take place several times a day.

The client is always dressed very neatly; she cannot stand hairs or dust on her clothes. Every day she takes several showers, changes clothes for working, for cleaning, and for eating. She avoids receiving visitors as much as she can. When people do come to visit her, she takes careful notice of where they walk and sit and what they touch. As soon as the visitors leave, she thoroughly cleans the places where they have been and the things they have touched. This is also the reason why she will not take anyone with her in her car. The client feels compelled to engage in sports every day. Afterwards she must take a good shower. Although this physical training seems to show obsessive-compulsive characteristics (i.e., when she cannot do her exercises because of illness she becomes very tense), she is not prepared to include this aspect into the treatment. The client is also very precise: things like paintings, chairs, books, and so on all have their fixed place.

History

As a child the client suffered from asthma and was very sensitive to dust. Because of this her parental home was kept meticulously clean. She no longer suffers from asthma. At that time she was often subject to temper tantrums. These had already started in her kindergarten years. Her mother could not handle her so she often went to an aunt who spoiled her. This aunt was a house-proud housewife and was very precise. When she was about 10 years old, the client started to dress very neatly. She cannot remember what induced her to do this. But her sensitivity to dust has probably played a part as well as the excessive neatness of her aunt.

At the age of 15 the family moved and she had to attend a different school, where she did not know anyone. She felt very insecure and it was then that the rituals started.

Assessment

Three information sessions were held. In addition, the patient filled out a number of questionnaires: The Maudsley Obsessive-Compulsive Inventory (MOCI), the Social Anxiety Scale (SAS), the Self-rating Depression Scale (SDS) of Zung, and the Hostility and Direction of Hostility Questionnaire. Starting with the first session, the patient was requested to monitor daily on 0–8 scales how much she was troubled by obsessive-compulsive behavior, depressed mood, and feelings of hostility. Since the first part of Sarah's treatment was conducted within the context of an experimental study on the effects of exposure in *in vivo* therapy, the information sessions were primarily directed at a micro-analysis of her obsessive-compulsive behavior.

The client apparently tries to avoid the following situations, and if she fails she feels compelled to wash her hands and/or take a shower: reading the newspaper (dirty hands), traveling by train, using public telephones, touching keys and money, touching bottles, putting her bag on the floor, touching shoeshine implements, touching her glasses, walking barefoot, and receiving people. The more visitors she receives, the tenser she gets; indeed, she cannot keep track of all the things they touch. The cleaning of her house must always take place in a specific order. If there is any deviation from this specific order, she starts all over again. Her precision-compulsion is further expressed in the fact that everything has its fixed place, paintings have to hang straight, and so on.

At home she suffers more from her compulsions than at work. Although there is quite a lot of dust at the place where she works – a library archive – it does not worry her very much. She works in a separate room so that contamination through other people seldom occurs.

The client has no concrete thoughts about falling ill or contaminating other people. She experiences great tension and anxiety when contaminated, but she herself does not know the reason for it. Her boyfriend seems to reinforce her obsessive-compulsive complaints. He takes her complaints into account as much as possible. He seldom invites people. Also, he never leaves his things lying about because she cannot stand this. Furthermore, he helps her clean up the house.

With respect to the obsessive-compulsive disorder, the following five main targets for treatment were formulated; each of these situations was rated by the patient on a 0–8 scale for anxiety and discomfort.

- Not cleaning the house for a week.
- Traveling by train without washing hands, taking a shower, or putting on clean clothes afterwards.
- After work, not cleaning and brushing her coat.
- Not cleaning the kitchen after having done the dishes.
- After shopping putting the goods away without cleaning them first.

Table 5.1 provides the scores on the questionnaires and the mean anxiety/discomfort score (0–8) on the target situations.

In the third session the treatment rationale of self-controlled exposure *in vivo* was explained to Sarah. It was explained that by giving in to the urges to clean and to wash her hands and to be very precise, she actually maintained her obsessive-compulsive behavior. By exposing herself to situations that provoke anxiety and tension without ritualizing, in the long run her anxiety and discomfort will decrease and with it the urge to ritualize. It was further explained that exposure would be gradual, starting with relatively easy situations. To see just how much she had understood the rationale, Sarah was requested to write it down in her own words when at home and to give this to her therapist in the next session.

Table 5.1. Scores at the Pretest

	Pretest
Target ratings compulsions (0–8)	6
Obsessive-Compulsive Inventory	14
Social Anxiety Scale (SAS)	24
Hostility (HDHQ)	21
Depression (SDS)	50

Subsequently, a detailed inventory was drawn up of situations that provoked anxiety and led to rituals. All listed situations were written down on notecards and scored by her by means of an anxiety bar (0–100). Then, a hierarchy was constructed, ranging from easy to difficult assignments.

It was agreed that she would practice the hierarchy items for at least 90 minutes twice a week. At the end of the last session, the following homework assignments were given to her to practice in the first two homework sessions.

- Walk barefoot through the house. Don't wash your feet.
- Do not wear your special eating sweater when eating. Eat in your ordinary working clothes.
- Visit people without first taking a shower or changing.
- Hang your paintings crooked. Leave them like this for a week.
- After you have been to the masseur, soap yourself only once when taking a shower.
- Do not dust more than once a week.

Course of Treatment

Session Four

Sarah had done all of these assignments and was quite pleased about it. Walking barefoot through the house had at first been difficult, but nevertheless she had gone to bed without washing her feet. It was agreed that she would repeat the previous assignments. If these were to go well once again, the following assignments would be added.

- Put away your clothes within a minute.
- Sit behind your desk in your special eating clothes, but do not clean the desk afterwards.
- Prepare a hot meal. Do not take a shower afterwards. Do not change. Wear the same clothes in the evening and wear them again to work.
- Do not polish your shoes more than once a week.

Session Five

Sarah said that things did not go all that well this week; she still felt compelled to clean her glasses and her watch thoroughly (assignments which had not yet been given to her) and feels very guilty about this. She gives the impression of being very tense. She had succeeded in doing nearly all of the assignments which had been given to her, the new ones included. She had failed to dust only once a week. She had, however, noticed that tension decreased when she did not give in to the urge to ritualize. The therapist emphasized that there was no reason at all to feel guilty about failing to do an assignment and that it was not wise to do more assignments than was agreed. In addition to repeating the old assignments, she had to carry out the following assignments (for the next session).

- Put on your glasses, go out for five minutes. Do not clean your glasses.
- Do not wash your hands before dinner.
- Put the chairs in a different position. Leave them like this for a week.
- Shake leaves off a plant. Let them lie about.
- Go to the bank, make a withdrawal, and do not wash your hands afterwards.
- Eat in your house clothes, without putting on your special eating clothes.
- Take a shower at home. Do not take your keys with you under the shower.

Session Six

Again Sarah was very tense, although she had succeeded in doing nearly all of the assignments. Only the assignment with the keys had failed. This, however, had made her so angry that she had lashed out at Bob, her live-in boyfriend. Her relationship with Bob is going through a bad period; Sarah feels misunderstood and this is probably also a reason why she has been so tense lately. Before dealing with her relationship problems, however, Sarah wants to finish the exposure assignments. She is given the following assignments for the next session.

- Do not wash your hands after meals.
- Take several coins and banknotes from your purse and hold them in your hands for at least two minutes. Do not wash your hands.
- Use a public telephone. Do not wash your hands or face.
- Go through the house. In every room touch at least 20 objects. Do not clean anything afterwards.

- Take your mail to your desk. Go through it, parcels included. Do not clean your desk, do not clean your hands, do not clean the mail.
- Make a stain on your door. Do not clean it.
- Mop the kitchen only once a week. Do not take longer than usual.
- Mop the bathroom once a week. Do not take longer than usual.
- Mop the shower once a week. Do not take longer than usual.

Session Seven

Again she had done the assignments reasonably well. Using a public telephone and touching money had been very difficult, but she had not given in to the urge to wash her hands. But she had not put the receiver against her ear so as not to be contaminated. It was agreed that she would try this again, but this time she had to touch herself with the receiver. The assignments not to mop more than once a week had failed; she had mopped the floors twice because she had had visitors.

Sarah now sees a clear connection between external events (a quarrel with Bob, problems with her boss at work, insecurity in social situations) and her obsessive-compulsive behavior. When such events upset her, she is much more troubled by her obsessive-compulsive complaints. She is reasonably satisfied about her progress. Because of her gradually increasing ability to do things without ritualizing, she begins to feel that she can solve her obsessive-compulsive problems.

Session Eight to Session Eleven

Carrying out the assignments (see Table 5.2) gave her little difficulty. But more and more it became clear that her obsessive-compulsive behavior was influenced by insecurity in social situations and her problems with Bob. At the end of this period, Sarah was able to do most of the assignments without tension, but the hierarchy had not yet been completed. Sarah filled out the questionnaires once again. The results on the target ratings scale and on the other scales do not indicate much progress (see Table 5.3). This can be partly explained by the fact that three out of five target situations were not practiced during treatment, because they ranked too high in the hierarchy. It was suggested to her that she continue treatment after the summer holidays, but Sarah would rather stop treatment for a while because

Table 5.2. Hierarchy Items Used in Session Eight to Eleven

1. Read a book from the library at your desk. Do not clean your desk and do not wash your hands.
2. Go out in your house clothes. Keep them on for the whole evening.
3. Do not sweep the floor of the shed more than once a month.
4. Do not sweep the hall near the front door more than once every two weeks.
5. Wear your special eating clothes the whole evening. Do not clean anything in the house.
6. Vacuum only once a week.
7. Read a newspaper at your desk. Fold it out on your desk. Do not clean your desk and do not wash your hands.
8. Go to a gas station. Go back home and do not wash your hands.
9. Put five books in the book case and leave them there for a week.
10. Go out and do some shopping. Put away the goods without cleaning them. Do not wash your hands.
11. Do not clean the doors more than once a week and do not take longer than usual.
12. Do not wash your car more than once a month.
13. Throw your clothes on a chair. Do not cover them with a sweater. Leave your boyfriend's clothes lying about too.
14. Read the newspaper. Immediately after that, touch at least 10 objects in the house and clutch them tightly. Do not clean anything and do not wash your hands.
15. Wear the same clothes "day and night" for four days. Do not avoid touching or using things, especially not the couch.
16. After taking a shower put on the same clothes you have worn all day.
17. Do not put the shoes you want to polish in the shed but in the kitchen.
18. After dinner do not clean the table with a cloth.
19. Do not take a shower for a day.
20. Buy a book without plastic wrapped around it. Put it in the book case among the other books without having a further look at it or cleaning it. Do not wash your hands.
21. Pet a dog thoroughly. Do not wash your hands.
22. Put at least 10 books in a place where they do not belong.
23. Use your glasses when you have to drive your car. Do not clean your glasses more than once a day. This must never take longer than 20 seconds. Clean only the lenses, not the frame. Do not wash your hands and face more often than usual.
24. Leave your glasses anywhere in the house without putting them in their case.
25. Sit behind the desk in the clothes you have worn all day. Do not clean your desk. Do not wash your hands.
26. Do not clean the washstand every morning, but only once a week.
27. Drive your car across a muddy track. Do not wash it.

Table 5.3. Scores at the Pretest, Posttest, and Follow-up, Six Months After Treatment

	Pretest	*Posttest*	*Follow-up*
Target ratings compulsions (0–8)	6	5.6	3.6
Obsessive-Compulsive Inventory (MOCI)	14	12	11
Social Anxiety Scale (SAS)	24	23	45
Hostility (HDHQ)	21	24	28
Depression (SDS)	50	48	65

she needed time to study for an important examination after the summer holidays. But she did want to keep on doing the exposure assignments that had not been practiced yet, at her own pace.

Broad-spectrum Therapy

About six months after exposure treatment there was a follow-up interview with Sarah. She was very tense and depressed and had suicidal wishes. Her obsessive-compulsive problems, however, showed further improvement (see Table 5.3). Aside from the target problems and Maudsley Obsessive-Compulsive Inventory, the questionnaires showed a deterioration of all other problems: Sarah proved to be more depressed, more socially anxious, and more hostile than before the treatment. The situation at home with her boyfriend proved to have become untenable and this was the immediate cause of her suicidal wishes. Sarah herself wanted to continue the treatment. In view of the crisis atmosphere at home, it seemed advisable to invite Sarah's boyfriend (Bob) to attend the next interview. Sarah agreed.

Communication Training. The purpose of this interview was to evaluate their relationship problems. During the initial interview it became clear that both partners were distressed and dissatisfied with the relationship. Both had seriously entertained the idea of separation but had not discussed the issue with each other. Bob was increasingly troubled by Sarah's aggressive moods and her remaining obsessive-compulsive problems. Bob still could not receive friends because of Sarah's problems, although he too found that the rituals had improved. Sarah felt that Bob did not understand her and therefore she felt lonely. When she was very tense, she smashed her crockery or phoned Bob, who then had to come home immediately to comfort her. Bob reinforced Sarah's behavior by immediately giving in to her wishes and taking her on his lap. It was explained to the couple that

Sarah's aggressive moods had been learned in her childhood and had first been reinforced by her mother and aunt. Now they were reinforced by Bob. Both readily accepted this explanation of Sarah's behavior, and a contractual agreement was reached in which it was specified that Bob should not give in to Sarah when she was in an aggressive mood. Since both partners were unable to express their emotions directly toward each other, communication training was proposed to the couple, which they both accepted. At this stage, the therapist made explicit that the goal of the communication training was not necessarily to improve their relationship, but to teach them skills to express their feelings more directly, which eventually could result in a mutually agreed-upon separation.

During communication training, conflict situations which had occurred in the previous week were rehearsed in role-playing. Both had good listening skills, but their main problem was that they were unable to express their wishes in a clear way, which prevented conflict resolution.

In communication training emphasis was directed to spontaneous expression of feelings, assertiveness, and empathy training. Behavior rehearsal was used as the primary therapeutic vehicle, which involves the partners acting out relationship problems with each other in role-plays. The therapist's office permitted the couple a safe place to change their behavior and to practice new ways of communication. Specifically, the therapist began by asking the couple to explain as much about a particular situation as needed to allow the therapist to play the role of both partners. Next, the therapist asked Bob and Sarah their goals in the situation (i.e., what did they want to say). Then, in a series of role-plays, the partners attempted to change their behavior. The therapist modeled appropriate behavior where necessary by alternately playing the role of either partner. At the end of these sessions partners were encouraged to use their newly learned skills in their daily interaction.

The contractual agreement which had been agreed to in the initial interview with the couple was effective in that Sarah's aggressive moods disappeared. The progress that both partners made with respect to their communication skills was remarkable. In the fifth session Sarah and Bob told the therapist that they had decided to separate for some time to find out what they felt for each other and to see whether they could live without each other. In the past week they had been able to discuss this openly with each other for the first time, and both were satisfied with this solution. It was agreed that they would live apart for a month and that they would have no contact at all with each other. Therapy was interrupted during this period.

After this month Bob and Sarah saw each other again in the therapist's office. Bob was very satisfied about living alone, a heavy load had fallen off his shoulders, and he wanted to make the separation definite. Sarah too was satisfied about the separation, but she indicated that she would like to maintain a friendly relationship with Bob. Bob made it clear, however, that he did not want that, and so Sarah accepted a definite separation. Both felt relieved that the die had been cast, and both were happy that they had been able to convey their wishes to each other. In addition, there was consensus that the treatment should be continued on an individual basis with Sarah.

Reevaluation and Treatment Planning. The next two sessions were devoted to a reevaluation of Sarah's problems. Sarah was still socially anxious and depressed, although no longer suicidal. Although the obsessive-compulsive rituals had improved, Sarah kept avoiding a number of situations, in particular those which involved having contact with other people, such as receiving visitors. Inspection of the daily records of obsessive-compulsive complaints, depressed mood, and hostility revealed that these problems seemed to (co)vary from one time to another. From reexamination of the notes that had been made from interviews, it appeared that there was some relationship between obsessive-compulsive problems and social situations. Her obsessive-compulsive complaints (and to some extent her hostility and depression) appeared to increase on account of stressful interpersonal events. It now seemed plausible that the obsessive-compulsive behavior might also provide reinforcement in the form of tension reduction and temporary relief from the worries caused by Sarah's social difficulties. It was further hypothesized that Sarah's depressed mood was partly the result of a lack of social reinforcers, and partly the result of irrational cognitions.

On the basis of this analysis, the following treatment plan was formulated. To deal with the social anxiety that was presumed to underlie the remaining obsessive-compulsive problems, assertion training was proposed. Further, cognitive restructuring seemed appropriate to deal with the irrational cognitions. Finally, to overcome the remaining compulsive problems, Sarah was instructed to continue to practice difficult *in vivo* exposure tasks on her own.

There was a consensus on the problems and goals of therapy, and it was decided to start with assertion training on a once-a-week basis. The reason for giving priority to assertion training over dealing with the irrational cognitions was twofold. *First,* part of her current depressed feelings were presumably related to grief due to the loss of her partner. Since grief is a normal reaction to the loss of a love object, there seemed no need for a therapeutic intervention to deal with this. Since it was anticipated that the mourning process could interfere with the cognitive restructuring approach, it was decided to postpone cognitive therapy for some time. The other reason for beginning with assertion training was that it probably would be easier to change irrational cognitions when Sarah already had the necessary social skills and engaged in social interactions, rather than treating irrational cognitions in a vacuum of social relationships. Generally, assertion training using role-playing to change behaviors can be used without worrying about cognitions unless there are clear indications that these cognitions will interfere with the practice of assertion skills in daily life.

Assertion Training. The next 10 sessions were devoted mainly to assertion training. The first two sessions were devoted to a more detailed analysis of Sarah's assertion problems. Inspection of her social anxiety scale had already provided a number of social situations in which Sarah found it difficult to express herself. In these sessions a number of social situations were role-played to observe Sarah's behavior in such situations. Difficult situations for Sarah were refusing a request and giving and receiving of negative expressions. Receiving and giving positive expressions (such as a compliment) were less of a problem. Further, Sarah's nonverbal behavior, such as eye contact, distance and posture, and voice quality, were generally good. Therefore, it was decided to focus on the training of (1) refusal skills, (2) the expression of negative emotions, and (3) receiving criticism. Since one situation was not clearly more difficult than another, there was no need for using a hierarchy ranging from less anxiety arousing situations to situations that provoked high anxiety. To increase Sarah's motivation, it was decided to use only situations that she encountered in real life. Therefore, Sarah was instructed to record difficult situations on precoded sheets and to bring these with her to the therapy session. Each session started with a brief discussion of the assertive problems that she had encountered. Then, a few of these problems were rehearsed in role-playing, the therapist modeling more appropriate behavior when necessary. When enough progress was made in role-playing, Sarah was instructed to practice this particular behavior as homework assignment. Examples of situations that were rehearsed in this way are:

- Inviting people to visit her.
- Being invited herself to visit people.
- Telling a lesbian acquaintance who wants her to stay the night that she is not interested.

- Making it clear to her neighbor, who really wants a relationship with her, that she is interested only in drinking a cup of coffee with him occasionally.
- Making it clear that she likes a man and inviting him for dinner.
- Accepting criticism from her boss at work.
- Criticizing acquaintances and her boss.

After eight of these sessions, progress was evaluated. Sarah now had a number of social contacts; she regularly went to a bar after work with some colleagues; and both Sarah and the therapist found that the assertion skills had improved remarkably. Her obsessive-compulsive complaints also had continued to improve. Sarah had regularly received visitors without having been overly concerned about what they touched. Neither did she feel compelled to clean the entire house after the visitors left.

She seemed to have dealt with her separation from Bob reasonably well. Therefore a cognitive therapy was started to change the irrational cognitions that had remained unchanged.

Cognitive Therapy

Ellis (1962) uses an A-B-C framework of *rational-emotive therapy*. *A* refers to an *A*ctivating event or experience, *B* to the person's *B*elief about the activating (A) event, and *C* to the emotional or behavioral *C*onsequence, assumed to result from the *B*eliefs (B). The critical elements of treatment involve determining the (irrational) thoughts that mediate the negative feeling (e.g., depression, anxiety) and confront and modify them so that undue anxiety or depressed feelings are no longer experienced. After having explained the rationale of this therapy, Sarah was instructed to read a booklet describing the basic principles of rational emotive therapy. The first stage of cognitive therapy was directed to training Sarah to observe and record her cognitions. By using precoded A-B-C homework sheets, Sarah learned to discriminate between the actual event and her own thoughts. Sarah readily understood the relationship between irrational cognitions and negative feelings, and she was able to offer a number of irrational cognitions associated with her negative feelings after the first week of monitoring these thoughts.

The next stage of therapy involved rationally disputing the irrational cognitions. First, the therapist challenged the irrational beliefs in a Socratic-like fashion and later on Sarah was instructed to do this on her own as homework assignment.

At least four major themes run through the cognitive therapy:

1. She needed to have a relationship in order to be happy, but was unfit for such a relationship since her previous relationship had become a failure due to her faults.
2. She had to engage in sports every day and was not allowed to eat "fat food"; otherwise she would not have a good figure and hence would be unable to find a lover.
3. If she was not precise and neat, she would feel insecure and "loss of control" would be intolerable.
4. Tension is intolerable and must immediately be given in to by means of rituals or aggressive moods (e.g., smashing crockery).

It is important to note that the irrational beliefs depicted above operated on a preconscious level in a more or less automatic fashion. That is, they only became part of Sarah's conscious awareness after training in discriminating these beliefs through her homework assignments and through the therapist's intervention during therapy sessions. After rationally disputing these ideas, Sarah received behavioral assignments. For example, when it had become clear to Sarah on a cognitive level that it was an irrational idea that she could find a partner only if she would participate in sports every day and eat as little as possible, she was given the homework assignment not to do sports for a week and to eat well without paying attention to calories and without checking whether she had gained weight. After this week, Sarah was able to skip sports when she did not feel like it and her eating habits had changed without her becoming fat. After 10 sessions of cognitive therapy, the situation was reevaluated. Sarah was markedly less depressed and had a number of satisfying social relationships and the obsessive rituals were no longer problematic.

Because there were still a number of exposure assignments left, which Sarah could not bring herself to do on her own, it was decided to do one *in vivo* exposure session at her home, to tackle the remaining bits of her obsessive-compulsive problem. During this session the therapist contaminated all kinds of objects in the house and Sarah had to touch the ground, her clothes, and bed clothes, without washing her hands or cleaning anything. Although Sarah *dreaded* doing this, her tension did not increase very much (a maximum of 6 on a 0–10 anxiety scale). After half an hour, tension had decreased, and after an hour it had completely disappeared.

At the next session it appeared that Sarah had succeeded in not

cleaning anything and that she had repeated a number of these assignments. Because Sarah did reasonably well, it was decided to
terminate regular therapy on a weekly basis. There were seven follow-
up visits over a period of nine months, during which period progress
appeared to continue.

Follow-up

Sarah was reassessed at the last follow-up visit nine months after the
end of formal treatment. Results on the rating scales and questionnaires over the course of therapy are shown in Figure 5.1. At this time
Sarah did extremely well. The obsessive-compulsive problems had
markedly improved and she was no longer depressed. She now enjoyed social relationships and had had an affair that had lasted for
five months. In addition, she had recently started a new relationship.

Overall Evaluation

The focus of this case was a change in the obsessive-compulsive problems of the client. During the course of therapy a number of other
treatment targets emerged that seemed partly related to the obsessive-
compulsive behavior and had to be dealt with separately. Although
treatment was broad-spectrum, it was behavioral in that strategies
applied were training procedures specifically directed to deal with the
various target problems in succession. In this case it was felt necessary to deal with the "underlying" problems (e.g., social anxiety) to
eliminate the obsessive-compulsive problems. Exposure therapy alone
was not very effective until assertion training and cognitive therapy
were implemented to deal with social anxiety and irrational cognitions. It is unlikely, however, that assertion training and cognitive
therapy on their own would have resulted in a definite improvement
of the obsessive-compulsive problems. It should be noted that when
starting therapy, Sarah was so much distressed by her obsessive-
compulsive problems that these problems had to be dealt with first.
Moreover, at the start of therapy Sarah was unaware of her uncertainty in social situations, as shown in her low score on the Social
Anxiety Scale at the pretest. Only during the course of exposure
therapy dealing with her compulsive behavior did the problems in
social situations become evident to her.

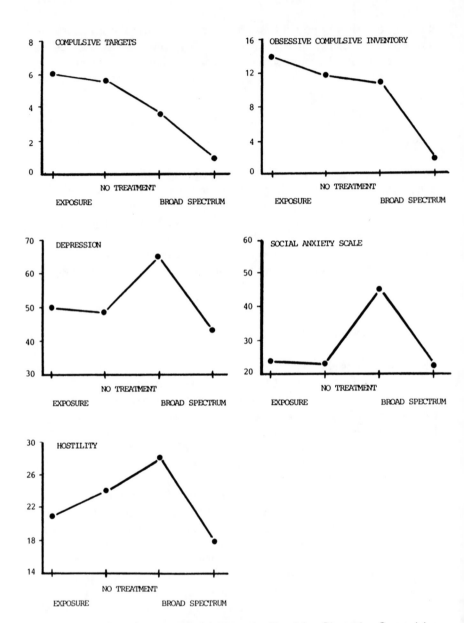

Figure 5.1. Results on compulsive targets, Maudsley Obsessive-Compulsive Inventory, Zung Self-rating Depression Scale, Social Anxiety Scale, and Hostility and Direction of Hostility Questionnaire.

References

Ellis, A. (1962). *Reason and emotion in psychotherapy.* New York: Lyle-Stuart.

Emmelkamp, P. M. G. (1982). *Phobic and obsessive-compulsive disorders: Theory, research and practice.* New York: Plenum.

6

Nonbipolar Depression

Michael E. Thase

Description of Depression

The term *depression* may be used to describe a variety of dysphoric states, ranging from normal grief and reactive sadness to long-standing unhappiness and dissatisfaction. However, the clinical depressive syndromes currently classified as major affective disorders are distinguished by three factors: (1) persistent and relatively pervasive sadness or loss of interest, present nearly every day for a period of at least two to four weeks, (2) presence of an accompanying constellation of behavioral, cognitive, and neurovegetative changes (including motoric retardation and/or agitation, insomnia or hypersomnia, excessive guilt, self-denigration, suicidal ideation and/or hopelessness, fatigue or anergia, poor appetite and weight loss, or food cravings and weight gain, difficulty concentrating, anhedonia, and loss of libido), and (3) impairment in interpersonal and/or vocational functioning or a level of severity sufficient to lead an individual to seek treatment. It is important to note that no single sign or symptom is diagnostic of depression, and a number of nonaffective psychiatric and medical conditions may present with dysphoric features. Clinical depressions tend to be episodic, with episodes lasting from weeks to years in duration and, if untreated, associated with increased risks of mortality from suicide and cardiovascular diseases. As many as 10% of the adult population will experience a major depressive episode at some point during their life spans.

In this chapter, assessment and treatment of an individual with nonpsychotic, nonbipolar major depression is described. This is the most common form of affective disorder treated in outpatient settings. During the past decade, considerable effort has been devoted to developing cognitive and behavioral approaches for assessment and effective treatment of nonbipolar depression. Other less prevalent affective disorders, such as psychotic (delusional) depression and bipolar disorder (i.e., episodes of depression alternating with at least one period of mania) have received less extensive study by cognitive-behaviorally oriented investigators and are more commonly seen in inpatient and medication clinic settings.

Case Identification

William G., a 23-year-old white, single, first-year graduate student, came to the Diagnostic and Evaluation Center of an urban, university-affiliated clinic seeking treatment. Mr. G. had no previous history of psychologic/psychiatric treatment. He had been urged to seek help by several family members.

Presenting Complaints

Mr. G. requested treatment for depression, stating that he was feeling increasingly agitated and afraid that he would "lose it." He described being unable to get over breaking up with his girlfriend.

History

Mr. G. had been doing fairly well until about two months prior to the initial contact. He denied long-standing adjustment difficulties and, in fact, had maintained an above average GPA in college, was socially active, and felt that he was well-liked by others. About one year prior to the start of this episode, his application to medical school had been turned down. He described handling this setback with only a modest degree of disappointment, being buffered by the chance to begin graduate school in the Fall at a major university located in his home town, the opportunity to improve his application and try again the following year, and the fact that he recently had begun his first serious dating relationship.

This relationship subsequently flourished, and for approximately six months Mr. G. and his friend Ms. L. were daily companions and sexual partners. Mr. G. related that he felt Ms. L.'s love had finally enabled him to become a "whole" person. They began to make plans for marriage at some indefinite point in the future. Six months prior to beginning therapy, Mr. G. returned home to begin graduate school. He devoted himself to his studies and worked part time as a research assistant. He initially maintained the relationship with Ms. L. via frequent phone calls and occasional weekend visits. However, four months later, Ms. L. told him that she was no longer sure about the relationship, and that she wanted the opportunity to date others. Although hurt by this, Mr. G. agreed that it was a good idea. Upon returning home, he found that he had lost his zeal for school. He had trouble concentrating, lost his appetite, and began having difficulty falling asleep. His thoughts were frequently about Ms. L., and he began to ruminate about her whereabouts, choice of companions, and the like. He called Ms. L. repeatedly, alternating between feeling hurt and needy or angry and demanding. After several weeks of progressively worsening upset, he impulsively left school one weekday and drove 300 miles for an unannounced visit with the intention of "working things out." Unfortunately for Mr. G., his surprise visit turned into a nightmare, as when he arrived at Ms. L.'s apartment he found her in bed with another man. Moreover, Ms. L. was furious because of the unannounced visit, and indignantly broke off the relationship, chastising Mr. G. for being immature and "clinging."

During the following weeks, Mr. G. grew increasingly depressed. His attendance at school became sporadic, and he stopped shaving, only rarely left his apartment, and refused all social invitations. He experienced daily crying spells and periods of restlessness, and ate only one small meal each day, ultimately losing nearly 20 pounds. His mood became predictably worse in the morning, when he would stay in bed and ruminate about his lost love. He lost interest in sex and described being unable to feel any joy or pleasure. His sleep disturbance worsened, such that he was sleeping only three to five hours per night, with multiple arousals and final awakening at least two hours earlier than usual each morning. He began to think of himself as a "reject" and a "fool," ridiculing himself for his many perceived shortcomings and inability to maintain the relationship. Although he did not contemplate suicide, he did feel empty and hopeless, doubting his prospects for ever becoming successful in life. He continued to ruminate about his former girlfriend, feelings which intensified when she did not return his letters or phone calls. Finally, after a bleak holiday visit with his family, he decided to enter treatment.

Assessment

Results of a detailed intake interview were consistent with a moderately severe episode of major depression, nonbipolar type, with prominent features of melancholia (endogenous depression). Indeed, on examination Mr. G. appeared intensely dysphoric, gaunt, agitated, and bleary eyed. His mood state remained persistently sad and tearful throughout a 1½ hour interview, showing no signs of reactivity to immediate therapeutic support. Hospitalization was discussed, although Mr. G. declined, stating that he would like to try outpatient therapy and that he *would not* contemplate suicide. He was given the clinic's emergency number, and a second appointment was arranged for two days later to provide further crisis-oriented support and to complete the assessment. At that time Mr. G. remained quite depressed. A semistructured research interview was completed, revealing no evidence of other, antecedent psychiatric disorders or substance abuse, and two commonly used depression scales were administered. He scored in the severe range on both the Beck Depression Inventory (BDI), a self-report scale, and the clinician-rated Hamilton Rating Scale for Depression (HRSD) (see Table 6.1). A physical examination and routine blood work revealed no evidence of intercurrent medical problems. It was noted that the patient's father had suffered one epi-

Table 6.1. Changes in Beck (BDI) and Hamilton (HRSD) Scores During a Course of Cognitive Therapy

Week	BDI	HRSD
Pretreatment	36	24
1	33	22
2	26	16
3	22	—
4	29	13
5	13	—
6	10	7
7	8	6
9	6	6
12	5	4
14	4	3
20	5	4
32	5	3
44	4	2

sode of depression, which responded to antidepressant (tricyclic) medication during a psychiatric hospitalization.

Selection of Treatment

At this point, various outpatient treatment strategies were discussed with Mr. G. Because of the prominent neurovegetative changes in sleep, appetite, weight, activity level, and libido, as well as the family history of depression, antidepressant treatment with a tricyclic agent seemed prudent. Mr. G. stated that he had an aversion to taking medication and he requested a psychological therapy. Moreover, he identified wanting to cope better with his feelings and to learn more about himself as equivalent priorities to symptomatic relief. Given his motivation for such a treatment, it was decided to begin treatment using Beck's cognitive-behavioral therapy (CBT: Beck, Rush, Shaw, & Emery, 1979). This approach seemed appropriate, since it has been shown to at least match the efficacy of tricyclics in several clinical trials (see Beck et al., 1979; Thase, 1983) and provides an individually tailored combination of cognitive and behavioral strategies for coping with many of the target symptoms reported by Mr. G., such as ruminations, loss of interest, insomnia, and agitation/anxiety. Other more strictly behavioral or cognitive methods (e.g., social skills training, pleasant-events task assignment, relaxation training, or self-control training) may be incorporated, as needed, as components in Beck's multimodal approach to depression. However, while being technically eclectic, this form of therapy is theoretically grounded in the notion that distorted cognitive processes, such as automatic negative thoughts, logical errors, and reductionistic thinking, contribute to and maintain the depressive syndrome. Further, in depression-prone individuals, it is hypothesized that more durable, underlying cognitive processes, referred to as silent assumptions and schemata, provide rigid and faulty basic beliefs about one's self and the world, which may trigger logical errors, faulty information processing, and automatic negative thoughts during periods of vulnerability (e.g., following rejection by a lover).

It was decided to monitor progress using weekly administrations of the BDI and biweekly HRSD ratings (see Rehm, 1981, for a detailed discussion of the various assessment inventories for depression). Given Mr. G.'s severe insomnia and clinical presentation of melancholia, two consecutive all-night electroencephalographic (EEG) sleep studies were obtained to provide objective measurements of the degree of sleep disturbance and rapid eye movement (REM) sleep latency, a biological "marker" of endogenous depressions. It has been proposed that individuals who show a rapid onset of the first REM period (i.e., <60 minutes after sleep onset) have a physiological disruption which necessitates treatment with either pharmacotherapy or ECT (Rush & Shaw, 1983; Thase, 1983). Sleep studies would be repeated following either response or nonresponse to the course of cognitive therapy. Results of the initial studies confirmed Mr. G.'s reports of insomnia, documenting poor sleep continuity (75% of the night spent asleep compared to an age-normative value of 90–95%), but REM latency was within the normal range, with a mean value of 74 minutes (mean 90 minutes ± 25 minutes).

Course of Treatment

Therapy was initiated with twice-weekly sessions. Such frequent visits are preferred with severely depressed patients to provide an increased level of monitoring and therapeutic support, to facilitate participation with homework, and to maximize the probability of observing modest clinical gains which are a direct result of the interventions employed (and frequently overlooked or minimized by depressed patients). The focus of such early sessions is often quite behavioral, in that a functional relationship between cognition and mood has not yet been demonstrated within the single-case design of therapy. Also, symptomatic distress still is quite high.

During the initial sessions, Mr. G. still was noted to be quite depressed (see Table 6.1). The session began with the therapist briefly providing an overview of what CBT was like. This offers a clear rationale for the "why" and "how" of therapy, as well as emphasizing that this form of treatment focuses on coping with, and alleviating, depression. The importance of working as a collaborative team and the rationale for utilizing homework assignments also were introduced. An initial treatment contract for 12 twice-weekly sessions was agreed upon. Mr. G. was then asked whether he had any questions or comments, at which point he replied, "Well, I'm not sure it will work, but I'm willing to give it a try." Next, the most recent BDI was jointly reviewed, with attention given to identifying the most pressing difficulties. One priority for therapists during any form of treatment for depression is continual assessment of suicidality and hopelessness. In this case, Mr. G. was not suicidal and seemed modestly hopeful about his prospects with treatment. Mr. G. identified a broad goal of "getting over Ms. L. and getting on with my life." The therapist was then able to introduce the concept of moving from the general to the specific and pointed out that it would take some time to get over such a deep love affair which ended on such a sour note. The idea of getting on with life was operationalized:

> *T*:   What would it take in order for you to feel like you were beginning to move on?
>
> *C*:   Just to get L. out of my mind (tearful).
>
> *T*:   Well, I think we both know that goal will take some time to reach. What else?
>
> *C*:   I guess being able to get back to work in the lab and being able to get out of my apartment more.
>
> *T*:   Okay, let's start with those goals and work from there. I think a good way to get a handle on how you're spending your days would be to have you keep track, on an hour-by-hour basis, of your daily activities. Here are three log sheets to use until our next appointment. Does this homework assignment make sense?
>
> *C*:   You want to take a baseline.
>
> *T*:   That's true, but more importantly, it will give us a chance to begin to identify, on a day-to-day basis, just where we need to concentrate our energies.

It always is important to ascertain whether the patient understands the reason for the homework and its potential importance to his or her ultimate response. This ensures the highest probability of completion of the assignment. The therapist also assigned reading a short pamphlet summarizing CBT and asked Mr. G. to underline any sections he wished to discuss further or which particularly applied to him.

During the next several visits, the initial theme of "getting on with life" was pursued by use of activity monitoring and specific homework assignments to increase the likelihood of attending previously valued social/recreational/academic behaviors. As in many other behavioral interventions, a graded, progressive approach is taken, with emphasis on setting obtainable goals. For example, Mr. G. had previously enjoyed jogging and, with some support, he was able to begin a regular running program, first in the afternoon when his energy level was higher and subsequently in the morning as a coping alternative to lying in bed and ruminating. Concurrently, his attendance at school and the lab increased, perhaps solely as a consequence of self-monitoring or in concert with an overall increase in activity level. During these early sessions, Mr. G. was asked to put his temptations to call Ms. L. "on the shelf" until he was better able to cope with the expected high probability of further rejections. Thought stopping was employed to gain some control over intrusive ruminations about Ms. L., and a relaxation tape was used to help decrease tension he experienced at bedtime. In each case, these specific techniques were first practiced as "experiments" during the session and, when found to be of some use, were assigned as homework to improve coping with distressing symptoms.

By the third week of treatment, a modest, yet consistent pattern of decline in depression, agitation, and insomnia was apparent. Mr. G. joined an intramural basketball program, and he went out socially once with friends. Nevertheless, he criticized himself: "I'm just going through the motions." Upon discussion, this pessimistic feeling state was reframed in terms of objective, evidence-based behavior, namely, that improvements had been made, but much work remained to be done.

Between weeks 3 and 5, the focus of therapy shifted toward more cognitively oriented material. By this point, the rationale for such a shift was clear, and Mr. G.'s progress with previous homework assignments had created a feeling of therapeutic momentum. Thoughts and feelings about Ms. L., and their perceived implications about Mr. G.'s self, the world, and his future (i.e., Beck's cognitive triad) are illustrated in Table 6.2. This three-column worksheet was used to identify a situation associated with increased dysphoria and begin to catalogue some of the automatic negative thoughts experienced at these times. The three-column approach led to identification of "hot" cognitions, centering around themes of being incomplete without a girlfriend and being insignificant. This set the stage to begin to test the validity of the automatic thoughts and develop more rational, evidence-based alternative cognitions.

It is important to keep in mind that the process of testing negative automatic thoughts is not simply a matter of cajoling the patient into accepting the therapist's viewpoint, nor is it explaining away realistic difficulties. For example, with respect to the thought "L. doesn't love me anymore," all available evidence indicated that this was likely to be true. However, regarding the cognition "I drove her away," a list entitled "Reasons L. Jilted Me" was constructed (see Table 6.3). While the list initially included several depressogenic explanations, as other possible alternatives were explored it became ap-

Table 6.2. Three-column Worksheet for Establishing Associations Between Events, Mood, and Cognitions

Situation	Mood	Automatic Thoughts
1. Walking to lab, thinking about where L. might be now	Sad; lonely	I'll never get over her. That was the love of my life. I was so happy then, I'm miserable now. L. doesn't love me anymore.
2. Daydreaming after dinner	Sad; lonely	I drove her away. I'm such a jerk. I'm empty without her. L. doesn't love me anymore.

parent that several more neutral and credible possibilities existed. The specific believability of each alternative was weighed by examining the evidence. In the case of the statement "I drove her away," Mr. G. ultimately decided that this was partly believable (he had, after all, repeatedly called her, barged into her apartment without calling first, and behaved in a demanding and/or "whiney" fashion), but he

Table 6.3. "Reasons L. Jilted Me"

Before Restructuring		After Restructuring	
Reason (rank ordered)	Believability (%)	Reason (rank ordered)	Believability (%)
She doesn't love me	100%	She doesn't love me	100%
I'm a boring jerk	80%	Lonely—found someone to take my place	100%
Found somebody else	70%	Long-standing pattern of dumping boyfriends	90%
I drove her away	70%	Angry at me for moving away	70%
		I drove her away	20%
		I'm a boring jerk	0%

was able to recognize that (1) he was inexperienced in coping with dissolving relationships, (2) he was trying to hold on to someone he loved, and (3) L. was already withdrawing from him when he began to behave in that fashion.

During the next phase of treatment, the therapeutic contract was renegotiated for six additional weekly visits. Work continued on identifying automatic thoughts and testing their validity by weighing the evidence and considering alternative explanations. Between weeks 4 and 9, Mr. G.'s ratings on both the BDI and HRSD dropped down into the recovered range (see Table 6.1). He continued to experience intermittent periods of sadness and still reported diurnal mood variation with a mild degree of early morning awakening. However, his interest in school and social activities had returned, his sleep was otherwise normal, and he had regained five pounds.

During the final three weekly visits, Mr. G. was able to identify a more basic, silent assumption, "I'm empty without a girlfriend." A homework assignment helped to differentiate the things he liked about having a girlfriend (i.e., preferences) from the absolute necessities of life, and linked more generic preferences about having a girlfriend with aspects he liked in his relationship with Ms. L. Symptomatic status remained quite stable and within the range of remission (see Table 6.1). Mr. G. elected to arrange a final visit with Ms. L. Prior to this meeting, a session (#12) was devoted to role-playing and rehearsing various possible scenarios and outcomes from this meeting. The meeting with Ms. L. was described as awkward and detached, but provoked no major adverse reactions and added to a growing sense of self-efficacy.

Termination

A single session (#14) was devoted to review of progress and discussion of termination. Mr. G. reported (and the therapist agreed) that all major goals were obtained. He volunteered that the processing of "catching" and testing automatic thoughts had itself become almost automatic. Regular therapy visits were terminated, and an infrequent series of follow-up visits was agreed upon. The therapist also offered to be available during this period as a "consultant" if the need arose between follow-up visits. A repeat series of EEG sleep studies revealed normalization of sleep continuity indices, with no change in REM latency values.

Follow-up

Three follow-up visits took place over the next six months. Mr. G. remained in remission, and reported that he occasionally would use various strategies learned in therapy to help make difficult decisions or to understand what was going on "cognitively" when he felt down in the dumps. He had elected to try to reapply to medical school and was progressing satisfactorily toward his master's degree.

Overall Evaluation

One problem with using a multimodal approach is that it is often difficult, if not impossible, to identify the active ingredient(s). In this case, was it activity scheduling, use of cognitive strategies, more nonspecific therapist support factors, spontaneous remission, or jogging? This is a question that will remain unresolved, although Mr. G. personally attributed his recovery to the use of cognitive techniques. Obviously, research employing large groups of clinically depressed patients either randomly assigned to component treatments or sequentially given various components will be needed to test the relative power of each factor. Research in this area conducted to date has yielded rather inconclusive results, with Lewinsohn and associates (e.g., Lewinsohn & Hoberman, 1982) suggesting a commonality of effects engendered by an approach providing four ingredients: (1) an elaborated, well-planned rationale, (2) training in coping skills applicable in enhancing daily life, (3) structure and guidance such that skills are appropriately applied *in vivo*, and (4) belief that improvement is due to the individual's increased skillfulness, not the therapist's skillfulness. Obviously, Beck's form of CBT meets these criteria, as do most of the other newer short-term psychosocial treatments for depression. Until sufficient empirical data are available to guide implementation of particular techniques, it seems intuitively appropriate for behavioral clinicians to continue to tailor interventions to meet the specific needs of their patients.

A related issue pertains to the potential long-term benefits of treatments like CBT. As suggested by this case, such treatments may indeed provide improved coping skills applicable in the patient's natural environment. This offers one clear advantage for the more costly and time-consuming cognitive and behavioral therapies relative to pharmacotherapy, particularly given the high relapse rates seen in depression (Thase, 1983). Preliminary evidence is beginning to accumulate to support this point, although investigations employing large samples and follow-up periods extending past conventional 6- to 12-month designs are needed.

Finally, it is of some interest that while Mr. G. appeared to be an ideal candidate for tricyclic medication, he showed a full response to CBT. Alternatively, as he was young, bright, articulate, and motivated, it could be argued that he was an ideal candidate for any form of psychological therapy. It is likely that the groups of patients who respond to these divergent modalities overlap to some degree, a circumstance which will make the task of identifying differential indicators of response all the more difficult. In this case, it seems that application of a relevant set of interventions was sufficient for improvement despite the patient's prominent neurovegetative symptomatology, an observation now supported by data from several controlled, outpatient clinical trials (see Thase, 1983). Here, the relevance and efficiency of the CBT interventions for dealing with the major presenting problems may be critical, as we have found high attrition rates in equally symptomatic outpatients treated with other forms of psychosocial therapy when either no precipitating stressors were apparent or when therapy did not facilitate coping with distressing symptoms such as agitation or insomnia (Thase, Monroe, Hersen, Bellack, & Himmelhoch, unpublished observations). Nevertheless, since Mr. G.'s REM latency values were neither markedly shortened prior to treatment nor increased during recovery, it might be argued that his degree of "endogeneity" did not fall into the range which necessitates a biological intervention. Regardless, it appears that a multimodal cognitive-behavioral therapy offers a viable alternative for treatment of many outpatients with nonbipolar major depression.

References

Beck, A. T., Rush, A. J., Shaw, B. F., & Emery, G. (1979). *Cognitive therapy of depression.* New York: Guilford.

Lewinsohn, P. M., & Hoberman, H. M. (1982). Depression. In A. S. Bellack, M. Hersen, & A. E. Kazdin (Eds.), *International handbook of behavior modification and therapy* (pp. 397–431). New York: Plenum.

Rehm, L. P. (1981). Assessment of depression. In M. Hersen & A. S. Bellack (Eds.), *Behavioral assessment* (pp. 246–295). New York: Pergamon.

Rush, A. J., & Shaw, B. F. (1983). Failures in treating depression by cognitive behavior therapy. In E. B. Foa & P. M. G. Emmelkamp (Eds.), *Failures in behavior therapy* (pp. 217–228). New York: Wiley.

Thase, M. E. (1983). Cognitive and behavioral treatments for depression: A review of recent developments. In F. J. Ayd, I. J. Taylor, & B. T. Taylor (Eds.), *Affective disorders reassessed: 1983* (pp. 234–243). Baltimore: Ayd Medical Communications.

7

Rape Trauma

Dean G. Kilpatrick
Angelynne E. Amick

Description of Disorder

Rape is generally defined as the use of force or threat of force to obtain sexual relations from a nonconsenting person. Victims perceive rape as a life-threatening situation and fear that they will be killed or seriously injured. During rape, victims suffer extremely high levels of cognitive and physiological anxiety. They feel terrified and helpless. They experience tachycardia, muscle tension, rapid breathing, and other signs of physiological anxiety. Via classical conditioning, stimulus generalization, and higher order conditioning, stimuli and situations associated with the rape acquire the capacity to evoke clinically significant levels of fear and anxiety. Thus, encountering stimuli or situations that are rape-related evokes cognitive feelings of apprehension and dread, physiological anxiety symptoms, and behavioral avoidance. Rape-related fear often causes victims to drastically restrict their life-style, behavior, and ambition. Fear-induced reductions in activity levels often produce depression. Additionally, depression can be produced by feelings of learned helplessness engendered by rape or through self-blame and other types of cognitive distortions rape victims frequently experience. Not surprisingly, victims often develop sexual dysfunction and diminished sexual desire, because rape-induced anxiety has become associated with sexual behavior, sexual thoughts, and sexual desire. Consistent with the diagnostic criteria for Post-traumatic Stress Disorder, victims frequently experience rape-related intrusive thoughts, flashbacks, and dreams, the occurrence of which is often accompanied by considerable distress.

There is no evidence that rape-induced problems disappear spontaneously, and without treatment problems can last for many years. Additionally, a rape experience fundamentally changes a victim's view of the world and of other people. No longer is the world a safe place where people are to be trusted. Rather, the world is a dangerous place where no one can be trusted.

Case Identification

Linda* was a 21-year-old, single black female who was referred for treatment by the local rape crisis center. She had been the victim of multiple sexual assaults committed by three or four 18- to 22-year-old members of a street gang on two separate occasions over a one-week period, approximately nine years prior to treatment. Linda had never told anyone about the incidents until she confided in her boyfriend immediately before seeking treatment.

Presenting Complaints

The constellation of symptoms presented by Linda centered around her sense of being out of control, being about to die, or "going crazy." She reported having had her symptoms for approximately one year. She reported becoming anxious when she encountered rape-related cues in the media and groups of men on the street. Particularly disturbing were frequent, intrusive thoughts about violently murdering her assailants. Her dreams, as well as waking thoughts, included revenge-oriented violence with guns and knives.

Somatic symptomatology contiguous with rape-related anxiety and homicidal thoughts included headaches, nausea, itching scalp, tightness in her chest, and shortness of breath. Depressive symptomatology included early morning wakening, decreased appetite, difficulty concentrating, and social withdrawal. Linda used the hypnotic sedative meprobamate and alcohol in an attempt at self-medication for her anxiety. Although generally a nonsmoker, she also reported

*This client's name has been changed to protect her confidentiality.

smoking one-half pack of cigarettes per day in response to her highly anxious state.

Finally, Linda cited as problematic her relationship with her grandmother, who tended to excessively discuss rape and other crimes. She also expressed frustration with being unable to organize her life and return to school. A somewhat peripheral complaint was her fear of driving an automobile.

History

At the time of initial contact, Linda was unemployed and living with a boyfriend. She had moved from the major Northeastern city where the rapes occurred to her grandmother's home in Charleston approximately five months before seeking treatment.

Family/Social History

Linda was reared an only child by her mother. Her parents divorced when she was seven years old. Her father remarried and is a restaurant owner. She had no contact with several half-siblings while growing up.

Linda described herself as very close to her mother but withdrawn from others in her neighborhood. She began dating at age 17 and has had several boyfriends. She reported having a few female friends at school.

Educational/Occupational History

Linda attended a private Catholic high school and then college for a few months before leaving the North. She has held a variety of jobs, including work as a file clerk, movie ticket salesperson, and nursery worker.

Psychiatric History

No psychiatric difficulty or history of treatment was reported prior to the year preceding treatment. Linda reported normal sexual functioning and desire.

History of Rape Experience

Although her memory of the rape experience was clouded, Linda estimated that the sexual assaults had occurred when she was in junior high school. She recalled that a gang of several 18- to 22-year-old men forcibly entered her home on two occasions while she was alone after school. Two gang members raped her while the others looked on, laughing and jeering. Although she remembered vividly a particular song playing on one of the assailant's radio and the semen stains on her pants, Linda had great difficulty recalling other details such as the exact year in which the incidents took place.

After the assaults, Linda was terrified to go out in her neighborhood because the assailants had attacked her on two separate occasions and had boasted of the assault to others in the neighborhood. Her fear generalized to men encountered on the street, and she became hypervigilant when outside or on public transportation. Linda described often refusing to do errands for her mother because of her fears. However, she remained adamant about her total refusal to disclose the incident to anyone.

Linda's rape-induced problems gradually improved, and she was relatively problem-free until about one year prior to seeking treatment. At that time, she was faced with a series of violent incidents that appeared to elicit memories of the assaults and provoke a delayed Post-traumatic Stress Disorder. A particularly crucial factor in exacerbating Linda's symptomatology was an encounter with one of the assailants. He asked her to "get high" with him, and upon her refusal, he verbally degraded her. Also during the year prior to her presentation for treatment, Linda was in her father's restaurant during an armed robbery, her best friend was raped, and she was physically beaten by her boyfriend. As a result of these experiences, she reported a dramatic increase in her rape-induced intrusive thoughts, revenge-oriented ideation, and other symptomatology. The recurrence of rape-related problems, the strength of her homicidal urges to obtain revenge, and general feelings that she had lost control of her life prompted Linda to move to Charleston. The move helped initially, but her problems remained sufficiently disturbing for her to finally seek treatment.

Assessment

Elsewhere (Veronen & Kilpatrick, 1983), we have argued that it is useful to follow Lang's (1968) tripartite model in assessment and treatment of rape-related anxiety. Thus, problems are conceptualized and assessed in three major "channels": (1) physiological or autonomic, (2) cognitive or mental, and (3) behavioral or motoric.

Physiological or Autonomic Channel Assessment

The physiological components of Linda's presenting complaints were assessed by a multimethod approach, including psychophysiological assessment and behavioral self-monitoring of anxiety-related physical symptoms. Psychophysiological assessment was conducted in an Industrial Acoustics Corporation (IAC) sound-attenuated chamber, using a Grass Model 7A polygraph and a Con-Sol BSR-GSR solid-state monitor to measure exosomatic electrodermal activity. After electrodes were attached, Linda was informed that she would remain alone for a five-minute adaptation period, after which a therapist would enter the room to interview her regarding the sexual assault experiences. During the adaptation and interview periods, heart rate, resting skin conductance, electrodermal responses, and frontalis electromyographic activity were continuously recorded. Data collected during the interview were used to pinpoint the content of rape-related ideation that was most anxiety producing for the client. Treatment efficacy assessment focused upon physiological activity during the five-minute adaptation period prior to the interview. Activity during this period was conceptualized as reflecting anticipatory physiological anxiety. Mean heart rate, EMG, basal skin conductance, and nonspecific electrodermal responses (increases in skin conductance of .002 microohms or greater) during each of the five one-minute segments were determined. The psychophysiological assessment procedure was repeated after treatment was completed.

Since Linda reported several physiological symptoms that appeared to be stress-related, she was asked to self-monitor on a daily basis the following physiological symptoms: headaches, itchy scalp, nausea, sleep disturbance, and sensation of tightness in chest.

Cognitive or Mental Channel Assessment

In this channel, assessment included several self-report inventories that have proven useful in detecting rape-induced problems, both with respect to distinguishing between rape victims and nonvictims and in detecting clinical changes in symptomatology (Kilpatrick & Veronen, 1984):

1. The Derogatis Symptoms Checklist (SCL-90-R), a 90-item symptom checklist that generates three overall scores and nine symptom dimensions: somatization, depression, anxiety, hostility, phobic anxiety, paranoid ideation, obsessive-compulsive activity, interpersonal sensitivity, and psychoticism.
2. The Veronen-Kilpatrick Modified Fear Survey, a 120-item inventory of potentially fear-producing items and situations. Each item is rated on a scale of 1 (not at all disturbing) to 5 (very much disturbing). In addition to an overall score, scores are obtained on the following subscales: animal fears, classical fears, social-interpersonal fears, tissue damage fears, miscellaneous fears, failure/loss of self-esteem fears, and rape fears.
3. The Profile of Mood States Scale, a 65-item measure of six transitory mood states: tension-anxiety, depression-dejection, anger-hostility, vigor-activity, fatigue-inertia, and confusion-bewilderment. On all but vigor-activity, high scores reflect greater mood disturbance.
4. The Impact of Event Scale, a 15-item scale developed to measure two key diagnostic criteria for Post-traumatic Stress Disorder: (a) event-related intrusion (intrusively experienced ideas, images, feelings, or bad dreams) and (b) event-related avoidance (consciously recognized avoidance of certain ideas, feelings, or situations).*

Aside from the cognitive dimensions of Linda's symptoms measured by the inventories, two other cognitive areas were assessed. The first involved intrusive thoughts of revenge against the assailants and about the rape experiences. The client was requested to monitor the frequency of such cognitions on a daily basis over a one-week period prior to the onset of treatment. Linda initially used a wrist counter to record the frequency of disturbing cognitions. However, this strategy was modified by having Linda record the duration of intrusive cognitions since one intrusive cognition would often lead to an extended period of rumination. Additionally, Linda proved unable to separate revenge cognitions from cognitions of the rape experiences per se because the association between the two had become so great.

A second cognitive area to be assessed was irrational cognitions

---

*References for these scales, information about their reliability, validity, and norms for rape victims are presented elsewhere (Kilpatrick & Veronen, 1984).

and beliefs about the assault and her responsibility for it. These cognitions took the form of a strong belief on her part that others would blame her for the assaults because she knew her assailants and was attacked by them on more than one occasion. She also expressed extreme concern about others' evaluations of her, stating that she would be overwhelmed with embarrassment if peers and family were to discover that she was raped. Inherent in this belief system was Linda's feeling of self-blame about her responsibility for the attack. Since it is unreasonable to believe that an 11- or 12-year-old girl should be able to fight off three or four male gang members, all of whom were much older and stronger than she, we felt her self-blame was irrational. Similarly, we felt it was unlikely that others would blame her for the assault should she tell them about it, particularly given her age at the time of the assaults and the fact that there were multiple assailants.

These irrational beliefs and disclosure about the assaults were assessed via Linda's interviews with the therapists. The frequency of her dreams of murdering the rapists was assessed using the same method.

Behavioral Channel Assessment

Problematic behaviors were delineated through an interview, and some behaviors assessed via self-monitoring. Interview data indicated Linda to be socially withdrawn, fearful of driving an automobile, and experiencing interpersonal difficulty with her grandmother. Also among behavioral deficits, Linda listed her inability to return to school and organize plans for getting on with her life. Pretreatment self-monitoring of substance use revealed Linda to be using 800–1200 mg of meprobamate, 3–4 alcoholic drinks, and one-half pack of cigarettes per day.

Goals for Treatment

After reviewing Linda's assessment data, we determined that there were several target behaviors that required therapeutic intervention. The following target behaviors and goals for treatment were first reviewed with Linda and then were mutually agreed upon as therapeutic goals:

1. To reduce autonomic hyperactivity and resulting somatic symptomatology associated with rape-related stimuli.

2. To reduce frequency of intrusive thoughts about the rape and about seeking revenge.
3. To reduce use of alcohol, drugs, and smoking as a maladaptive method of reducing stress associated with rape-related anxiety.
4. To reduce irrational beliefs about her responsibility for the assault.
5. To increase willingness to discuss the assault with other people.
6. To increase ability to assertively communicate with grandmother regarding the upsetting nature of constant references to crime and rape.
7. To increase ability to implement plans and behaviors consistent with independent living, putting rape into perspective and going on with her life (e.g., learning to drive, resuming her education).

Diagnosis

Linda's symptoms and problems met the *DSM-III* criteria for the diagnosis of Post-traumatic Stress Disorder, Chronic and Delayed. An interesting and atypical aspect of Linda's case was that she experienced not only intrusive thoughts about the rape itself but also about achieving revenge by murdering her assailants.

Selection of Treatment

Selection of treatment procedures in this case was guided by several general assumptions about appropriate treatment for rape victims as well as by some specific aspects of Linda's case.

Our first general assumption is that it is inappropriate and unethical to attempt to reduce anxiety and fear associated with being raped, per se. There is ample evidence that the incidence of rape and other forms of violence against women is high (Kilpatrick, Veronen, & Best, in press), so rape victims' fears of being revictimized are not unrealistic. Unlike combat veterans, who are removed from the situation that produced their Post-traumatic Stress Disorder (PTSD), rape victims cannot remove themselves from a situation where the possibility of being attacked is always a grim reality. Thus, rape victims' fears of being revictimized are not unrealistic and should not be eliminated via treatment. Rather, treatment should focus on help-

ing the victim put fears into perspective by taking appropriate pre-
cautions to increase her safety while not unduly restricting her life-
style and behavior.

Our second general assumption is that an important aspect of
effective treatment is helping victims understand the etiology of their
symptoms. A victim who becomes terrified when she sees a man who
resembles her assailant or when her husband approaches her sexually
often thinks she is losing her mind. Giving her information that her
reactions are normal and were acquired through classical conditioning
provides her with reassurance as well as a way of understanding her
rape-induced problems. We believe that victims can tolerate having
symptoms as long as they understand why they are having them and
that such symptoms are normal.

Our third general assumption is that the complex, multifaceted
symptoms and problems experienced by most rape victims are best
treated with a strategy that focuses upon teaching the victim to use
a variety of techniques to cope with her problems rather than to use
one technique to eliminate problems. Providing victims with a variety
of coping skills also enables victims to use the techniques with other
problems as well as with rape-related problems.

There were also two specific aspects of Linda's case that influenced treatment selection. The first was that Linda's neighborhood
in a large Northeastern city is a dangerous, high-crime area. Since
her plans included the possibility that she would return to her home,
her fear of victimization had a particularly realistic basis. Thus, it
was important to pick a treatment that focused upon teaching her
to cope with fear of victimization rather than one that focused upon
elimination of such fear. Second, Linda's intrusive thoughts and impulses about seeking revenge by having her assailants killed or seriously injured were extremely strong and disturbing to her. Obviously,
it would have been ill-advised to use a treatment designed to reduce
anxiety associated with these homicidal impulses and fantasies.

Given these considerations, we ruled out the use of systematic
desensitization or exposure techniques such as implosion. However,
a modification of the Stress Inoculation Training (SIT) treatment approach developed by Veronen and Kilpatrick (1983) appeared to be
ideally suited for use with Linda. As originally designed, this SIT
treatment package lasted for 20 hours and focused on treatment of
specific rape-related fears. Preliminary evaluation of treatment efficacy was good (Kilpatrick & Veronen, 1984; Veronen & Kilpatrick,
1983), and SIT was recently identified as a treatment strategy for
rape-related problems that holds great promise (Holmes & St. Lawrence, 1983).

Course of Treatment

Treatment Procedures

We made three major modifications in Veronen and Kilpatrick's SIT treatment package for use in Linda's case. First, SIT was presented to Linda as a treatment that would teach her a variety of skills to be used in coping with her rape-related problems, not as a treatment specifically for rape-related fear and/or phobic avoidance. Second, the SIT treatment package was streamlined and reduced from 20 hours to 8 hours, excluding homework assignments. Third, the focus in the coping skills application phase was changed from confronting a specific stressor to using coping skills whenever appropriate in a more general manner. Treatment was conducted by the second author using a one-session per week, one-hour per session individual treatment format.

Rationale and Educational Phase. Linda was instructed about typical victim reactions to rape and told that her fears had been originally elicited via classical conditioning during the rape situations and had generalized to a variety of other rape-related cues and stimuli. It was pointed out that, although the rapes took place years ago, a recent series of violent incidents had reelicited many old rape-related fears and anxiety. The three channels (physical, cognitive, and behavioral) through which she was experiencing anxiety were explained. Linda was assured that, although she often found herself suffering from a number of anxiety-related symptoms, her fear responses were not all-or-none phenomena. She was educated about the importance of detecting early signs of anxiety and using these symptoms as cues for effective coping strategies. She was informed that she would be trained in the use of several coping skills to be used in dealing with her problems.

Additionally, the therapist told Linda that, because of the severity of her fears, intrusive thoughts, and associated somatic symptomatology, she was spending a great deal of time "taking care of her rape-related problems." She was encouraged to redirect her energy toward "taking good care of herself" by mastering the more adaptive coping skills we would teach. Importantly, Linda was reassured that her behaviors were typical and predictable and that she was not "going crazy." Finally, we addressed her strong desire to obtain revenge via murdering her assailants by encouraging her to consider the value of obtaining revenge by living a productive life. The essence of this idea was captured by the 17th century English author George Herbert, who stated: "Living well is the best revenge." Herbert's statement was discussed with her, and she was asked to carefully consider it.

Coping Skill Acquisition and Application. Several behavioral techniques were used to facilitate coping with specific rape-related problems. These techniques are described in greater detail elsewhere (Veronen & Kilpatrick, 1983).

1. Jacobsonian tension–relaxation contrast training was used to reduce autonomic hyperactivity associated with rape stimuli. An audiotape of relaxation training was provided for at-home practice. Three treatment sessions were devoted to this training procedure.

2. Thought stopping has been used to counter the ruminative or obsessive-thinking characteristic of the rape victim (Forman, 1980). Although it was originally utilized to eliminate self-devaluative and negative internal dialogue related to social censure and criticism, its use in breaking up obsessional thoughts of being harmed and of harming others is a natural extension of the technique.

Linda was taught to employ thought stopping to control her obsessions about the rape and plans for revenge. An example of Linda's ruminative thinking is given in the following situation:

Linda is relaxing in front of the television at home. An old "Dragnet" episode comes on the screen. The officers mention briefly the incidence of rape in the city. The word *rape* cues such thoughts as, "Why do men rape innocent women? Like those animals that raped me. They aren't really men and don't deserve to live. I'd like to shoot them all. They would lie dying in their own blood and see me standing above them, laughing."

Thought stopping was taught by having Linda think about the rape and her plans for revenge. After she continued these thoughts for 30–45 seconds, the therapist, in a loud, commanding voice, said, "Stop," and asked Linda what happened. Linda replied that the thoughts stopped. This process was repeated several times. The next step was to have Linda say, "Stop," aloud when the thoughts began. Finally, she was able to stop the thinking by silently verbalizing "Stop." Following her use of the stopping procedure, Linda was encouraged to engage in or imagine pleasant activities incompatible with rape-related rumination. One session was used to teach this treatment procedure.

3. Cognitive distortions about self-disclosure and self-blame were challenged by educating Linda to typical self-accusatory victim reactions. The value of social support in a victim's adjustment process as well as the probability of actually receiving such support from sig-

nificant others were discussed. Two treatment sessions were devoted to the use of this procedure.

4. Linda's communication difficulties with her grandmother were addressed by suggesting assertive ways of expressing herself. Specifically, role-play was employed, which allowed Linda to practice conveying to her grandmother her aversion to crime- and rape-related conversations. One session was devoted to this technique.

5. General goal attainment was facilitated by discussing with Linda the necessity of setting achievable successive steps to her goals, rather than becoming overwhelmed by the perceived enormity of her aspirations. Linda's ultimate goal was a career in the criminal justice system. Immediate steps targeted were learning to drive a car and applying to technical school. Two treatment sessions were used to address these issues.

6. Although excessive substance usage was not directly treated, these behaviors were described as maladaptive coping responses elicited by anxiety. It was suggested that more adaptive skills, taught through the course of therapy, would replace substance use as coping behaviors for dealing with stress.

Treatment Outcome

Presentation of outcome data will focus upon evaluation of the extent to which each of the seven therapeutic goals was achieved. Additionally, Linda's performance on the self-report pre- and posttreatment will be presented.

Goal 1. Reduction of autonomic hyperactivity and resulting somatic symptomatology associated with rape-related stimuli: An inspection of Table 7.1 indicates that treatment produced a significant reduction in anticipatory EMG, nonspecific electrodermal response, and basal skin conductance activity. Reduction in heart rate also occurred but was not statistically significant. Examination of Linda's pre- and posttreatment self-monitoring data revealed that dramatic improvement occurred after treatment with respect to the physiological symptoms of headaches, itchy scalp, nausea, sleep disturbance, and tightness in chest. Linda reported that using her relaxation skills in response to early somatic indicators of anxiety was quite successful in reducing these symptoms. All of these symptoms were reduced in frequency to zero levels.

Goal 2. Reduction of intrusive thoughts about rape and seeking revenge: Linda had difficulty understanding some of the Impact of

Table 7.1. Psychophysiological Assessment Data

Psychophysiological Measure	Pretreatment Minute						Posttreatment Minute						
	1	2	3	4	5	Mean	1	2	3	4	5	Mean	t
Heart rate (beats per minute)	91	90	105	89	89	92.8	89	91	85	88	86	87.8	1.39
EMG (microvolts)	18.9	21.2	20.9	18.6	18.8	19.7	19.5	16.9	17.1	16.5	16.4	17.3	2.80[a]
Nonspecific EDRs (frequency per minute)	5	4	3	7	6	5.0	0	1	0	1	2	1.8	7.20[c]
Basal Skin Conductance	.0040	.0040	.0038	.0040	.0040	.0040	.0032	.0025	.0026	.0026	.0028	.0029	4.52[b]

[a]significant at $p < .05$
[b]significant at $p < .01$
[c]significant at $p < .005$

Event Scale items. Thus, her posttreatment scores were indicative of considerable intrusion and avoidance. During posttreatment assessment, confusing items were clarified for Linda and she was asked to respond to the inventory a third time, answering first as she would have before treatment and then as she felt after treatment. On this revised administration, she reported that event-related intrusion had been reduced by two-thirds at posttreatment; whereas event-related avoidance was unchanged. One plausible explanation for the continued elevation of avoidance scores is that her newly acquired coping skills (e.g., thought stopping) provided Linda with more adaptive ways to continue "avoiding" problematic stimuli. Interestingly, her estimate of her pretreatment levels of intrusion and avoidance were virtually identical to her actual pretreatment scores. It is also important to note that, although reduced by two-thirds, some intrusive thoughts were still occurring after treatment. However, Linda stated that they were less disturbing to her since she could use thought stopping to keep them from developing into a long string of ruminations and could use her relaxation training skills to cope with the anxiety they produced.

Goal 3. Reduction of use of alcohol, drugs, and smoking behavior: Posttreatment self-monitoring data indicated that Linda had become completely abstinent regarding her usage of meprobamate and tobacco. Her alcohol consumption was also reduced from a pretreatment average of three to four alcoholic drinks per day to approximately three glasses of wine per week.

Goal 4. Reduction of irrational beliefs about responsibility for the assault: Analysis of posttreatment interview data revealed that little progress was made toward achieving this goal. Linda expressed that she blamed herself somewhat less than prior to treatment, but she still contended that others would react in an accusatory manner toward her if she confided in them and was equally concerned that people would gossip about her if they knew she had been victimized.

Goal 5. Increasing willingness to discuss the assault with other people: For reasons that were discussed above, Linda remained quite reluctant to discuss her assault with others. Her fears of doing so were quite strong and her avoidance behavior regarding disclosure was well-developed. It is interesting to note that her fears persisted in spite of the fact that the one person (excluding us) that she ever told responded very supportively. We viewed Linda's continued reluctance to discuss her assault as problematic, but she did not. Because her overall functioning was so improved and because of her failure to see this area as a problem, we elected not to pursue this therapeutic goal further.

Goal 6. Increasing ability to assertively communicate with grandmother regarding references to crime and rape: Linda reported that she had successfully achieved this goal after treatment by using the skills she had learned in role-playing and assertively asking her grandmother to not talk about crime and rape because of the distress it produced. Interestingly, Linda did this without telling her grandmother that the topic was upsetting because Linda herself had been raped.

Goal 7. Increasing behavior consistent with independent living, putting the rape in perspective and going on with life: During a follow-up interview, Linda proudly announced that she had been accepted into a technical school, was applying for a student grant, and was taking driving lessons. Linda also reported instigating a meeting with her half-sister, whom she had not seen in approximately 12 years.

An important theme in Linda's therapeutic progress was the idea that she must stop "taking care of" her rape-related problems and redirect her energy into reaching her goals. Linda was able to experience her progress, both in symptom reduction and in increased productivity, as "the best revenge."

Improvement in Self-report Measures

Linda exhibited substantial improvement on all of the self-report measures. This improvement is illustrated by the pre- and posttreatment SCL-90-R data presented in Figure 7.1. Inspection of this figure reveals an across-the-board reduction of symptomatology. Examination of Linda's pre- and posttreatment mood state profile as measured by the POMS in Figure 7.2 indicates that Linda's negative mood states decreased after treatment while her positive mood state of vigor increased. Data from the MFS mirrored this trend, reflecting a posttreatment reduction in both Rape Fears (Pretreatment M=108; Posttreatment M=91) and Overall Fears (Pretreatment M=255; Posttreatment M=208).

Termination

Termination was indicated by Linda's acquisition of the coping skills and her generally positive posttreatment assessment data. In addition to these factors, we observed Linda's growing inclination to as-

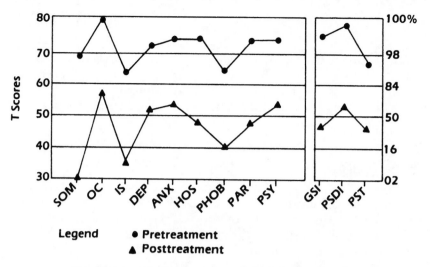

Legend   ● Pretreatment
         ▲ Posttreatment

Figure 7.1.   Pre- and posttreatment SCL-90-R profile.

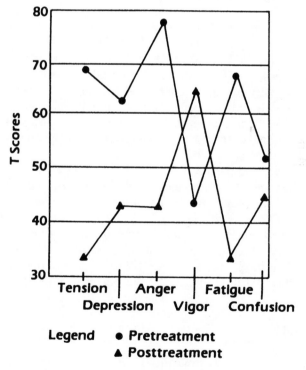

Legend   ● Pretreatment
         ▲ Posttreatment

Figure 7.2.   Pre- and posttreatment POMS profile.

sume responsibility for following through on goal-directed behaviors such as seeking driving lessons and applying to technical school. Treatment was, therefore, terminated by fading session frequency from once per week to once per two weeks, three weeks, four weeks, and so on.

Follow-Up

An in-person follow-up interview was conducted at two months post-treatment. At that time, both Linda's self-report and her assessment data indicated that all therapeutic gains had been maintained. At three months posttreatment, Linda reported via a telephone follow-up that she was doing extremely well. This latter follow-up was conducted immediately prior to completion of this chapter.

Overall Evaluation

In general, we believe that the modified version of SIT that we used with Linda was highly successful. Most of the therapeutic goals were achieved by the end of treatment and maintained at follow-up. In addition to helping reduce her rape-related intrusive thoughts and symptomatology, treatment also helped Linda to resume realistic planning regarding her future and to give up her obsession of achieving revenge by having her assailants murdered. Moreover, the coping skills she learned in treatment are ones that she can use to deal with new problems as they arise.

The only cloud in this silver lining was Linda's lack of improvement with respect to self-blame and willingness to talk about the assault with other people. Her self-blame is obviously well-entrenched and difficult to change.

It is worth noting that the treatment we used with Linda was noninvasive and required relatively little treatment contact. We believe that this modified version of SIT has much to recommend it as a treatment for Post-traumatic Stress Disorder resulting from rape.

References

Forman, B. (1980). Cognitive modification of obsessive thinking in a rape victim: A preliminary study. *Psychological Reports, 47,* 819–822.
Holmes, M. R., & St. Lawrence, J. S. (1983). Treatment of rape-induced trau-

ma: Proposed behavioral conceptualization and review of the literature. *Clinical Psychology Review, 3,* 417–433.

Lang, P. J. (1968). Fear reduction and fear behavior: Problems in treating a construct. *Research in Psychotherapy, 3,* 90–102.

Kilpatrick, D. G., & Veronen, L. J. (1984, February). Final report, NIMH Grant No. MH29602, *Treatment of fear and anxiety in victims of rape.*

Kilpatrick, D. G., Veronen, L. J., & Best, C. L. (in press). Factors predicting psychological distress among rape victims. In C. R. Figley (Ed.), *Trauma and its wake.* New York: Brunner/Mazel.

Veronen, L. J., & Kilpatrick, D. G. (1983). Stress management for rape victims. In D. Meichenbaum & M. E. Jaremko (Eds.), *Stress reduction and prevention* (pp. 341–373). New York: Plenum.

8

Social Inadequacy

Mary Jane Black
Harold E. Schroeder

Description of the Disorder

Social inadequacy is an important component of many psychological disorders. It is prominent among psychiatric patients, in affective disorders, and among "shy" individuals with heterosocial difficulties. Few clients, however, are referred specifically for help with social deficits; the majority initially define their difficulties in other ways. Clients may express concern over their self-image, their mood, or a variety of problems secondary to limitations of social skill. Clinicians identify problems of depression, anxiety, anger, family conflict, and so on.

One of the most important and common social deficits is the inability to interact in conversation. The ability to interact verbally with others in a variety of situations is personally enriching and effective behavior. Conversely, deficits in conversational skill impose limitations on social and vocational functioning. Among college students, minimal and frequent daters can be discriminated by their ability to initiate and maintain conversations. Depressives engage in fewer conversations and derive less social reinforcement from verbal interactions than nondepressives. Posthospital adjustment of psychiatric patients is facilitated by conversational competence. Since conversational difficulties are such a prominent and crucial feature of social inadequacy, we have selected a case in which the focus is on training conversational skills.

Case Identification and Presenting Complaints

Roger was a slim, pale, 23-year-old man who came to therapy at the urging of a longtime friend. The friend had repeatedly expressed concern over Roger's pessimistic outlook and his social isolation. During the initial interview, Roger acknowledged that he generally had felt discouraged about his life since his graduation from high school five years before. In recent months these feelings had intensified. He sought treatment when he found himself thinking of suicide, an act that was not only frightening but that also conflicted strongly with his religious values. Anxious and near tears, he said he knew he was depressed and needed help.

History

Roger was the third of four children. The household had been organized around a domineering, dogmatic father. An alcoholic, Roger's father had nonetheless managed to hold a responsible position from which he was retired. He had stopped drinking and was no longer physically abusive, but remained angry and critical. A shy and self-effacing child, Roger had always been a special target of his father's wrath. His mother was a quiet woman who had devoted her life to protecting the children from their father. She arranged for the youngsters to spend much time with their cousins in the homes of various aunts and uncles.

Roger's two older brothers moved out of state after they finished their college educations. The youngest child, a daughter, was Roger's close companion until she left home to be married. Although he frequently considered living on his own, Roger remained at home with his parents. After work, he generally stayed in his room, reading or listening to music. There were occasional angry accusations from his father about his lack of ambition. His typical response was to accept his father's criticism meekly, and then withdraw to ruminate about his shortcomings. Occasionally, he allowed himself to indulge in angry fantasies, which then provoked further guilt and self-criticism. The father made no effort to encourage his son to move away; instead, he repeatedly pointed out the impracticalities of his attempting to survive financially on his current wages.

Roger depended on his siblings and cousins for socialization. As they all began to go their separate ways, he experienced acute loneliness. His few dates in high school had been arranged by others. He tried to make friends when he began to work, but shyness and lack of confidence always intruded. The happiest period of his young adult life was the few months when he played guitar with a small band on evenings and weekends. For the first time he felt he was important to someone. He was comfortable talking with his friends about music. During this period he had several brief, awkward heterosexual relationships which seemed to have been characterized by intense dependency and exaggerated expectations on Roger's part. When the musical group disbanded, these experiences ceased as well. He was able, however, to maintain a friendship with one high school classmate. Their relationship was still close, but the frequency of their contacts had diminished since the friend's recent marriage. Sadly, Roger expressed hopelessness about ever making friends or establishing a family.

Roger's work life was as unrewarding as his social life was painful. An average student in high school, he had made no college or vocational plans. After graduation, he drifted from one menial job to another. He knew he should be more productive, but income and self-esteem remained low. He gained little satisfaction from his work and expected that this would always be true. Initially, he said that he had never had any career ambitions. However, in a later interview he talked with unusual animation about an interest he had developed just prior to his high school graduation. At that time he had been staying with an uncle who sold insurance for a living. This man had often taken Roger along with him when he called on potential customers. These were stimulating and pleasurable experiences. The youth quickly picked up a substantial amount of knowledge about the business. His uncle was impressed and offered to help his nephew enter the field. When he was asked why he had not taken advantage of this opportunity, Roger said that the thought of having to converse with people in their homes or offices was too terrifying.

He wanted desperately to be with other people, but Roger only accepted jobs which permitted him to work in relative isolation. Friendly co-workers were acknowledged, but kept at a distance. He was often commended for his reliability and competence. He had been offered promotions to better paying and more responsible jobs. He actively avoided these because they invariably required greater interpersonal involvement. On one occasion, he manufactured an excuse to quit a job because he was embarrassed to admit his feelings of social inadequacy when a promotion was offered to him. At the time he began therapy he was working as a stock man in a supermarket. Having been complimented repeatedly on his diligence, he was again fearful of being considered for advancement.

Initial Assessment

Assessment of Roger's depression and the risk of suicide were immediate therapeutic concerns. Subjective distress was obvious. His affect was sad, and he looked dejected and discouraged. He expressed dissatisfaction with every aspect of his life: his work was unfulfilling, he regarded his home environment as intolerable and unchangeable, and he complained of loneliness and social isolation. He was preoccupied with negative thoughts and expectations for the future. His appetite was not affected, but he did admit to a sleep disturbance. On work days he arose regularly at 7:00 A.M., after about eight hours' sleep. However, on days off he slept an average of 14 hours, sometimes spending an entire day in bed. Complaining of low energy, Roger nonetheless continued to do his job effectively. He rarely drank, and used no drugs or medications. His social ties were minimal, but well maintained. He communicated regularly with his friend by telephone and had an occasional dinner at the friend's home. He was looking forward to a visit from his sister and her husband the following month. Suicidal ideation was infrequent and vague. Roger's religious affiliation was an important aspect of his life; he believed strongly in his church's injunctions against self-destruction. He found comfort in regular church attendance. Overall, he was considered seriously depressed and in need of immediate treatment, but not actively suicidal.

Social inadequacy was the most potent and pervasive contributor to Roger's depressive behavior. He was a bored underachiever whose social apprehensions interfered with opportunities for vocational advancement. His wages were at the poverty level; he could not afford to move out of the conflictual and blaming atmosphere of his family home. Even if finances no longer became a barrier to independent living, it was unlikely that he would choose to be on his own. Emotional dependency was reinforced by relatives. Nearly friendless, he lacked the skills and confidence to develop mature relationships to sustain him outside the family circle. Significant improvement in any area of Roger's functioning could be achieved only by direct treatment of social inadequacy as the critical, underlying problem in his depression.

Treatment

The client readily agreed to a minimum of 12 therapy sessions, with an evaluation of progress at the end of that period. As an additional support, he was given the option to telephone the therapist between weekly appointments, should he become acutely distressed. His depression was acknowledged as understandable in the context of his isolation and lack of fulfillment. He was told that social skill problems were a major cause of his depression; as his skills improved, he would experience an improvement in his affective life. Therapy was described as a process of learning these and other skills to promote constructive change.

Several goals were identified during the first therapy session. Career advancement and independent living were long-term targets of achievement. One short-term goal was interruption of the cycle of guilt and anger provoked by the client's encounters with his father. Roger was instructed to leave the room immediately whenever his father made critical comments toward him. Another goal was increased activity. For the first week, Roger was to record the time he awakened on his days off. Using the average of these times as a baseline, each succeeding week he was to set his alarm 15 minutes earlier, until he was sleeping no longer than 10 hours on his days off. He was to get out of bed within five minutes after the alarm had rung and get dressed. Each day he was to spend time out of the house engaging in some activity, if only to walk around the block. In addition, he was to maintain his regular church attendance.

Conversational skill training was selected as the specific treatment for Roger's social inadequacy because it had the greatest potential for enhancement of interpersonal effectiveness in all areas of his life. In treating severe conversational deficits such as his, it is very difficult to generate behavior on which to build skills. Particularly when there is a learning history that includes a threatening, punitive parent, silence and avoidance become more reinforcing than talking. Therefore, to encourage social activity of any sort, demands and risk must be low, but the behavior constructive. Our training technique is a highly structured, integrated system of skill development. Learning is progressive, beginning with systematic exposure to discriminative stimuli which signal conversational content. Basic skills are taught for simple, time-limited conversations. Skills are strengthened by practice and elaborated to enable the learner to engage in more complex, open-ended interactions.

Training incorporates four elements identified by Rich and

Schroeder (1976): (1) cognitive restructuring, (2) response acquisition, (3) response reproduction, and (4) response shaping. The fifth component in their classification – response transfer – has been an especially vexing problem for researcher and clinician alike. The present therapeutic program is unique because response transfer is embedded in each of the other components through practice and real-life experimentation. Similarly, assessment is an ongoing process by which progress is monitored in several modes by client and therapist. With sufficient in-session instruction, the major portion of the client's training can be accomplished on his or her own time. This procedure fosters response transfer in the natural environment and facilitates efficient use of the therapy hour. It is particularly advantageous for clients like Roger who have other important clinical issues, such as depression and anger, which must be addressed concurrently. The conversational skill-building process utilized for this case is typical of our customary training sequence; a more detailed description is available in Schroeder and Black (1985). The major emphasis for the remainder of this chapter will be conversational skills training since it was the major focus of therapy. Progress on other behavioral goals will be reported within this context.

The first training element, *cognitive restructuring*, begins when conversational behavior is conceptualized for the client as a skill which is learned like any other skill. Proficiency is achieved through the learning of basic skills on which more complex responses can be built. Learning is described as an active process involving recognition of needs and strengths, instruction, practice, experimentation in real life, and constructive evaluation of outcomes. Conversation is defined as more than just talking; it is a mode of communication in which effective listening and interpersonal sensitivity are crucial factors.

Another step in cognitive restructuring is a thorough analysis of conversational problems to discriminate behavioral, emotional, and cognitive sources of difficulty. Some individuals have true skill deficits because of poor learning experiences. Others have adequate skills, but anxiety or negative thinking interferes with performance. The usual case is one in which an individual has a combination of difficulties. Assessment on all dimensions allows both the therapist and the client to pinpoint problem areas which deserve special attention. Roger was given self-evaluation forms to complete at home and bring with him to his next therapy session. These included the range of his current social interactions, rewarding experiences he hoped to achieve through improved skills, anxiety rating scales, and a checklist of cognitive factors which influenced his social behavior. These materials were important assessment devices and also gave Roger something concrete to do to begin a systematic approach to his problems.

When he returned for the next therapy session, Roger reported that he had experienced a brief period of hopefulness that his social problems could be resolved. Then he sank into discouragement once again. In the necessary process of confronting the particulars of his conversational difficulties, he overwhelmed himself with accusations of incompetence. He was told these reactions were understandable considering his overall depressive outlook and lack of learning opportunities. As a form of resistance, however, they had to be countered firmly and specifically. Throughout therapy, Roger needed frequent reminders that the learning of complex skills required hard work. It was also pointed out that he had skills on which to build: he had been able to converse with his musician friends, he had interacted sufficiently well during job interviews to get hired, and so forth.

Roger's self-reports included multiple difficulties. Most of them could be traced to faulty cognitions. His thinking was characterized by negative self-evaluations, disastrous expectations about his performance, and social disapproval. The result was, of course, intense anxiety that prevented attempts to talk with others. Cognitive restructuring, based on Ellis' rational-emotive therapy (Ellis, 1962), was utilized to begin the process of anxiety reduction.

The therapist modeled and the client practiced making more rational, less inhibiting self-statements about conversations and other life problems. Like many clients, Roger assumed that every aspect of his behavior had to be perfect in order for him to consider himself worthwhile. This demand for absolute success is an especially strong obstacle to constructive behavior change. Roger was instructed to reinforce himself for his efforts, rather than to demand a flawless performance. He also insisted on change in his father's hostile attitude, in spite of a family history of interactions suggesting that this was not likely to occur. As Roger relinquished this demand, he expended less energy in angry frustration and more on his own efforts to change. Other helpful techniques taught and practiced were anxiety management through relaxed breathing and covert rehearsal of satisfying interpersonal encounters. All in-session work was backed up by written materials, which included assignments to be done to reinforce learning.

By the third therapy session, Roger was ready to begin the *response acquisition* component of conversational training. Instructions are an important and necessary part of all phases of response acquisition. Devising appropriate instructions to address the behavioral complexities inherent in all conversations is a difficult problem. General instructions such as "talk about something you know well," are rarely sufficient to facilitate social approach even in basically competent individuals. For clients like Roger whose experiences have been severely limited, general instructions provoke additional resistance and discouragement. Very specific instructions may be useful on one occasion but misapplied on another, resulting in awkwardness or even worse consequences. For Roger, specific instructions only encouraged his faulty belief that there was one, and only one perfect way to behave.

To take advantage of the best features of general and specific instructions while minimizing their disadvantages, we taught Roger a comprehensive technique for all conversational behavior. It is a *general* stimulus–response strategy which is applicable to any *specific* conversation. Conversations were simply conceptualized for him as the interaction of two types of behavior: observation and reaction. "Observation" was defined as information gathering – learning to notice aspects of each conversational situation (e.g., the setting), the other person (e.g., what the person is doing), and the emotions perceived (e.g., happiness). Observations are cues to be used to initiate conversations and are usually the most appropriate content. "Reaction" was described as one's internal responses to environmental or conversational stimuli such as thoughts, feelings, opinions, curiosity, and the like. Reactions facilitate the mutuality of conversational encounters.

In the next two sessions, Roger was taught to develop his observational skills for conversations, beginning with what he noticed in the therapy situation itself. He was instructed to put his observations into words as preparation for the covert rehearsal he was to do as homework outside of therapy. His observations would be the basis of *response reproduction* for the short conversations he would initiate in future weeks. He protested that he could not possibly talk with anyone who did not speak to him first, especially a stranger. He was assured that he could do so when he was "ready." All such resistance was interpreted as lack of readiness rather than lack of ability.

There was more resistance to homework assignments which directed the client to make observations on his own and list them on worksheets provided by the therapist. Roger said he "didn't go anywhere to see anybody he could talk to," and therefore had no settings in which to make observations. A review of Roger's customary daily routine elicited numerous, previously ignored opportunities to converse with someone if he chose to. He listed these on a worksheet to provide structure for his homework. All homework assignments were labeled as "experiments" – "just to see what happens." This bit of cognitive restructuring minimizes performance demands and makes it more likely that the client will expose himself to situations in which the target behavior would naturally occur. As an additional focus for learning, in the process of making observations Roger was to select three persons with whom he would like to talk briefly "when you are ready."

By the fifth therapy session Roger appeared more relaxed, and there were noticeable changes in his mood. It was still difficult for him to get out of bed on days off, but he had managed to cut two hours off his sleep time. It was his own idea to save small errands to do on those days so that he would have some purpose in leaving his house. He could recognize the association between aversive interactions with his father and acute episodes of depression, but it was still hard for him to resist being drawn into conflicts with this parent. Sundays were especially tense because both of them were generally in the house most of the day. The therapist suggested that Roger go to a restaurant for brunch after church to give himself something pleasurable to do and to reduce the opportunity for altercations with his father. He said he had no money to do this, and furthermore, he did not "deserve" to treat himself this well. Nonetheless, the following week he did initiate a Sunday routine which included brunch and, ultimately, reduced-price movies shown during the afternoon at a local university. His sister's visit about this time was a factor in maintaining Roger's motivation to change. He tended to dismiss the therapist's acknowledgment of his efforts as "what a therapist does," but he was much more accepting of his sister's social reinforcement for the same behavior changes.

With increased activity, Roger's exposure to social stimuli increased as well. He had become a good observer through homework assignments and was able to find conversational material in many settings. His real-life experiments now included "instant conversations." These were defined as conversations that had natural time limits (e.g., speaking with the gas station attendant). The initiation of conversations could therefore be practiced, while content demands remained low. The client was given checklists on which he was to evaluate specific behavioral components of his performance, such as introducing a topic relevant to the situation. This procedure was designed to avoid negative, global evaluations. Rather, particular strengths and weaknesses were assessed realistically.

Because he was still quite hesitant about social approach, Roger missed many conversational opportunities. Recapitulations of these were utilized for in-session response acquisition and reproduction through modeling and role-play. Roger's report of an interesting event led to the *response shaping* phase of treatment. He had finally begun to make a few comments to the friendly waitress who regularly served him at Sunday brunch. During one of their short conversations she remarked that she enjoyed talking with him, but had initially hesitated to do more than greet him because he looked so aloof. This impression is all too frequently created by shy people. In their effort to portray a confident attitude they do not feel, they unknowingly present themselves as distant or uninterested. This experience helped Roger understand how his own behavior could contribute to social rejection. In-session modeling and practice then began on the nonverbal components of conversational skill such as facial expression, eye contact, and body language. Paralinguistic elements were also stressed. These included a clear, well modulated voice, meaningful, expressive language, and emotional tone appropriate to conversational content. Self-evaluation forms for future real-life experimentation included a checklist for these components.

In succeeding sessions, Roger was introduced to the second part of the conversational strategy-reaction. Reactions were described as his natural responses to conversational events. His first step was to learn to become actively aware of thoughts, feelings, questions, and the like, that arose in the context of the conversational situation itself. Verbalizing these allowed him to engage in longer conversations and to share in the responsibility for maintaining them. For example, he was taught to ask open questions and to talk about experiences of his own that were relevant to what another person said. Both the observation and reaction components of the strategy provided structure for all conversations and helped him manage anxiety more effectively through focused attention to his immediate experience.

In many areas of his functioning, Roger made slow but steady progress. By the twelfth session, he was sleeping no more than 10 hours on his days off. He spoke of increased energy and expressed more interest and pleasure in his own activities. He made some acquaintances among the regular attendees at the Sunday movies. He gradually began to carry on casual conversations with co-workers. One of them invited Roger to his apartment to listen to music. After an awkward beginning, Roger considered the evening enjoyable and a success. He was still subject to episodes of depression, but these had decreased in frequency; they occurred on an average of only twice a week instead of daily, as they had at the beginning of therapy.

Roger was able to maintain his behavioral gains, but there were significant impediments to his further growth. Dependency was one of these. He often spoke of moving, but remained in the family home. With his sister's encouragement, he had followed up on the therapist's instructions to begin making specific plans for independent living. However, when his sister's visit ended, so did his motivation. His social circle had widened dramatically, relative to his initial isolation, but he had made no sustained friendships that could support his transition to living on his own. He repeatedly spoke of his frustration over his inability to develop deeper relationships. He generally was able to interact superficially with a variety of people, but he wanted longer lasting and more intimate ties. He wanted to ask a young woman at work for a date, but postponed doing so. He complained that nothing important or meaningful came of his conversational attempts.

Part of Roger's difficulty was his reluctance to share his reactions in conversations. Fearing rejection if anyone "really knew me," he disclosed little of himself. Conversations were often one-sided. His silence could easily be interpreted as lack of interest, making it unlikely that he would be sought out again. He failed to ask for clarification of comments that puzzled him and, consequently, he sometimes would respond inappropriately. Problems in timing of remarks and interpersonal sensitivity also were matters for concern. With a learning history of punishment for self-expression, he was most resistant to offering an opinion or reacting with feeling. There also was the suspicion that Roger's defensiveness and chronic resentments were interfering factors. He denied that he expressed himself angrily, but in role-plays there had often been nonverbal or paralinguistic behaviors that suggested otherwise. All of these interactional components had been addressed repeatedly and specifically in therapy sessions without success.

Individual therapy sessions were becoming less and less productive. Roger had affiliative desires that could not be satisfied until he had learned to recognize and master the complexities of social interactions more effectively. He needed an accepting, responsive atmosphere in which his skills could be practiced and shaped in a more natural environment. Realistic sources of support were necessary in order for him to become less dependent on his family and his therapist. For these reasons, group therapy was chosen as an additional intervention.

The purpose of the group was to improve Roger's interpersonal functioning through behavior change. The group process is interactional. It is a closed group to which new members are added only at 12-week intervals. Since many clients remain in the group for as long as a year or more, there are always experienced members available to model norms for new members. These include the acceptance of new members, self-expression in the form of disclosure and feedback, confrontation of maladaptive interpersonal behaviors, the establishment of behavioral goals by therapists and group members, and consistent emotional support for positive behavior change.

The group was described to Roger as an important opportunity to develop and practice additional social skills with others who were working on the same goals. He was anxious about joining, but agreed to participate in this "experiment" once a week for a 12-week period. For the first three weeks he participated in both individual and group therapy. After that time, individual sessions were scheduled only for specific purposes. To minimize dependence on the therapist, Roger was directed to work out appropriate issues with his peers in the group, rather than during individual sessions. This procedure was the first phase of the termination process.

Because Roger's therapist was also one of the group leaders, there was ample opportunity to observe his interpersonal behavior. He was readily accepted into the group, and was able to interact quite well on a superficial level. For the most part, however, he remained silent or was quite skillful in diverting attention from himself to other, more verbal members. When the group members insisted on his involving himself more fully, many of the obstacles to his social progress noted earlier were evident. Group feedback was helpful in making him aware of his underlying hostility and how he expressed it nonverbally through silence and withdrawal. This behavior was demonstrated explicitly when he informed the therapists privately that he would not return for the next 12-week session of group meetings. He cited financial and other reasons for his departure. It was obvious to the therapists that he was actually reacting angrily about a difference of opinion he had had with one member of the group. Fortunately, before the next series of meetings began, he was telephoned by another group member who was empathic, but insistent that he return to the group. Roger was able to respond to this emotional support and did remain in the group. His acceptance in the group in spite of conflicts with members was instrumental in motivating him to leave his family within the next two months. He moved into an apartment with the co-worker with whom he shared an interest in music.

Termination

Roger was in individual and group therapy for a total of 18 months. His decision to leave treatment was endorsed by the therapist, who agreed that he had accomplished his behavioral goals within the group and should expand his skills independently beyond the therapeutic environment. By that time he had formed friendships with two group members and made several friends outside the group. In the final weeks of group sessions, through empathic disclosures about his own interpersonal struggles, he contributed to the growth of other members.

Follow-up

Roger periodically telephones the therapist to report life changes. One of these is his new occupation as an insurance trainee. Roger is still vulnerable to brief depressive episodes when he experiences stress. At one point, he returned to therapy for a month to work out conflicting and confusing feelings about the unexpected death of his father.

Overall Evaluation

Roger's case illustrates the complexity of treatment for social inadequacy. From the beginning, Roger presented multiple problems which required multilevel interventions. It was necessary to deal with his distorted and unhealthy self-perception, depressed mood, anger, level of aspirations, guilt and self-criticism, social isolation, anxiety, family and other relationships, distortions in interpreting the behavior of others, and so on. Such a multifaceted treatment approach is common because of the pervasive influence of social skill deficits. In addition, difficulties common to all forms of therapy, such as client resistance, are not avoided through a behavioral approach. Treatment of social inadequacy is a complicated and lengthy procedure which may require periodic follow-up sessions to deal with particularly difficult situations.

References

Ellis, A. (1962). *Reason and emotion in psychotherapy.* New York: Lyle-Stuart.

Rich, A. R., & Schroeder, H. E. (1976). Research issues in assertiveness training. *Psychological Bulletin, 83,* 1081–1096.

Schroeder, H. E., & Black, M. J. (1985). Unassertiveness. In M. Hersen & A. S. Bellack (Eds.), *Handbook of clinical behavior therapy with adults.* New York: Plenum.

9

Tension Headache

Frank Andrasik

Description of the Disorder

Tension headache is one of the most common bodily complaints of individuals today, exceeded only by cold, flu, and the like. It is characterized by a persistent bilateral pain that is experienced as a dull, gnawing, bandlike ache, which builds and resolves slowly. Tension headache is best viewed as a "stress-related" disorder; the headache is believed to be due to sustained contractions of shoulder, neck, scalp, and facial muscles that occur when attempts at managing pressing environmental demands or stressors are ineffective. These contractions stimulate pain receptors in the affected muscles and produce ischemia by compressing intramuscular arterioles. Once a headache has begun, management efforts which meet with minimal success may serve to create additional stress, which may then further intensify symptomatology. The muscle contraction etiological model of headache is being questioned at the moment, though, and may undergo some revisions in the not too distant future. Depression is often an accompaniment of tension headache, and some clinicians suspect that it may be the primary cause of the headache in many cases. Finally, the headache respects no social, racial, educational, or intellectual boundaries, although it is unevenly distributed across

Preparation of this manuscript was funded in part by a Research Career Development Award made available to the author by the National Institute of Neurological Communicative Disorders and Stroke (NS00818).

gender. Females clearly predominate in community and outpatient surveys, but this might be due in part to an increased willingness of females to admit to and to seek treatment for this problem.

Case Identification

The patient was a 36-year-old unmarried female, who was visually impaired since birth. She presently was enrolled in doctoral study, was employed as a work-study student at her university, and volunteered her services to an agency serving individuals with special needs.

Presenting Complaints

The main reason for seeking treatment was the presence of a continuous headache, rated as moderate to very intense. She described the headache as "ever present" and noted that the musculature and arteries in her forehead and both temple areas were very sensitive to touch. She would occasionally become nauseous when the headache reached an intense level, but vomiting never occurred at these times. She noted that her headache was worse when she became angry, when she was required or asked to do something she did not want to do, and when the weather was "rainy" or the sky was overcast (this made it difficult for her to ambulate outdoors). Headache significantly interfered with her ability to work and recreate and often required periods of bed rest for recuperation.

Additional complaints consisted of periodic bouts of gastrointestinal distress, occurring every two to three months and lasting approximately two weeks. The patient reported concern about her weight and recently had enrolled in a program for weight control. Finally, she expressed concern over her inability to make progress on several important projects.

History

The patient was relatively headache free and contented while attending schools for the blind. When she reached junior high school she was placed in the regular classroom and soon thereafter began to experience headache. In a short while she began to treat her headache with a number of over-the-counter preparations, and then was consuming these medications at levels far beyond those recommended by the drug manufacturers. She described herself as experiencing a number of adjustment difficulties throughout life, primarily interpersonal and social in nature, attributing many of these to her visual handicap. At age 25 she began to seek therapy to promote a more positive adjustment to her blindness and a more appropriate degree and frequency of socialization. The next two years were spent receiving regular therapy from a Rehabilitation Counselor. This individual therapy was followed by a two-year course of group psychotherapy, consisting largely of transactional analysis and periodic marathon sessions. This was subsequently followed by a brief exposure to Erhart Seminars Training. These activities were stopped when she began "to know about as much as my therapists." All of this helped to decrease her "worrying" and made it easier for her to "take things as they come." Yet her headaches continued unabated. She was being followed by a general practitioner and chiropractor for the care of her headache and GI distress, the latter of which had begun around the time she was discovered to have polyps in her abdomen (two years prior to this intervention).

Assessment

At the first appointment the patient was asked to begin keeping a "headache diary" on a daily basis. Ratings of headache activity were made at four discriminable times per day (breakfast, lunch, dinner, and bedtime) on a scale ranging from 0="no headache" to 5="intense, incapacitating headache." The weekly sum of these ratings served as the primary measure of outcome. A one-week baseline was initiated prior to treatment, and her total score for this week was 43. Several additional measures were derived from the diary to monitor progress: (1) the number of days per week the patient was completely free of headache, (2) the single highest or peak rating occurring for a given week, which indicates whether treatment is "taking the edge off" the more debilitating headaches, and (3) the sum of only those ratings above a value of "1," as a way to distinguish between clinically significant and nonsignificant headache. In the rating scheme employed, a value of "1" was defined as a "slight headache; I'm aware of it only when my attention is directed to it," and headaches assigned this value were of little consequence to the patient. All medications taken for headache were recorded in this diary as well. The patient took 41

Extra Strength Tylenol and 22 Coricidin D tablets the week prior to treatment. The diary also included a space for her to record factors that she believed elicited, exacerbated, and/or maintained her headaches. The diary quickly became an important communication aide, as the patient would readily enter in it material she was reluctant to share with the therapist face-to-face.

The patient was advised to seek consultation from a physician with special expertise in headache to rule out any physical causes for headache and complications due to sinus problems. Positive physical findings are rare for headache sufferers, especially those having a consistent pattern of headache for several years. However, when problems are present they can have life-threatening consequences. For example, out of the first 100 or so patients seen at our research clinic for nonpharmacological treatment, 2 individuals were found or suspected to have brain tumors. In medical settings the base rates are higher.

Baseline physiological recordings of muscle tension levels were obtained from the patient's neck/shoulder and forehead areas, as these were the typical sites of her headache. Electromyographic readings were excessively high at both areas, documenting the contribution of muscle contractions to the headache. Resting muscle tension levels obtained by an Autogen HT-1 portable myograph from the neck/shoulder area were in the range of 12–15 microvolts and 9–12 microvolts from the forehead area. Further, the patient was unable to decrease these high tension levels when requested to do so. Her degree of muscle tension was readily visible because of her stiff, rigid appearance and posture.

Information obtained from interview and diary reports during baseline revealed that the patient was quick to employ negative or self-deprecating statements. Instructors at schools for the blind reportedly had taught her "to value the opinions of persons with sight more than my own." Consequently, she was hypersensitive socially and quick to change her opinions whenever disagreements with others occurred. Her diminished self-worth made it difficult for her to accept credit for any of her accomplishments and left her stagnated with respect to certain immediate goals – completion of her doctoral thesis, the only requirement remaining for graduation, and training and showing her guide dog, something she was told "an unsighted person should never do." Many days were spent doing little but "lounging around the apartment." (See Andrasik, in press, for further details about assessment procedures for use with headache patients.)

Selection of Treatment

Four general problems identified and targeted for treatment were ranked as follows: (1) excessive medication consumption and the possibility that this was now serving in part to maintain headache, (2) abnormally high levels of tension in the muscles of the neck/shoulder and forehead, (3) maladaptive beliefs about her self-worth and a consequent inability to express her true feelings and opinions to others, and (4) a failure to make progress on her educational (dissertation) and avocational (training and showing her dog) goals and general inactivity.

Recent research suggests that chronic consumption of large quantities of analgesic medication can serve to intensify symptoms of tension headache and may even begin to produce tension headache-like symptoms in individuals taking analgesics as a palliative agent for other forms of headache. It is speculated that analgesics exert this apparent paradoxical effect by suppressing function of the antinociceptive system or those pathways concerned with regulation of dull pain (Kudrow, 1982). It is becoming the practice at many headache specialty clinics to begin treatment by first withdrawing patients from all analgesics, as well as other medications and substances producing chronic vasoconstriction (caffeinated beverages, decongestants, etc.). Preliminary data from Kudrow's (1982) clinic suggests that a sizable proportion of individuals become markedly improved by analgesic withdrawal alone. It is speculated further that certain other types of medications can be antagonistic to and may impede progress in self-regulatory therapies and more appropriate medical procedures. For example, Stroebel (personal communication, November 11, 1983) reports that regular consumption of benzodiazepines may impede progress in biofeedback therapy by nearly 50% (i.e., takes a patient twice as many sessions to benefit from treatment). The patient's high level of analgesic consumption fell within this "abuse" range and suggested that withdrawal might be helpful in and of itself. The decongestant taken by the patient contained aspirin, which is noted for causing stomach distress as well.

Withdrawing an individual from high levels of analgesics or other harmful medications in the absence of "active" treatment is often difficult, though, because symptoms may initially increase and an intense "rebound headache" may occur in the first two to three weeks following complete cessation of the medication. Further, many individuals are reluctant to give up their only form of treatment, even though not optimally effective, without being provided new means for coping with headache symptoms. The present patient shared this reluctance, so medication withdrawal was begun concurrent with initiation of biofeedback treatment to reduce the excessive muscle contractions underlying her headache.

It appeared that the patient's maladaptive cognitions were contributing in part to the stress and tension she was experiencing, thus mediating headache. These negative beliefs rendered her somewhat hopeless about the prospects of ever being able to cope effectively with her headaches and related problems. Treatment for these problems did not start until the patient was beginning to profit from biofeedback. Many individuals find a physiologically based approach easier to "buy" initially and, consequently, to learn. It was hoped that initial success at biofeedback (most patients show measurable gains at controlling the target response in the first few sessions of treatment) would increase the patient's confidence in her ability to profit from treatment, which would in turn make her more receptive to examining her errors of thinking and her maladaptive ways of interacting with others. Treatment for the remaining problem (#4) was unnecessary as the patient began to make progress in her daily life in response to the improvements made in the other problem areas.

Course of Treatment

Treatment began at week 2 and continued through week 12, with 9 individual sessions held during this period. Her response to treatment as revealed by 2 separate measures of headache is shown in Figures 9.1 and 9.2. At the first treatment session the patient was informed that current medications probably were contributing to her headache and stomach problems, and she was advised to reduce and ultimately eliminate them. She elected to withdraw her medication gradually over several weeks and had reduced it by nearly ¾ within 2 weeks. She experienced great difficulty dispensing with her medication entirely and continued to take small doses on a periodic basis for some time.

She was then provided a rationale for pursuing biofeedback and cognitive-behavioral treatment, similar to the following:

> The type of headache you are experiencing is caused by prolonged, painful contractions of the scalp, shoulders, neck and facial muscles. People usually are not aware that their muscles are becoming tense until they experience a headache, nor are they aware of the things that cause

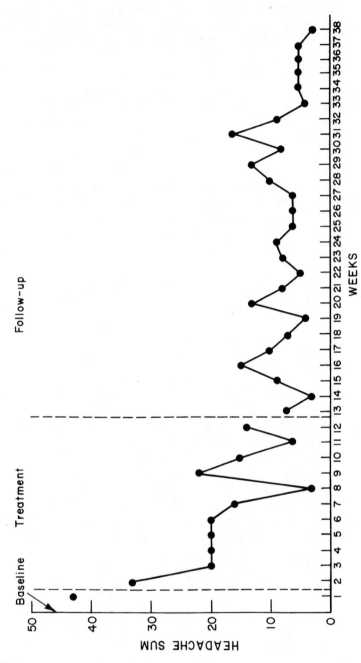

Figure 9.1. Weekly headache sum scores for all headaches occurring during baseline, treatment, and follow-up.

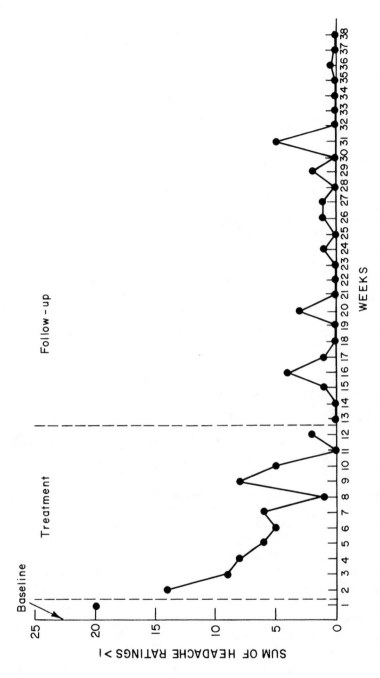

Figure 9.2. Weekly headache sum scores for only those headaches rated 2 or greater (on a 0 to 5 scale) occurring during baseline, treatment, and follow-up.

them to become tense in the first place. One way to deal with headache is by providing biofeedback, which will help you to relax your muscles, before they become tense enough to produce a headache. Another way to alleviate headache is to deal with those things or events that make you tense in the first place. We call these stressors, and they include many things which upset or bother us. Some examples of stressors we have already talked about include difficulties in interpersonal relationships, deadlines and other demands at work or school, memories of past unpleasant things that have happened, and even the headache itself, which can become stressful when it does not quickly go away. We all experience these things, but the way we react to them determines whether or not they become significant problems for us and eventually lead to a headache. Thus, a second way you can learn to manage your headaches is by learning to control your reaction to stressors by changing the way you think about or interpret certain situations. Today we will begin with biofeedback to help you learn to reduce the painful muscle contractions in your neck, shoulder, and forehead areas. In future sessions we will talk more about ways to change your reactions to things that upset you.

Biofeedback was begun at the first treatment session and followed the procedures developed by Budzynski, Stoyva, and colleagues (see Budzynski, 1978, for a review). Briefly, sensors were attached alternately to the patient's shoulder/neck and forehead areas to record the muscle activity at these sites. The myograph used contained a device that would emit an audible tone which sped up or slowed down in direct proportion to the amount of muscle tension detected by the recording sensors. The patient was instructed during treatment to begin to identify ways to lower the tone as this would be indicative of lowered muscle tension. She was encouraged in the initial sessions to experiment with a variety of strategies to accomplish this end, as well as to become aware of what activities or events led to increases in muscle tension so these could be reduced or avoided in the future. Suggestions for achieving relaxation initially were provided by the therapist (slow, deep, even breathing; altering body posture; pleasant imagery; self-suggestions to relax; implementation of tension/release cycles when needed), but the patient was free, and in fact was encouraged, to select whichever strategies worked best for her.

The first few feedback sessions were particularly illuminating to the patient. Lacking appropriate visual proprioceptive feedback, she noticed that she tended to exaggerate muscle movements at times when she wanted to communicate certain cognitive or emotional states. For example, she held her eyes extremely wide open and kept her upper body quite rigid when she wanted to indicate a high level of interest in what another person was saying. Her first efforts to relax the musculature of her forehead likewise were unsuccessful because, when it was suggested that closing her eyes might be helpful, she closed them so tightly that her forehead tension actually rose. At a subsequent session she stated that she suspected she had been doing this all along but she was too self-conscious to ask others to verify her hunch. She then began to seek direct feedback from the therapist about her general appearance, demeanor, and posture. With increased attention to this, the excessively high levels of muscle tension soon dropped to the range of 3–5 microvolts, still abnormally high.

Biofeedback was provided at all nine sessions, with the patient continuing to show further reductions in her tension levels. Probe readings in the absence of feedback taken at the beginning of each session revealed steady decreases in her basal or resting levels of muscle tension across time at both training sites. At the fourth treatment session the patient reached a "learning plateau" and became frustrated at her temporary lack of progress at biofeedback. It was instructive that this happened because she began to lapse into her former style of defensive-coping by bracing her musculature. She noted for the first time that she clenched her teeth and contracted her forehead when she became "heavy in thought."

Later it was discovered that she became very tense when ambulating, when accompanied by her guide dog and when using her sonic guide device alone. Feedback was provided during movement to enable her to maintain a more relaxed state at these times. At session 6 she decided to enter her dog in competition, and biofeedback was provided while she practiced her show routines with her dog. Around this time she began spontaneously to resume progress on her dissertation proposal.

Feedback trials ranged from 30 to 40 minutes initially and from 15 to 20 minutes near the end of treatment. Periods of no feedback were interspersed with treatment to see whether the patient could control her muscle tension level without assistance and to see whether she could discriminate subtle increases in tension. Twice-daily home practice of strategies learned during treatment was encouraged in order to augment treatment effects and to promote generalization. The patient reported high compliance to this request. Once the patient reliably showed the ability to discriminate heightened tension states and to decrease them when present, she was instructed to begin to apply these skills in a coping or contingent manner. This involved a rather constant monitoring of her muscle state and engaging in lowering when needed.

From week 6 on, treatment began to focus additionally on her cognitive and emotional responses to stress and headache (Holroyd & Andrasik, 1982). The patient was first taught a number of coping or positive self-statements to replace her more typically negative ones. Examples include: "This situation is not impossible – I can handle it. Don't worry; worry won't help anything. Here's what I need to do. I knew I could handle this; I'm doing well." Cognitive reappraisal or restructuring was also used in an attempt to modify more directly a number of her maladaptive or inappropriate cognitions. For example, a pervasive belief was that her opinions were inferior to those of others. For these and related maladaptive beliefs the patient was "pushed" to examine the consequences of the hypothesized belief. For example: "You worry continually over what you are about to say next and the possibility that you will make a mistake. Even trivial matters make you upset. All the good ideas you have go entirely unnoticed. Later you often find out your ideas were just as good as, and often superior to, those of others. You become angry and jealous when people receive credit and are praised for lesser achievements. This constant state of alertness keeps your body tensed and worked up and ultimately leads to headache." The recognition of these consequences helped the patient to begin to dispute this unproductive way of thinking. The patient noticed at one point that her headache often would intensify after a therapy session. Her own analysis revealed this to be due to her overconcern with pleasing the therapist and doing well. Behavioral assignments, such as accepting x compliments without attempting to refute them and stating x opinions in public for a given week were used to motivate the patient to begin to behave in a manner consistent with her modified, more appropriate beliefs. The patient selected and ordered audiotapes for a popular text on assertion training during this last phase of treatment and began to use strategies contained in it as well.

Termination

From week 2 through week 8 the patient experienced steady improvement. She attributed the minor setback experienced at week 9 to corneal karotitis, which required brief medical treatment. By week 12 the patient showed marked ability to lower her neck and facial muscle tension. Readings in the absence of feedback taken at the last few sessions revealed that the patient could quickly achieve and reliably maintain levels in the range of 1–3 microvolts. She reported that she had gained a new awareness of factors leading to headache and recognized how certain of her former beliefs had contributed to her headaches. She realized further that she would need to continue to use her relaxation and cognitive coping skills as well as to refrain from medication in order to keep her headaches at their new, more manageable level. She felt for now that she had acquired all of the basic skills needed to manage her headaches.

At this last session the patient was asked to list all changes made as a function of treatment. The list included: (1) "happier, life is more enjoyable," (2) "more self-confidence and self-esteem regarding my abilities," (3) "more energy," (4) "interested in new activities," (5) "more aware of body and facial expressions," and (6) "people talk more to me now; maybe because I feel more relaxed and appear more relaxed." She acknowledged that "negative cognitions" continued to be problematic for her and recognized that this was an area in need of constant monitoring.

Follow-up

The patient elected to continue her diary recordings on a daily basis for the next six months, as this served to prompt and motivate her to practice and apply the skills acquired during therapy. Weekly headache recordings throughout follow-up revealed maintenance of therapy gains. Figure 9.2 reveals that most of the headaches she experienced during this time were of minimal clinical consequence. Relative increases in headache activity were noted at weeks 16 and 20, when multiple stressors impinged on her (interviewing for a new job, receiving complaints from her landlord about her dog, scheduling of a dissertation proposal meeting, beginning to show her dog), and the Christmas holiday season, which was spent alone (week 31).

Continued accomplishments were reported: she completed her dissertation proposal during week 14 and successfully defended her proposal during week 19; during week 20 she purchased an exercise bike and began to use it regularly; she took up a number of new activities, including participation in a theater group and horseback riding and starting a small, private business. Follow-up encompassed winter, a time she feared because of increased ambulation difficulties due to ice and snow. At last report she stated: "I am finding that I can relax myself and as a result haven't fallen once – we just walk very slowly and I keep relaxing myself when I feel tension building. I still don't like winter but now at least I can survive it."

At week 18, or six weeks after the completion of treatment, the therapist obtained ratings from a close friend of the patient in order to provide an independent estimate of improvement. Ratings made on a 10 cm visual analogue scale indicated 93% improvement. Upon the rating form, her friend commented: "This answer is based on *not* seeing (patient's name) take aspirins several times during the course of a day. She is not taking *any* at the meals we have shared! (Patient's name) does not seem to tire as easily and there is a definite reduction in aspirin consumption. She talks through her 'problems' and has now begun to prioritize tasks. She is beginning to set more realistic goals."

Overall Evaluation

Several aspects deserve comment. First, the patient's headaches were assumed to have multiple causes and were treated accordingly by multiple procedures. Use of a multifaceted intervention makes it impossible to determine the relative contributions of each, nor whether each was indeed even necessary. Second, following application of a fairly rigorous bio-cognitive-behavioral treatment, the patient was not completely free of headaches. Complete cessation of headaches is an unrealistic goal for most chronic headache sufferers. Rather, the more appropriate goal is to reach a point where the patient believes headaches can be managed effectively and the presence of a headache is no longer intimidating or overly discomforting to the patient. The patient's comments about coping with winter weather conditions illustrate this desired outcome. Third, the reader may ask why biofeedback was employed over other forms of relaxation, which do not require sophisticated equipment for administration. Biofeedback was felt to have a better chance for reducing the excessively high levels of muscle tension observed during assessment. Also, recent findings suggest that biofeedback may be helpful for certain patients who have failed to respond to relaxation training alone (Blanchard et al., 1982).

Finally, even though some aspects of the present case may seem idiosyncratic to individuals with visual handicaps, all can be found in nonhandicapped individuals. The extreme tension elevations resulting, for example, from exaggerated eye closing or opening stand out only because of their increased magnitude. The "typical" tension sufferer may display similar types of muscle bracing, but to a much lesser degree.

References

Andrasik, F. (in press). Assessment of headaches. In J. A. Blumenthal & D. McKee (Eds.), *Applications in behavioral medicine and health psychology: A clinician's source book*. Sarasota, FL: Professional Resource Exchange, Inc.

Budzynski, T. (1978). Biofeedback in the treatment of muscle-contraction (tension) headache. *Biofeedback and Self-Regulation, 3*, 409–434.

Blanchard, E. B., Andrasik, F., Neff, D. F., Teders, S. J., Pallmeyer, T. P., Arena, J. G., Jurish, S. E., Saunders, N. L., Ahles, T. A., & Rodichok, L. D. (1982). Sequential comparisons of relaxation training and biofeedback in the treatment of three kinds of chronic headache, or the machines may be necessary some of the time. *Behaviour Research and Therapy, 20*, 469–481.

Holroyd, K. A., & Andrasik, F. (1982). A cognitive-behavioral approach to recurrent tension and migraine headache. In P. C. Kendall (Ed.), *Advances in cognitive-behavioral research and therapy* (Vol. 1, pp. 275–320). New York: Academic Press.

Kudrow, L. (1982). Paradoxical effects of frequent analgesic use. In M. Critchley et al. (Eds.), *Advances in neurology* (Vol. 33, pp. 335–341). New York: Raven Press.

10

Insomnia

Richard R. Bootzin

Description of Insomnia

Insomnia refers to a group of disorders in which the individual has
difficulty initiating or maintaining sleep. During the past decade considerable progress has been made in the assessment and diagnosis
of insomnia. As a result, much has been learned about the many different causes of chronic insomnia. Among them are physical illness
(e.g., rheumatic, back, or cardiac pain), physiological disorders (e.g.,
sleep apnea or nocturnal myoclonus), drugs (e.g., caffeine, nicotine,
dependence on sedatives), circadian rhythm dysfunction, diet, psychopathology, stress, environmental conditions, and poor sleep habits.
Because of the multiple causes of insomnia, a thorough assessment
is essential.

Case Identification and
Presenting Complaint

The case to be described is a 27-year-old woman (L.) who is married
and has a two-year-old daughter. L. complained of severe problems
in both initiating and maintaining sleep. She reported that it often
took her more than two hours to fall asleep, that her sleep was restless and fitful, and that she had frequent awakenings accompanied
by long periods of wakefulness. On the days following a poor night's
sleep, L. would feel fatigued, irritable, and incapable of meeting the

ordinary demands of everyday life. To cope with her insomnia, she had been taking benzodiazepines (Valium) nightly. Although her insomnia persisted, she, nevertheless, became dependent on Valium. She was convinced that she needed Valium in order to get what little sleep she was getting.

Shortly before seeking a nonpharmacological treatment, L. became pregnant. Since her gynecologist insisted that she stop taking Valium while pregnant, she did so. However, L. experienced considerable distress during withdrawal from Valium and her inability to sleep continued. This led to her decision to seek an alternative to drugs for her insomnia.

History

L. reported that up until the birth of her daughter, two years earlier, she had had no sleep problems. In the first few months after her daughter's birth, L. was vigilant at night and slept poorly. Her insomnia and daytime fatigue continued even as her daughter matured and no longer required attention at night.

After one year of insomnia, L. went to a sleep disorders center for evaluation. On the basis of two all-night sleep recordings, the personnel at the center concluded that L. did not have a physiological sleep disorder but that her sleep pattern was consistent with endogenous depression. They recommended that she see a psychiatrist.

Although L. was anxious and fatigued, which she attributed to her inability to sleep, she did not feel depressed. Nevertheless, she sought out the help of a psychiatrist. After seeing her for a few sessions, the psychiatrist concluded that L. was not clinically depressed and prescribed Valium for her sleep problems and daytime anxiety. As mentioned earlier, she became dependent on Valium, which she took daily until she became pregnant.

Assessment

The assessment of insomnia is a complex task. The nature of the sleep disturbance (see *Diagnostic Classification of Sleep and Arousal Disorders*, Association of Sleep Disorders Centers, 1979) must be accurately described. Each of the possible contributing causes must be assessed. The components of a complete assessment of sleep disturbance include (1) a physical examination and medical history, (2) a detailed personal history, (3) psychological inventories, (4) daily sleep diaries, (5) all-night polysomnogaphy, and (6) daytime mood and performance measures (Bootzin, Engle-Friedman, & Hazlewood, 1983).

In L.'s case, the physical examination had been performed by her physician, and two nights of sleep had been recorded a year earlier at a sleep disorders center. Since the sleep disorders center provided summaries of the two all-night recordings of L.'s sleep, it was not necessary to repeat the all-night evaluation.

The information obtained from polysomnography is an important component of the assessment of insomnia. First, it is the most accurate means of ruling out disorders such as narcolepsy, sleep apnea, and nocturnal myoclonus (for information about these disorders see Williams & Karacan, 1978). Second, there are some insomniacs whose sleep complaint is not verified by polysomnography. This type of insomnia, called subjective insomnia, may require different treatment strategies than are effective with those whose complaint is corroborated by polysomnography, called psychophysiological insomnia. Only by means of polysomnography is it possible to differentiate between subjective and psychophysiological insomnia. Third, the information obtained from polysomnography also has treatment uses. Many insomniacs are reassured to learn that the sleep they obtain is normal in many important respects; for example, that they have normal rapid-eye-movement (REM) sleep cycles, or that they are getting more sleep than they thought. The feedback from polysomnography can be a means of reducing anxiety about sleep.

The polysomnography report regarding L.'s sleep stated that on the first night she slept less than two of almost five hours in bed. Further, more than a third of the two hours was spent in Stage 1 (a transition stage between waking and sleep). On the second night, a more complete record was obtained. L. slept 85% of the seven-hour period for a total of about six hours of sleep. The sleep was distributed among sleep stages as follows:

Stage I	15.0%
Stage II	56.0%
Stage III and IV	2.9%
REM sleep	26.1%
Latency to Stage I	24 minutes
Latency to REM	55 minutes
Number of awakenings (>60 sec.)	8
Time awake after sleep onset	37 minutes

There was no evidence for narcolepsy, sleep apnea, or nocturnal myoclonus. The noteworthy features of this record were the markedly reduced percentage of deep sleep (Stages III and IV) and the frequent awakenings. Normally, about 20% of the night's sleep consists of Stages III and IV, while L. had only 3%. The best way to characterize her sleep is that it was light, restless sleep.

The client also showed a shortened latency to REM sleep and a slightly increased percentage of REM. The normal values are about 90 minutes latency to the first REM period and a total REM% of 20–25%. As noted by the sleep disorders center, this pattern is consistent with endogenous depression. However, these values for REM are not markedly deviant, and the decreased sleep in Stages III and IV coupled with the frequent awakenings also are consistent with insomnia caused by tension, hypervigilance, and cognitive ruminations.

During her first interview, L. was articulate and appropriately animated. She was distressed about her sleep and daytime fatigue, but did not appear depressed. However, her Beck Depression Scale score was 18 (mildly depressed) and her Taylor Manifest Anxiety score was 31 (highly anxious). Thus, as is commonly found among insomniacs, L. had elevated scores on both depression and trait anxiety.

Sleep diaries are perhaps the most critical component of any attempt to assess insomnia. They are a practical and efficient means of obtaining sleep information over an extended period of time while the insomniac sleeps at home in his or her own bed, and they provide a measure of the client's view of the disorder (Bootzin & Engle-Friedman, 1981). They also play an important treatment role in providing a means for documenting the frequency of the problem and providing feedback regarding the effects of treatment interventions. It sometimes occurs that insomniacs overestimate the frequency of their disturbed sleep. Thus, self-monitoring may help document the actual frequency of their sleep problems and communicate that they are getting more sleep than they thought. The sleep diary employed contains entries for nap taking, sleep latency, number and duration of awakenings, total sleep, quality of sleep, and feeling upon awakening (see Bootzin et al., 1983). L. was encouraged to use the back of the sheet to note the occurrence of events that might have affected the night's sleep, such as the use of sleep medication or alcohol, sickness in the family, or emotional distress.

L. was given two weeks of sleep diaries and daytime mood measures for a baseline period. She was told that it would be helpful if during these two weeks she experienced the full intensity of her insomnia so that the information necessary to design an effective treatment would be available. There were two reasons for stressing the desirability of poor sleep during the baseline period. First, it accurately describes the purpose of having a baseline period. This helps reduce the pressure on the therapist to begin therapy before a thorough evaluation has been completed. Second, it may, nevertheless, have therapeutic consequences, as a paradoxical intervention, by helping to reduce the insomniac's anxiety about the necessity of getting a good night's sleep. If that occurs, it may help demonstrate to the client that some of the problem was self-induced through worrying about sleep. Thus, temporary improvement can be used as a means of focusing attention on the role of the individual's cognitions in maintaining the problem and in producing improvement.

L. returned for her second session with the baseline data. She was somewhat embarrassed as she admitted that her sleep during the past two weeks had been better than usual. On only two of the 14 nights had she awakened exhausted in the morning, and on only one night had she obtained less than five hours of sleep. In fact, her average nightly total of sleep was over 6.5 hours. Nevertheless, she had awakenings totaling more than 30 minutes almost every night while her sleep latency averaged more than an hour and was more than two hours on two nights. However, compared to her expectation of a miserable night's sleep every night, she slept quite well.

L.'s report of improved sleep during baseline could have been due to a number of factors. First, in the absence of self-monitoring, it might have been that L. just was unaware of how frequently she had a poor night's sleep. Thus, the self-monitoring may have helped document that her problem was not as bad as she thought. Second, since the regular use of depressants such as Valium produce disrupted sleep, L., who was now drug free, may have begun to experience the benefits in improved sleep of having withdrawn from Valium. And, third, her improved sleep might have been due to the reduction in worry about sleep as described above.

Although her problem was not as severe during baseline as she had anticipated, L. did not consider the problem solved. Therefore, continued assessment and treatment aimed at improving and maintaining the gains experienced during baseline were begun. Information about sleep and its consequences were discussed, and L. was instructed to keep another two weeks of records.

The next session was delayed a few weeks because L. had a miscarriage. She experienced considerable grief and emotional distress in response to the loss. Her insomnia continued and she again began to take Valium occasionally. She resumed treatment determined to free herself from the need to take Valium, as she eventually planned on becoming pregnant again.

Selection of Treatment

Both assessment and the selection of treatment are part of an ongoing, interactive process. It is not the case that assessment ends once treatment begins or that the selection and carrying through of treatment depend only upon an earlier, formal assessment. Additional treatment elements may be added depending upon the client's response to earlier elements or to the therapist's improved understanding of the nature of the client's problem. All of this is by way of emphasizing that the selection of techniques for L. did not take place only at the end of the initial assessment. Thus, the discussion of the selection of treatment techniques will sound somewhat more structured and planned than actually occurred.

A number of features of L.'s sleep problem made her a good candidate for behavior therapy: (1) her insomnia appeared to be under the control of situational cues, that is, it developed suddenly in response to changed family circumstances and was likely being maintained in part by situational cues for arousal; (2) L.'s sleep pattern and response to personality inventories indicated a pattern that was likely due to anxiety and cognitive intrusions; and (3) the improved sleep L. reported during baseline indicated that her sleep pattern was malleable and probably responsive to cognitive restructuring.

There were four components of the therapy: (1) supportive exploration of L.'s response to her miscarriage, (2) information about sleep and cognitive restructuring, (3) stimulus control instructions, and (4) stress management and social skills training.

Support

The first few sessions after treatment resumed focused on L.'s reactions to her miscarriage, including her feelings of loss, its impact on her sense of self-worth, its effect on her relationship with her husband, her reaction to others who were pregnant, and her anxieties about becoming pregnant again. The goal of this component of therapy was to help L. come to terms with her thoughts and feelings about the miscarriage.

Information and Cognitive Restructuring

A primary goal of treatment was to change L.'s view of her sleep problem from one in which she was a victim of a disorder to one in which she was someone capable of coping with the problem. This was a particularly appropriate goal in this case since there were repeated indications that contributing to the problem were L.'s anxious ruminations about sleep and fatigue, both of which she considered out of her control. Thus, throughout treatment an emphasis was placed on providing accurate information about the consequences of sleep loss and on pointing out the links between cognitive rumination and sleep disturbance.

L. was informed about sleep stages, developmental changes, and the effects on sleep of tranquilizers, alcohol, caffeine, naps, and sleep environment factors. Two additional points were stressed. First, there are large individual differences in sleep needs. Some people have lived long, productive, satisfying lives getting less than two hours sleep a night for as long as they can remember. In general, the body will get the amount of sleep that it needs. One possibility for L. to consider was that she did not need as much sleep as she believed necessary. For example, L. was getting about six and a half hours of sleep while spending ten hours in bed. In response to this discussion, L. started delaying her bedtime from about 10 P.M. until about 11:30 P.M.

The second point that was stressed was that it is not a calamity to go without sleep. One night's total sleep deprivation produces very few effects. There are performance deficits following even prolonged periods of reduced sleep. And, although fatigue and irritability are frequently reported after prolonged sleep deprivation, it should be noted that many factors, in addition to sleep loss, determine fatigue and arousal. Tasks that capture the individual's interest produce alertness even after sleep loss. In addition, fatigue and arousal follow a daily circadian rhythm. Even if individuals go without sleep entirely, they will be alert during the day and fatigued at times when they ordinarily sleep. Thus, the day's performance is not as dependent on the previous night's sleep as L. assumed.

Stimulus Control Instructions

The goals of stimulus control instructions are to help the insomniac acquire a consistent sleep rhythm, to strengthen the bed as a cue for sleep, and to weaken it as a cue for activities that might interfere with sleep (Bootzin et al., 1983; Bootzin & Nicassio, 1978). One component of sleep disturbance is that the insomniac never may have acquired a consistent sleep rhythm. This may occur as a result of inconsistent bedtime and/or time of arising in the morning. During the baseline period, L. showed moderate variability in the times she went to and got up from bed. Another component is that insomniacs may engage in activities in the bedroom at bedtime that are incompatible with falling asleep, such as reading, watching television, or worrying. For L., the behavior engaged in at bedtime that was incompatible with falling asleep was cognitive activity. At bedtime, she frequently re-hashed the day's events and worried about the next day. The goal of treatment was not to eliminate worrying, some of which might have involved a useful rehearsal of potentially stressful events, but to relocate it to another time and place. Thus, the client was instruct-ed to find a comfortable chair in a room, other than the bedroom, for worrying and planning.

The following rules constitute the stimulus control instructions (Bootzin & Nicassio, 1978):

1. Lie down intending to go to sleep *only* when you are sleepy.
2. Do not use your bed for anything except sleep; that is, do not read, watch television, eat, or worry in bed. Sexual activity is the only exception to this rule. On such occasions the in-structions are to be followed afterward when you intend to go to sleep.
3. If you find yourself unable to fall asleep, get up and go into another room. Stay up as long as you wish and then return to the bedroom to sleep. Although we do not want you to watch the clock, we want you to get out of bed if you do not fall asleep immediately. Remember, the goal is to associate your bed with falling asleep *quickly*! If you are in bed more than about 10 minutes without falling asleep and have not gotten up, you are not following this instruction.
4. If you still cannot fall asleep, repeat Step 3. Do this as often as is necessary throughout the night.
5. Set your alarm and get up at the same time every morning irrespective of how much sleep you got during the night. This will help your body acquire a consistent sleep rhythm.
6. Do not nap during the day.

Stress Management and Social Skills Training

As indicated by the elevated depression and anxiety scores, there was more causing discomfort in L.'s life than just poor sleep. However, L. sought out treatment specifically for insomnia and that was the major focus of the therapy. Time also was spent on a number of more general issues such as the use of relaxation as a coping skill to deal with *in vivo* stress, learning to say "No" to unreasonable demands, and exploring ways of bringing more enjoyment into L.'s life.

Some of these more general issues related directly to L.'s sleep complaints. For example, L. complained that she was so fatigued during the day from lack of sleep that she was unable to handle many burdensome social obligations. A goal of therapy was to help her learn to deal more effectively with reducing her commitments, so that she need not rely on her symptoms as an excuse. Another example is that although L. complained of considerable daytime fatigue, she admitted that she found that she was bored much of the time. Thus, a goal of therapy was to explore ways of bringing more enjoyment into her life by having her initiate more activities that she found enjoyable and interesting.

The topics, goals, and techniques of dealing with stress and assertiveness waxed and waned throughout therapy. Although they may have contributed importantly to L.'s general improvement, no formal records of progress in these areas were kept. These topics were dealt with as secondary and complementary to the primary focus on the sleep disorder itself.

Course of Treatment

After the initial assessment, L. was seen for seven sessions over a 15-week period. The first two sessions focused on her thoughts and feelings about her miscarriage. Although her grief and general distress diminished, her insomnia worsened. In fact, a crisis revolving around L.'s sleep was developing.

L. was becoming increasingly worried about a winter vacation she and her family were to take at her in-laws in California. As the date for departure approached, L.'s insomnia worsened. The week before they were to leave, she averaged over two and a half hours a night to fall asleep and averaged only five hours a night of sleep. L. was agitated over the possibility that her insomnia would continue while they stayed at her in-laws. First, she felt she would not be able to follow the stimulus control instructions she had just begun to use. The household would be crowded and she was worried that she would disrupt the sleep of others by getting out of bed and being awake. Second, if she did not sleep, she was concerned that she would be fatigued and irritable during the day and yet would be forced to participate in family activities.

The focus of the fourth session, which took place a couple of days before departure, was on L.'s misconceptions about sleep and ways of coping while in California. For example, it was pointed out that many insomniacs sleep better away from home than they do at home. The novel environment does not have the same cues for disrupted sleep as are present at home. In addition, ways of coping with lack of sleep were discussed. L. had received relaxation training and it was suggested that she use relaxation during the day as a way of restoring energy. However, she was reminded that even after poor sleep, she would probably be able to participate in all activities, as the activities themselves would likely be interesting and increase arousal. This discussion was directed at helping L. reduce her anxiety about the consequences of inadequate sleep by emphasizing that she had the tools available to cope with any problem that might occur.

L. returned from her vacation three weeks later refreshed and enthusiastic. She had had only sporadic nights of insomnia while at her in-laws and had found that, indeed, she could cope with them. She followed the stimulus control instructions without difficulty and used relaxation during the day when she became overly fatigued. She participated in almost all family activities. She was now persuaded that her earlier worrying about being unable to cope with sleep loss had contributed to her insomnia.

The next three sessions were spent consolidating the gains. Increasingly, sleep became a less important focus of the therapy while more attention was given to stress management and social skills issues. The final session was scheduled one month after the previous one to ensure that she possessed the resources to maintain the improvement on her own. At the end of therapy, L. was averaging about 45 minutes to fall asleep and averaged seven hours of sleep a night. She still had a poor night's sleep about once a week, but now felt that she was capable of dealing with it without resorting to medication. She no longer considered herself an insomniac. Therapy terminated with the understanding that she would get back in touch with me if there was a recurrence of her insomnia.

Follow-up

Four months later, L. called for an appointment. She was pregnant again and had started having some difficulty sleeping. She was seen for two sessions during which we reviewed the procedures and information she had previously learned. We also discussed her concerns about another miscarriage. L.'s sleeping problems abated as she successfully passed the point in her pregnancy when she previously had had a miscarriage. Once that point had passed, her anxieties about another miscarriage diminished and she started sleeping better again.

Overall Evaluation

Two important aspects of this case should be noted. First, good therapy is not solely the application of previously evaluated procedures to a circumscribed problem. In fact, this case illustrates the interdependence of different areas of functioning. L.'s sleep problems were influenced by her social skills, her ways of handling stress, and the emotional turmoil of her miscarriage. Although the focus of the therapy was on insomnia, it was important to deal with all of L.'s problems both to have a better understanding of her resources and to develop an alliance with her. Therapeutic alliances are particularly important in behavior therapy where so much of the therapy depends upon the willingness of the client to carry out therapeutic instructions.

Second, although this case presentation emphasized the cognitive aspects, it should be remembered that it was a multicomponent treatment. Cognitive restructuring was certainly important, but may have depended upon improvement produced by other techniques such as regularizing sleep rhythm, stimulus control instructions, and use of relaxation as a coping tool during the day. In the clinical application of procedures, it is not necessary to apply only one procedure. The therapist uses the combination of procedures previously found to be effective that seems appropriate to the problem. This is not a fixed formula and procedures should be reevaluated depending upon the feedback received from the client's success or failure with those techniques.

References

Association of Sleep Disorders Centers. (1979). Diagnostic classification of sleep and arousal disorders. *Sleep, 2*, 1–137.

Bootzin, R. R., & Engle-Friedman, M. (1981). The assessment of insomnia. *Behavioral Assessment, 3*, 107–126.

Bootzin, R. R., Engle-Friedman, M., & Hazlewood, L. (1983). In P. M. Lewinsohn & L. Teri (Eds.), *Clinical geropsychology: New directions in assessment and treatment.* New York: Pergamon.

Bootzin, R. R., & Nicassio, P. M. (1978). Behavioral treatments for insomnia. In M. Hersen, R. M. Eisler, & P. M. Miller (Eds.), *Progress in behavior modification* (Vol. 6). New York: Academic Press.

Williams, R. L., & Karacan, I. (Eds.). (1978). *Sleep disorders: Diagnosis and treatment.* New York: Wiley.

11

Obesity

Marsha D. Marcus

Description of Obesity

Obesity, commonly defined as a body weight 20% or more above the desirable range of weight for height, poses a significant public health hazard. Twenty to 30% of the adult population is overweight, and the prevalence of obesity is probably increasing. Obesity has been identified as a risk factor in a variety of diseases including hypertension, diabetes, gall bladder disease, degenerative diseases of the weight-bearing joints, and heart disease. Despite the seriousness of the problem, treatment efforts have been only moderately successful. The average weight loss produced by all types of therapy is approximately 12 pounds, while the average client is more than 50 pounds overweight at the start of treatment. Nevertheless, constrained by considerable social pressures to remain thin, people often diet repeatedly in chronic efforts to lose weight.

The behavioral group treatment of obesity is also associated with modest in-treatment weight losses and large interclient variability. However, behavioral weight reduction programs appear to have some advantages over other outpatient treatments in that fewer patients drop out of treatment, fewer untoward responses occur with behavioral treatment and the tendency to regain weight after treatment may be less pronounced than with other types of programs. Thus, it seems worthwhile to try to improve the outcome of behavioral treatments for obesity.

One potential method to enhance treatment outcome is individualized behavioral therapy. Such an approach allows the therapist an opportunity to conduct a thorough behavioral analysis and to develop a weight loss program incorporating components which focus upon the particular needs of the client. Moreover, clients seeking behavior therapy for obesity may have related problems that complicate treatment. An individual approach allows the utilization of strategies to address coexisting problems. Any program for a client seeking behavior therapy for obesity should include (1) nutrition and exercise information; (2) self-control strategies, particularly self-monitoring; and (3) stimulus control techniques. Additional techniques may be incorporated when they are indicated by the results of the behavioral assessment.

Case Identification

Joyce A. was a 28-year-old, white, single female who was 5 feet 5 inches tall (165.1 cm) and weighed 189 lb. (85.81 kg). She was 43.2% overweight. Ms. A. had a master's degree in business administration and worked in the marketing department of a large corporation. She was referred for treatment by her family physician because of increasing desperation about her obesity and her concern regarding her ability to control her eating behavior.

Presenting Problem

Ms. A. reported a 10-year history of overweight and preoccupation with dieting. She described herself as "slightly pudgy" during her high school years but gained 20 lb. during her first year away from home at a large Midwestern university. Ms. A. reported that she went on a high-protein, low-carbohydrate diet and rapidly lost 25 lb., which was quickly regained. This began an alternating pattern of weight gain and stringent attempts at dieting that persisted over the next 10 years.

On diet days, Ms. A. skipped breakfast, had a piece of fruit and a small scoop of cottage cheese for lunch, and chicken or fish and a small salad for dinner. Several times a week, however, Ms. A.'s strictly controlled eating behavior was disrupted, resulting in an episode of binge eating during the evening. She reported ingesting huge amounts of high-calorie, palatable foods (i.e., pastries, snack foods, ice cream) in a period of one to three hours. Ms. A. stated that binge eating was likely to occur when she was hungry or feeling frustrated or angry.

Binge episodes were followed by intense remorse, guilt, and self-loathing along with more renewed determination to become a "perfect" dieter. In fact, while Ms. A. described herself as generally "emotionally intense," she reported that her affective state closely paralleled the degree of control she had over her eating behavior. That is, she felt a sense of optimism and well-being on days that she dieted successfully and was pessimistic, ashamed, and dysphoric when she overate.

At the point Ms. A. sought behavior therapy, she felt that her obesity and overeating episodes were contributing to increased social withdrawal, feelings of hopelessness, and depression. Ms. A. denied neurovegetative symptoms of depression or sustained changes in mood. However, she did describe a probable episode of major depression at age 23 which occurred subsequent to the termination of a year-long love affair. Ms. A. reported the rapid gain of 20 pounds, hypersomnia, tearfulness, sadness, difficulty concentrating, marked irritability, and social withdrawal. The episode lasted approximately six months. She did not seek treatment at that time, but acknowledged two brief intervals of psychodynamic psychotherapy during her early 20s. Ms. A. denied any current or past history of substance abuse or suicidal behavior.

History

Ms. A. was the youngest of three children of Eastern European immigrants. Her father was a certified public accountant, while her mother was a musician. Ms. A.'s older brothers were 35 and 33 years old at the time of referral. Both were married professionals who lived in different states with their respective families.

Ms. A.'s growing up years were characterized by a family atmosphere described as "an emotional pressure cooker." Her mother was moody and volatile and her father was taciturn and withdrawn. Mr. and Mrs. A. had frequent arguments but were in apparent agreement about their high expectations for their children. Mr. and Mrs. A., who had experienced periods of hunger and deprivation during their adolescent years in war-torn Europe, placed an emphasis on plentiful meals and family conversation at the dinner table. Nevertheless, the evening meal was a time of frequent husband–wife conflicts and family disagreements. Ms. A. reported that she often went to her room after her kitchen clean-up chores with a knot in her stomach. Later, feeling hungry, she would sneak to the kitchen and "stuff down left-overs."

Ms. A. worked hard to achieve academically, but, despite considerable success, always felt "second best" to her "brilliant" brothers. Moreover, she felt that her parents favored their sons, which caused her to repeatedly seek to win her parents' approval.

The client had many girlfriends during high school and participated in several extracurricular activities. While she was viewed by classmates and teachers as enthusiastic and competent, she felt herself to be a social failure because she dated only occasionally.

During her second year of college, Ms. A. fell in love and became involved in her first sexual relationship. She reported that her feelings for this young man were far more intense than his for her, and that she was always worried that he would terminate the relationship. Not surprisingly, this boyfriend felt that Ms. A. was "too fat," which exacerbated her preoccupation with diet. Further, she believed that her relationship problems would vanish if she could achieve her ideal weight. The romance ended badly after two years with a predictably negative effect on Ms. A.'s self-esteem.

Ms. A. did not become seriously involved with a man again until after graduate school. At that time, she became engaged to a research engineer whom she met at work. Her fiancé was undemonstrative and critical and complained about her dependence and "constant need for reassurance." Although Ms. A. was not happy with the relationship, the engagement ultimately was terminated by her fiancé. Ms. A. was devastated, and the previously mentioned period of depression ensued. Her heterosocial relationships following the broken engagement were sporadic and unsatisfying. The client believed that if she could lose weight she would meet "Mr. Right."

Ms. A. described herself as conscientious and competent in her work, but she felt ill-used by her boss. That is, she felt that she was overworked and underappreciated. Further, she felt that her boss often made unreasonable demands on her time and asked her to perform tasks more appropriate for someone with less training. Ms. A., however, was not able to discuss her concerns with her boss. She felt that some of the problem was due to her overweight, that is, that a heavy woman was perceived as less competent and valuable than a thin one.

Ms. A.'s relationship with her parents during her adult years continued to be a difficult one. On the one hand, she was dependent on them for emotional support, advice, and approval. On the other, she resented their intrusive behavior and critical attitude. Despite her intense ambivalence, Ms. A. frequently went to see her parents after work and often ate her dinner at their home.

Assessment

The assessment phase lasted three weeks and included the use of a clinical interview, self-report assessment measures, and an eating and exercise diary. A clinical interview was used to obtain a detailed weight and diet history as well as to assess the presence of other psychological or interpersonal difficulties. In assessing the obese patient, it is important to determine whether it is appropriate to focus treatment on obesity or whether a coexisting problem requires intervention. Ms. A. presented a history which indicated long-standing difficulties with overweight and disordered eating behavior. However, she also reported a history of depression as well as current depressive symptomatology. Thus, if Ms. A. had been clinically depressed at the time of assessment, it would have been advisable to treat the depression prior to beginning a weight control program. The clinical interview data indicated that Ms. A. was not currently clinically depressed, but that she suffered marked dysphoria associated with her eating behavior.

Similarly, it is important to assess the possibility of medical problems that could effect treatment. For example, the use of psychotropic medications is frequently associated with significant weight gain. An individual with arthritis may be unable to participate in an exercise program. Morbid obesity (100% or more overweight) is unusually refractory to treatment and is probably best treated by a physician (i.e., a modified protein-sparing fast or gastric bypass surgery may be indicated). Ms. A. was referred by her physician, who reported that she was in excellent health. In general, however, it is advisable for clients seeking treatment for obesity to obtain written permission from a physician to participate in a weight-loss program requiring moderate caloric restriction and exercise.

There was no contraindication to a weight reduction program for Ms. A. However, the interview data yielded the picture of a chronic weight problem complicated by binge eating. Binge behavior is thought to negatively effect the outcome of behavioral weight control programs. Nevertheless, this eating pattern is common among individuals seeking behavioral treatment for obesity. One study found that 70% of an overweight group applying for behavioral treatment had problems with binge eating (Gormally, Black, Daston, & Rardin, 1982).

These researchers developed a self-report questionnaire, the Binge Eating Scale (BES), which was found to be highly effective in discriminating among three levels of severity for binge eating in the obese. The BES is readily administered and scored and provides a useful adjunct to clinical interview data. While there currently are no norms available for the three severity levels of binge eating, Gormally et al. observed a weighted mean on the Binge Eating Scale of 30 ± 7 for serious bingers and a weighted mean of 14 ± 6.7 for individuals with little or no problem. Ms. A. scored 38 on the BES placing her in the serious problem range. She also reported extreme preoccupation with controlling the urge to eat as well as guilt and dysphoria after a binge. This clinical picture is similar to that presented by obese individuals with serious binge eating in the Gormally et al. study. To assess the current severity of depressive symptoms, the client was asked to complete the Beck Depression Inventory (BDI) (Beck, Ward, Mendelson, Mock, & Erbaugh, 1961). She scored 22 on the BDI, indicating a significant degree of depressive symptomatology. In summary, the self-report findings from the BES and BDI corroborated data from the clinical interview.

The third component of the assessment consisted of an eating and exercise diary. Ms. A. was asked to record all food and drink she consumed and to assign the appropriate calorie values (books listing calorie values of common foods are readily available). In addition, she recorded the time and place of each eating episode and noted thoughts and feelings which occurred before, during, and after eating. Finally, she was expected to monitor her activities by recording type and duration of all exercises.

The eating and exercise diary is probably the single most important tool for assessment and treatment planning of an obesity program. It allows for the collection of baseline calorie and energy expenditure information, as well as the identification of problem eating patterns and maladaptive or unrealistic attitudes about dieting. The diary also provides information about the antecedents and consequences of binge eating or episodes of overeating.

Diary entries indicated that Ms. A. consumed at least 2,000 calories during her binges, which occurred two or three times a week. It is easy to see that Ms. A. would gain weight rapidly unless calories were sharply restricted between binges. Moreover, it was anticipated that a moderate weight control program with an average weight loss goal of 1.5 to 2 lb. per week would not be successful unless the frequency of binge episodes decreased. Thus, the amelioration of binge eating was considered to be an important focus of treatment.

The information recorded in Ms. A.'s eating diary allowed for a functional analysis of binge eating behavior. Loro and Orleans (1981) have set forth guidelines for such an analysis and also have listed suggested behavioral interventions. In the case of this client, the primary antecedents of a binge were hunger, anger or frustration, self-critical thoughts, and anxiety related to work or heterosocial relationships. In sum, Ms. A. had learned to overeat in response to a variety of physical, affective, and cognitive stimuli. After a binge, self-loathing, guilt, depression and shame often led to renewed vows to diet. Thus, the consequences of the episode perpetuated the cycle of dieting and binge eating.

The final phase of the assessment is the creation of a problem list and establishment of reasonable treatment goals. This is done with the active participation of the client. While the problem list and corresponding goals may be revised, the goal-setting process may be viewed as the initiation of active treatment. That is, since obese clients, particularly those with binge eating problems, often have unrealistic expectations about dieting and weight loss, the setting of goals may aid the client in formulating more reasonable expectations for herself. Ms. A.'s problem list and goals are summarized in Table 11.1.

Selection of Treatment

The selection of treatment interventions derives directly from the behavioral assessment. In the case of Ms. A., the major problem areas were determined to be obesity and binge eating. However, it was important to assess her depressive symptoms and nonassertive behavior and to understand how these difficulties were implicated in the development and maintenance of Ms. A.'s eating problems. For the purposes of her treatment program, the depressive symptomatology and nonassertive behavior were conceptualized as problems contributing to the disordered eating behavior. The interventions for obesity, binge eating, and related difficulties will be discussed in turn.

The behavioral treatment of obesity is based on the assumption that obesity results from overeating and underexercising. Further, it is assumed that healthy eating and exercise patterns can be learned. Behavioral weight loss programs utilize an empirically validated multicomponent package of techniques. As mentioned previously, the mainstays of treatment are nutrition and exercise information, self-monitoring, and stimulus control techniques. A full discussion of these techniques is beyond the scope of this chapter and are described in detail elsewhere (see Stuart & Davis, 1972).

In the case of Ms. A., the treatment of obesity was complicated by serious binge eating problems. The management of binge eating is not independent from the treatment of obesity. In fact, many treatment strategies that have been recommended for binge eating are integral parts of behavioral programs for obesity. For example, behavioral treatment emphasizes habit change within the context of moderate caloric restriction and reasonable goal setting. Virtually all investigators have advised against restrictive dieting and unrealistic weight loss goals for binge eaters. Behavioral weight control strategies such as planning ahead for high-risk overeating situations and developing substitute activities for eating have also been suggested for management of binge behavior. While the treatments of obesity and binge eating overlap, components that focus specifically on binge eating were included in Ms. A.'s treatment.

Ms. A. was provided didactic information and a rationale for treating binge eating. First, the relationship of overly strict dieting and subsequent binge behavior was explained. Particular emphasis was placed on the manner in which regular, nutritionally balanced meals and the gradual weight reduction program would prevent hunger and serve to minimize the likelihood of a binge. Second, binge eating was defined as a learned response to a variety of internal and external pressures. The data from the food diary was used to identify the antecedents and consequences of binge eating and to demonstrate how cognitions, affect, and interpersonal problems were involved in the maintenance of binge behavior.

Next, strategies to deal with the urge to overeat were developed. For Ms. A., a binge was most likely to occur in the early evening. She decided to prepare several meals for the freezer, so she could warm them in her microwave oven immediately upon her return from work, and thus avoid a binge due to hunger. In addition, Ms. A. was asked to select an activity as an alternative to binge eating. She chose exercise (other possibilities are relaxation exercises or phone contact with a friend). Ms. A. joined a health club with a friend and went to the gym two nights a week. She also found that walking home from work when the weather permitted was relaxing as well as an aid to weight reduction.

Finally, it was necessary to clarify the consequences of binge eating and to minimize the negative emotions resulting from a binge. This was done by explaining that binge eating was an attempt to ameliorate a variety of problems, and consistently challenging Ms. A.'s belief that she was a failure because of her eating problem. A variety of cognitions that are typical of depressive individuals then

Table 11.1. Problem List

Problem	Goal
I. Obesity	I. Weight reduction to goal weight of 132 lb. (59.9 kg)
A. Unrealistic expectations about weight loss	A. Weekly weight loss of 1.0–2.0 lb. (.45–.91 kg)
B. Rigid dieting	B. Daily quota of 1,200 calories
C. Irregular meal pattern	C. Three meals daily
D. Avoidance of dietary carbohydrate	D. Consumption of carbohydrates 40–50% of daily intake
E. Lack of exercise	E. Walk 30 to 60 minutes five times per week
II. Binge Eating	II. Reduction of Binges
A. Antecedents	A. Clarification and minimization of binge antecedents
1. Hunger	1. Avoid hunger
2. Cognitive factors	2. Identification and correction of maladaptive or distorted cognitions
a. Self-critical attitude, low self-esteem	
b. Perfectionistic, "all or nothing" attitude about eating behavior	
3. Affective factors	3. Identification and minimization of affective factors; use of alternative coping strategies
a. Depressive symptoms	
b. Anxiety related to pressure of work and heterosocial relationships	

4. Interpersonal factors
   a. Passive, dependent, nonassertive behavior at work, with parents, and in heterosocial relationships

B. Consequences
   1. Short-term
      a. Enjoyment of food
      b. Relief of hunger
      c. Relief from negative emotional state
   2. Longer term
      a. Self-loathing, guilt, dysphoria
      b. Social withdrawal
      c. Weight gain

4. Reduction of interpersonal conflict through utilization of alternative coping strategies

B. Clarification and minimizations of binge consequences
   1. Short-term
      a. Increase enjoyment of food at meals; decrease fear of "forbidden foods"
      b. Utilization of alternative strategies
   2. Longer term
      a. Minimize affective factors
      b. Decrease social withdrawal
      c. Weight loss program

were identified. For example, Ms. A. had a generalized belief that she was a failure. She persistently maintained a self-critical and self-demeaning attitude. Further, she continually expected criticism and disappointment from those around her. Following Beck's (1967) recommendations, Ms. A. was challenged about her erroneous thinking patterns. She learned to identify self-defeating cognitions and to counter them, and also was asked to rehearse positive self-statements. She practiced using positive self-verbalizations at home between sessions.

Ms. A. also demonstrated generally nonassertive behavior at work, with her parents, and in heterosocial relationships. She was asked to generate a list of situations which she had found difficult to handle. Then using role-play, feedback, and rehearsal, she practiced using appropriately assertive responses. Ms. A. also practiced her newly acquired assertive skills between therapy sessions.

Course of Treatment

The client was seen for 35 sessions held over a period of 11 months. Initially, sessions were scheduled weekly. After four months, Ms. A. was seen on a biweekly basis for a three-month period. Finally, she was seen only monthly.

Ms. A. was weighed at the beginning of each session. Then, time was spent reviewing the eating and exercise diary and discussing diet-related problems. The remainder of the session was used to focus on other problems.

Initially, Ms. A. found it difficult to self-monitor on a consistent basis. This is a time-consuming and tedious task and often is the focus of client resistance. It seems particularly difficult for individuals to record the amounts and caloric values of food eaten during binges, since binge eating is associated with a lack of self-awareness. The client sometimes would cancel or fail to appear for appointments when she did not self-monitor (and/or had gained weight).

Further, the therapist's directive to self-monitor also may have elicited the client's previously learned tendency to rebel. For example, Ms. A. often responded to her mother's demands to diet in a maladaptive fashion by overeating. Similarly, Ms. A. frequently resisted her boss's arbitrary demands by procrastinating or going home and binge eating. Therefore, Ms. A.'s failure to comply with the self-monitoring may have been a form of passive rebellion. Her resistance was handled by the therapist adopting a calm, matter-of-fact attitude about her failure to record, discussing difficulties encountered, and reframing her failure to comply as an opportunity to learn about the eating problem.

Eventually, Ms. A. self-monitored faithfully, and the diary data were used to structure sessions throughout the course of treatment. Examination of the antecedents and consequences of binge eating afforded the opportunity to discuss maladaptive cognitions and behavior patterns not directly related to eating behavior. A perfectionistic, "all-or-nothing" attitude characterized Ms. A.'s approach to her work as well as her diet. Similarly, heterosocial anxiety was a general problem as well as a frequent antecedent to a binge. As the food-related difficulties receded, more time was spent in discussion of these and other day-to-day problems.

Ms. A.'s binge eating decreased from two or three episodes a week to an average of one episode a week during the first six weeks of treatment. Binge frequency remained constant until month 4, when the number of binges dropped to an average of two a month. Contrary to her fears, Ms. A. did not gain weight by eating moderately between binges. As binge episodes diminished, she began to lose weight. The rate of weight loss improved during the spring when energy expenditure increased through walking an average of 40 minutes daily. The client lost a total of 51 lb. (23.2 kg) during the course of treatment. This represented a weight loss rate of approximately 1.1 lb. (.5 kg) a week.

Ms. A. became markedly less dysphoric as she learned to self-manage her eating behavior. She also learned to recognize negative thoughts and expectations and to counter them with positive self-statements. In fact, Ms. A.'s score on the Beck Depression Inventory decreased from an initial pretreatment score of 22 to 12. Her score during the final treatment session was 7, which is in the nondepressed range.

Ms. A. also made substantial gains in her ability to deal more comfortably with her parents and the demands of work. She found role-playing particularly helpful in this regard, and was able to utilize the strategies developed in therapy both at work and with her family. However, Ms. A. was less successful in her efforts to enhance her social life. She continued to avoid situations in which heterosocial contacts were likely to occur, and thus did not practice the skills that were learned during therapy sessions.

Termination and Follow-up

As Ms. A. improved during treatment, the frequency of sessions was decreased to once every two weeks. Then, when weight loss was progressing and binge eating was minimal, termination was planned and sessions were scheduled on a monthly basis.

Ms. A. was asked to anticipate potential problems and to plan strategies to deal with them. Her major concern was that she would gain weight and/or resume binge eating once therapy sessions were terminated. It should be noted that it is particularly important for the therapist to stress that occasional binge episodes are likely, if not certain, to occur, and to help the client plan for them. Ms. A. had continued to have occasional binge episodes during treatment and knew that she could resume a healthy eating pattern afterward. Therefore, the therapist and client were able to review situations that previously had triggered binge eating, and focus on ways to cope with future relapses. Ms. A. felt confident that she had learned cognitive strategies for countering "feast or famine" eating behavior. However, she agreed that anxiety about heterosocial relationships was likely to continue to be a high-risk situation for binge behavior in the future. Unfortunately, as mentioned above, efforts to alter her behavior in such situations were not successful.

Weight loss maintenance was also discussed during the termination phase. It is relatively common for weight loss clients to begin to regain weight as they approach their target weight, since they tend to believe, erroneously, that they can resume their former eating and exercise patterns once they are thin. Thus, it is important to stress the importance of permanent habit change *throughout* treatment. In addition, it is often useful to help the client plan a strategy to deal with small weight gains. Ms. A. decided that she would resume self-monitoring and calorie counting if she gained weight.

Telephone contacts were initiated at six and nine months following treatment. Ms. A. had maintained her weight loss and binge episodes were infrequent. She reported that she was no longer preoccupied with food or the desire to achieve a model-thin body weight (her weight at nine months posttreatment was 136 lb./61.7 kg). Her mood was good and she looked forward to the future. In addition, she had maintained the gains she had made in her relationships with her parents and colleagues.

By contrast, Ms. A. continued to experience heterosocial problems. She felt ill at ease and perpetually disappointed during her intermittent social contacts with men. Thus, she decided to completely avoid romantic entanglements, although she stated that she hoped to marry "some day."

Overall Evaluation

The behavioral treatment of obesity may be complicated by the presence of other problems. The client whose treatment was described in this chapter was a 28-year-old professional woman with a 10-year history of overweight and disordered eating behavior with concomitant depressive symptomatology and nonassertive behavior. The major goals of assessment were to rule out contraindications to obesity treatment, to identify coexisting problems, and to gather data for a multifaceted behavioral program. Treatment lasted 11 months, and included behavioral strategies to deal with binge eating, depressive symptoms, and nonassertiveness, as well as with obesity. Major clinical issues were dealing with client resistance and managing relapse behavior. The treatment of this client's overweight and disordered eating patterns was quite successful and was accomplished by a remission of depressive symptoms and an improvement in social skills. Her nonassertive behavior in the context of heterosocial relationships was not modified.

References

Beck, A. T. (1967). *Depression: Causes and treatment.* Philadelphia: University of Pennsylvania Press.

Beck, A. T., Ward, C. H., Mendelson, M., Mock, J., & Erbaugh, J. (1961). An inventory for measuring depression. *Archives of General Psychiatry, 4,* 53–63.

Gormally, J., Black, S., Daston, S., & Rardin, O. (1982). The assessment of binge eating severity among obese persons. *Addictive Behaviors, 7,* 47–55.

Loro, A. D., Jr., & Orleans, C. S. (1981). Binge eating in obesity. Preliminary findings and guidelines for behavioral analysis and treatment. *Addictive Behaviors, 6,* 155–166.

Stuart, R. G., & Davis, B. (1972). *Slim chance in a fat world: Behavioral control in obesity.* Champaign, IL: Research Press.

12

Alcohol Abuse

Joseph R. Cautela

Description of Alcohol Abuse

In my clinical practice, individuals are referred or self-referred for the following reasons:

1. They feel they cannot control the ingestion of alcohol once they have taken a drink, and they continue to drink until in a stupor.
2. They ingest so much alcohol that it interferes with important functions, such as work, social interactions, and sexual behavior.
3. Significant others tell these clients that their drinking is a problem and suggest they seek help.
4. Significant others demand that these clients seek help and threaten such actions as divorce or, as in the case of a problem drinker's parents, to shut off allowance or college tuition.

In my discussion with clients, I make it clear that I am not concerned with whether alcohol abuse is a disease or whether they could be labeled alcoholic. Instead, I am concerned with the following: (1) Does alcohol interfere with daily life? (2) How does alcohol interfere with daily life? (3) Do they want to change their drinking behavior? (4) Can we work together, with the help of others, to eliminate problem drinking?

Case Identification

The client in this case was an attractive 33-year-old female, childless and divorced for 10 years. At the time of her initial visit, she was vice-president in charge of personnel for a large department store chain.

When the client was age 15, her parents were divorced. As a result, there were many problems concerning financial matters and the custody of the client. According to her, her father was a successful businessman who tried to dominate and intimidate everyone. He died of a heart attack one month after she entered college. Reportedly, she did not grieve because she never felt close to him. At the time of treatment, the client's mother was still living, but they visited very infrequently.

Presenting Complaints and History

The client claimed that she had been depressed as far back as she could remember. She started drinking in college to get her through the stress of exams, but she was under control enough so that she was able to take the exams and do well. The September after graduating from undergraduate school, she began graduate school. She was married for six months while in graduate school, but called her marriage a "disaster." She stated that she began drinking more and more in graduate school due to the increasing pressure of her marriage and exams. In her marriage there was constant arguing, screaming, and some physical abuse, but the husband was the one who finally decided to leave.

After graduate school, she obtained a position in the personnel department of a department store chain. She worked her way up to being vice-president in charge of personnel. During the three years that she was working in this capacity, she engaged in occasional alcohol binges and experienced blackouts on weekends and evenings. For the most part, she was able to perform her job well during the day. However, she reported that, during the last six months her performance at work had slowly deteriorated.

Previously, the client had gone to a therapist who prescribed Antabuse. She abstained from drinking for about six weeks, but then stopped taking the medication and subsequently began to drink more and more. She then joined AA and stopped drinking, and became involved with another AA member. When her lover ended the relationship very abruptly (after he met another woman), the client became quite upset and started drinking again and having blackouts. Sometimes she found herself at home in bed and later discovered that some friends had taken her there.

She then became involved with a married man at work, but, after a few months, he ended the relationship. At this time, she stopped seeing a therapist, stopped going to AA, and started drinking again. Now, feeling lonely and distrustful of men, she socialized occasionally with female friends, and with her boss and his wife. She told them about her heavy drinking and her unfortunate relationships, and, in general, complained about her life.

Before coming to me for treatment, she again had attended AA for a month but still felt very depressed and went on occasional drinking binges. One of the precipitates to seeking treatment was that, twice within the previous month, the client had awakened after a party in a stranger's bed. On the second of these occasions, she found herself with two strange men she vaguely remembered having met at a party. She stated that although she was trying to do something with her life, there was nothing she really enjoyed any more. In addition, she was becoming increasingly concerned that she would black out.

Assessment

My general method in treating maladaptive approach behaviors, such as excessive alcoholic intake, is to:

1. Directly target the maladaptive behavior and define it in terms of its frequency, duration, intensity, and latency.
2. Attempt to modify the antecedents and consequences of the maladaptive behavior.
3. Increase the general level of reinforcement.
4. Reduce as many sources of stress as possible, whether or not they are clearly identified as antecedents or consequences of the maladaptive behavior.
5. Encourage the client to attend Alcoholics Anonymous.

Assessment procedures for this case consisted of a behavioral inventory developed by the author (Cautela, 1977), interviews with the client, and interviews with the client's best friend. On the behavioral inventory, the client recorded the frequency of drinking, nature of the alcoholic beverage, where and when drinking occurred, who was present, and what occurred before, during, and after drinking.

Behavioral analysis revealed a number of antecedent conditions to drinking. For example, the client typically would drink when a man with whom she was involved would not respond to her passive, clinging, and demanding behavior. The nature of her relationships with men is depicted in the excerpt below:

Client: I don't know why, it seems like when I get seriously involved in a relationship and I care about the person he dumps me.

Therapist: Why do you say that?

Client: Because that's the fact. It's happened so many times.

Therapist: Tell me how your relationships evolve.

Client: Well, at first the man pays a lot of attention to me. He practically sweeps me off my feet. As I begin to care for him, I become more passive, dependent, and afraid of rejection.

Therapist: Why do you change after you feel you really care?

Client: Well, then I have more to lose.

Therapist: What do you mean by, "I become passive and dependent?"

Client: I don't express what I want. I do whatever he wants to do.

Therapist: In what areas?

Client: In every area.

Therapist: For example . . .

Client: I do whatever he wants, socially and sexually.

Therapist: Even though you don't agree?

Client: Yes.

Therapist: Do you think that it makes the man lose respect for you?

Client: I guess so. I never thought of it that way. I thought he would like me more because I did what he wanted.

Therapist: Well, it would seem to me that if you get your way all the time with people you lose your respect for them. Maybe what you need is assertiveness training. That way, you can feel better about yourself and gain the respect of other people, especially men.

Client: I guess I really need that.

The client also would drink following stressful meetings at work, and when she was feeling resentful of her superiors and peers, whom she thought took advantage of her.

The behavioral assessment also revealed that the client was very indecisive, and that she constantly ruminated over the possible negative consequences of her decisions. Finally, it should be noted that her general level of reinforcement (GLR) (Cautela, 1984) was low, that is, she experienced very few rewards or positive events in her life. As a result, reinforcement from drinking alcohol was quite powerful. In order to ensure her cooperation in giving up alcohol, which was one of her few sources of pleasure, her GLR needed to be increased.

Assessment also indicated that several potentially reinforcing events often co-occurred with or followed drinking. For example, the client gained a good deal of attention from others by complaining about her drinking and her life. Ingesting alcohol and becoming incapacitated in social situations helped her to avoid heterosexual relationships. Moreover, drinking excessively at parties helped decrease her anxiety concerning how people would respond to her, thus aiding her to avoid negative reactions or social rejection. Finally, the altered state produced by alcohol attenuated her ruminations and feelings of helplessness.

Selection of Treatment

The following target behaviors were selected for intervention: (1) reduction of stress level, (2) abstinence from drinking alcohol, (3) elimination of strong and weak urges to drink, (4) reduction of negative thinking, especially concerning relationships with men and being able to live an alcohol-free life, (5) appropriate assertive behavior toward superiors and subordinates at work, (6) assertive behavior toward men in general, (7) desensitization of fear and rejection, especially by men, (8) desensitization of stressful work situations, such as meetings and confrontations with superiors and subordinates, (9) increase confidence in decision making, and (10) increase in recreational activities.

When I encouraged the client to attend AA meetings, she responded, "I tried AA before. It doesn't work for me. That's why I'm coming to you." I suggested that perhaps AA would be a good combination with my treatment. She said, "I don't need it. I have enough support." I did not bring the matter up again. I was concerned that the client would think I wanted AA as a supplemental treatment approach for her because I was not confident with my own approach.

Four covert conditioning procedures were used to make the drinking of alcohol aversive and to increase self-control in this area (i.e., making the decision not to drink when tempted) (Cautela, 1977). These will be described briefly below.

Covert Sensitization

When employing covert sensitization, the client is asked to imagine performing the behavior to be decreased and then to imagine aversive consequences. A list of places where the client usually drinks was drawn up. The time of day and the nature of the alcoholic beverage also were noted. As with all covert conditioning procedures, the client was asked to sit in a comfortable chair, close her eyes, and pay close attention to my directions. She was asked to listen carefully to what I said and *really* become involved in the scenes I described. She was told to try to experience the scenes as real, and not as imaginary. The following is an example of one of the scenes we used:

> You are at a party. The only person you know is the hostess. You feel uneasy. Everyone around you is drinking an alcoholic beverage of some kind. You feel at a disadvantage and left out. You look at your ginger ale and say to yourself, "To hell with it. I am going to have a drink." As soon as you say that, you start to feel a tightness at the pit of your stomach. As you walk toward the liquor table, you start to feel nauseous, weak, and faint. When you are about a foot away from the liquor table, you feel weak and cold. Food particles are coming up into your mouth; you swallow them back down. You barely make it to the table. You grab a bottle of Scotch and a glass. As you pour the liquor into the glass, you have an overwhelming feeling that you are going to vomit. You continue to fill the glass anyway. You are feeling crampy, nauseous, weak, and lightheaded as you put the glass to your lips. Suddenly, you start to vomit all over your hands, right into the glass of Scotch and all over the liquor table. You can smell the brown and green vomit all over the table, on your hands and in the glass. Your hands feel sticky and slimy. You continue vomiting all over your clothes. Snots come out of your nose. You really feel sick. As you look around, you see everyone looking at you covered with vomit, holding a glass of liquor. You let go of the glass. You turn around and head for the bathroom.

Covert Extinction

Covert extinction is similar, in many respects, to overt extinction procedures. When employing it, the therapist instructs the client to imagine performing the behavior to be reduced, and then to imagine that reinforcement does not follow. Accordingly, this client was given the following instructions:

> You raise the glass to your lips. You start drinking (e.g., Scotch, whiskey, bourbon, etc.). The Scotch has no taste whatsoever. Absolutely no taste. You know it is a liquid, but it has no taste. It doesn't even taste like water. You swallow the Scotch, and even though you know you are swallowing something, you have no sensation of the liquor going down your throat. After a minute or two, you feel no different than before you had the drink. Now, five minutes later, there is still no effect.

The client was asked to practice this scene in my office until she could follow the instructions and actually imagine the scenes with each alcoholic beverage that she was accustomed to drinking. She also was instructed to practice the scenes at least five times each day at home.

Covert Reinforcement

Covert reinforcement was used to increase self-control. The client was asked to imagine the following scene:

> You have just come out of a meeting. It has not gone well for you. You start to think, "I can't wait until I get home and take a belt." As soon as you say that, you start to think, "What the hell am I doing? That's how I've been screwing up my life." Then you say firmly, "I am not going to do it."

After the client indicated that she could experience the scene vividly, she signaled, and I said, "reinforce." At this time she was instructed to imagine a pleasant scene. This procedure was used with all the possible sources of "temptation." Eventually, scenes were put on tape, and the client was asked to play the tapes every day.

The client was instructed to employ covert sensitization, covert extinction, and covert reinforcement procedures every time she erred and took a drink. If she had a few drinks in the afternoon, she was to do scenes appropriate to that situation during the evening or next morning. In addition, she was instructed to utilize scenes that represented those situations in which she actually had drunk. For example, if she accepted an invitation to go out for drinks, she was to practice with a scene that included the particular bar or restaurant in which she had had a drink. Thus, she would first imagine the scene and that she got sick and vomited (covert sensitization). Then, she would imagine she was tempted to accept the invitation but decided not to, and then reinforce herself (covert reinforcement). She would further imagine that when she drank the liquor it had no taste (covert extinction).

Self-control Triad

The client was taught to use the self-control triad (Cautela, 1983) whenever she had a temptation to drink and whenever she felt uncomfortable. At these times, she was instructed to say "stop" to herself in a firm and loud voice, then to take a deep breath, relax, and imagine a pleasant scene. In addition, the client was asked to say the following each morning before she got out of bed, "If I am tempted to drink or if I get depressed or nervous today, I will use the self-control triad until the temptation goes away and I calm down."

Social Behavior

In addition to the covert conditioning procedures described above, the client was taught to refuse invitations to drink using behavioral rehearsal. When she had some trouble asserting herself with men, even after the behavioral rehearsals were practiced, covert reinforcement also was employed. Here, she imagined that she was being assertive and feeling good about it, and then imagined a reinforcing scene. Covert reinforcement scenes also were used for conquering her fear of rejection by men, and for getting her to stop complaining. In addition, she used the self-control triad whenever she was about to complain.

The client was desensitized using covert reinforcement for fears she experienced during staff meetings, such as making a suggestion and having other board members (all men) laugh, looking nervous, and not having information "at her fingertips." She was asked to imagine herself at the meetings, feeling calm and comfortable (reinforcement). We also conducted behavioral rehearsals and covert reinforcement on being assertive at meetings. She was to use the self-control triad when she started to become fearful during meetings.

Increasing the General Level of Reinforcement

A reinforcement "menu" was devised to provide alternative behaviors to substitute when the client had the urge to drink. Some of the alternative behaviors were: listening to the stereo, reading a bestseller, calling friends, playing a relaxation tape, and engaging in creative fantasy, that is, imagining she was the central figure in a story in which she continually was being reinforced.

The Reinforcement Survey Schedule (Cautela & Kastenbaum, 1967) and a number of interviews revealed possible sources of reinforcement. We discussed ways to engage in as many of the reinforcement activities as possible. Furthermore, she was encouraged to go bowling with her friends at least on a weekly basis. She expressed concern over her performance and interacting with the people. I employed covert reinforcement to desensitize her to these fears.

I brought in a list of courses available at a nearby adult education school. She chuckled as she noticed a course entitled "Stand-up Comedy." I asked her if she would be interested in such a course. She replied, "Well, I guess if I am laughing, I can't be depressed." I suggested that she go to the first class and see what it was like. The week after her first class, she was enthusiastic about the course and some outgoing people who had attended.

Relaxation Training

Finally, the client was taught both progressive muscle relaxation and imagery relaxation. She was instructed to practice progressive muscle relaxation once a day and to listen to the imagery relaxation tape once a day. After a few weeks, she said she preferred the imagery relaxation and that she was playing it twice a day and not using the progressive muscle relaxation.

Course of Treatment

Therapy sessions occurred once a week for the first six months, then every two weeks for two months, and, finally, once a month for the last three months. We developed excellent rapport. The client did all her homework assignments (keeping records, playing tapes, and practicing relaxation) with enthusiasm.

Alcohol Behavior

The client became abstinent from liquor after the third month. Strong urges disappeared after the fifth month. After six months and up until the eighth month she reported weak urges occasionally when she was under great stress. At the end of ten months, she did not experience urges, and even the thought of drinking alcohol was aversive.

Social Behavior

After the first two months, she was able to be appropriately assertive at meetings. After three months, she felt comfortable at meetings. After the fifth month, she was able to be assertive and comfortable with men who were in upper management. After the seventh month, she felt confident and was able to be comfortable with men in a heterosexual relationship. She ceased complaining to her boss about personal problems after the fifth month. She did occasionally tell him about her status in therapy. He agreed that she was looking more comfortable, especially at meetings. He also said she was doing better work.

After the third month, she took an adult education course in "Stand-up Comedy." She found the class stimulating and entertaining. She was constantly looking for new comedy material for her presentation, which was due at the end of the course. At the end of the course, after 10 weeks of class, she did a five-minute stand-up routine at the local Comedy Connection Nightclub.

She attended weekly bowling meetings with a league she organized with some of the employees. She kept a bestseller ready to read at all times. She went out to dinner and to the movies once a week.

Follow-up

The client called me one year later to "fill me in." She reported she was in love and engaged to be married the following month. She still used relaxation exercises twice a day and used the self-control triad when needed. A year after the phone call, the client sent me a postcard from Europe informing me that she was having a happy anniversary.

Overall Evaluation

In this case of alcohol abuse, the primary goals of therapy were achieved with one year of treatment. The reinforcing effect of alcohol was modified, the client's general level of reinforcement was increased, negative rumination was decreased, and coping and assertiveness skills were mastered.

References

Cautela, J. R. (1977). *Behavior analysis forms for clinical intervention.* Champaign, IL: Research Press.

Cautela, J. R. (1983). The self-control triad. *Behavior Modification, 7,* 299–315.

Cautela, J. R. (1984). General level of reinforcement. *Journal of Behavior Therapy and Experimental Psychiatry, 15,* 109–114.

Cautela, J. R., & Kastenbaum, R. A. (1967). Reinforcement survey schedule for use in therapy, training, and research. *Psychological Reports, 20,* 1115–1130.

13
Marital Distress

Gary R. Birchler

Description of Marital Distress

Criteria for ascertaining the existence of marital distress are difficult to pinpoint. Case referrals originate from inpatient and outpatient settings, from one or both partners, and from a variety of allied health professionals. Typically, couples wait too long before seeking professional help. The following guidelines indicate the appropriateness of professional assistance and the general symptoms of the problem: (1) when one or both partners are dissatisfied with the quality of their relationship and their own attempts to improve things have not been successful; (2) when either partner's cost or pain experienced in the relationship exceeds the rewards or pleasures; (3) when appreciable and continuing amounts of either partner's time and energy are devoted to *avoiding conflict* or *engaging in conflict*; (4) when either partner believes that marital communication is diminished or absent, that few activity interests remain in common, and that sexual and affectionate interaction is boring or absent.

Within these general guidelines, couples typically experience marital distress related to aspects of *structure, process*, and/or *content*. *Structure* can be conceptualized as the existence of certain sex-roles, situational factors, and relationship definitions adopted by the couple or imposed on the couple from external sources. These structural factors, typically operational by default rather than through discussion, help determine (1) who does what to maintain the relationship and accomplish its goals, (2) who has access to whom and when, and (3) how, in an intimate relationship, the difficult balance is achieved between personal independence and interpersonal dependence. *Process* pertains to *how* the partners interact, and in particular to the development and practical application of communication skills necessary for the definition and resolution of important relationship issues. Finally, *content* relates to the *what* of relationship problems. In this area, marital distress typically is a function of disagreements about sex and affection, money, household management, children, in-laws, personal habits, and so on. Keeping these dimensions in mind, the first step in the marital evaluation process consists of clients and clinicians working together to understand the nature of the dysfunctional structural, process, and content-related problems.

Case Identification

The case to be described here originated from an outpatient Mental Health Clinic located within a comprehensive V.A. Medical Center. Mr. Carlson had heard about the Family Mental Health Program from a friend and called to arrange for an initial conjoint appointment. David was 31 years old and Carol was 32. They had been married 12 years, and had two daughters, aged four and one. David worked for a bottled water company and was a part-time student pursuing a B.A. degree in business. Carol was a high-school educated homemaker and part-time babysitter.

Presenting Complaints

On the first phone contact David indicated a severe "lack of communication" and the need for help in learning how to talk together. During the initial interview the couple described a number of recent stresses in the family which included (1) financial difficulties related to husband's low pay, (2) the prospect of husband losing his job, (3) the necessity of wife having to babysit to supplement their income, despite (4) wife having significant physical problems, including obesity and hypertension secondary to toxemia of recent pregnancy, and (5) youngest daughter having a three- to four-month developmental delay.

In addition, Carol complained that "David holds things inside. I feel there's a wall between us, with me and the children on one side and him on the other." She reported his withholding knowledge of financial difficulties from her and that his pattern of noncommunication and withdrawal was a long-standing problem. For example: "Six years ago he withdrew for six months when we were planning to adopt a child, because he couldn't accept the idea of adoption." Four years previously Carol seriously considered divorce because "I wasn't going to hassle raising three kids — he's just like having another kid around. I would go to work to bail him out of money problems, but I didn't want to go to work." Other problems mentioned by Carol were her concerns that "my friends are uncomfortable around David. He never talks." Finally, Carol indicated that her husband does not discipline the children enough.

David presented the chief problem as, "I don't know how to communicate." He stated that Carol withdraws when she is angry with him. To resolve fights, "I come out and appease her but we're never close again for months." They agreed that they fight infrequently, but significant damage is done when fighting occurs.

History

A brief "family of origin" history was taken from each partner. David was one of seven children. His father was an alcoholic. When David was seven his parents began fighting; when he was 11 they divorced. His mother remarried and he has many half-siblings. His father moved away and has since suffered from cancer and a heart attack. No one in the family showed much affection; their interactional style was to fight or withdraw. David learned to keep everything to himself.

Carol was the second of four daughters. Her oldest sister had cerebral palsy. She described her father as a "bastard," while mom and the kids were "puppets" who "stayed close to each other to survive." She and her sisters were physically abused. Father is now deceased; mother and the two younger sisters have all been in therapy. As children, "we were not allowed to express emotion — the only emotion I ever saw was Dad getting angry. The only emotion I know is anger."

Once married the Carlsons reported a difficult relationship history. David has had repeated jobs, most of them seriously unsatisfying or low-paying. He once tried to get into the bottled water business for himself, but succeeded only in draining the emotional and financial resources of the family. Carol had much difficulty getting pregnant, but finally had two daughters. However, the second pregnancy was quite traumatic for all. It resulted in major health problems for Carol, emotional problems for the older child, and a developmentally retarded baby. Amidst this history, they reported poor ability to communicate, problem solve, and manage conflict. However, through all this they established a positive and supportive connection to their church and succeeded in maintaining a fairly good base of affection and sex. At the time of the intake interviews, they were very discouraged about their relationship (and their lives) and were actively considering divorce.

Assessment

The author has developed a behavioral-systems approach to the assessment and treatment of marital distress. The model is presented in Figure 13.1 and is described in detail elsewhere (Birchler, 1983; Birchler & Spinks, 1980). The clinical assessment phase (see Figure 13.1) is designed to gather diagnostic information, to establish trust and rapport with the clients, and to orient them in the language and perspectives of the therapeutic approach. Initial interviews elicited the presenting complaints and brief personal histories. In addition, the Marital Relationship Assessment Battery (MRAB) and a Communication Sample (CS) were obtained to complete the multimethod evaluation procedure.

Marital Relationship Assessment Battery (MRAB)

The MRAB consists of the following seven self-report inventories which are completed independently by each spouse. These descriptions indicate the kind of information deemed important in the assessment phase of behavioral marital therapy.

Locke-Wallace Marital Adjustment Scale (LWMAS).   This scale is a commonly used self-report measure of global marital satisfaction. General areas of agreement and disagreement on major topics within the relationship are indicated. Empirically derived scale scores discriminate maritally distressed from nondistressed couples. Scores range from 0 to 158. A score of 100 is used as the cutoff point. Higher scores indicate greater satisfaction.

Marital Status Inventory (MSI).   In this scale, 14 true–false questions assess the degree to which each spouse has sought dissolution of the relationship. Scores range from 0 to 14. Higher scores indicate more steps toward divorce.

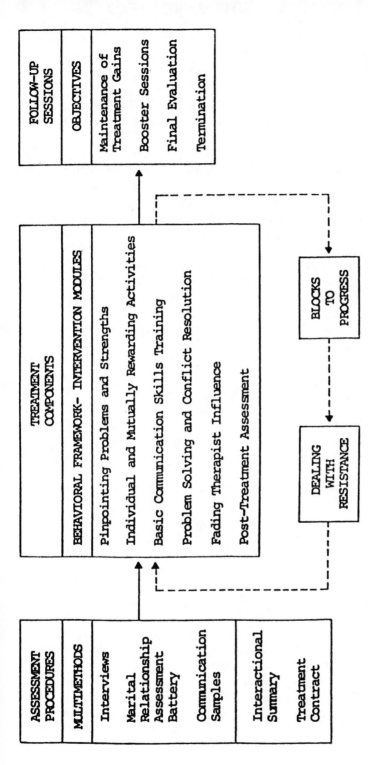

Figure 13.1. Behavioral-systems marital therapy: Assessment and intervention components. [From Birchler, G. R. (1983). Behavioral-systems marital therapy. In J. P. Vincent (Ed.), *Advances in family intervention, assessment and theory* (Vol. 3, pp. 1–40). Greenwich, CT: JAI Press; and from Spinks, S. H., & Birchler, G. R. (1982). Behavioral-systems marital therapy: Dealing with resistance. *Family Process, 21*, 169–185. With permission.]

173

Areas of Change Questionnaire (ACQ). In this questionnaire 34 areas of typical marital conflict are assessed by analyzing couples' requests for behavior change in self and spouse. Scores range from 0 to 68. Higher scores represent a greater number of areas of marital conflict.

Self-Description Inventory (SDI). This is a self-report questionnaire which includes three scales designed to assess individuals' sense of self-esteem, psychological distress, and physical symptoms. The SDI helps indicate individuals' tendencies toward depression, anxiety, denial, and somatic preoccupation. Self-esteem and psychological distress scores range from 0 to 8; physical symptoms scores range from 0 to 5. Higher scores on self-esteem and lower scores on psychological distress and physical symptoms are indicative of health.

Response to Conflict (RTC). This scale provides an index of the relative proportion of time that each person engages in maladaptive interaction. Each spouse indicates both partners' reactions to conflict situations. Scores range from 0 to 8. Higher scores represent more maladaptive responses to conflict.

Inventory of Rewarding Activities (IRA). This questionnaire assesses recreational activities engaged in alone, with spouse only, with spouse and other adults, with family, and with others (excluding spouse) over the previous four weeks. The measure also indicates what percentage of time in a typical week is spent working, sleeping, and engaging in rewarding or nonrewarding activities.

Summary of Current Important Issues. Used as the final MRAB self-report instrument, each spouse lists his or her perception of the four most significant relationship and personal strengths and weaknesses.

Table 13.1 presents the pretherapy and posttherapy MRAB scores for Mr. and Mrs. Carlson. Highlights of the pretherapy MRAB data indicate that (1) both partners had significant marital dissatisfaction, with David more so than Carol, (2) Carol had achieved 11 of 14 steps toward divorce, (3) Carol had significantly elevated psychological distress and physical symptom scores, (4) the Response to Conflict scores were in the maladaptive range with the exception of David's self-appraisal (his maladaptive behavior suggested passive, withdrawal tendencies; Carol was more active and aggressive), (5) David's Inventory of Rewarding Activity (IRA) scores were very high for *working* hours (70 hours a week for work and school activities). Carol's IRA scores were relatively low for *spouse only* activities, somewhat high for *with adults, not spouse,* very low for time engaged in *rewarding* activities, and very high for *nonrewarding* activities. Overall, MRAB information documented a moderate to severe level

Table 13.1. Pre- and Posttherapy Results of the Marital Relationship
Assessment Battery (MRAB) and Marital Interaction Coding System (MICS)

	Pretherapy		Posttherapy	
MRAB Inventory	*David*	*Carol*	*David*	*Carol*
Locke-Wallace Marital Satisfaction	48	85	105	114
Marital Status Inventory	5	11	1	4
Self-Description Inventory:				
Self-esteem	5.6	6.9	5.8	6.4
Psychological distress	2.9	3.6	2.4	2.1
Physical symptoms	0.6	2.2	0.4	1.0
Areas of Change Questionnaire	18	18	2	1
Response to Conflict Scale:				
Appraisal of self	1.8	3.7	0.5	1.3
Appraisal of spouse	3.3	4.1	0.6	0.9
Inventory of Rewarding Activities—				
Activity Distribution (%):				
Alone	27	25	21	29
With spouse only	35	19	43	32
With spouse/other adults	13	15	11	9
With family	23	29	24	26
With adults, not spouse	0	12	0	3
Time Distribution (%):				
Working	42	0	24	24
Sleeping	30	29	31	31
Rewarding activities	23	4	34	12
Neutral or nonrewarding	5	67	11	32
MICS Behavioral Category[a]				
Problem Solution	.80	.80	2.44	.67
Positive Verbal	.30	.50	.70	.89
Positive Nonverbal	3.60	4.00	5.22	3.78
Negative Verbal	.30	.00	.00	.00
Negative Nonverbal	.30	.00	.00	.00

[a]*Note*: Behavioral frequencies are expressed in terms of rates per minute.

of marital distress and a relationship complicated by a combination
of personal, structural, process, and content problems.

Communication Sample

A very important part of behaviorally oriented marital therapy is to
obtain *a sample of interaction behavior*. We have learned from existing research that the communication and problem-solving skills

demonstrated by distressed relative to nondistressed couples are significantly different. Therefore, observation of marital conflict interaction by means of live or videotaped methods is extremely useful for assessment and is highly recommended as a pre/posttherapy outcome measure.

During the *Communication Sample* (see Figure 13.1), the couple was asked to spend about 10 minutes attempting to resolve an identified marital conflict. They were told that they might not solve the problem in 10 minutes, but that the therapist was interested in observing how they go about it. At this point the therapist left the room and videotaped the negotiation, which then was evaluated for purposes of diagnosis and baseline measurement. With research in mind, a variety of coding systems have been developed to interpret and quantify videotaped interactions. The most prominent scoring system is the Marital Interaction Coding System (MICS). It was developed at the University of Oregon in the 1970s and requires trained coders. The MICS features 30 verbal and nonverbal codes that can be summarized into the following behavioral categories: Problem Solution, Positive Verbal, Positive Nonverbal, Negative Verbal, and Negative Nonverbal.

The pretherapy negotiation topics for this couple were (1) David's going to school four nights a week, and (2) discipline of the children. Carol requested that David not go to school four nights "because the kids need him." He tended to minimize her concerns and quickly switched to the mechanics of getting a degree, which courses to take, and so on. After six minutes with no resolution of the problem, David changed the topic to the issue of discipline. On this issue they quickly achieved consensus that things were better. To the therapist-observers, David's change of subject appeared to be an effective maneuver designed to avoid conflict and personal responsibility. During therapist debriefing, the couple reported that the interaction was not representative of home behavior, in that the discussion was more prolonged than those at home. Carol stated that at home "things don't get resolved, David doesn't want to talk anymore and that's it," a statement with which he agreed. They again described one another as withdrawing to an extreme degree when angry and shutting each other out.

Table 13.1 also presents the pre- and posttherapy MICS data. Relative to available norms for distressed couples, this couples' MICS data reflect the typical paucity of Problem Solution behaviors and an even lower rate of both Positive and Negative Verbal support behaviors. This pattern typifies a conflict-avoidant style of communication, whereby both partners assiduously avoid the expression of negative affect (lest a catastrophical fight occur). This expressive in-hibition also restricts their communication of positive affect. Partners who collaborate in a conflict-avoidant style of communication shape one another into a self-fulfilling prophecy. They fear that the expres-sion of anger will result in an escalating, uncontrolled, and destructive outcome. Therefore, they hold all their emotions inside. Inevitably, these emotions build up to the necessary (and sometimes destructive) ventilation point, whereupon intense emotion is released out of pro-portion to the original stimulus. This outcome, in turn, reinforces holding emotions inside. Behavioral marital therapy can help couples modify this destructive, self-perpetuating pattern.

Interactional Summary

The third and final assessment session included an interactional sum-mary. The objectives were to present the multimethod assessment information to the couple in a way which they could accept and which facilitated their entering into a treatment contract. The therapist first provided an overview of the findings from the MRAB, as the couple reviewed a written summary. The presentation emphasized both strengths and weaknesses in the marriage. Second, observations from the *Communication Sample* were integrated with other interview in-formation about the couple's style of communication, problem-solving ability, and conflict management. These were summarized for the couple in a way which implicated a faulty *system* of interaction rather than implying fault with the individuals. The MRAB feedback and interactional summary led naturally into a discussion of goals for treatment and agreement upon a treatment contract.

Selection of Treatment

This couple seemed ideal for the behavioral-systems approach for treating marital distress. Both partners had acquired faulty com-munication skills from their families of origin and, once together, had been unable to develop an effective style on their own. Their mutually reinforced conflict-avoidant interaction interfered not only with daily transactions but also with their ability to problem solve and provide fundamental support, understanding, and intimacy for one another.

The treatment components suggested for and accepted by Mr. and Mrs. Carlson (see Figure 13.1) closely followed the information obtained during the assessment phase. The major *structural* problems consisted of David spending most of his time away from family either working or going to school and Carol's virtual absence of rewarding activities both independent of and together with David. The *process* problems concerned their collaborative set to "bottle up" their accumulative anger inside, with Carol eventually blowing up and David completely withdrawing or otherwise escaping from the situation. Their basic communication skills, their general problem-solving ability, and their conflict-resolution skills were all in need of improvement. David's general unassertiveness and Carol's tendency to "mother him" and "nag at him" were also discussed as interactional problems. Finally, David's major *content* problem areas related to employment and school, his lack of time with and attention to the family, his lack of adult socialization activities, and his discipline of the children. Areas of improvement for Carol involved giving appreciation to and spending time with David, paying attention to her appearance, and increasing her independent rewarding activities.

Course of Treatment

Many of the structural-, process-, and content-based problems presented by this distressed couple are typical of such couples and thus were addressed well by the basic behavioral-systems treatment components (see Figure 13.1; see Birchler, 1983, for further details). Accordingly, the first six weeks of treatment were devoted to enriching the partners' mutually and individually rewarding activities, improving their basic communication skills, and improving their general problem-solving and conflict-resolution techniques.

Two procedures were employed to assist Carol and David enhance their quality time together. First, the Caring Activities assignment was instituted. In this exercise each partner was given a worksheet which had several examples of simple, pleasing behaviors which one partner could perform for the other, e.g., "Give me a compliment," "Give me a back rub," and so on. Partners were asked to edit and extend the list of examples so that 7 to 10 potential caring activities were identified for each person. These behaviors were edited to exclude any relationship problems.

Over the course of the next three to four weeks, the therapists helped the couple to develop and implement these small but symbolic caring behaviors to the point where they were more aware of the importance and positive influence of these exchanges. After the Caring Activities assignment yielded considerable success, more substantial rewarding relationship activities were gradually introduced. For example, from the fourth through the sixth week of treatment the following assignments were made: (1) Carol obtained babysitting help from David and friends and began a twice-weekly exercise class for herself. (2) David was given increased sanction to pursue his night school classes, but at a reduced rate (i.e., two vs. four nights per week). In exchange, the family would participate in one evening activity per week of his choosing (e.g., a movie, sports event, dinner out, etc.). (3) Finally, the couple planned and carried out weekly activities just for the two of them (e.g., a walk around the neighborhood, a dinner out, etc.).

As is typically the case in psychotherapeutic, behavior-change efforts, both partners demonstrated some initial resistance to these assignments. In particular, Carol failed to follow through with her assigned individual activities and David was less than enthusiastic initiating couple-oriented activities. Carol's resistance was handled using three interventions: (1) graduated assignments beginning with brief (i.e., 30–45 minute) shopping trips, (2) enlisting David's support to watch the children (whom at first she reluctantly left with babysitters), and (3) continually reframing her participation in independent activities as strengthening her ability to be a good wife and mother rather than it being perceived as neglect and abandonment. Similarly, David responded to the therapist's strategy to shape his couple-oriented behaviors. Beginning assignments featured brief periods of contact (e.g., a 15-minute walk after dinner) or activities which required little dyadic interaction (e.g., going to a movie or sporting event). As these were successful, activities requiring more communication and/or time together were introduced.

The second objective, basic communication skills training, also was pursued in the first four treatment sessions. Through the use of brief lectures, therapist modeling, coaching, behavioral rehearsal, videotape feedback, and specific homework assignments, Carol and David were taught to send short clear "I-statement" and "feeling" messages and to engage in the standard active listening techniques of eye contact, supportive bodily gestures, paraphrasing, and validation of expressed feelings (see Birchler, 1983, for further detail). About half of each treatment session was devoted to these activities. As adjunct bibliotherapy, chapters from *A Couples Guide to Communication* (Gottman, Notarius, Gonso, & Markman, 1976) were assigned weekly in parallel to the sessions.

At first, Carol had considerable difficulty acquiring active listening skills. She appeared to be impatient with David's passive, soft-

spoken, and tentative style of expression. She had a tendency to inter-
rupt him and to "mind read" or anticipate his thoughts and feelings.
When she did this, David would withdraw from the discussion even
further. After general coaching and verbal feedback failed to modify
this pattern, the therapists decided to use videotape feedback. It was
first explained to Carol that her impatient response to David's very
deliberative style of communication was understandable since her
own style was to get to the point and be action oriented. However,
keeping in mind that her ultimate goal was to increase David's communication with her, she (and David) was asked to study videotaped
interactions on two occasions and to notice the paradoxical effect that
her response to David was having. The videotape feedback illustrated
that Carol's interruptions and general inability to listen carefully had
the effect of inhibiting David's self-disclosure of thoughts and feelings. In training sessions thereafter, the better she listened (with
coaching and therapist reinforcement), the more expressive David became. Before long, notable gains were made in the *way* in which this
couple communicated and the confidence with which they approached
the next objective: problem solving.

The approach to problem solving/conflict management was similar to that described in detail by Jacobson and Margolin (1979). The
couple was helped to identify and work on increasingly difficult content-related marital problems by applying a five-step problem-solving
model: (1) agenda building, (2) selection of issues, (3) brainstorming
solutions, (4) selecting and implementing a solution, and (5) follow-
up evaluation. Mr. and Mrs. Carlson first chose to work on sharing
the parenting responsibilities during their vacation. Partly because
of their training in basic communication skills, they did very well on
their first several content area conflict resolutions.

Beyond general problem solving, they were taught conflict management techniques having to do with the timely initiation of open
communication when conflicts emerged, the appropriate use of time-
out procedures, and subsequent resolution of issues when anger, timing, or other situations prevented immediate resolution of the problems at hand. Once again, for this couple self-disclosure skills were
more in need of encouragement than conflict-avoidant techniques.

By the end of eight treatment sessions, David and Carol had
made significant gains in (1) the expression of caring and attention
to one another, (2) basic communication skills, and (3) discussing and
at least proposing solutions for the following problems: disciplining
the children, David's school activities, Carol's independent rewarding
activities, David being more assertive regarding expression of posi-

tive and negative emotions, Carol reinforcing versus inadvertently punishing David's self-disclosure, Carol's weight problem, David's smoking problem, and the possibility of Carol going to work to help out with the finances.

In general, this couple was well motivated for therapy. Their failure to improve their relationship on their own was more related to skill deficits (i.e., poor parental models) and lack of self-confidence and self-esteem than to issues of interpersonal control, competitiveness, or maladaptive manipulation. Accordingly, the therapist interventions required to deal with their particular resistant behaviors were largely of the educational, social reinforcement, and light interpretation variety. The more sophisticated, countermanipulative therapist intervention options for dealing with resistance (e.g., the use of paradoxical, confrontational, and antisabotage procedures or individual sessions) were not indicated.

In particular, the major stumbling blocks to the success of this case were David's tendency to withhold emotions in the face of Carol's real or anticipated response, and Carol's tendency to mother, nag, and overprotect David in the context of her requesting more assertiveness from him. These problems were dealt with in two ways. One consisted of practicing assertive skills during therapy sessions and at home. The second involved interpretation of the couple's prior self-defeating interactional style through carefully placed therapeutic comments.

Termination

Parts of the final three treatment sessions were devoted to termination activities and issues. Basically, termination consisted of two activities: (1) fading the therapist's influence by turning over the agenda and direction of therapy to the couple, and (2) completing the post-therapy assessment measures.

In the former case, the therapist took an increasingly less directive role in deciding the details of interaction at home and in the sessions, but nonetheless encouraged Mr. and Mrs. Carlson independently to identify and address important relationship issues. This was accomplished through regularly scheduled "talk times," that is, twice-a-week meetings designed to provide the structure and forum for processing relationship issues. In addition, a brief handout was distributed to provide a general list of important preventive concentration areas.

The posttherapy assessment procedures were the same as for pretherapy: The *MRAB* and a *Communication Sample*. Table 13.1 also
presents the posttherapy measures for this couple. As can be seen,
significant improvement was noted for both David and Carol on marital satisfaction, the Marital Status Inventory (the steps toward divorce since therapy started), each partner's level of Psychological
Distress, the Areas of Change Questionnaire, both self- and spouse-
related Responses to Conflict, and proportion of rewarding activities
engaged in with spouse alone. In addition, Carol improved significantly
on her Physical Symptoms score. Based on their MRAB scores, Mr.
and Mrs. Carlson made significant improvements in their marriage.

The results of the Communication Sample are less dramatic for
this couple than many, but some improvement was noted. Following
therapy, David increased his Problem Solution behaviors threefold.
In addition, both partners showed improvement on their rates of Positive Verbal behaviors. Finally, David increased his Positive Nonverbal behaviors and Negative Verbal and Negative Nonverbal behaviors were absent from the posttherapy interaction assessment. It
should be noted, however, that this couple was extremely low in the
overt expression of negative affect even at the beginning of therapy.

Follow-up

At the time of termination (i.e., after three evaluation and nine treatment sessions) a follow-up meeting was scheduled for one month later.
The meeting is called a "booster" session, designed to review progress
made during and after therapy. Between termination and follow-up,
Mr. and Mrs. Carlson were encouraged to have at least one weekly
"talk time." In addition, two long-term interactional projects were
suggested. David was to continue being assertive (with both positive
and negative issues), and Carol was to respond positively to his assertiveness. Progress was to be reviewed weekly. Carol was to continue some rewarding activity for herself, and David was to limit
work and school activities while initiating a family-oriented activity.

At the follow-up meeting, the couple indicated reasonable success
with both of these projects. David had begun a new job with a different bottled water company and also had expressed his desire that
Carol consider part-time employment to help with family finances.
Carol agreed to look for work so long as David limited his school activities and continued with his commitment to family time. For her

part, Carol had joined an innovative babysitting co-op, in which, on a rotating basis, one mother watched several mothers' children while the others shopped, went to exercise classes, visited one another, or just enjoyed time alone.

Regarding marital communication, both partners indicated somewhat less regularity in talking than during therapy, but both were satisfied with the current amount. They denied any extended periods of interpersonal "cold war," which characterized their pretherapy conflict management interaction.

Overall Evaluation

This case is fairly representative of those accepted for behavioral marital therapy in outpatient clinics across the country. Mr. and Mrs. Carlson were relatively well-educated, had two children, and came from broken or dysfunctional families that were plagued by alcoholism, spouse abuse, and child abuse. Each partner practiced a style of communication and conflict (anger) management which was incompatible with a satisfying marriage. They were attracted to one another as they reacted against certain parental models in their families of origin, but over time they resented the unfamiliar personality characteristics in their partners. Their attempts to solve these problems only seemed to polarize their maladaptive responses to conflict. Eventually, lest they separate, they sought marriage counseling. Multimethod assessments, including interviews, questionnaires, and behavioral observations, confirmed significant marital distress involving structural-, process-, and content-related problems. The standard treatment components of behavioral-systems marital therapy were applied: development of individually and mutually rewarding activities, basic communication skills training, and problem solving/conflict management techniques. Comparison of pre- and posttherapy assessment batteries and Communication Samples indicated significant and broadbased improvements for this couple. Moreover, at the follow-up session, these gains appeared to be maintained.

Fortunately, resistance to change was nominal in this couple. The reader is referred to Spinks and Birchler (1982) for a discussion of how to handle cases in which resistance to behavioral-systems marital therapy is more pronounced. The literature suggests that behavioral marital therapy assists at least two-thirds of the couples seeking help for marital distress. This case study represents one of these successes.

References

Birchler, G. R. (1983). Marital dysfunction. In M. Hersen (Ed.), *Outpatient behavior therapy: A clinical guide* (pp. 229–269). New York: Grune & Stratton.

Birchler, G. R., & Spinks, S. H. (1980). Behavioral-systems marital and family therapy: Integration and clinical application. *The American Journal of Family Therapy, 8,* 6–28.

Gottman, J., Notarius, C., Gonso, J., & Markman, H. (1976). *A couple's guide to communication.* Champaign, IL: Research Press.

Jacobson, N. S., & Margolin, G. (1979). *Marital therapy: Strategies based on social learning and behavior exchange principles.* New York: Brunner/ Mazel.

Spinks, S. H., & Birchler, G. R. (1982). Behavioral-systems marital therapy: Dealing with resistance. *Family Process, 21,* 169–185.

14

Sexual Dysfunction

J. Gayle Beck

At its inception, sex therapy for the full range of heterosexual dysfunctions was heralded as the "new psychological penicillin." Success rates were high, and public and professional interest alike was focused on this rapid, problem-oriented treatment. In particular, attention was directed at disorders of arousal and orgasm in women, problems that previously had not been addressed fully by existing therapies. Accumulation of time and experience produced the gradual realization that sex therapy, much like other forms of behavior therapy, was facing increasingly complex cases which called for more refined assessment and treatment. This chapter will describe the treatment of a couple with secondary orgasmic dysfunction and illuminate the importance of viewing this problem within the broader context of the marital system. While specific changes in sexual functioning were noted, the interaction between increased sexual arousal and improvements in communication was particularly salient in this case.

Description of Secondary Orgasmic Dysfunction

Loss of the ability to achieve orgasm (i.e., secondary orgasmic dysfunction) has been attributed to a variety of factors in the clinical literature. This problem often co-occurs with a broader picture of sexual

The author gratefully acknowledges the assistance of Sandra Leiblum for her comments on an earlier draft of this chapter.

inhibition, low arousal, and general marital distress between partners. Relevant contributing factors include inadequate genital stimulation, poor communication of both sexual and nonsexual needs, pervasive moral beliefs about the inappropriateness of sexual abandonment in women, and, occasionally, diminished ability for lubrication resulting from menopause or surgery such as a hysterectomy. The development of this problem often generates considerable anxiety for the woman who is aware that she is not responding as she once was and attributes this change to some personal deficiency. When coupled with a pattern of impaired communication, this can lead to avoidance of all sexual activity.

Some women accept their lack of arousal and orgasm as a "natural" part of aging and may never seek professional treatment. Alternatively, help can be sought for a variety of reasons, including the following: (1) the woman has developed a chronic pattern of heightened anxiety and avoidance which her partner is unwilling to tolerate, (2) marital disharmony has reached proportions severe enough that separation is considered, and (3) the woman, whose view of herself has been radically altered, attempts to uncover the cause of her "personal deficiency." The presenting problem usually is one aspect of a larger picture that includes many or all of the elements reviewed above. The following case illustrates this clinical picture and demonstrates treatment with the use of several intervention strategies.

Case Identification

The couple consisted of Sarah, a 49-year-old hospital technician, and her husband, Bill, a 56-year-old maintenance worker. They had been married for 31 years and had two sons, ages 27 and 30. Both Sarah and Bill were socially skilled, although neither was psychologically sophisticated. Sarah had completed a two-year nursing program and Bill had dropped out of school after the ninth grade to work.

Presenting Complaints

The chief complaint was, in Sarah's words, "I can't face sex – it makes me anxious and I can't reach orgasm anymore. I can't get aroused but I feel like I should. If we have sex, it's painful because I'm not aroused, which only makes me more anxious."

In addition, Bill had developed a pattern of deliberately ejaculating immediately upon vaginal penetration, to reduce the discomfort of prolonged vaginal irritation. Their sexual pattern consisted of months of abstinence, punctuated by intercourse at Bill's request. Sarah complied at these times, out of "duty," and usually was depressed for several days afterward. They were referred for sex therapy by a psychologist whom Sarah had seen for a related problem.

History

Sarah's sexual functioning initially was adequate; she was orgasmic and easily aroused during the beginning years of the marriage. Her sexual problems began following a complete hysterectomy at age 31. She noted at this time finding intercourse difficult due to diminished lubrication, but was able to reach orgasm if Bill provided adequate manual stimulation. A trial of hormone replacement therapy was initiated when Sarah was 34 but was discontinued due to the development of breast fibroids. Sarah continued to have difficulty reaching orgasm and grew gradually more apprehensive about sexual contacts. At age 36, she began experiencing anxiety in public places and had severe panic attacks, which often precipitated visits to the local emergency room. She found herself increasingly reliant upon Bill for reassurance and safety when venturing outside of the home. As her agoraphobic pattern became more severe, the couple redirected their attention toward constructing a life-style around Sarah's panic attacks. She quit her nursing job and remained isolated at home, totally dependent on Bill as her source of social and emotional support.

Sarah had begun treatment for her agoraphobia with a behaviorally oriented therapist at age 47. She had made remarkable gains during the year she was in treatment, was able to travel alone, resumed work, and felt much more sure of her own coping abilities. She had not experienced a panic attack in over a year at the time of her presentation for sex therapy.

Bill provided a similar account of their sexual history together, placing much greater emphasis on the burden of responsibility he felt for his wife and his constant worrying about her physical well-being. He revealed dissatisfaction with their sexual relationship throughout the course of Sarah's agoraphobia, but stated he didn't want to pressure her by making sexual demands. Bill reported a history of not expressing his needs directly to Sarah and feeling that he had to adjust himself to whatever symptoms she experienced. He was considerably more comfortable with the marriage since the resolution of

Sarah's agoraphobia but was unsure of the future. Additionally, he held little hope for lessening their communication gap, given the chronic history of this problem.

Based on the initial contact, it was felt that this couple had a variety of relational problems, in addition to their dysfunctional sexual pattern. They individually reported impaired communication. In addition, careful questioning revealed a well-developed set of expectations about how they should approach one another to avoid disputes. Their sexual pattern reflected these beliefs and was worsened by Sarah's high level of sexual anxiety. While the etiology of these expectations was unknown, Sarah's history of agoraphobia compounded these beliefs and helped to create a rigid interaction system.

It appeared that Sarah and Bill had evolved a dysfunctional *sexual script*, that is, a plan or code that directed their sexual behavior and guided their expectations of each other. As discussed by Gagnon, Rosen, and Leiblum (1982), the script concept can be a useful organizing scheme for understanding the cognitive, social, and emotional interplay in sexual disorders. A script for sexual interaction includes the choice of partner (Who), circumstances under which sexual activity is appropriate (When and Where), the type of behavior engaged in (What), and underlying motives (Why). Script development begins during childhood, with sex-role socialization, and continues to be elaborated and expanded throughout the life cycle. Dysfunctional scripts in adulthood are characterized by several features: (1) there is a discrepancy between actual behavior and desired patterns for each partner; (2) there frequently are discrepancies for each client in cognitive and performance elements of the script; (3) differences may occur between partners with respect to the desired range or diversity of sexual behavior; and (4) a relatively rigid pattern often has stabilized between the two partners.

In applying this scheme to sexual dysfunction, these four dimensions warrant thorough assessment. For Sarah and Bill, the salient dimensions of dysfunction appeared to be marked discrepancies between actual and desired behavior for each other and a stable pattern of abbreviated communication between them. These hypotheses were based on information gathered in the initial interview and were explored further in the assessment phase, discussed below.

Assessment

Prior to designing treatment, both clients were given a battery of surveys which included scales intended to assess sexual information, attitudes, marital happiness, and the degree of arousal and anxiety to a range of heterosexual behaviors. This battery was readministered mid-treatment and at termination. Table 14.1 shows this couple's scores. At pretreatment, Bill demonstrated below average information about sexuality and conservative attitudes concerning the roles that men and women should adopt in a sexual relationship. Sarah reported considerable anxiety to most forms of sexual behavior and indicated low levels of arousability. Additionally, both clients were moderately dissatisfied with the relationship, particularly with the use of leisure time, career decisions, and definitions of independence.

To follow up the script formulation outlined above, a detailed assessment of Bill and Sarah's sexual interaction was conducted. Their behavioral script was discussed, from initiation of sexual contact through intercourse and afterplay. Both clients described their usual pattern as Bill initiating contact by stating that he was feeling sexy and beginning to undress. Sarah described a marked increase in anxiety at this time, stating that she often worried about experiencing pain but kept these feelings to herself. Foreplay was brief, involving kissing and breast stimulation. Immediately upon achieving an erection, Bill initiated intercourse and attempted to ejaculate quickly to diminish Sarah's discomfort. As soon as Bill achieved orgasm, all sexual contact was terminated.

Both Bill and Sarah articulated dimensions of their cognitive script which included expectations that they held as necessary for sexual and marital harmony. Sarah revealed that she felt that she

Table 14.1. Self-report Scores, Pre-, Mid-, and Posttreatment

	Pre		Mid		Post	
	Sarah	*Bill*	*Sarah*	*Bill*	*Sarah*	*Bill*
Sexual information[a]	21	14	missing		22	19
Sexual attitudes[a]	24	8	25	9	29	12
Marital happiness[b]	68	79	75	71	97	88
Sexual arousal[c]	+2	+7	+53	+47	+48	+30
Sexual anxiety[c]	23	15	2	0	5	0

[a]Subscales of the Derogatis Sexual Functioning Inventory. Norm for Information scale = 21 (lower scores reflect less information), male norm for Attitude scale = 23, female norm = 17 (lower scores reflect conservatism) (Derogatis, 1976).
[b]Marital Happiness Scale. 0–110 scale (lower scores reflect less marital satisfaction) (Azrin, Naster, & Jones, 1973).
[c]Adapted from the Bentler Heterosexual Behavior Hierarchy. Higher scores reflect higher levels of arousal and anxiety (Bentler, 1968).

should keep her feelings to herself, especially those involving sexual anxiety, and her belief that she should resolve her sexual problem herself. Bill's expectations included his belief that he should not allow his own feelings to upset Sarah and that it was his responsibility to ensure her happiness. Extended semistructured role-play assessments indicated that these expectations influenced their verbal behavior with each other. Neither ever directly expressed their own needs to the other and both would try to second guess how their spouse was feeling at any given instance. In contrast, Bill and Sarah each described their ideal sexual encounter as characterized by open communication, extended foreplay, relaxation, and diminished pressure for intercourse.

Based on this assessment, the predominant areas for script modification were as follows:

1. To increase Sarah's ability to relax during sex and diminish Bill's pressure for intercourse, with the aim of enhancing arousal through nonintercourse pleasuring.
2. To increase direct feeling expression and diminish attempts to second guess each other's needs and desires, with the aim of reducing the discrepancy between ideal and actual communication styles.
3. To redefine Sarah's sexual problem as a couple problem, to reduce the responsibility Sarah felt to resolve this problem on her own, and to diminish Bill's expectation to ensure her happiness, with the aim of enhancing mutual problem solving by clarifying cognitive and performance aspects of the script.

Selection of Treatment

Treatment was designed to address these aspects of their sexual script and was conceptualized as addressing the sexual and marital dimensions simultaneously, given the overlap in scripts in these areas. A male and female co-therapy team was chosen, based on the rationale that this would facilitate modeling of communication styles. Given that the three areas for script modification involved both intrapersonal and interpersonal functioning, several behavioral approaches were selected to facilitate clarification of problem areas and to illustrate behavioral options to the clients.

To address the rigidity in their dysfunctional sexual script, a Masters and Johnson approach (Masters & Johnson, 1970) was chosen utilizing sensate focus and other pleasuring exercises to facilitate arousal. This treatment approach scales sexual contact by beginning with nongenital touching and gradually progressing to more intimate behaviors. It was felt that, in light of Sarah's sexual anxiety, this gradual exposure would facilitate relaxation and arousal, much as exposure techniques have proven therapeutic for other anxiety-based disorders. Intercourse was prohibited during this treatment phase in order to eliminate performance pressures. An integral component of this treatment approach was providing feedback and expressing needs. At first, this was accomplished most easily during treatment sessions in discussion of homework exercises and by therapeutic reinterpretation of specific communications. As the clients became more skillful at expressing themselves, the therapists became less active.

Intercourse was reintroduced at the point at which the clients were able to pleasure each other to high levels of arousal and when Sarah had achieved orgasm. A number of suggestions were made, concerning sexual positions and the inclusion of manual stimulation during intercourse. A trial of the squeeze technique was planned, if Bill's pattern of rapid ejaculation proved to be resistant to change. The emphasis on clear and open communication remained throughout this phase of treatment.

The marital script was approached using a combination of education and communication training. The first phase of this intervention consisted of discussing implicit aspects of Bill and Sarah's marital pattern, specifically areas involving feeling expression, definitions of independence, and use of leisure time. As both clients had a number of expectations for relating to each other, the first step involved airing these and examining whether Bill and Sarah were accurate in their beliefs. This type of discussion, while emotionally charged, highlighted discrepancies between cognitive aspects of the marital script and actual behavior with each other. Bill was asked to read sections of a male sexuality self-help book (Zilbergeld, 1978) to assist in clarifying myths about his role in providing emotional and sexual comfort to Sarah. The process of changing dysfunctional aspects of the marital script involved a number of specific recommendations to modify how they responded to each other's moods, redivision of household responsibilities, and the creation of new leisure activities that both would enjoy.

Following this phase, communication training was implemented, using the intervention model of Gottman, Notarius, Gonso, and Markman (1976). This consisted of specific recommendations for requesting behavioral change, sharing positive and negative feelings, and giving and receiving feedback. These exercises were included to maintain and advance the script changes that Sarah and Bill had made previously.

The two types of interventions were delivered simultaneously and modified according to Sarah and Bill's progress. During the course of treatment, 10 weeks were spent in script redefinition and 9 in communication training. Concomitantly, 13 weeks were devoted to sensate focus and 6 weeks were spent resolving problems related to intercourse. Treatment sessions were held on a weekly basis. Sarah and Bill were seen together on all but one occasion, when an individual session was held. Treatment lasted 19 weeks, with a three-month follow-up.

Course of Treatment

Both clients were initially quite motivated for treatment, although at the outset, Bill was somewhat uncomfortable with discussing his sexual functioning. In contrast, Sarah appeared to rush the pleasuring exercises and revealed that this pressure arose from her perception that she held complete responsibility to reverse her anorgasmia. The resolution of this issue proved critical in clarifying and explaining an important dysfunctional aspect of the marital script, as evidenced by the following excerpt from week 5 of treatment:

Sarah: Bill is not satisfied with my progress. I think he expects much more.

Bill: That's not so! I think we're getting better at touching and you're starting to get turned on — it's just fine.

Sarah: But you don't act like that (angrily).

Therapist: It sounds like there's a missing link in your communicating. Sarah, maybe you could explain what you mean when you say that Bill expects more.

Sarah: Well, we have been doing the touching exercises and I'm starting to feel more relaxed. I feel like I should be going faster, that I should be very aroused and having sex and all. Bill seems to want that, too.

Therapist: It sounds like you're saying several things, Sarah. First, you seem to be owning all of this and pressuring yourself to fix it, fast.

Sarah: Sure, like we talked about last week. I hadn't thought of it like that before. It's going to be hard to change my thought that it's all up to me, but Bill will help, if I let him.

Over time, Sarah came to believe in Bill's shared role in treatment, which diminished the pressure she put upon herself for change. Additionally, Bill began to relax more during sexual contacts and to allow Sarah to pleasure him. This shift occurred gradually following discussions such as this, where unarticulated and rigid expectations were aired. This type of intervention illustrates the interplay between marital and sexual components of the script, as well as exemplifying the use of communication strategies.

At the onset of treatment, both clients were asked to keep structured logs of sexual arousal and anxiety ratings during the exercises and ratings of satisfaction with marital communication.* These records were helpful at the beginning of treatment in order to clarify goals, and provided an objective basis to examine the course of treatment. Figures 14.1 and 14.2 display Sarah's and Bill's scores, respectively, for sexual anxiety, arousal, and marital communication across the course of treatment. As can be seen, Sarah's sexual anxiety dropped during the initial four treatment sessions and she began to experience more arousal during sensate focus. She experienced her first orgasm at week 8. As treatment progressed, she noted several sudden returns of sexual anxiety, which were closely linked to failures in communication and attempts to progress through treatment too quickly. The reintroduction of intercourse evoked considerable anxiety, as well. In the preceding weeks, this couple had learned effective strategies for reducing Sarah's anxiety, such as returning to nongenital pleasuring and sharing their feelings with each other, and were able to have mutually pleasurable intercourse. Sarah's arousal remained high; she was orgasmic during 75–80% of all sexual contacts by the end of treatment, although, like most women, she was not orgasmic with intercourse alone. Her marital satisfaction showed a less pronounced change over the course of treatment, relative to Bill's.

Bill's ratings revealed a different pattern of change. While his level of sexual arousal was relatively stable, he responded favorably to alterations of the marital script. His satisfaction with communication rose gradually across the 19 weeks of treatment, especially when intercourse was reintroduced. Bill experienced a sharp increase in

---

*Copies of the sexual anxiety and arousal scales and semistructured initial assessment role-plays are available, upon request, from the author.

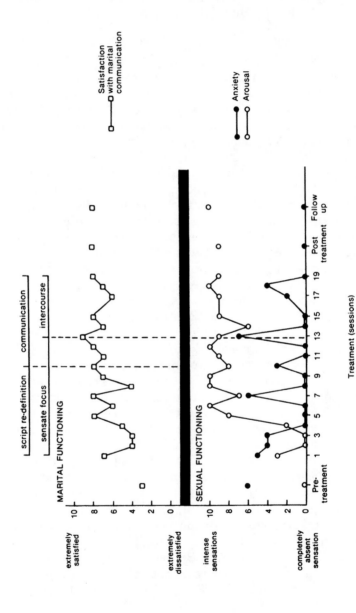

Figure 14-1. Anxiety, arousal, and marital satisfaction throughout treatment: Sarah.

194

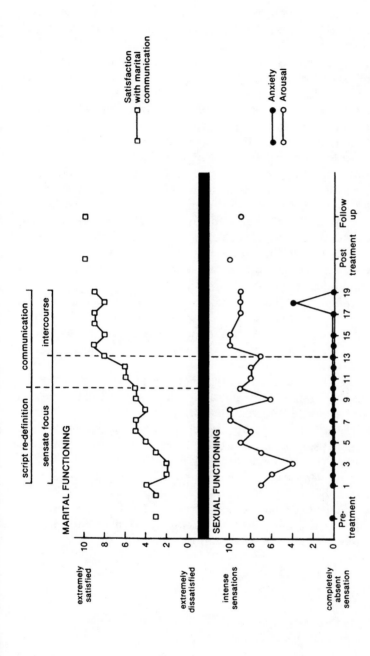

Figure 14.2. Anxiety, arousal, and marital satisfaction throughout treatment: Bill.

195

anxiety at week 18, when the squeeze technique was initiated. This technique was introduced at Bill's request to prolong intercourse, although neither was unhappy with their sexual interactions at this point. Both clients responded to the squeeze technique with fears that Bill would be hurt or uncomfortable due to the disruption created by this intervention. It was decided to discontinue the use of the squeeze technique after discussion of their current satisfaction with the sexual script. Bill's request to prolong intercourse was based, in part, on his desire to provide Sarah with more pleasure, a desire that was addressed by introducing other forms of stimulation.

As treatment progressed, Bill and Sarah took more initiative for modifying portions of their sexual and marital scripts. For example, at week 12, they decided to take a camping trip to a nearby lake to break the monotony of their day-to-day pattern. They also initiated the purchase of several popular sexuality books and explored a range of new behaviors. Termination was initially discussed at week 17, when it appeared that stability and satisfaction were occurring in both sexual and marital functioning. At this point, Bill raised the topic of prolonging intercourse and two additional sessions were held to explore their use of the squeeze technique. At week 19, both Bill and Sarah felt comfortable with their ability to handle problems, including anxiety, "mind-reading" other communication gaps, and diminished arousal.

A posttreatment assessment was conducted two weeks after the final treatment session. As can be seen in Table 14.1, Bill had gained more accurate sexual information during the course of treatment, while Sarah reported considerably less anxiety and heightened arousal to a full range of sexual behaviors. Both agreed that the discussions about the roles that they had been adopting and the rigidity of this pattern had proven helpful. Sarah found the gradual reexposure to sexual intimacy beneficial in reducing her anxiety and, coupled with better communication about specific forms of touch and stimulation, facilitating her arousal. Bill found communication training helpful for direct expression of feelings and requests for behavior change.

Follow-up

Three months after termination, Bill and Sarah were contacted for a follow-up appointment. During this session, Sarah reported reaching orgasm on a more consistent basis and routinely experiencing high levels of arousal during sexual contact. Their marital relationship remained stable and both were contented with the communication styles that had developed, including means for conflict resolution and clarification of needs. Bill and Sarah had recently joined a community club to expand their social activities and had begun dancing. Sarah felt supported by Bill without feeling that she had to keep her feelings to herself. Bill similarly felt able to directly express his feelings without the burden of protecting Sarah. They both expressed increasing confidence in their ability to relate as individuals and as sexual partners.

Overall Evaluation

The most striking aspect of this case was the beneficial interplay between interventions designed to address orgasmic dysfunction and marital communication problems. Because therapy addressed aspects of their script for interaction in both domains, it progressed rapidly and change in both areas occurred. While the term "script" was never used in sessions with Bill and Sarah, this concept proved helpful for the therapists in understanding the nature of their problem and in designing interventions. Bill and Sarah were able to articulate the *roles* they each had adopted in the marriage and the *cues* to which they responded. This language proved helpful for them in clarifying areas for change, as well as training in maintenance of therapeutic gains.

One consistent trend that occurred in both sexual and marital functioning was a reduction in the discrepancy between ideal and actual behavior of the script. This was due, in part, to detailed assessment and discussion of dysfunctional aspects of their sexual and nonsexual communication. The airing of private assumptions and clarification of expectations enabled both members of this couple to form a shared perspective on their marriage and to work together for change. The inclusion of specific behavioral assignments provided them with a testing ground for script modification. Since both Bill and Sarah were motivated to improve their sexual relationship, therapeutic suggestions were viewed as a means to understand their dysfunctional patterns and as opportunities to experiment with enacting their ideal scripts. Had more resistance been encountered, change most likely would not have occurred as rapidly or as smoothly, and further exploration of relevant factors, such as a desire for separation, would have been necessary. In the present case, concordance of cognitive and performance aspects of each individual's script occurred as the dysfunctional pattern was changed.

While the issue of the number and gender of therapists necessary for effective sex therapy has yet to be resolved empirically, the inclusion of a dual therapist team in this case seemed extremely important. Bill initially voiced his apprehension and doubts concerning the probability for change during an individual intake session and was able to establish rapport with the male therapist through this disclosure. The sharing of these concerns was critical for increasing Bill's motivation and helping him to explore aspects of the script with Sarah. Additionally, the fact that Sarah had prior experience in therapy seemed to contribute to the rapidity of treatment, since she was able to apply her previously learned anxiety-management skills to sexual contacts with Bill.

The outcome of this case generally was positive, owing to these factors. While the treatment goals appeared extensive at the outset, the integration of sex and marital therapy provided a context which was broad enough to encompass both. The explicit emphasis on reducing the discrepancy between ideal and actual behavior in the script helped to integrate changes as they occurred and provided a rationale which Bill and Sarah could apply to problem solving outside of therapy. Relapse was not noted at follow-up, although a complete determination of outcome would require further assessments. While every case of sex therapy does not follow this course (e.g., Everaerd, 1983), this case does demonstrate the complexity of sex therapy as practiced in the 1980s and highlights the importance of including a broader assessment of the couple's marital system. The script concept proved to be an important organizing scheme for clarifying larger units of interpersonal behavior between Bill and Sarah, while maintaining a focus on intrapersonal processes. While emphasis was given to the cognitive and performance dimensions of this couple's fixed pattern, it would have been equally feasible to incorporate affective responding within this conceptual framework. As this case highlights, this broader, more sophisticated approach enables the use of a more complex definition of sexual dysfunction and captures more completely the intricate nature of designing and implementing sex therapy.

References

Azrin, N., Naster, B., & Jones, R. (1973). Reciprocity counseling: A rapid learning-based procedure for marital counseling. *Behaviour Research and Therapy, 11*, 365–382.

Bentler, P. M. (1968). Heterosexual behavior assessment, I: Males, and II: Females. *Behaviour Research and Therapy, 6*, 21–30.

Derogatis, L. R. (1976). Psychological assessment of the sexual disabilities.

In J. K. Meyer (Ed.), *Clinical management of sexual disorders*. Baltimore: Williams and Wilkins.

Everaerd, W. T. A. M. (1983). Failure in treating sexual dysfunctions. In E. B. Foa & P. M. G. Emmelkamp (Eds.), *Failures in behavior therapy*. New York: Wiley.

Gagnon, J. H., Rosen, R. C., & Leiblum, S. R. (1982). Cognitive and social aspects of sexual dysfunction: Sexual scripts in sex therapy. *Journal of Sex and Marital Therapy, 8,* 44–56.

Gottman, J., Notarius, C., Gonso, J., & Markman, H. (1976). *A couple's guide to communication*. Champaign, IL: Research Press.

Masters, W. H., & Johnson, V. E. (1970). *Human sexual inadequacy*. Boston: Little, Brown.

Zilbergeld, B. (1978). *Male sexuality*. Boston: Little, Brown.

15

Sexual Deviation

Barry M. Maletzky

The fabric of deviant sexual desire presents such diverse weaves as to confound simple diagnostic schemes. Nonetheless, while each new case seems to present unique features, a few general categories comprise the majority of patients seen and treated for sexual abuse. Among 730 sexual offenders having recently completed at least one year of treatment in our Sexual Abuse Clinic, 56% were diagnosed as heterosexual pedophiles, 20% as homosexual pedophiles, 15% as exhibitionists, and 4% as mixed heterosexual and homosexual pedophiles. Thus, 95% of this large sample could be encompassed within these four diagnostic categories, leaving a smattering of other offenders (rapists, obscene telephone callers, "frotteurs," transvestites, etc.) comprising a minority of those treated.

These figures are typical of the experiences of other large sexual abuse clinics about the country and indicate that a case report of the treatment of a heterosexual pedophile should be offered as representative of clinical work in this field. To demonstrate certain clinical and theoretic points, however, the case of a combined heterosexual and homosexual pedophile will be presented. Fortunately, many, but not all, of the characteristics of the heterosexual and homosexual pedophile and the treatment techniques offered for him match those in the treatment of other sexual offenders.

Description of Sexual Deviation

Despite popular opinion to the contrary, our work indicates that most pedophiles are stably married men who have been steadily employed. Their pedophilia originated as fantasies of sexual activity with youngsters when they were between the ages of 12 and 17 and progressed from these fantasies to actual pedophiliac incidents, usually when these men were in their 20s to 30s. Many, but not most, have had prior sexual charges by the time they first are sent for treatment. Though most pedophiles are exclusively heterosexual *or* homosexual, there is a somewhat greater risk that an identified heterosexual pedophile will also show sexual arousal to young boys and vice versa.

The majority of pedophiles have had sexual experiences with playmates of both sexes before the age of 10, but this finding is not specific enough to explain pedophilia. The same is true of our data indicating that between 25 and 30% of pedophiles were themselves victims of pedophilia at an early age. It is also clear that pedophilia cannot be adequately explained as a lack of a normal sexual outlet. As is so often the case in the behavioral disorders, effective treatment techniques are at hand in the face of inadequate explanations of the mechanisms of sexual abuse.

Despite the large acceleration in public awareness recently, heterosexual and homosexual pedophilia are probably not growing phenomena; it only appears so because of the increasing publicity these problems receive and the encouragement offered through the media and schools for victims and their families to report instances of sexual abuse. Studies indicate that over 25% of females and 10% of males in our country have been the intended or actual victims of sexual abuse. Other reports amply demonstrate the sexual, emotional, and physiological problems attendant upon such victims, even years after the abuse has ended.

With the advent of powerful behavioral treatment techniques and the availability of assessment techniques to measure their efficacy, all sexual offenders should be offered the option of treatment, though not all can be given free access to the community while undergoing it. Failure to guarantee access to such treatment techniques may be almost as serious a crime as the abuse itself.

Case Identification

Patient R.L. was a 54-year-old married male in excellent physical health with no history of drug or alcohol abuse. He had worked as a logger most of his adult life and continued to do so throughout the present treatment course.

Presenting Complaints

R.L. was reported to a metropolitan county's Children's Services Division by the teacher of his 11-year-old granddaughter, after an approximate one-year history of sexually molesting her at a frequency of approximately twice per week. Subsequently, allegations were also made of sexual abuse of this girl's 8-year-old brother over the same time course, though at a lesser frequency.

History

Following a school presentation of the facts of sexual abuse, Karen, R.L.'s 11-year-old granddaughter, was noted by teachers to be acutely upset. Following questioning by her favorite teacher, Karen admitted that her grandfather had been sexually molesting her for almost a year. Her description of these events was at first denied by R.L., but he subsequently agreed with her general story, though markedly minimizing his participation. Eventually, under treatment, he essentially agreed with events as she described them.

R.L.'s sexual activity with Karen had begun with what appeared to be harmless wrestling and tickling. R.L. admitted, however, that he would occasionally fantasize sexual touching with her, at times even during intercourse or masturbation. He became bolder in his play with her, letting his hands "stray" to brief, apparently accidental, touching of breast and genital areas. When she didn't object he began to fondle these areas directly, at first over and then under her clothing. When she resisted he referred to the act as "our games in secret," promised her special presents and favors (which he delivered), and occasionally persisted by holding her forcibly down while he fondled her. If she screamed or cried, he would immediately desist. For approximately four months prior to discovery, he would remove her pants and panties, lick her vaginal area, and insert his finger into her vagina, even occasionally if she insisted it hurt. He caused no physical damage. On three occasions he removed his erect penis and forced Karen to stroke it, and on one occasion, the last, he forced her to lick his penis. He did not ejaculate nor ever attempt penile penetration.

These events occurred approximately once per week while R.L. was babysitting his granddaughter and they were alone in his house, or with his other grandchildren. R.L. told Karen that if she told about this "secret" it could cause great trouble for them both.

Because of these events, R.L.'s stepson and daughter-in-law, the victim's parents, informed their two remaining children what had occurred. As they did so, Steven, their 8-year-old son, exclaimed: "but that's what Grandpa did to me too!" Subsequent investigation revealed that R.L. had begun to include Steven in the sexual abuse of his sister approximately six months before entering into treatment. He would forcibly direct Steven to fondle his sister's genital area while he would fondle the boy. He also had Steven stroke and lick his erect penis and on two occasions had committed fellatio on the boy. R.L. had used bribes and threats similar to those with Karen. On two other occasions he had molested Steven without Karen's presence.

Two charges of sexual abuse in the first degree were brought against R.L. for these activities. He pleaded guilty to both and received a suspended sentence with the following requirements on probation:

1. No contact, supervised or unsupervised, with either victim.
2. No unsupervised contact with any child under the age of 18.
3. Mandatory treatment.
4. Periodic evaluations of treatment via:
   a. The penile plethysmograph.
   b. The polygraph.

R.L. admitted to molesting two other young girls many years earlier, though no legal charges were forthcoming at that time. On six to eight occasions he had molested a stepdaughter when she was 11 through 13; penile penetration had occurred on one occasion. The girl reported this to her mother, the patient's current wife, who confronted him strongly; they both "prayed about it," and she considered the matter finished. She did not learn until later of a second molestation, this of a 9-year-old girl, a friend of another stepdaughter, which occurred on three occasions several years later.

R.L. reported occasional fantasies of sexual activity with young girls and boys dating back to his early teenage years, but he successfully fought the majority of these urges. When he found himself in the company of an attractive youngster with whom he had had physical contact he found the urges increasingly compelling.

Developmental History

R.L. knew of no pregnancy or birth complications reported by his parents regarding him. His parents had also reported no developmental milestone delays. He recalled, however, that they had complained of some temper tantrums when he was a youngster and teachers had noted an inability to sit still and concentrate in school, traits he rapidly outgrew, however.

He recalled a close relationship with his father, whom he described as tolerant and accepting. He was somewhat alienated toward his mother, whom he described as erratic and cold; she rarely offered encouragement and was critical of his best efforts, especially in school. As he grew into adolescence, he found himself growing more distant from both and could not share emotional problems with them. He did not enter a period of adolescent rebelliousness, however, but seemed to passively resist some of their directions. He eventually developed a closer relationship with his parents in his 20s which lasted until their deaths many years later.

Educational History

Although R.L. had difficulty concentrating at first in school and had subsequent difficulty learning to read, no specific perceptual problems were apparent. He eventually progressed to grade level in reading, though this subject, along with spelling, remained his worst throughout school. He was stronger in mathematics and science. He maintained moderate grades through junior and senior high school, but quit in the eleventh grade to join the service, believing further schooling would be irrelevant and longing to achieve independence from his home situation. He received no further formal education.

Military History

He entered the Army hoping to train for a career but instead was assigned to the infantry and never consistently raised the issue of demanding the training he was originally promised. He suffered no disciplinary action in the service and received an honorable discharge after three years.

Vocational History

Upon discharge from the service, he obtained a job at an uncle's laundry. He disliked working indoors "cooped up" and after a year attempted to quit to enter logging. His uncle prevailed upon him to help out in the laundry for another year, but during this time he developed a rash, subsequently diagnosed as "neurodermatitis," attributed to the pressure of work within a confined setting. He summoned the courage to tell his uncle he was quitting. He obtained a job with a logging company and had continued to work for this company until the time of his arrest and subsequent treatment, a duration of some 30 years. He was known as a hard and loyal worker and had never been terminated from any position.

Social and Marital History

R.L. was always known as a shy youngster, a loner who seemed to lack confidence around peers. He had just one close friend through high school but gained some confidence in the service and increased his circle of friends thereafter.

While working in the laundry, he met his only wife, a woman four years his senior who had two children by a previous marriage, both infants at that time. He denied sexual interest in them as a motivation for increasing interest in her. They shared many interests and he saw her as possessing traits he admired but lacked, as she was active, outgoing, and confident, someone upon whom he could occasionally depend and who would offer support when he needed it. He described their subsequent relationship as stable, though he recognized that he had again reverted to being rather solitary. He withdrew interest in friends and engaged in activities mostly with his family. He was viewed as a devoted father to his step- and then his biological children. He perceived no difficulties within the marriage around the time of the molestations (though also see below under sexual developmental history). He and his wife had been married for 32 years at the time of referral. The two stepchildren and the two biological children were at that time fully grown and had moved out of the house.

Sexual Developmental History

R.L. recalled early sexual games with two cousins, a boy and a girl, when he and they were approximately six to eight years of age. These consisted of mutual exposure and fondling of genital areas. For several years following this he masturbated to fantasies of these sexual activities. His parents learned of these activities and severely rebuked him for them. Sexual matters were otherwise not discussed at home.

At the age of 10 he was approached sexually by an uncle who

seemed inordinately fond of him. On four or five occasions this uncle felt his genital areas underneath his clothing, then warned him not to tell. He was petrified of consequences should he do so and talked of this activity for the first time in his life only during treatment.

He recalled increasing sexual awareness of girls his own age during adolescence, with conventional sexual fantasies during masturbation but with occasional fantasies persisting of sexual activity with younger children. He was too shy to date; his first sexual experience with a girl occurred in the service and this was enjoyable. For a time he lost any sexual interest in children.

Following his marriage he enjoyed an apparently normal sexual relationship with his wife for many years. However, as his stepchildren grew, he began to fantasize sexual activity with them and did so occasionally during intercourse with his wife. Approximately two years before the present sexual activity began with his stepgrandchildren, R.L.'s wife was diagnosed as having diabetes mellitus. Her illness reduced her libido and their frequency of sexual interactions decreased by approximately 33%. R.L. was uncertain as to whether this led to an increased sense of unfulfillment and desire. Sexual activity had occurred earlier with his stepchildren in the midst of apparently adequate sexual relationships with his wife.

Religious History

As a youngster, R.L. was exposed to a strict religious household in which sexual topics were not discussed. He rebelled against this as an adolescent and young adult, but as his family grew he gradually renewed an interest in the church, partly secondary to his wife's fundamentalist beliefs.

Following apprehension on the present charges, R.L. suddenly became "born again," in his own words. He insisted that mortal punishments and treatment were tolerable but unnecessary as the Lord had now enlightened him and no such sexual transgressions could possibly recur.

Medical History

Aside from an appendectomy at an early age, R.L. had no past history of medical treatment, serious illness, or head trauma with unconsciousness. He had undergone no prior counseling. There were no allergies and he denied the abuse of drugs or alcohol.

Legal History

The present charges were the only ones ever cited against him.

Genetic History

The same (maternal) uncle who had molested R.L. had a long history of alcoholism. There was no other history of psychiatric illness, alcoholism, or apparent sexual deviation within the biological family.

Assessment

Mental Status

On the first and second examinations, R.L. appeared as a rugged, conservatively dressed man of approximately his stated age. He spoke with normal latencies and duration of utterance. He was oriented in all three spheres with recent and remote memory intact. He demonstrated adequate retention, mathematical, and abstracting skills. His vocabulary and fund of information were normal and his intelligence was estimated to be within normal limits.

R.L. showed slightly flattened but appropriate affect. There was no loosening of associations nor other evidence of a thought disorder and no suicidal or homicidal ideation.

R.L. stated that he knew he was guilty of the present offenses and had to serve his "penalty." However, he indicated it mattered little what mere men or women could do to him as he was "under the province of God." No evidence of delusions was seen, however. While agreeing to undergo treatment, he was honest in stating that it was only to satisfy his probationary requirements. When asked why what he had done was wrong, he answered in terms of "moral transgressions," ignoring the consequences to the victims, though when these ideas were supplied, he agreed with them. He was cooperative, pleasant, and readily agreed to initial homework assignments.

R.L.'s wife was also seen. She was supportive of him, suspicious of treatment, but amenable to assisting with it in any way possible.

Psychological Testing

No psychological tests were undertaken as part of the initial assessment.

Frequency Records

R.L. was asked to keep daily records of:

- Covert pedophiliac activity: pedophiliac urges, fantasies or dreams.
- Overt pedophiliac activities: actual pedophiliac activity or masturbatory pedophiliac fantasy.

These were reported to the therapist at each treatment session.

The Penile Plethysmograph

The penile plethysmograph is the most objective means of measuring male sexual arousal (Abel, Blanchard, Murphy, & Becker, 1980). This device assesses male sexual arousal by measuring circumference changes in the penis. While not infallible, it can detect changes so slight that the patient himself may not be aware of them. It is therefore difficult, but not impossible, to "cheat" the instrument. As with any medical test, it cannot be relied upon solely in assessment and treatment, but it forms one of the most important means of verifying treatment success.

In R.L., measurements made over several evaluation sessions led to an understanding of which materials (stories, slides, movies, etc.) were most arousing. Figure 15.1 demonstrates an early plethysmograph record documenting arousal to heterosexual and homosexual pedophiliac material, as well as to adult heterosexual material. Readings are expressed as a percentage of full tumescence. As with all offenders, three deviant stimuli which had elicited the highest readings in each classification were isolated as test stimuli and presented from time to time during treatment to assess progress. These stimuli were never paired with aversive stimuli so that generalization of treatment effects could be adequately measured. For R.L. plethysmograph measurements were made twice monthly during active treatment and then every three months during booster phases.

Polygraph

Although its validity has been repeatedly questioned, the polygraph, or "lie detector," has proven useful in following the course of a variety of offenders (Jason, Williams, Burton, & Rochat, 1982). In our expe-

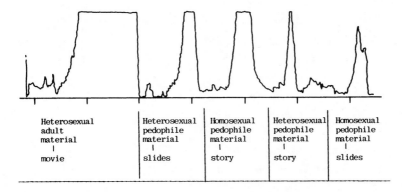

| Heterosexual adult material | Heterosexual pedophile material | Homosexual pedophile material | Heterosexual pedophile material | Homosexual pedophile material |
| movie | slides | story | story | slides |

←— Time

Figure 15.1. The penile plethysmograph recording from the fifth treatment session for patient R.L.

rience, it cannot be relied upon to conclusively determine adequacy of treatment but often serves as a useful adjunct. For R.L. polygraph tests were conducted every three months during treatment and every six months during booster phases. Relevant questions were: "In the past (three or six) months, have you sexually molested any young girls or boys?" "In the past (three or six) months, have you had any urges to sexually molest young girls or boys?"

Legal Records

Statewide computerized police files were searched monthly during treatment and follow-up to learn of any charges of deviant sexual activity.

Assessment of Safety

R.L. was accepted into an *outpatient* treatment program and deemed safe to be at large (within the confines of his probationary restrictions). A number of factors in our experience have been associated with reduced risk of immediate reoffense and convinced us of R.L.'s safety:

1. Restriction of victims to the immediate family. ⎫ Lack of
2. Location of offenses within a home environ- ⎬ preying
   ment. ⎭ behavior

3. Admission of guilt.
4. Amenability to treatment.
5. Placement on probation.
6. Employment stability.
7. Marital stability.

Some negative factors occurred but were deemed less significant:

1. Multiple victims.
2. Combined heterosexual and homosexual pedophilia.
3. Use of some physical force.

In our experience, the following factors have been neutral in that they do not bear on safety to be at large:

1. Duration of problem.
2. Frequency of deviant acts.
3. Use of threats.

Selection of Treatment

Treatment of the sexual offender must proceed not by adherence to rigid schools of thought but in accordance with the literature demonstrating efficacy. Accordingly, the following treatment techniques were selected:

1. *Aversive Techniques*
   a. *Assisted covert sensitization.* This behavioral treatment pairs stories, slides, and movies of deviant sexual activity with aversive stimuli, chiefly a foul odor. The technique has been more extensively described in Maletzky (1984). The aversive odor is also combined with aversive story elements. Examples for R.L. will be detailed below.

      The odor, in this case rotting placental tissue, is delivered via a special odor machine that can also present other foul odors, to prevent accommodation, as well as fresh air and pleasant odors for aversion relief. Tapes of scenes were produced for R.L. and a vial of odor sent home with him for homework practice.
   b. *Electric shock aversion* (Evans, 1980). Aversive therapy is most effective when different noxious stimuli are presented. Accordingly, electric shock was also selected to be delivered

to the fingers of R.L. in place of aversive odor on a random basis, but in the ratio of odor:electric shock of 5:1. In our experience, more frequent administration of shock can increase treatment nonacceptance and undue anxiety. The therapist self-administered shock before each session in the presence of R.L. to diminish his anxiety.

c. *Foul taste aversion*. Tablets of propantheline, and anticholinergic medication for ulcer, were sent home with R.L. and he was instructed to chew a tablet upon encountering any pedophiliac urge. This pill, harmless even ingested whole, has a highly aversive taste when chewed.

2. *Orgasmic Reconditioning*. Most workers in this field have stressed the importance of fantasy in keeping alive deviant sexual urges. For a more complete description of these techniques and the theories underlying their use, see Foote and Laws (1981). Two orgasmic techniques make use of this crucial component in the development of sexuality.

a. *Masturbatory fantasy change*. R.L. was asked to masturbate to deviant (pedophiliac) fantasies until reaching ejaculatory inevitability. At that point he was asked to quickly switch his fantasies to those of normal adult sexuality. He was then asked to make this switch-over point earlier and earlier in the course of masturbation until finally he was masturbating to normal fantasies only.

b. *Masturbation satiation technique*. The patient was also asked to masturbate to ejaculation completely with normal adult sexual fantasies; then he was requested to continue to masturbate for an additional 15 minutes to deviant fantasies. This associated the deviant fantasies with a period of time when sexual desire was at its lowest: just following ejaculation.

3. *Aversive Behavioral Rehearsal*. Although this technique has been described in the literature solely for exhibitionism (Wickramaserka, 1980), we have enjoyed some success with it in pedophilia as well. As originally described, the exhibitionist was to have exposed on cue to disinterested parties, thereby associating extreme anxiety with the exhibitionist act. For R.L. we modified this technique by asking him to demonstrate to a group of therapists how he molested both his victims. By carrying out the sexual behaviors on anatomically correct large girl and boy dolls, extreme distress was evoked in R.L., an unfortunate but necessary effect of this treatment.

4. *Biofeedback*. The penile plethysmograph can be used not only to assess treatment response but to enhance treatment by functioning as a biofeedback device (Laws & Pawlowski, 1973). Thus while undergoing plethysmograph evaluation on a biweekly basis, R.L. was also given feedback via a series of colored lights concerning the level of arousal with differing stimuli. His assigned task was to keep the red light (the signal for high deviant arousal) off when exposed to deviant stimuli and keep the green light (the signal for normal arousal) on when exposed to nondeviant stimuli. Most patients adapt well to such tasks, as did R.L., who perceived this part of treatment as under his own control.

5. *Ancillary Techniques*.
   a. *Assertive training*. Because of historical documentation of subassertive behavior and a *possible* link to marital and sexual dissatisfaction, several sessions of assertive training were undertaken with the following components:
      (1) Reading the book *Your Perfect Right* (Alberti & Emmons, 1978) and taking notes on how it applied to him and how he could apply it to his own life.
      (2) Turning down two requests each week.
      (3) Disagreeing with a prevalent opinion twice each week.
      (4) Keeping an assertion log.
   b. *Brief marital counseling*. Four sessions were held with R.L. and his wife to focus on the need for increasing sharing of emotions, basic communication techniques, and airing of past grievances and mistrusts. With the history of a *possible* relationship between decreasing sexual activity on Mrs. L.'s part associated with an increase in deviant sexual arousal in R.L., such sessions were felt to carry potential benefit.

6. *Techniques Not Used*. It is important to describe some potential techniques felt not to be necessary or useful in the present case:
   a. *Sexual education*. R.L. seemed to have a good grasp of general sexual information.
   b. *Positive conditioning*. These techniques, such as desensitization, success imagery, and positive olfactory conditioning using amyl nitrate to enhance sexual pleasure (Maletzky, in press) were deemed unnecessary because of R.L.'s relatively good adult heterosexual responses.
   c. *Group therapy*. Although R.L. had led a relatively sheltered life-style focused on his family, he was not seen as grossly deficient in social skills and not in need of group techniques.
   d. *Depo-provera*. While depo-provera, an antiandrogen, can

decrease overall sexual drive (Berlin & Meinecke, 1981), its use is not indicated except in cases in which a patient is at large yet judged marginally safe to be so. This was not believed to be the case for R.L. because of the safety factors mentioned above.

Course of Treatment

Table 15.1 demonstrates the entire treatment course for R.L. with the timing of each phase and of each mode of treatment. It took four initial sessions for evaluation and some trust building prior to testing on the plethysmograph and the initiation of aversive procedures. Thereafter, the time course of treatment proceeded for R.L. in a fashion similar to most offenders.

The table, however, must be interpreted with some caution. Each session within each phase was not identical to the next. Moreover,

Table 15.1. The Timing and Mode of Treatment During the Treatment Course for Patient R.L.

Phase	Frequency	Duration	Techniques
Active phase	Once/week	4 months	Assessment Trust-building Assisted covert sensitization Electric shock aversion Plethysmographic biofeed-back Orgasmic reconditioning
Intermediate phase	Twice/month	3 months	Assisted covert sensitization Electric shock aversion Plethysmographic biofeed-back Aversive behavior rehearsal
	Once/month	3 months	Assertive training Marital counseling
Booster phase	Once/3 months	12 months	Assisted covert sensitization Electric shock aversion Plethysmographic biofeed-back

each assisted covert sensitization session was not identical to each other one, and so on. More or less time might be taken on certain slides or stories depending on the plethysmograph response. In addition, certain sessions were occupied to a greater or lesser extent with explanations of homework assignments.

Treatment for R.L. can be conceived as occurring over three general phases: in what is called the *active treatment phase* R.L. was seen weekly for four consecutive months and at almost each session assisted covert sensitization and electric shock aversion were accomplished. Several typical though abbreviated ACS scenes for R.L. are reproduced in Table 15.2. Each scene contained three parts:

1. Building deviant sexual arousal.
2. Aversive consequences associated with deviant arousal.
3. Escape (usually) from aversive consequences associated with escape/avoidance of deviant sexual contact.

Such scenes were read to the patient through a microphone/earphone setup. In addition, however, R.L. was asked to read and/or make up his own sexual scenes that were similarly paired with aversive odor or occasionally electric shock. Slides and movies of deviant sexual material were used as alternate stimuli and interspersed randomly with scenes and presentations.

It can be seen that treatment of *both* the heterosexual and homosexual pedophilia was carried out – scenes, slides, and so on for each were deemed necessary and were interspersed. While it would have been of theoretic interest to separate heterosexual and homosexual pedophiliac sections of the treatment, it was felt important to decondition both deviant arousal patterns rapidly.

Portions of these sessions were devoted to explaining homework assignments. Typical assignments are listed in Table 15.3. From time to time R.L. would be asked to demonstrate and/or explain how he followed through on such assignments. His wife was also asked for her observations on how well he followed through.

Through the *intermediate treatment phase*, R.L. was seen twice per month for three months, then once per month for three more months, and more time was then taken in each session on aversive behavior rehearsal and then assertive training and finally marital counseling. It was felt that the proven efficacy of the conditioning techniques justified their use later in treatment.

A reversal of this trend is commonly seen in the *booster phase*, a one-year period of time in which R.L. was seen every three months.

Table 15.2. Several Typical (Though Abbreviated) Assisted Covert Sensitization Scenes for Patient R.L.

Scene 1: You're all alone with Karen and you've taken her to your bedroom. You're touching her all over now, over her clothing and now underneath. She's letting you do whatever you want! You take off her top, then her pants and panties. You can see her young naked body lying on the bed, so pretty and innocent. You let your hands roam over her body at will, touching everywhere—her nipples, and genital area. You push your finger inside her vagina slowly, feeling how tight and wet it is inside . . . but suddenly Karen screams—you've hurt her! She's bleeding; you've ripped her open. She's screaming and blood is gushing out all over. It's disgusting and you're getting sick to your stomach, hurting Karen so much. You've got to get away! Quickly you run out of the room and the house. Now you can breathe the fresh air now that you're away from molesting Karen. You can relax again.

Scene 2: You've got Steven all alone with Karen in your bedroom, and you've made both of them undress. They're completely naked and you're touching both of them anywhere you want. You can feel Steven's small penis in your hand as you stroke it back and forth. You're really getting hard as you feel what it feels like! You start to suck his penis—you can feel the shaft and head of it in your mouth and on your lips . . . but suddenly there's a foul putrid odor. You look and see a huge sore on the underside of Steven's penis. It's red and full of pus and some of the pus has oozed into your mouth and down your throat. You feel sick to your stomach, that smell is driving you wild! Chunks of vomit catch in your throat and you can't gag them down. Vomit fills your mouth and you throw up all over you and Steven. Chunks of vomit dribble down your chin and onto his penis—it's disgusting to be there, sucking and fondling him like that. You run away, clean up, and get outside. You can breathe the fresh air again and relax now that you're away from molesting young children . . . you can settle back, breathe deeply and relax.

Scene 3: You and Karen are on a picnic all alone. You lean her back on the blanket and start to undress her. You can see her naked body come into view as you take off her blouse, then her shorts and panties. You can feel her young body with your hands as you fondle her nipples, and then her vagina. You start to go down on her, licking her small clitoris and feeling it with your tongue as she just lies there letting you have your way with her. But suddenly there's a noise . . . it's your wife and stepson! They've been watching and they've seen everything—they come running up, yelling at you . . . the police are with them . . . you've been caught red-handed. Everyone is glaring at you, you feel sick and embarrassed, nauseous, and that horrible odor comes back, making you even sicker. But suddenly you get away—it was only a dream—you can relax and breathe the fresh air again, glad that you're away from molesting young children.

Table 15.3. Typical Homework Assignments for Patient R.L.

Phase	Assignment	Frequency	Duration
Active phase	Sexual autobiography	Once	1 week
	Overt and covert frequency records	Once/week	Entire active phase
	Assisted covert sensitization: tapes with self-applied odor	4 times/week	Entire active phase
	Foul taste aversion—chewing pill when pedophiliac urge occurred	As needed (averaged twice/week during first 2 months)	Entire active phase
	Orgasmic reconditioning—Fantasy change	3 times/week	Entire active phase
Intermediate phase	Overt and covert frequency records	Once/week	Entire intermediate phase
	Assisted covert sensitization: tapes with self-applied odor	3 times/week	Entire intermediate phase
	Orgasmic reconditioning: Satiation technique	3 times/week	First 2 months of intermediate phase
	Assertion homework assignments (see text)	As directed (see text)	Last 4 months of intermediate phase
Booster phase	Assisted covert sensitization: tapes with self-applied odor	Once/week	Entire booster phase

In these sessions primary emphasis was again placed on the aversive techniques in an effort to guarantee that they had "taken hold" and were generalizing to situations outside the office setting. Similarly, more time was spent in plethysmograph assessment during those later sessions to confirm continuing treatment efficacy as frequency of treatment was being reduced.

The course of treatment for R.L. proceeded relatively smoothly and typically for the usual sexual offender. Despite his initial protests over treatment, he adapted well to the techniques and equipment employed and began to actively participate in devising his own assignments. Approximately midway through treatment he admitted that at the start of therapy he had continued to harbor sexual fantasies about youngsters of both sexes but that deviant arousal was becoming much reduced. His plethysmograph responses (see below) seemed to bear out these self-observations.

Assessment of Treatment Efficacy

Frequency Records. Figure 15.2 presents R.L.'s self-report data on covert pedophiliac behaviors only, monthly during treatment. No overt behaviors were reported over this time period. The first four weeks of records were arrived at by R.L. retrospectively as he had originally denied any such covert behaviors, then recanted and, as explained above, admitted that these had been present. Nonetheless,

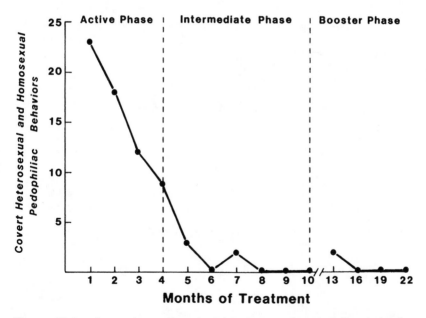

Figure 15.2. Covert heterosexual and homosexual pedophiliac behaviors monthly during the three phases of treatment for patient R.L.

they appear to fit a typical pattern and are probably reasonably accurate. The rapid decline in deviant urges, fantasies, and dreams after the fourth week of therapy of the active treatment phase is typical in our experience.

The Penile Plethysmograph. Figure 15.3 depicts the plethysmograph at the next-to-last booster session (19 months after the initiation of treatment) and indicates no arousal to deviant stimuli. Figure 15.4 demonstrates plethysmograph results during all treatment phases. The figure shows averaged responses, as percentage of full tumescence, for the three test stimuli, at monthly intervals during treatment and follow-up, and documents a close correlation between this objective measure and the frequency reports. Again, the rapid decline after approximately one month of active treatment is typical; the continued low readings, within normal limits, as treatment frequency was tapering was reassuring. At the last booster session, 22 months after initiation of treatment, plethysmograph results continued to be essentially normal.

In the light of these findings, a decision was reached with the patient to terminate treatment, and this decision was communicated to his probation officer, who had received regular progress reports on treatment to date. However, R.L. was asked to continue listening to his tapes and using foul odor with them at home for another year at a frequency of once per month, and he was urged to contact us if any deviant sexual urges recurred.

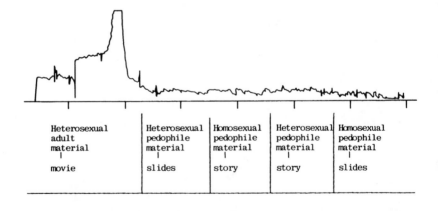

Figure 15.3.   The penile plethysmographic recording for the next-to-last booster session (19 months after initiation of treatment) for patient R.L.

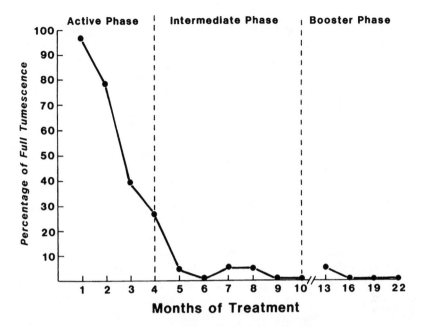

Figure 15.4. Average penile plethysmograph recordings for three test stimuli monthly, as percentage of full tumescence, during the three phases of treatment for patient R.L.

Polygraph. R.L. passed each polygraph examination.

Legal Charges. No charges were filed against R.L. during his treatment course or during follow-up.

Follow-up

As part of an ongoing research project, R.L.'s plethysmograph is being assessed at yearly intervals since termination of his "booster phase." Two such evaluations have now been obtained and revealed no return of deviant sexual arousal. A check of legal records indicates that no charges have been filed.

Overall Evaluation

The patient R.L. had a long history of deviant sexual arousal to both young girls and boys. His history raised interesting questions of etiology:

- Was alienation to his mother a stimulus to generalize hostility toward all females?
- Did early sexual games, perhaps occurring at some crucial time of sexual central nervous system development, play some role?
- Was subassertion a factor in diminishing his ability to get needs directly met?
- What role did his sexual victimization play?
- Was there a genetic component increasing the likelihood of deviant sexual arousal, perhaps transmitted through his mother's side of the family (c.f. his maternal uncle's behavior)?

While there will not likely be an end to speculation regarding the etiology of these disorders, treatment options now seem clear. The presence of deviant sexual arousal dictates the incorporation of behavioral measures into a treatment program (though other measures may be necessary as well), and these usually will involve aversive conditioning. Moreover, the penile plethysmograph should be employed as one assessment device to monitor treatment efficacy. While not infallible, it represents the best instrument yet developed for objectively measuring treatment effect in these areas.

R.L. was an "involuntary" patient. Indeed, there are few "voluntary" sexual offender patients as most are brought to treatment either under direct legal duress, such as R.L., or under the imminent threat of it; others enter "voluntarily" but under pressure from their families, ministers, or the like. While seeming to contradict common sense, such involuntary patients achieve results as beneficial as those of voluntary patients (Maletzky, 1980).

The results in the present case match that of over 90% of sexual offenders treated on an outpatient basis in our clinic. We cannot be too satisfied with these results, however, because they come too late: some of R.L.'s victims developed signs of sexual abuse that may affect certain areas in the remainder of their lives; his stepdaughter is said to be unusually shy, has never married, and is chronically anxious; his stepgranddaughter is beginning to develop problems in school.

Perhaps the time to have identified and treated R.L. was when he was first developing sexual fantasies about young children. He had what appear to be the hallmarks of a developing sexual offender: he was shy and introverted, rarely dated, and was a victim of sexual abuse himself. Our development of some understanding in these areas may combine with the increasing awareness of, and earlier referral of, the *adolescent* sexual offender for treatment in order to help break the destructive cycle of sexual abuse.

References

Abel, G. G., Blanchard, E. B., Murphy, W. D., & Becker, J. V. (1980). Two methods of measuring penile response. *Behavior Therapy, 12,* 320-328.

Alberti, A. E., & Emmons, M. L. (1978). *Your perfect right.* San Luis Obispo, CA: Impact Publishers.

Berlin, F. S., & Meinecke, C. F. (1981). Treatment of sexual offenders with anti-androgenic medication: conceptualization, review of treatment modalities, and preliminary findings. *American Journal of Psychiatry, 138,* 601-607.

Evans, D. R. (1980). Electrical aversion therapy. In D. J. Cox & D. J. Daitzman (Eds.), *Exhibitionism: Description, assessment, and treatment* (pp. 59-61). New York: Garland.

Foote, W. E., & Laws, D. R. (1981). A daily alternation procedure for orgasmic reconditioning with a pedophile. *Journal of Behavior Therapy and Experimental Psychiatry, 12,* 267-273.

Jason, J., Williams, S. L., Burton, A., & Rochat, R. (1982). Epidemiologic differences between sexual and physical child abuse. *Journal of the American Medical Association, 247,* 3344-3348.

Laws, D. R., & Pawlowski, A. V. (1973). A multipurpose biofeedback device for penile plethysmography. *Journal of Behavior Therapy and Experimental Psychiatry, 4,* 339-341.

Maletzky, B. M. (1980). Self-referred versus court-referred sexually deviant patients: success with assisted covert sensitization. *Behavior Therapy, 11,* 306-314.

Maletzky, B. M. (1984). Assisted covert sensitization. In A. S. Bellack & M. Hersen (Eds.), *Dictionary of behavior therapy techniques.* New York: Pergamon.

Maletzky, B. M. (in press). *The treatment of the sexual offender.* New York: Wiley.

Wickramaserka, I. (1980). Aversive behavioral rehearsal: a cognitive-behavioral procedure. In D. J. Cox & R. J. Daitzman (Eds.), *Exhibitionism: Description, assessment, and treatment* (pp. 123-149). New York: Garland.

16

Multiple Personality

Glenn R. Caddy

The dissociative disorders generally and multiple (including dual) personality in particular are viewed as exotic peculiarities of the human condition. Despite intriguing popular titles such as *The Three Faces of Eve* (Thigpen & Cleckley, 1957) and *The Five of Me* (Hawkesworth, 1977), and probably because of the extreme rarity of multiple personality, there has been little presented in the professional literature regarding this condition.

Description of Multiple Personality

The essential feature of multiple personality is the existence within an individual of two or more distinct personalities, each of which is dominant at a particular time. In accordance with current diagnostic conceptualizations (American Psychiatric Association, 1980), multiple personality is a dissociative disorder.

> Each personality is a fully integrated and complex unit, with unique memories, behavior patterns, and social relationships that determine the nature of the individual's acts when that personality is dominant. Transition from one personality is sudden and often associated with psychosocial stress . . . The individual personalities are nearly always quite discrepant and frequently seem to be opposites (APA, 1980, p. 257).

Commonly, the original personality (also referred to as the core personality) has no knowledge of any of the alternate or subpersonalities. When there are more than two subpersonalities in one individual, each of these subpersonalities typically is aware of the existence of the others to at least some degree.

Presenting Complaints

Audrey H. had been a quiet, but very bright student in a psychopathology class that I taught. Several weeks following the final exams in that course, she made an appointment to see me in my private practice, her telephone call reflecting that she "kept on seeing herself in many of the disorders discussed in the class." Audrey attended the appointment dressed in a black skin-tight pants-suit. Her state of substantial emotional distress notwithstanding, she had buttoned her outfit quite provocatively.

Audrey's complaints were numerous but may be best characterized, in the order in which they were discussed, as follows:

1. Despite being in weekly therapy with a psychiatrist for the past two years, she felt that she was not improving, and that her clinician was becoming desirous of an emotional rather than a professional relationship with her. She needed to see someone who "could really help me."
2. She reported the constant fear that she was about to "go mad." She often felt "crazy" (though she reported no clear indices of psychoses during brief questioning at that point), and "spacey."

In terms of this latter feeling, Audrey reported that she had been involved in numerous minor motor vehicle and other accidents, and that she was "wacked out" much of the time on her medication. (The brief review of her current medication usage which followed this remark indicated that she was taking up to 60 mg of Valium daily and was inconsistently taking Haldol and several antidepressants.) Also in regard to her affective state, Audrey reported feeling anxious and upset much of the time, feeling scared about her emotional well-being, and feeling depressed. Beyond the aforestated symptomatology, she did not provide any indication of her subsequently admitted capacity to dissociate.

History

At the time of the first consultation, Audrey had just turned 29 years old. She had been separated from her husband, Robert, for about six months. She had two children, a girl 10 years old and a boy age 8. The two children she regarded as the only real joy in her life, save perhaps her religion. Audrey reported a family history that was both fascinating and remarkable. Her mother was one of 18 children born into a wealthy Austrian family who moved to New York and brought many of the "old ways" with them. Audrey reported growing up during her early childhood in a rather idyllic country mansion with a black nanny who took care of her and her three older siblings. This woman was a source of much love and affection for Audrey. Her mother, on the other hand, she reported to be caring but distant. Her mother's main concern, she recollected, "was always that I was clean." Her father died suddenly when Audrey was six years old. She remembered her father as handsome, tolerant of her mother, and very loving toward his children.

Following the death of her father, Audrey reported her own feelings as total despair. She got over this despair, she reported, only through the help of her imaginary little friend, Annishka, who was always good and showed her what she could do to overcome her troubles. Thereafter, Audrey's history into and through adolescence appears normative. At age 18 she began dating Robert, and while she stated that she had never really valued Robert a great deal, having become pregnant, she married Robert soon thereafter.

The marriage brought Audrey little sense of emotional fulfillment and so, despite her strong Catholic upbringing and current belief, from about the age of 23 she participated in and often initiated a series of typically brief sexual liaisons with "professional men who could see her during the daytime." Of particular significance here was the number of these encounters, a figure that Audrey presented matter-of-factly as involving in excess of one hundred men over the course of about six years. She reported no particularly distressing symptomatology during the early years of her marriage, except "never being happy" and "feeling bored."

The first indication of Audrey's "mental illness" occurred at age 24. She was in the bathroom of her home and experienced pain in her chest, a sense of doom, and great fear. She fainted and was transported to a local emergency room and held overnight for observation. Despite the fact that her blood and other test results showed no evidence of myocardial infarction and that her physician indicated the likelihood of an "emotional collapse" (panic attack), Audrey became convinced that she had suffered a minor heart attack. Following this incident she did not immediately seek further professional care. Within a few weeks of being home, however, she became phobic while showering (because she feared that the bathroom door would shut and that she would have another attack and be unable to summon help). She also exhibited a marked increase in her general anxiety level, some of which she attributed to ongoing difficulties both with her mother and with Robert. It was, however, the sudden death of her doting father-in-law that same year, an event that brought back much of the pain she had experienced at the death of her own father, that produced such depression in Audrey that she felt compelled to seek professional assistance.

Audrey's mental health care over the next five years was unfortunate. Despite substantial quantities of various (including antipsychotic) medications, two hospitalizations (with diagnoses of depression), and two long-term psychiatric relationships, during one of which she was given to believe that she was mentally ill, perhaps psychotic, and would require many years of therapy, Audrey never acknowledged to her clinicians the existence of her multiple personalities. Neither was this material revealed until some eight weeks into the therapy to be reported.

Assessment

During the earliest consultations, Audrey was so under the influence of the various medications she was taking that it was impossible to undertake an evaluation of her basic level of emotional functioning. Hence, the first task both from an assessment and therapy point of view, was to facilitate supportive withdrawal of the medication she was taking and to motivate her to realize that this was a crucial first step. This initial treatment and assessment phase was conducted over an eight-week period by providing directive and supportive therapy, two to three times weekly, together with the assistance of a psychiatric colleague who initially prescribed Ativan in place of the Valium. As Audrey's medication abuse was eliminated, a comprehensive functional analysis of her behavioral repertoire was undertaken. This procedure involved data gathered both from traditional instruments (such as the Minnesota Multiphasic Personality Inventory and the Thematic Apperception Test) and from ongoing observation of Audrey's emotional state, and the development of an understanding of the cognitions which she held regarding many of the ambiguities in her life.

It was these ambiguous and/or conflicting cognitions that were focused on for development and clarification during the early assessment phase, for such a procedure was commonly employed by the present clinician in the development of treatment planning with patients exhibiting anxiety and depression (see also Beck, 1976; Meichenbaum, 1974). Moreover, the discrepancies and ambiguities between much of Audrey's behavior and her cognitions were of such major proportions that they fostered the already existent desire on the part of the clinician to explore them further. It is noteworthy also that the analyses of Audrey's functioning, in her relatively drug-free state, revealed her to exhibit specific phobias (the aforementioned phobia of being in a small closed room, especially a bathroom, and a related phobia focused on the possibility of a heart disorder; a phobia related to freeway automobile driving; and a phobia about crowds). Audrey was also profoundly nonassertive.

I had developed a treatment plan based on essentially cognitively oriented behavioral procedures and I was beginning to implement a relaxation training sequence during the eighth session, when Audrey became tearful and indicated essentially the following:

> There is something I haven't told you. I have never told anyone this before because it scares me. Despite what you have been telling me about mental illness and the fact that I am anxious and depressed and not crazy, and that I have a lot of abilities to develop and thoughts to modify, when you hear this you will change your mind. Remember I told you about Annishka my little childhood friend, well, she is still with me. Many times when I feel sad or when I go to bed at night I become Annishka. And sometimes if somebody upsets me, in fact, almost always when I get propositioned by men or when I interact with a man, it is Anna that takes over.

Clearly, following this unanticipated revelation additional assessment was required. This further assessment resulted in the following conclusions: (1) Audrey believed that Annishka and Anna were separate personalities who took over from Audrey at certain times, in particular under conditions of sadness in the case of Annishka and when sexually provoked or interpersonally stressed, in the case of Anna. (2) Annishka was described by Audrey as about six years old and "a sweet, innocent child who would always comfort me." Audrey acknowledged that she could largely control Annishka's appearance and that this appearance was like her (Audrey) regressing to the role of a child. Annishka would always disappear, however, during sleep. Thus, the Annishka alternate would exist for only several hours at a time, and, depending on Audrey's emotional state, might appear most days of the week, or less frequently. Annishka did not understand Audrey, however, and was not aware of Anna's existence. (3) Anna, on the other hand, was a controlling, sexually and otherwise aggressive woman who always got what she wanted from people. She was the same age as Audrey and wore Audrey's clothes, but with a different effect. Her facial expressions, patterns of eye contact, and posture, unlike those of Audrey, reflected self-assurance and provocation. When annoyed, Anna was extremely cutting and often quite vulgar. She was aware of Audrey and regarded her as an incompetent, confused woman, a person with a lot of religious "hang ups," a woman to be pitied. Anna was not cognizant of the existence of Annishka. Anna would appear whenever she wanted to, and, in particular, when Audrey was experiencing interpersonal difficulties. Audrey could only sometimes control Anna's appearance. Her disappearance would occur as quickly as her appearance, the change back to Audrey occurring when the interpersonal stress experienced by Audrey had dissipated.

The assessment of the dynamics of these various alternate personalities was accomplished over the next three sessions, almost exclusively through interviews with Audrey. I never met Annishka, though there were glimpses of her that were obvious in Audrey at various times. Anna, on the other hand, emerged as a consequence of some wry comment I made to provoke and motivate Audrey to action during our ninth session. Anna also emerged during a number of subsequent sessions, and in fact, it became possible for me to provoke her into emerging with relative ease.

Selection of Treatment

The revelation of Audrey's alternate personalities in no way detracted from the observations about Audrey made previously. In fact, it actually helped explain the degree of contradiction existent within the cognitions of the patient. Moreover, because I view human behavior and the cognitions which support it to be a function of learning, I hypothesized the dissociative process to be lawful and functioning to serve the interpreted best interests of the personality, which in this case was Audrey. I regarded this process to be no less an attempt to cope by the primary personality than the emergence of anxiety, depression, and the like. In accordance with a cognitive behavioral perspective, these various states of disruption were all hypothesized to be the product of an array of distorted, confusing, and ambiguous cognitions that coexisted with limitations in the capacity of the patient to master her interpersonal world.

Given this theoretical framework, the therapeutic plan which was developed after the revelations was not substantially different from that which had been initially proposed for resolving the other disorders reported by Audrey. A presumption of greater complexity and more time to completion was made; and by the time the therapy began, it was becoming obvious that Audrey's seductive hystrionics vis-à-vis the clinician would require special attention. Otherwise, though, the procedures employed in this case were largely those cognitive behavior therapy techniques which are applied in the management of severely anxiety disordered and depressed patients. Within the context of these procedures, I chose to aid Audrey in the development of behavioral/interpersonal competence and to attempt an integration of the various subpersonalities or elements of my patient and thereby structure an "effective" Audrey.

Course of Treatment

Following the stabilizing of Audrey's psychotropic medication usage to a quite minimal dosage level (a process which had been accomplished by the ninth week of therapy), the following therapeutic goals were developed jointly with Audrey:

1. It was mutually agreed upon that therapeutic success could not occur unless an extremely honest and mutually respectful therapeutic relationship could be developed. While such a relationship is important in therapy generally, given Audrey's assessed propensity to interpersonal manipulation, the lack of relationships of integrity in her life, her cognitions regarding and her distrust of men, and the fact that her clinician was male, the relationship matter was of critical importance in this instance. It was agreed that we would aim to achieve just such a relationship within a period of three months.

2. It was agreed that Audrey would learn to reduce anxiety and tension using progressive muscular relaxation training and EMG biofeedback procedures. The relaxation techniques would be employed at home at least once a day on at least five days weekly. The timetable set to achieve the goal of learning the techniques was three weeks from the date of being introduced to them.

3. The third goal involved employing education and both imaginal and, thereafter, *in vivo* systematic desensitization, to aid Audrey in overcoming her phobic reactions to the prospects of a heart attack in small enclosed rooms, her "real discomfort" in going shopping, especially in large stores, and her fear of driving on the freeway. The date of achievement of this goal was set initially at four months from the beginning of therapy.

4. The fourth goal involved the development in Audrey of a series of assertive repertoires to aid her in dealing effectively in her interpersonal relationships, especially with men. It was agreed that this goal would be achieved by the sixth month of therapy.

5. Coexistent with each of the preceding goals, it was agreed to base the therapy on a cognitive behavioral model (after all, the previous chemotherapeutic and general supportive "talk" approaches had accomplished very little). In accordance with this model, the problems experienced by Audrey were conceptualized in terms of the interaction between interpersonal skill deficits (which were not all that substantial), and dysfunctional cognitions (which were severely pathological in this instance). In this regard, the analyses of Audrey's cognitive difficulties had indicated the need to focus on the following specific problem areas: (a) her ambiguity regarding the judgment of human worth, her conflicts regarding her own sense of worth, and hence, her uncertainty regarding her rights in relation to others and her responsibilities regarding herself; (b) the conflicts between the behavior and belief systems of Audrey and Anna, and to a far lesser extent, Annishka, and the need to develop a rational Audrey who could meet the basic needs expressed by both Anna and Annishka within one integrated and self-reinforcing system; and (c) the development of specific rationally based cognitive analytic strategies designed to confront the cognitive basis of the anxiety overlay and the more deeply involved depressive state which characterized Audrey.

Achievement of the first goal, the establishment of an honest and mutually respectful relationship, was achieved to an adequate degree in accordance with the proposed timeline. But Audrey's history of distrust and fear of people, especially men, and her constant tendency to alternate with Anna in order to control her interpersonal relations made the process of achieving a high-quality therapeutic relationship exceedingly difficult. It took nearly one and a half years, in fact, before I was satisfied that it was the personality of a strengthening Audrey who was really permitting me the relationship which I had indicated at the beginning of therapy to be the goal.

The second goal, involving anxiety reduction through relaxation training, was no less difficult to achieve than the aforementioned therapeutic relationship. Audrey reported benefit almost from the outset, as she compulsively employed the progressive relaxation sequences in an effort to relieve her anxiety. Despite her conscientiousness with the procedures, however, her progress was slow because the positive effects she experienced from the relaxation were only transitory. It was not until the subsequently discussed cognitive restructuring procedures were well and truly underway that Audrey's level of generalized anxiety became really manageable.

Essentially, the same sequence of events followed introduction of desensitization procedures designed to deal specifically with Audrey's phobic repertoire. Audrey took to the procedures quite agreeably, was able to appreciate the theory underlying the approach, and experienced substantial benefit from the techniques. Having been trained to employ deep breathing exercises, for example, Audrey came to realize that she could eliminate the possibility of hyperventilation, which meant she could control the escalation of her anxiety into a panic attack, which previously had resulted in her fainting. Thus, logically, she now had a strategy which permitted her no longer to fear the possibility of panic attacks, which were the basis both of her phobias regarding shopping and, to a degree, being in small rooms. Within the framework of these cognitively oriented and behaviorally based sequences, desensitization procedures were applied with substantial benefit, though not with total success.

Achieving the fourth goal, acquisition of assertion skills, as in the previous procedures, represented somewhat of a "which to do first" problem. Enough of the work addressing the previous goals had been conducted with Audrey (and Anna) so that by the 16th week and approximately the 35th session, it was possible to begin to focus on Audrey's assertiveness difficulties. Some cognitive restructuring dealing largely with Audrey's need to experience a sense of self-control and personal responsibility for her state of mind had already been initiated via the relaxation and desensitization sequences. Given, however, that Audrey had such a low sense of self-worth and a lack of clarity regarding her rights as a person, training her in the technical utilization and application of assertiveness repertoires without first or coincidentally engaging her in cognitive restructuring would only have produced skills that would have been neither fully understood nor usable. It was at this point in the treatment, therefore, that the primary focus of therapy was turned to cognitive restructuring, with the specific techniques of assertiveness training being introduced coincident with this restructuring. Using this joint approach, by the sixth month of therapy Audrey had developed a thorough appreciation of the importance of assertiveness, and she had gained a considerable ability to generate assertive patterns of communication in the therapeutic setting. She was, however, so vulnerable to returning to her old routines, both cognitively and behaviorally, that it took another year of therapy before Audrey was consistently able to deal effectively (assertively) in stressful interpersonal interactions.

Over the course of that year, the use of rationally based argument, often provocatively and confrontively presented, the use of paradoxical intention procedures, the continued focus on personal control and responsibility, a commitment to personal awareness and growth, and the use of critical and logical analyses of one's own cognitive processes were all applied in order to provide both a process and a structure for Audrey's recovery. All these procedures, together with substantial levels of support, were provided within a framework involving ongoing assessment in order to ensure that the therapy was being efficiently and appropriately targeted to meet the therapeutic needs of the patient.

The focus on cognitive restructuring occupied much of virtually every weekly session from the sixth to approximately the 20th month of therapy. During this period, numerous issues were examined and dealt with, often both in terms of general philosophy and, thereafter, as they applied specifically to Audrey. In the early stages, the therapy focused on the proposition that it was the lack of internal consistency, the conflict and ambiguity which existed between many of the belief systems and the behavioral routines of Audrey and her alternates, which created the anxiety and depression and other difficulties which she experienced. Further, it was argued that it was these problems of internal consistency which provoked the need for (the functional utility of) the dissociative processes which produced Anna and Annishka. Having accepted these propositions as reasonable, and having been motivated to work toward a reconciliation of these ambiguities, given the structure of therapy, it became possible for Audrey to systematically evolve rational and internally consistent cognitions regarding many of the issues which had caused her difficulties.

The result of the aforestated sequence of events was that Anna's appearance was slowly extinguished as Audrey's coping capacities were increased. Moreover, while at least for some time Audrey experienced a deepening of her depression (a circumstance produced largely because she missed the excitement and strength of Anna, and also because she was becoming more in tune with her own feelings of profound sadness), a substantial lifting of her previously constant state of anxiety also became apparent. Thereafter, it became possible to focus specifically on the cognitions that were supporting Audrey's depression. By aiding her in rationally dealing with her pain, it became no longer necessary for either Anna or Annishka to be involved in its management. At the same time, Audrey and I continued to build her assertive and other behavioral repertoires, in order to facilitate the sort of reinforcements that would act against the depressive states she was experiencing.

There were numerous other specific targets for cognitive restructuring in this most complex patient. Far too many, in fact, to present herein. Suffice to say, however, that within 22 months of Audrey's entering therapy, she made such gains that she had not experienced any dissociation in eight months, she was no longer experiencing anxiety or depression, nor was she still phobic, and she had acquired a sense of her own competency and value as a person.

I continued to see Audrey for therapy on a monthly basis for the next six months. Thereafter, I saw her every two to three months over the course of the next year. During this last phase of therapy, the focus involved reinforcing many of the issues dealt with at earlier stages and aiding Audrey by making what I regarded as "refinements" in her day-to-day management of difficulties she was facing.

Follow-up

I moved from the area approximately three and a half years after beginning Audrey's therapy, but she continued to maintain contact with me via occasional telephone consults over the next five years. Audrey's life during that period was rather tragic, for not only did a second marriage terminate in divorce after two years, but at about the same time she also was diagnosed as having multiple sclerosis. These circumstances notwithstanding, she experienced no further dissociation and only moderate levels of reactive depression.

Overall Evaluation

The treatment of Audrey was surely one of the most interesting and rewarding therapeutic relationships I have experienced. Having suffered substantially from the lack of structure that characterized her previous therapies, Audrey proved willing and capable of embracing both the philosophical framework and the technical demands of the cognitive behavior therapeutic approach. Moreover, given the targets provided by the focus of such an approach, she showed slow but constant progress in the direction of these goals until one by one she achieved them. Perhaps most impressive of all is the fact that her success was so reinforcing for her that it offered external validation for the procedures being employed, which further motivated her to complete the process she had begun. There can be little question that both patient and clinician were greatly satisfied with the outcome of this first attempt ever to employ a cognitive behavioral approach in the treatment of multiple personality.

References

American Psychiatric Association. (1980). *Diagnostic and statistical manual of mental disorders* (3rd ed.). Washington, DC: Author.

Beck, T. A. (1976). *Cognitive therapy and the emotional disorders*. New York: International Universities Press.

Hawkesworth, H. (with T. Schwarz). (1977). *The five of me*. New York: Pocket Books.

Meichenbaum, D. (1974). *Cognitive behavior modification*. Morristown, NJ: General Learning Press.

Thigpen, C. H., & Cleckley, H. M. (1957). *The three faces of Eve*. New York: Popular Library.

17

Fear and Avoidance of Dental Treatment

Robert K. Klepac

Description of the Disorder

Few rational people pursue dental treatment as a leisure-time activity. Most see dentistry as a mildly noxious, sometimes uncomfortable, and occasionally painful experience which is one of those necessities to be borne for the sake of health and well being. For an estimated 5-6% of the U.S. population, however, dental treatment is much, much more than that. These people find the prospect of a dental visit so terrifying that they are unable to seek out and receive the dental treatment which they themselves feel they need. These are the "fearful avoiders" in the jargon of our dental behavior research clinic, and the present case is exemplary of this group. Other strategies may be needed for "goers and haters" – fearful patients who lose sleep and work surrounding each dental visit, but who are religious in their dental care, and those who do not receive dental treatment for other reasons, such as expense, gagging, or other nonfear factors. There is no single mechanism by which dental fear is acquired: direct experience of painful or frightening treatment at the hands of a dentist

This work was done with support from NIH Grant #DE 04976 awarded to the author by the National Institute of Dental Research. The author is grateful to Dr. Elizabeth Lander for her assistance in this project.

is one way, but an even larger proportion of people attribute their fear to vicarious learning – from movies and cartoons, stories from malicious siblings, or seeing a parent lamenting his or her plight after a dental appointment. Other sources have also been reported, albeit less frequently.

Case Identification

Gloria was 29 years old at the time of her intake interview. She had been working as a librarian steadily since receiving her Master's degree in library science five years earlier. She reported being happily married for six years, and had two children, ages one and four. An extensive interview and screening with the MMPI, Eysenck Personality Inventory, and the Geer Fear Survey Schedule revealed no evidence of serious psychopathology, nor of other notable fears. Her manner was poised and confident, and she spoke freely about herself and her situation throughout our sessions, though voicing concern about her "weakness" in facing dental treatment.

Presenting Problem

The client was referred to the clinic by a former client. Approximately two months earlier she had experienced some swelling and tenderness in the gum tissue surrounding a molar and had forced herself to make and keep a dental appointment. Seated in the dental chair, she fainted when the dentist approached her to ask her about her tooth. When she recovered, she refused further examination and left the dentist's office claiming that she would schedule another appointment when she was feeling better. The problem with her gums dissipated within days, and she could not bring herself to return to the dentist, despite urgings and pleas from her husband.

She decided to seek behavioral treatment at this time, in part because this incident convinced her that she might be unable to seek and receive dental treatment even if she felt it were seriously needed. A second reason offered for her decision to seek treatment was her concern for her four-year-old daughter, who was ready for an introduction to dentistry. Gloria could not bring herself to accompany her daughter to the pedodontist's office. Moreover, she was afraid that her own fear might be apparent to her daughter and that she would "inflict on her what I've been suffering with all these years."

History

There was no evidence of prior counseling, therapy, or psychiatric treatment of any kind, and no evidence of psychiatric problems in Gloria's family.

Gloria reported that she had been fearful of dental treatment as long as she could remember, and recounted a bad initial experience at about age four. While portions of the experience were vividly recalled, she was not sure whether other aspects of the episode were directly recalled or were in fact constructions based on her hearing accounts of the story from her family.

Prior to her first dental visit, her older brother and she were engaged in an ongoing "fight." On a drive with her parents during the week before her first dental appointment, they passed a workman breaking up pavement with a jackhammer. Her brother taunted her with the idea that that is what would happen to her at the hands of a dentist. She reported nightmares during that week, high levels of anxiety despite parental reassurances, and utter panic when being carried to the dentist's office. She recalls little about the treatment she received during that visit, but recalls being held down by two dental assistants while the examination took place.

During her grade school years Gloria was taken to the dentist regularly. She reported always being panicked, but "usually" cooperating with her kind and gentle dentist, though she reports having panicked on more than one occasion during this period, requiring restraint and reassurance before treatment could proceed. In high school, treatment continued to be fairly regular, with scheduling and transportation arranged by her parents, though she was able to become "too busy" and hence delay appointments on occasion. She had visited a dentist only once between the time that she left home for college (11 years earlier) and the recent unsuccessful visit: her parents arranged for a visit during a vacation period at home, and informed her of the fact only while en route to the office. She reportedly felt faint during that visit, but required only a routine prophylaxis (examination and cleaning). She is, by report and appearance, an excellent dental hygienist, brushing and flossing religiously in order to preclude the need for visits to the dentist. She was not able to recall any highly painful experiences with dentists, though she had had several restorations (fillings). The pattern of visits and the obvious fear and occasional loss of control were verified by her childhood dentist and by her father, who wrote to us at Gloria's request.

She voiced no undue apprehension regarding physicians or medical treatment currently or in the past, which was also supported in her father's letter.

Assessment

The self-reported pattern of dental visits, verified by Gloria's dentist and her father, were seen as a loose "base rate" for comparison with posttreatment visits. This, in fact, was the client's primary goal in treatment: she felt that if she could simply keep to a regimen of regular dental visits, without fainting, she would be satisfied.

To get a more detailed picture of her fear, the Dental Fear Survey (Kleinknecht, Klepac, & Alexander, 1973) was administered. This is a 23-item questionnaire which lists elements of the typical dental office and treatment situation and asks clients to rate the extent to which each elicits fear; it also asks the extent to which various physiological, cognitive, and behavioral events reflect that fear, and solicits an overall fear rating. This client was so severely avoidant that she could not report actual behavior and reactions based on memory or recent experience, and so she was asked to fill it out as best she could anyway, giving us her best guess as to how she would react. Our intent was to use this material as the best available means of predicting troublesome stimuli and probable reactions to them as a basis for later discussion and planning for her first posttreatment visit. All items were rated either "4" or "5" on the 5-point scales. The DFS thus provided little useful information; it was very difficult for Gloria to discriminate between more and less frightening aspects of the dental treatment situation. One useful bit of information was derived, however. We had assumed, since Gloria reported no recall of a painful dental experience, that pain was not a factor to be weighed in treatment planning. To our surprise, Gloria gave a rating of "5" to the item "fear that I might feel pain." In discussing the DFS with her, she acknowledged that this was a major consideration for her despite the fact that she did not believe she had ever been hurt unduly by a dentist.

For reasons to be outlined below, we decided to get a pretreatment measure of Gloria's ability to tolerate pain and to observe her reactions during pain assessment. Using apparatus assembled specifically for this purpose, Gloria was administered five trials in which constant current electrical stimuli were administered to an intact, healthy incisor. (*Note:* Tooth pulp testers available from dentist's offices and dental supply houses should *not* be used in this application.

They are crude and unreliable instruments intended to detect the simple presence or absence of sensation. Their constant voltage output often leads to wild fluctuations in sensation on repeated presentations at the same nominal intensity, and are likely to "jolt" a client, possibly aggravating an already intense fear.) Each trial was begun at intensities so low that no sensation was reported and increased in 5 μA increments until she first reported sensation. The series was then continued until she reported that the sensations were first painful, and to the point of tolerance, defined as "the point at which the sensations are highly painful, and beyond which you are not willing to proceed on this series." Tolerance levels were averaged across the five trials to provide a pretest assessment. Gloria averaged 42.5 μA on this tolerance measure. This measure was not compared to others in a psychometric sense; rather, it was treated as a sort of baseline against which later changes could be assessed. We had anticipated a fair degree of resistance to this assessment from Gloria, but she gave us none. The measure had been introduced as a means of gauging her ability to tolerate pain, which might play a major role in her apprehension, and which might be expected to change as treatment progressed. This apparently was enough to enlist her full cooperation. Nonetheless, she was extremely apprehensive during the procedure. Her hands were shaking visibly, and she perspired slightly despite an intentionally cool room temperature. As we prepared to administer the first stimulus, Gloria paled visibly and her breathing became erratic. The assessor stopped the trial and helped Gloria to relax. She was told that the data were potentially important to her treatment but not so important as to threaten her with a fainting episode. The safety features built in to the apparatus were again discussed, and she was reminded that she would feel nothing at all during the early trials and that she could stop the series at any point. She decided to continue and successfully completed the five assessment trials.

After a short rest and discussion, procedures directly analogous to those involved with tooth pulp stimulation were repeated with shock to the dorsal surface of her nonpreferred forearm, just above the wrist. While Gloria showed some apprehension during preparation for these trials, her behavior during this assessment was indistinguishable from that of myriad college students we have seen in contact with this apparatus and was in marked contrast to her intense reaction to the prospect of tooth shock. She logged a mean tolerance level of 9.25 μA. The final measure which was taken was a series of three "efficacy" measures. Gloria was asked to fill in the blank in the following statement: "I am able to tolerate the stress and pain of TOOTH SHOCK better than _____% of people my same age and sex." This same item was administered twice more, substituting "ARM SHOCK" and "DENTAL TREATMENT" as the targets.

Treatment Selection

Several treatments have been successfully employed with dental fear in our clinic and elsewhere: systematic desensitization, graduated exposure, modeling with guided practice, and cognitive restructuring, to name a few. We decided to use stress inoculation (SI) with Gloria for several reasons. First, our unsystematic observations across many clients suggest that SI is more consistently effective than some of the alternatives we have employed. Our guess is that the skill-acquisition, self-control framework inherent in this approach is credible to a wide range of people, and with a wider range of specific patterns of dental fear, than alternatives. With this particular client, however, this approach seemed especially likely to elicit a high level of motivation. Gloria was, in most aspects of her life, a very competent, "take charge" person, and she had voiced disappointment and some shame over her difficulties with dentistry. The notion that skills must be acquired and then practiced before proficiency is likely seemed to provide a means of accounting for her inabilities and a rationale for improvement consistent with her general views. Her near-fainting episode during tooth pulp pain assessment supported her self-report that the prospect of dental-specific pain was a particularly important factor to address in treatment, and the procedures for targeting pain in SI are well developed in our clinic. We have found that SI is seen as credible to more people than any other approach when pain tolerance is an issue. Systematic desensitization, for example, has been received quite well by clients who are not particularly concerned about pain, but often rejected when pain tolerance is a concern (Klepac, 1975). Stress inoculation seems to most people a particularly reasonable means of handling fear as well as their reactions to pain should pain occur.

Course of Treatment

The first session following assessment was spent explaining the rationale for SI and our reasons for its choice in words not unlike those presented above, but emphasizing potential effectiveness rather than credibility. She was told that stress inoculation requires the learning

of strategies which can both reduce pain sensations and increase one's
ability to tolerate those sensations that are experienced. The model
used in explaining pain reactions and control to Gloria was a watered-
down version of Melzack and Wall's (1970) gate control theory. Three
components of pain were described: a sensory component, an evalu-
ative component, an affective component, and illustrations of strategies which might be useful in controlling each of these components.
Detailed examples of such a rationale can be obtained from the author, and more general but highly useful examples appear in Turk,
Meichenbaum, and Genest (1983).

Her reaction to this explanation was hardly gratifying. She seemed
convinced of the plausibility of the rationale but voiced great doubt
about her ability to master such skills, and even more about her ability to use them in the dental treatment situation, given the severity
of her reactions during her most recent dental visits. In Bandura's
terms, her outcome expectations were high and positive, but her efficacy expectations were far from optimal. We explored with her at
some length evidence from her own life of her ability to master difficult skills and emphasized the gradual pace of such acquisition. Fortunately, her competencies in areas including sports, writing, and
cooking provided strong evidence of her ability to acquire and perfect
new skills, and she acknowledged that she probably could learn some
new tricks and could probably use them in the safety of our La-Z-Boy
recliner. She voiced continued skepticism, however, regarding her
ability to use these skills in the face of her intense reactions in the
dental chair. The following is a reconstruction of a portion of the conversation which occurred at this point (*K*=therapist; *G*=Gloria).

G: ... but the problem is not relaxing my muscles in your office where I'm in control of myself. The problem is relaxing them
in the dentist's office, when my mind is racing, my heart is pounding, and my head goes light!

K: Your description sounds a lot like what I saw you do during your first try at shocking your tooth.

G: That's right! I just don't believe that I could do anything but
panic. I nearly fainted when you were trying to get going with that.

K: But you didn't faint.

G: I was only able to do that by telling myself that it would be
over in a minute. I could never do that for a whole dental appointment. And I was still terrified. I never was sure I'd make it
through the whole thing until it was over.

K: You're absolutely right. You couldn't do it for a whole dental appointment – not today. Could you make it through one more trial of tooth shock right now?

G: Yes . . .

K: Yes, I think you could too. So think about what you are saying. With no particular training at all, you used a strategy to make it through five series of shocks, over a period of almost 15 minutes. What's more, you didn't hesitate a moment to say you could do one more trial right now. Yet that first trial nearly wiped you out.

G: It got easier after going through it, I guess.

K: Thank heavens for all of us, it usually does – and that's my point. You can now do what even I feared was impossible for you to do earlier, and I'm betting that what seems impossible for you now will seem easy for you with experience.

G: There's a difference, though. I knew that I could stop the tooth shock whenever I wanted to, and I knew about how much the next shock would hurt. It's not that way in the dentist's office. You're asking me to think about sunny beaches in your office, which I can do, and then to walk into a dentist's office and do it there, which I can't.

K: Suppose we could figure out some way for you to bridge that gap, some way to try your skills under fire, but in a situation easier than going through a real dental visit.

G: What do you have in mind?

K: Two things. First, once you have really mastered your skills in my easy chair, we can let you try them again with tooth shock and see if you can increase your tolerance for tooth pain – in small steps. Lots of people have decided to do just that, and it has worked well for them. If you think it's important, we can even make the shocks gradually less predictable, so that you won't know exactly what level of shock is coming next, or exactly when, but we'll go slowly so that you master one step before we take the next, and we'll keep the steps small enough so you're comfortable in trying, but big enough so you and I can both see progress. We'll even chart the progress on paper for you. Second, we can do some other things about the dentist and his office. We can tell you how to approach your dentist to arrange to have him stop for a moment if you need a break, just the way we did with the first tooth shock. We can also give you a chance to visit a den-

tist's office just to look, listen, and smell and to use your strategies to reduce your fear when you know that no treatment will
be done.

G: Won't that take a long time?

K: Less than seven years [the time between her last two appointments: she laughs]. Besides, the odds are very good that as
you gain confidence in your ability to manage these situations
and stresses, you'll decide that you really don't need some element that right now seems absolutely necessary. You and I will
plan each step together, and you will have the last say all the way
through. What do you think?

G: Can I think about it for a while?

Gloria called before her next appointment to tell us that she had
decided to give SI a try, and that I should gear up to get started right
away, "before I change my mind." From that point on, Gloria was a
model client.

We spent one session choosing strategies, and she selected three:
Benson's relaxation exercises, distraction via an imagined beach scene,
and positive self-talk. Three sessions were spent in practicing these
three strategies, and a fourth in discussing and practicing recognizing when to change strategies.

Four sessions were spent in stressed practice; three of these involved her using her strategies to increase her tolerance for tooth
shock presented exactly as done in the assessment. The fourth session was spent in an abrupt leap to presentation of shocks with
several parameters rendered unpredictable: intensity, duration, and
time of onset. During the last of these trials, Gloria even suggested
that I present some shocks at an intensity above the level of tolerance
determined on the last orderly series of shocks, which I did with some
apprehension.

In lieu of a series of sessions to gradually introduce her to the
dental operatory, Gloria decided to schedule a consultation session
with a dentist. She discussed with him what she had been doing, and
how they might proceed when she came in for an exam and possible
treatment. The dentist proved uncooperative, refusing to give her the
right to stop treatment, and asserting that his treatment was painless and required no special efforts on her part. Without consulting
our clinic, Gloria scheduled a similar consultation with a different
dentist and reached a workable arrangement.

Termination

Gloria was scheduled for a final session in which several of the assessment devices were re-presented. Her tolerance for tooth shock had increased from 32.5 to 91 μA, while her tolerance for arm shock increased from 9.25 to 13 μA. Ratings of efficacy mirrored these changes, increasing from 6 to 94% on tooth shock and from 50 to 65% on arm shock. Her efficacy for tolerating dental treatment changed from 2% to 65%. Measures of state anxiety during pain tolerance assessment decreased markedly during tooth shock and moderately during arm shock.

She had at that time scheduled a dental appointment and voiced optimism about her ability to deal with the visit. Gloria required three dental visits immediately following our treatment: one for cleaning and prophylaxis, one for filling a new cavity, and one for replacing an old, deteriorating filling. She reported that the appointments went without incident, and she had little trouble in using her strategies during these sessions and no need to stop the dentist to rest and muster her resources. She also reported a significant degree of fear during, and especially before, her first visit, which diminished over subsequent visits despite the fact that treatment was scheduled in the latter. Her report of dental treatment without incident was verified by Gloria's dentist.

Follow-up

Gloria returned for dental examinations 6 and 12 months after the dental treatment noted above, and had scheduled another routine visit at the time of our 18-month follow-up interview. She also reported with obvious pride that she had participated in preparing her daughter for her first dental visit and had taken her to the pedodontist herself.

In a phone contact 36 months after her first dental sessions, she reported receiving examinations every 6 months and having "survived" a series of root canal treatments shortly before our call. All of these dental visits were verified from her dentist's records.

Overall Evaluation

Treatment success was amply documented. It should be noted that the use of tooth shock during treatment seemed particularly important with Gloria: she was the most adamant of scores of patients we have seen regarding the difficulty of applying her office-derived skills in the dental operatory. With less recalcitrant patients we have successfully used arm shock as a training stimulus, *in vivo* visits to the dental office, and even imaginal presentation of dental office scenes in place of this difficult-to-instrument stimulus. For Gloria, dental fear and avoidance was a circumscribed fear: there was no evidence of other major problems in living. Many of our avoidant clients have fit that mold, though many have had other personal problems as well. The main obstacle to treatment of dental fear for these more complex cases is the maintenance of attention to the highly focused treatment procedures during training sessions rather than diversion into some other aspect of the client's situation – a problem far from unique to the treatment of dental fear. Stress inoculation and other interventions seem equally effective with these people, provided that a careful overall assessment is done, and attention paid to sequencing of dental and "other" problems.

As noted earlier, SI has been our treatment of choice for dental fear and avoidance for some time. In this area, however, we are blessed with an abundance of techniques which appear to be effective – perhaps equally so – and few guidelines for choosing among them. Research needed to identify useful predictors of differential success requires large numbers of subjects, which are difficult to attract in a timely fashion. This difficulty in attracting avoidant subjects has also hampered efforts at elucidating the theoretical mechanism(s) which might be involved in successful treatment. One observation from the current case has been rather reliably observed in our clinic and supported (albeit weakly, to date) in research: successful return to dental treatment is often preceded by a marked increase in efficacy expectations. It is quite possible that any treatment which increases a person's feelings of competence to tolerate dental treatment will work as well in returning that person to regular dental care. Stress inoculation's high credibility may render it a particularly apt intervention for increasing efficacy in applications which require tolerating physically uncomfortable stimuli. Procedures like those reported here have been used effectively with other painful medical procedures, though the role of self-efficacy in those cases is no clearer than in the present case.

Gloria's first visit to the dentist following treatment was her most fear-eliciting, though no treatment was performed. It is not clear how important that first successful (i.e., relatively painless) dental visit is to maintenance of fear and avoidance reduction. It is clear—from this case and others we have treated—that over the longer span of time successful patients can tolerate rather extreme and reportedly painful treatments without a subsequent return of fear or avoidance.

References

Kleinknecht, R. A., Klepac, R. K., & Alexander, L. D. (1973). Origins and characteristics of dental fear. *Journal of the American Dental Association, 86,* 842–848.

Klepac, R. K. (1975). Successful treatment of dental avoidance by systematic desensitization and pain tolerance training. *Journal of Behavior Therapy and Experimental Psychiatry, 6,* 307–310.

Melzack, R., & Wall, P. D. (1970). Psychophysiology of pain. *International Anesthesiology Clinics, 8,* 3–34.

Turk, D. C., Meichenbaum, D., & Genest, M. (1983). *Pain and behavioral medicine.* New York: Guilford Press.

III

Child and
Adolescent Cases

18
School Phobia

Cynthia G. Last

Description of School Phobia

School phobia typically is characterized by excessive and unrealistic fear of attending school, resulting in prolonged absence. It is distinguished from truancy by the presence of fear and anxiety and absence of antisocial behavior. Somatic complaints are common when the child is faced with the prospect of going to school, which often results in the youngster being brought to the attention of a physician. Prolonged school refusal also may be associated with poor academic performance, inadequate peer relationships, and social skill deficits. Moreover, the problem often occurs within the context of a separation anxiety disorder, in which case school refusal constitutes one of many ways in which the child attempts to avoid separation from his or her mother (or some other major attachment figure). The client described below illustrates such a case.

Case Identification

Mary was a 16-year-old adolescent who was referred for treatment at the suggestion of her school district. Because of her chronic school refusal, Mary was being tutored at home, rather than attending her local high school. She resided at home with her parents and older sister.

Presenting Complaints

In addition to her chronic school avoidance, Mary presented with a number of other fears, all of which appeared to be linked to anxiety concerning being separated from her mother. Thus, she avoided virtually all activities which involved her being apart from her mother, including staying at home or going out of home either alone or with other people. Occasionally, Mary's older sister could "substitute" for her mother, although mother always was the preferred companion. Attempts to confront feared situations usually resulted in panic attacks, which were characterized by a number of physical symptoms, including palpitations, chest pain, dizziness, and nausea. At these times of intense anxiety, Mary often feared that she would die, go crazy, or "lose control." She also reported that she constantly worried about "getting lost" and had several compulsive-like behaviors that were associated with this fear. Finally, the client admitted that she often was concerned that something "terrible" would happen to her mother, especially if they were apart.

History

According to her mother, Mary always had been a nervous child. In fact, she had been using minor tranquilizers on and off since the age of five. Her mother demonstrated a similar pattern of medication use and was known to have a history of agoraphobia. Her father was an alcoholic. While Mary's mother appeared to be very overprotective of her, her father tended to be passive and distant.

Although Mary had some difficulties with going to elementary school, the problem did not become a significant source of concern until age 14. At this time she had a panic attack while experimenting with marijuana. Her reluctance to be separated from her mother began immediately following this incident, progressively worsening over time. During the past year and a half she had refused to attend school and was being tutored at home.

Mary had undergone several different types of treatment (i.e., family therapy, individual psychotherapy, relaxation training) in the past two years, but none of them had been effective in alleviating her fears and avoidance behavior.

Assessment

In addition to an initial clinical interview, Mary completed a fear and avoidance hierarchy and a behavioral approach test prior to treatment (see Last, Barlow, & O'Brien, 1984, for a detailed description of these assessment techniques). These measures also were readministered during and after treatment. Thus, information obtained was used to evaluate baseline functioning, plan and execute treatment, monitor progress throughout treatment, and determine clinical outcome following treatment.

The *fear and avoidance hierarchy* listed 10 situations that caused Mary increasing levels of anxiety. Many of these items entailed walking or driving somewhere without mother, being alone at home, or going to school. Each situation was rated for degree of fear and avoidance behavior using a nine-point (0–8) scale. Mary's pretreatment ratings are presented below:

Description	Rating
1. Driving alone one block from home	2
2. Walking alone to Stewart's Ice Cream Parlor	3
3. Driving with a friend to the Grand Union Super-market	5
4. Being alone at home for three minutes	6
5. Driving alone to the Grand Union Supermarket	7
6. Going to the movies with a friend	7
7. Going to school for one class	8
8. Being home alone for 10 minutes	8
9. Driving alone to the next town	8
10. Walking alone for a one mile distance	8

Mary also participated in a *behavioral approach test* which was individualized and administered in her home environment. During the test, she was asked to engage in five feared activities selected from her fear and avoidance hierarchy. In addition to measuring her behavior, her anxiety level was recorded at various points during the test. Results from the test were as follows:

Item	Completed? YES	NO	Rating
1. Driving alone one block from home	X		2

| | Completed? | | |
Item	YES	NO	Rating
2. Walking alone to Stewart's Ice Cream Parlor	X		4
3. Being alone at home for three minutes		X	–
4. Going to school for one class		X	–
5. Walking alone for a one mile distance		X	–

Results from the clinical interview, fear and avoidance hierarchy, and behavioral approach test indicated that Mary met *DSM-III* (American Psychiatric Association, 1980) diagnostic criteria for separation anxiety disorder. The specific criteria for this diagnostic category are listed below:

Diagnostic Criteria for Separation Anxiety Disorder

A. Excessive anxiety concerning separation from those to whom the child is attached, as manifested by at least three of the following:
 (1) Unrealistic worry about possible harm befalling major attachment figures or fear that they will leave and not return.
 (2) Unrealistic worry that an untoward calamitous event will separate the child from a major attachment figure, for example, the child will be lost, kidnapped, killed, or be the victim of an accident.
 (3) Persistent reluctance or refusal to go to school in order to stay with major attachment figures or at home.
 (4) Persistent reluctance or refusal to go to sleep without being next to a major attachment figure or to go to sleep away from home.
 (5) Persistent avoidance of being alone in the home and emotional upset if unable to follow the major attachment figure around the home.
 (6) Repeated nightmares involving theme of separation.
 (7) Complaints of physical symptoms on school days, for example, stomachaches, headaches, nausea, vomiting.
 (8) Signs of excessive distress upon separation, or when anticipating separation, from major attachment figures, for example, temper tantrums or crying, pleading with parents not

to leave (for children below the age of six, the distress must be of panic proportions).

(9) Social withdrawal, apathy, sadness, or difficulty concentrating on work or play when not with a major attachment figure.

B. Duration of disturbance of at least two weeks.

C. Not due to a Pervasive Developmental Disorder, Schizophrenia, or any other psychotic disorder.

D. If 18 or older, does not meet the criteria for Agoraphobia.

Thus, Mary's chronic school refusal stemmed from a *fear of being separated from her mother*, rather than a fear of some aspect of the school environment (see Berg, 1980). In attempting to distinguish between these two types of school phobics, it is often useful to pose the following question to the child: "Could you go to school if your mother were to go to class with you?" In Mary's case, the response was affirmative, suggesting that her separation anxiety was responsible for her school avoidance.

Selection of Treatment

Although tricyclic antidepressants, particularly imipramine, have been reported to be effective in treating children with separation anxiety (see Gittelman & Klein, 1984), this treatment option was not selected primarily because both the client and her mother were strongly opposed to Mary taking antidepressants. Rather, a graduated program of *in vivo* exposure, which has yielded positive results with a variety of childhood and adult anxiety disorders, was chosen to reduce Mary's fear and avoidance behavior.

It was explained to Mary that the only way in which she would overcome her separation problem was to experience fear and discomfort in the very situations she had been avoiding. Through repeated, prolonged exposure to these anxiety-producing situations, her anxiety eventually would subside through the process of "relearning" and "habituation" of physiological arousal.

Although Mary initially was reluctant to agree to this treatment plan, after several sessions of discussion she finally consented to begin exposure therapy. During the next 12 sessions, she was exposed to increasingly difficult situations, some of which were selected from her fear and avoidance hierarchy. Each therapy session lasted from one and a half to two hours, including one hour of actual exposure experience, traveling to and from the location where the *in vivo* exposure was conducted, and discussion of homework and treatment progress.

Course of Treatment

At the onset of treatment, Mary's mother was enlisted to help modify her daughter's behavior. Historically, mother's attention had served as a very potent reinforcer. Unfortunately, mother had been attending to (and reinforcing) Mary's maladaptive avoidance behavior, instead of more adaptive coping responses.

In order for the *in vivo* exposure treatment program to be effective with this youngster, it seemed that the contingencies of reinforcement needed to be altered in Mary's home environment, as well as during formal therapy sessions. Therefore, the therapist instructed Mary's mother to "ignore the negative and reward the positive." In other words, Mother was to ignore crying and sobbing associated with avoidance behavior and reward approach behavior (coping) with attention and praise. Although ignoring Mary's distress initially was very difficult for her, mother eventually became more comfortable with her new approach as she saw its positive effect on Mary. It should be noted, however, that the therapist's support of mother was most critical in this regard, especially during the early weeks of treatment.

In vivo exposure sessions were held twice weekly during the first two months of treatment, and weekly during the third and final month. During these sessions, Mary gradually was exposed to walking alone, driving alone, and being alone at home. Exposure was graduated by having the client confront increasingly difficult levels of these tasks. For example, for "walking alone," Mary first was asked to walk a short distance (one block) accompanied by the therapist. Next, she was to walk the same distance alone. Following successful completion of this item, Mary walked with the therapist for two blocks, then walked them alone. Exposure proceeded in this manner until Mary was able to walk alone for one mile with minimal anxiety.

Throughout exposure sessions, Mary was asked to remain in situations that elicited high anxiety until the anxiety decreased or subsided. Therefore, even if she was unable to complete a task, it was stressed that she should not leave it until she felt better. In this way, she would no longer associate escape responses with relief from discomfort.

The client engaged in structured homework practice sessions between treatment sessions in order to (1) increase the number and types of exposure settings, and (2) facilitate the generalization of treatment effects to the natural (home) environment. Practice sessions consisted of self-initiated exposure to a variety of fearful situations, some of which already had been executed during therapist-assisted exposure sessions. As indicated earlier, mother was employed as the "therapist" for these homework assignments, encouraging, supporting, and rewarding Mary's attempts at self-exposure. In addition, Mary was requested to record information about each practice session (e.g., whether it was completed, maximum anxiety level reached) on a form provided for this purpose.

Graduated exposure during home sessions was utilized to overcome Mary's school refusal. Here, Mary was required to attempt a school-related task *each day* (these homework assignments were in addition to those focusing on her other fears). Part of the hierarchy used for these assignments, in ascending order of difficulty, is presented below:

1. Getting dressed to go to school
2. Driving with mother to school
3. Entering the front door with mother
4. Walking to classroom with mother
5. Attending class for five minutes while mother waits outside classroom
6. Attending class for 15 minutes while mother waits outside classroom
7. Attending an entire class while mother waits outside classroom
8. Attending an entire class while mother waits outside the school building
9. Attending an entire class
10. Attending two entire classes
11. Attending a half day of school (until lunch hour)
12. Attending a whole day of school

Following the first three weeks of treatment, Mary was able to attend her 9:00 A.M. mathematics class while her mother waited outside of the school building. The next week she completed the same task while her mother was *not* on school property. Two weeks later, school attendance (full days) was occurring on a regular basis.

Mary also showed slow and gradual progress in conquering her many other fears, during both home practice sessions and therapist-assisted exposure sessions. Following three months of treatment, all of her fear and avoidance ratings indicated minimal or no anxiety (ratings ranged from 0 to 3). Moreover, at this time she was able to complete all five items on the behavioral approach test with low levels of discomfort.

Termination and Follow-up

After the 12th week of treatment, the client, her mother, and the therapist agreed that Mary no longer was in need of weekly therapy sessions. However, Mary was encouraged to continue her "practice sessions" on a daily basis, since anticipatory fear (and avoidance) often recurs if exposure is discontinued immediately after termination. Mother's role in helping her daughter to maintain her treatment gains was discussed prior to termination.

The client and her mother were asked to contact the therapist if fearful behavior began to reemerge. Six weeks following the end of treatment, Mary's mother telephoned to report that Mary again was exhibiting some reluctance to attend school and to stay home alone. Following careful and detailed questioning, it appeared that mother was attending to signs of anxiety and fear in her daughter, in response to her own fear that Mary's problems would resume. The therapist reiterated the importance of ignoring such behavior and reviewed ways in which she could support and praise alternative coping behavior. It was agreed that mother would schedule an appointment in two weeks if Mary's behavior had not improved, at least partially, by that time. She contacted the therapist four weeks later and stated that Mary was doing well and no longer showed any indices of separation anxiety. Six months following termination, a therapist-initiated contact revealed that the client continued to maintain her gains.

Overall Evaluation

The above case depicts an adolescent school refuser whose avoidance stemmed from a more encompassing separation anxiety disorder. A clinical interview, self-report measure, and behavioral test were utilized to formulate the diagnosis and assess in detail the parameters of the client's fears and avoidance behavior. Treatment consisted of graduated *in vivo* exposure to anxiety-eliciting situations, including both therapist-assisted and self-initiated (home practice) sessions. The client's mother played an important role in the treatment program after learning to differentially reinforce coping behavior. As in this instance, enlisting the therapeutic assistance of the mother (or other family member to whom the child is overattached) can be critical in engendering short-term improvement with clients who demonstrate separation anxiety, and in having treatment gains maintained over time.

References

American Psychiatric Association. (1980). *Diagnostic and statistical manual of mental disorders* (3rd ed.). Washington, DC: Author.

Berg, I. (1980). School refusal in early adolescence. In L. Hersov & I. Berg (Eds.), *Out of school.* New York: Wiley.

Gittelman, R., & Klein, D. F. (1984). Relationship between separation anxiety and panic and agoraphobic disorders. *Psychopathology, 17,* 56–65.

Last, C. G., Barlow, D. H., & O'Brien, G. T. (1984). Cognitive change during treatment of agoraphobia: Behavioral and cognitive-behavioral approaches. *Behavior Modification, 8,* 181–210.

19

Childhood Depression

Cynthia L. Frame
Joan L. Jackson

Description of the Disorder

Although there has been some debate regarding the definition of childhood depression, it is generally agreed that a major feature is either a loss of interest or pleasure in previously enjoyed activities or a dysphoric mood, as evidenced by a sad facial expression or self-report of sadness or hopelessness. Other features frequently include (1) sleep disturbance, (2) loss of appetite, anorexia, and/or failure to display normal weight gain, (3) psychomotor agitation or retardation, (4) fatigue or loss of energy, (5) excessive self-criticism, guilt, and low self-esteem, (6) inability to concentrate, and (7) suicidal ideation, suicide attempts, or preoccupation with death. In addition, social withdrawal, change in school performance, and somatic complaints often are observed. Other factors currently hypothesized to be related to depression in adults, such as illogical thinking, inappropriate attribution of responsibility for events, deficits in self-reinforcement, low rate of response-contingent positive reinforcement, and social skills deficits, may also be useful in conceptualizing childhood depression.

Case Identification

Ben B. was an 11-year-old white male who was in the fifth grade in public school. He was of average height, somewhat slender, with brown hair and fair skin. Ben lived with his biological parents, Mr.

and Mrs. B., his older sister, Libby, age 13, and his younger brother, John, age 4. Both Mr. and Mrs. B. were high school graduates. Mr. B. worked as a plumber and Mrs. B. stayed at home, caring for the children and the home. The B.'s had been married for 14 years, during which time there had been considerable conflict between them. Mr. B. was an alcoholic and often became verbally abusive to Mrs. B. and the children when he was intoxicated.

Presenting Problem

Mrs. B. brought Ben to the clinic a few days following an incident in which he had threatened to jump from the car while being driven home from school by his mother. Upon questioning, Mrs. B. revealed that although this was the only attempt that Ben had made to harm himself, he had stated several times prior to this incident that he wished he were dead. She also expressed concern about Ben's refusal to eat and the fact that he was spending increasing amounts of time alone in his room.

History

Ben, who weighed 7 pounds, 3 ounces at birth, was the product of an uncomplicated, full-term pregnancy and normal delivery. Mrs. B. remembered him as a quiet baby who slept somewhat more than her other children and who reacted negatively to new experiences. For example, when left with a new babysitter, he would cry constantly until his mother's return. As he became familiar with the demands of a new situation, however, he seemed able to cope effectively. Mrs. B. recalled Ben's entrance into kindergarten as a stressful experience for them both. For nearly a month Ben cried and protested going to school each morning. However, with gentle insistence by Mrs. B. that he go, he finally seemed to adapt to and even enjoy school. Ben experienced no significant illnesses during infancy or early childhood, and he reached major developmental milestones at normal ages.

Ben's early elementary school years seemed relatively normal and uneventful. He performed well academically, earning mostly As and Bs, and exhibited no behavior problems. Though he was not extremely popular, he appeared to be accepted by his peers. Beginning in fourth grade, Ben periodically complained that his teacher's expectations for his academic performances were too high; however, his grades remained consistently good. On a few occasions, after failing to make an A on an exam, Ben had gone home and locked himself in his room for several hours. Each time, however, he seemed to have recovered by the next day. Mrs. B. noted that withdrawal was Ben's typical response to disappointment or punishment.

Two months prior to being brought to the clinic, Ben had been disappointed at not being selected to be a member of the school safety patrol. Ben said little about this event to his family and, in fact, began to decrease his interactions with them altogether, spending more and more time alone. During this time he also began to have difficulty falling asleep at night. Mrs. B. reported that she often heard him pacing back and forth in his room well past his usual bedtime. He started skipping meals, stated that he was not hungry, and upon awakening in the morning he complained of fatigue and headache, although extensive medical tests revealed no apparent basis for these symptoms. In addition, Ben's complaints about difficulty in completing his schoolwork increased and his grades began to drop. It was a few days after receiving a particularly low grade on an assignment that he began telling his mother he wished he were dead and threatened to jump from the car.

Assessment

Two types of initial assessment procedures were conducted with Ben, one for diagnostic purposes and another to identify and measure specific behaviors to target for intervention (see Costello, 1981; Kazdin, 1981). The diagnostic assessment consisted of several steps. First, Mrs. B. was interviewed about Ben's recent behaviors. Because of her report of suicidal ideation, poor appetite, and social withdrawal, the therapist (Dr. K.) questioned Mrs. B. about the presence or absence of each possible diagnostic feature of depression described in the first paragraph of this chapter. When she confirmed the presence of sleep problems, fatigue, difficulty concentrating, falling grades, and somatic complaints, the therapist felt fairly certain that Ben could be described as suffering from childhood depression (see Schulterbrandt & Raskin, 1977, for a discussion of the concept of childhood depression). To be more confident, however, she asked many other questions to rule out the possibility of medical problems which mimic depression and other psychological problems, such as an anxiety disorder or schizophrenia. The therapist also asked Mrs. B. to fill out a standard checklist which covered the characteristics of a number of childhood problems. When scored, the checklist indicated that most of Ben's symptoms fit into the syndrome labeled depression. However, because parents are not always accurate in reporting their children's behavior, the therapist also conducted a structured diagnostic interview with Ben. Further, he was asked to respond to multiple-choice items on a standardized self-report scale of depression for children. Both of these assessment procedures pointed to a diagnosis of depression.

Having made the diagnosis of depression, the therapist had some clues as to the starting point for assessing specific behaviors that might require treatment. (Kaslow & Rehm, 1983, provide a helpful guide to the assessment of depression-related behaviors.) Some of the most obvious problems Ben presented were suicidal ideation, social withdrawal, and poor school performance. The therapist speculated that since these seemed related to the child's depression, other factors probably were responsible for these problems. For example, declining academic performance could be the result of problems with concentration, lack of incentive to do schoolwork, or negative self-statements about achievement. Similarly, social withdrawal could be a function of negative self-statements about others' perceptions of oneself, lack of response-contingent positive reinforcement from others, or poor social skills. Finally, suicidal talk and plans could be triggered by any or all of these factors and maintained by parental attention and concern. Thus, a multifaceted behavioral assessment was undertaken.

Dr. K. first made a school visit to observe Ben's behavior in the classroom and on the playground. Armed with a timer and a list of behaviors to be observed, she watched Ben for 20 minutes while he was supposed to be working independently on a reading assignment. For each 10-second interval, she recorded whether Ben had been attending to his work or was off-task, that is, engaged in some other behavior. She found that he was working on-task only 18% of the time. Most of Ben's off-task activities included staring out the window with a sad expression on his face and engaging in repetitive movements such as pencil-tapping, hair-twirling, foot-jiggling, and rubbing his face. He seemed unaware that his behavior was somewhat disruptive to students sitting near him. Ben's teacher confirmed that Ben had been acting in this manner for the last couple of months and expressed some concern about how she might be of help. She was certain that he was capable of academic performance far beyond his present level because he had been a good student earlier in the year. She noted that he was also refusing to play with the other children

during recess, and that they had given up trying to talk him into joining their games. She could think of no event that could have precipitated the onset of Ben's depressed mood. However, when questioned by Dr. K., the teacher reported that Ben had not been selected
for participation in the safety patrol. Despite his eligibility, Ben had
been passed over because only a few children could be chosen. She
was surprised when the therapist speculated that this incident might
be of importance, since Ben had looked somewhat disappointed when
not chosen but he had never mentioned the matter again.

Dr. K. next chose to observe Ben on the playground at recess.
This time, for each 10-second interval, she recorded whether or not
Ben initiated or received any social interactions. Here, she found that
Ben was approached or talked to by other children less than 2% of the
time, and that Ben did not initiate interactions with his classmates.
Instead, he sat on the school steps with his back to the children and
his head in his hands. When the other children spoke to him, Ben
mumbled unintelligibly without looking at them. The other children
simply shrugged and walked away. Social interaction at school was
obviously at a minimum.

The therapist continued her behavioral assessment by having
Ben and his mother return to the clinic. Dr. K. was interested in learning what Ben was thinking about when "daydreaming" at school. At
first, Ben was very uncommunicative. However, he eventually was
able to discuss this with much assistance from the therapist, as the
following excerpt illustrates:

Dr. K.:   It seems like it's pretty hard for you to do your work
at school. (Pause) Is that right?

Ben: (Without looking at the therapist) I don't know.

Dr. K.:   Well, sometimes you don't get it done on time, right?

Ben: Yeah.

Dr. K.:   Sometimes it's easy for people to think about lots of
other things instead of their work. Does that ever happen to you?

Ben: Like what?

Dr. K.:   Oh, like riding a bicycle or remembering a favorite TV
show or something. (Pause) Do you find yourself thinking about
things like that instead of your schoolwork?

Ben: No.

Dr. K.:   Oh. What do you think about when you look out the window at school?

Ben: I don't know.

Dr. K.: Take time to think about that for a minute. (Pause)

Ben: I can't remember. (Puts face in hands.)

Dr. K.: O.K. Let's make it easier. Let's pretend you're at school now and you're supposed to be doing an arithmetic assignment. Are you with me? What's your assignment about? Addition?

Ben: No. We're on long division.

Dr. K.: Good, it helps me that you could tell me that. Now, pretend like you're doing the very first problem and there's a whole list of problems. Can you imagine that?

Ben: Yeah.

Dr. K.: Good, I appreciate how hard you're trying to help me out here. So you're working on the first problem. Forty-two into 640. What do you think? Will you get it right?

Ben: I don't know. (Pause) No. Maybe, but I'll never get done with all of them even if I do the first one.

Dr. K.: Oh? (Pause) Why not?

Ben: I don't know, I just won't, I can't . . .

Dr. K.: Can't tell me or can't do the work?

Ben: The work. It's too hard. I'm no good at it. I hate it. I hate school . . .

Dr. K.: So when you get an assignment, you feel like you'll never get it right and you'll never get it done?

Ben: Yeah. I just know I won't and I'm so tired. So why try?

Dr. K.: That sounds pretty rough. Do you ever tell yourself, "I did a good job" or "I bet I can do at least one problem today"?

Ben: No, that's stupid. I'd fail anyway.

From this conversation, the therapist gathered that Ben probably was not spending his time daydreaming about pleasant activities, but instead was focusing on negative statements about himself, school, and his ability to do his work. These negative cognitions appeared to be punishing any initial efforts that Ben put forth and precluded further inclinations to study harder. At any rate, it was clear that Ben was not making any positive self-statements about his schoolwork.

When questioned about his activities with other children, Ben expressed the same type of negative cognitions about his worth as a playmate. He claimed that the other children thought he was no fun and no good at games. He reported that he did not want to play with them anyway, because nothing was fun. With much assistance again, he stated that he often felt uncomfortable with other children because he didn't know what to say or do. At this point, the therapist asked Ben to participate in a standardized role-play task with her. Ben's response to various social situations were scored for appropriateness of content and voice quality. Scores indicated that he had the most difficulty when he was required to initiate a conversation or a request. At these times, his voice was low or unintelligible, and the content of his statements was not very appropriate. He was able to perform adequately in those situations when someone else initiated a conversation, but he stated that he preferred not to interact at all.

Finally, Dr. K. spent more time talking with Mrs. B. about Ben's problems at home. She reported that when Ben would come home from school he would go to his room until called for dinner. After dinner, he would return to his room and not emerge until he washed up at bedtime. While she was pleased that his TV watching was less this way, she was concerned about his failure to interact with family members. Furthermore, she observed that he did not do anything constructive during the time he spent in his room, but rather would sit or lie on his bed or pace around. His statements about wanting to be dead usually occurred when his father was not present. In response Mrs. B. and Libby tended to hug Ben and tell him not to talk like that because they loved him.

Both Mrs. B. and Ben claimed that the family had little contact with Mr. B., and that this was a preferable state of affairs. Mr. B. reportedly spent most of his free time with friends at a neighborhood bar or going on weekend hunting trips. He tended to ignore the children's presence when sober; when intoxicated, he became easily irritated, and the children avoided him. There seemed to have been little change in this family pattern for a number of years, and Mrs. B. saw little hope for future improvements. She stated, however, that Mr. B. was a "good man underneath it all" and was a good provider.

From the information she had collected by this point, Dr. K. was very confident about Ben's diagnosis of depression. Integrating results from school observations, interviews, and role-plays, she concluded that Ben's poor academic performance was closely related to a lack of positive self-statements about his competence and ability. She believed that his low frequency peer interactions were related to a number of factors. First, it seemed that other children were avoiding Ben because he was unpleasant to be around. They found his low voice tone, sad face, and withdrawn body positions aversive. Thus, Ben was engaging in behaviors that prevented interactions. Second, Ben did not seem to have the skills to let others know what he was thinking or wanting unless they asked him first. Since this rarely happened, Ben received very little positive reinforcement from the few social interactions in which he did engage. A good example of this was his failing to communicate to the teacher how important it had been to him to join the safety patrol. Moreover, his perceptions and self-statements that others thought negatively of him precluded his making any efforts to rectify the situation. All of this seemed to have generalized to his home life, where he continued his pattern of social withdrawal. Finally, in a desperate attempt to escape from this impossible situation, he resorted to talk about death. As a result, through his mother's concern and attention, he inadvertently received the social reinforcement he had been lacking, and this served to escalate his suicidal statements into suicidal actions.

Selection of Treatment and Course

Based on this extensive diagnostic and behavioral assessment, overall treatment goals and specific intervention targets were elaborated. The long-range goals were to improve Ben's mood, appetite, sleep, and school grades, and to eliminate suicidal ideation. These essentially were Mrs. B.'s presenting complaints and were considered to be the most important indicators of treatment success. More specifically, however, the therapist decided to target several particular behaviors for intervention. These included time spent on-task at school, number of social approaches received by Ben on the playground, number of social interactions initiated by Ben on the playground, time spent out of his room at home, and frequency of suicidal talk and threats. It was expected that depressive symptoms would decrease or abate when these target behaviors were modified successfully. Increasing time on-task at school was predicted to improve Ben's grades, and, thus, serve as a reinforcement to him. Likewise, increasing Ben's rate of social interaction, both at home and at school, should make life more enjoyable for him by increasing his rate of response-contingent positive reinforcement. It was anticipated that decreasing suicidal ideation would increase the opportunities for Ben's mother and sister to express positive emotions about his assets and successes, rather than his despair. In light of Mrs. B.'s description of Mr. B.'s relationship to the family, and her unwillingness to change that, no intervention was planned to involve him or Ben's interactions with him.

The first step in treatment was to establish a baseline of the target behaviors against which to measure improvement. The teacher-aide was taught to observe and record daily the classroom and playground behaviors of interest. Mrs. B. was asked to keep a record of the amount of time, in minutes, that Ben spent out of his room each evening and the number of suicidal statements made each day. To check whether measurement was being conducted reliably, Ben also kept a record of the time that he spent out of his room at home, and the therapist made occasional visits to the school to observe the on-task and social behavior. Records were collected for one week before treatment was begun. Baseline data indicated that Ben's rate of social interactions and time spent on-task were consistently low, and that he mentioned wanting to be dead twice during the week.

The treatment plan consisted of four components. First, Mrs. B. and Libby were instructed to ignore suicidal talk, while observing Ben unobtrusively to ensure that he did nothing to hurt himself. Instead, they were told to pay attention and respond with interest when he talked about other topics. For the other three components, the therapist would work with Ben in 30-minute individual treatment sessions twice per week.

The therapist wanted to begin with behaviors that would be easy to change to maximize the likelihood of success experiences. In addition, she wanted to start with skills that could be built upon to use with other problems later. For these reasons, Dr. K. spent the first treatment session teaching Ben to generate more positive self-statements about his academic work. He was given a school assignment and was instructed to verbalize some optimism about being able to accomplish the task, to take one step at a time, and to praise himself for each step he attempted. This initially required much coaxing and modeling by the therapist, but Ben eventually responded to the therapist's praise and soon was able to express a number of appropriate rewarding self-statements. The following is an excerpt of the final interaction for that session:

> *Dr. K.:* Here's your arithmetic assignment. You have 10 problems to do. What do you say?
>
> *Ben:* Sounds like a lot . . . But I'll just try them one at a time.
>
> *Dr. K.:* Good. Go ahead.

Ben: I know I can do this first one. Three plus five is eight. That was easy, but I could have made a dumb mistake and I didn't. That's good.

Dr. K.: Right you are! You are saying exactly the right things to yourself.

Ben: Oh, oh. This one's too, uhm, this one's harder . . . if I try, I can probably get it . . . Yeah. It might not be right, but I tried hard. I did good.

Dr. K.: That was an excellent self-statement. You've learned very quickly tonight, and I like how hard you've tried.

The therapist then had Ben practice saying positive statements to himself silently, and asked him to try it at school and when doing his homework. During the second session that week, Ben polished his skills and learned to vary the kinds of statements made for attempting assignments, completing them, and being correct. During this week, Ben's time on-task gradually rose to approximately 75%, which was considered the lower end of normal limits. However, his school and home social interactions remained low during that time period, and he once mentioned preferring to be dead.

Next, the therapist decided to try to decrease depressive behaviors that appeared to discourage other children from approaching Ben. She adapted a strategy that previously had been successful with another depressed child (see Frame, Matson, Sonis, Fialkov, & Kazdin, 1982). Here, Ben was taught to speak loudly and clearly in response to questions, to smile now and then, to look at the person who had spoken to him, and to refrain from turning his back or covering his face with his hands. To do this she used a large mirror and had Ben look at himself whenever he engaged in a depressive mannerism. In addition, they repeatedly role-played another child initiating a conversation with Ben, so that he could practice responding appropriately. Ben quickly stopped turning his back or covering his face. However, he had more difficulty learning the other skills, so an additional session was spent on these behaviors. As before, Ben was told to practice at school with the other children. The therapist also checked to make sure that Ben was still making positive self-statements about his schoolwork. During this week, Ben's on-task behavior reached about 85%, and the number of social interactions he received rose from two to seven. The time he spent with his family increased slightly, but his social initiations at school remained almost nonexistent.

The next step was to increase Ben's initiation of interactions with his classmates and family. Here, Dr. K. used two tools concurrently. She taught Ben appropriate words to say when making requests or beginning conversations and then role-played them with him. In addition, she helped him develop positive self-statements about his interpersonal competency. One week was spent on developing these skills. Again, Ben was to practice at school and at home. During the following week she taught Ben assertion skills, including how to let others know what he wanted and to communicate his disappointment, distress, or lack of understanding in an appropriate manner. These statements were hard for Ben to make, since he had rarely done so before, but he practiced a great deal and began to improve in this area.

Termination

Before embarking on treatment, the therapist established criteria to be met before treatment would be terminated. Ben's on-task behavior was to occur at a rate of 75% or greater, a rate that was considered typical for fifth-grade boys. Furthermore, Ben's rate of social interaction was to match that of the other boys in his classroom, who had been observed in order to determine their average rates of initiating and receiving social interactions. Furthermore, Ben was expected to spend the same amount of time out of his room that he had before becoming depressed, which was approximately two hours per evening. Of course, Ben's mood, appetite, sleep, grades, and suicidal ideation were expected to have changed in the desired direction before termination.

After the eight treatment sessions, Ben was on-task approximately 85% of the time, and his grades had returned to Bs and occasional As. The rate at which other children approached him on the playground had increased dramatically, and his number of social initiations showed a moderate increase. Both were now within normal limits, although there was still room for improvement. Both Ben's and his mother's recordings showed that he was spending from one to three hours with his family after school each day, and he had ceased talking about wanting to die. He reported not feeling sad any longer, and his appetite had returned. His mother no longer heard him pacing in his room after bedtime. A repeat of the diagnostic interviews and paper and pencil measures showed that Ben no longer qualified for a diagnosis of depression.

Follow-up

At three months and one year following the end of treatment, Ben was reassessed using all of the assessment techniques previously utilized. At these times, he showed no evidence of depression, his grades remained high, and his social interactions were well within normal limits for a boy his age. Now a successful member of the soccer team and a Little Leaguer, he commented that it was hard for him to believe that he had once felt bad enough to want to end his life.

Overall Evaluation

In Ben's case this combination of techniques for treating childhood depression appeared to be very successful. With a single client it is difficult to be certain that improvement in symptoms is not due to spontaneous remission or to some external event not under the control of the therapist, such as making the baseball team or changing classrooms. The fact that Ben's target behaviors tended to remain unimproved until each was treated specifically suggested that the improvements were, in fact, attributable to the treatment program and not simply to spontaneous remission.

The success of this treatment, however, was due not as much to the treatment techniques themselves as to the careful matching of the treatment to this child's specific strengths and weaknesses. In other cases, immediate hospitalization may be required to prevent suicidal behaviors, and antidepressant medications are sometimes necessary. Some children are so depressed that they do not have the energy to learn new cognitive and social skills immediately and require gradual shaping. Finding rewards for some depressed children may also be difficult because of their pervasive lack of pleasure. Finally, many times depression in children is transient or secondary to other problems such as enuresis or separation anxiety. All of these factors serve to underline the need for a complete and detailed assessment of each child's symptoms, behaviors, and social and family situations.

References

Costello, C. G. (1981). Childhood depression. In E. J. Mash & L. G. Terdal, (Eds.), *Behavioral assessment of childhood disorders* (pp. 305–346). New York: Guilford Press.

Frame, C. L., Matson, J. L., Sonis, W. A., Fialkov, M. J., & Kazdin, A. E. (1982). Behavioral treatment of depression in a prepubertal child. *Journal of Behavior Therapy and Experimental Psychiatry, 13,* 239–243.

Kaslow, N. J., & Rehm, L. P. (1983). Childhood depression. In R. J. Morris & T. R. Kratochwill (Eds.), *The practice of child therapy* (pp. 27–51). New York: Pergamon Press.

Kazdin, A. E. (1981). Assessment techniques for childhood depression: A critical appraisal. *Journal of the American Academy of Child Psychiatry, 20,* 358–375.

Schulterbrandt, J. G., & Raskin, W. (Eds.). (1977). *Depression in childhood: Diagnosis, treatment, and conceptual models.* New York: Raven Press.

20

Autism

Laura Schreibman
Alison E. Stanley
Debra L. Mills

Description of Autism

Early infantile autism is a severe form of psychopathology in children affecting approximately one child in 2,500. While it is a relatively infrequent disorder, its occurrence has a major impact on the family, schools, and community. This is well illustrated by the comments of one mother known to the authors who aptly described life with an autistic child when she said: "We don't go anywhere, we don't do anything, and we never have anyone over to our home when he's awake."

The syndrome is characterized by the presence of most, but not necessarily all, of the following characteristics. First, the children typically display profound and pervasive deficits in social attachment and behavior. This is evidenced by their failure to establish normal bonding with parents and others, poor eye-contact, resistance to affection, preference for solitary activity, and disinterest in peers. Second, there is typically a delay or failure in the acquisition of language. About 50% of (untreated) autistic children never develop functional

Preparation of this chapter and the treatment reported herein were supported by USPHS Research Grants MH 28231 and MH 28210 from the National Institute of Mental Health. The authors are grateful to the many therapists who have taken part in the treatment we have described in this chapter. Special acknowledgment is due Paco's mother for her determined efforts throughout her son's treatment.

language; those who do often display abnormal, noncommunicative speech such as echolalia (repeating the speech of others). Third, the children display an unusual unresponsiveness to their physical environment. Most have histories of suspected but unconfirmed deafness or blindness, prompted by their failure to respond to environmental stimulation. Fourth, the children often have a preoccupation with the preservation of sameness in their environment. They are highly sensitive to changes in their physical environment, routes of travel, or daily routine. Fifth, self-stimulatory behavior is often present. This consists of repetitive, stereotyped activity, which appears to serve no other function than to provide sensory feedback. Examples of this behavior include body rocking, hand flapping, spinning objects, and gazing at lights. Sixth, self-injurious behavior such as head banging, face-slapping, and self-biting is sometimes present. Seventh, autistic children sometimes display isolated exceptional skills, usually in the areas of music, memory, or mechanical ability. In addition to these features of the syndrome, autistic children frequently are mentally retarded, with about 60% having measured IQ's below 50. While retardation seems to be an independent condition, it seems often (but not always) to coexist with autism. However, autistic children typically show normal physical development and none of the physical stigmata often associated with retardation.

Case Identification

Paco was 25 months old when referred to the authors. The initial intake evaluation revealed a very attractive, pale, blond little boy who was brought to the clinic because of developmental delays and bizarre behavior. Observation of Paco and an interview with the mother revealed the following history and presenting complaints.

Paco was the product of a full-term pregnancy and C-section delivery. He had a brief bout of jaundice shortly after birth but otherwise his birth history was uneventful. However, since Paco was the second child born to this family, the mother realized within the first few months that something was wrong. The child was incessantly active and fussy. He had difficulty nursing and was difficult to hold. He would remain stiff and rigid when held, failed to establish eye contact, and cried during social contact. When he was a little older, his mother noted that he actively resisted affection and would scream, fight, and bite if people attempted to hold him. Also, it was very difficult to calm or quiet him, and often only prolonged rocking in a bed swing would induce sleep. He did not anticipate being picked up by raising his arms and preferred being alone. His mother reported that he did not "need" anyone, even her or his father. He would not mind if they left him (e.g., with a babysitter) and did not indicate happiness upon their return. He never spontaneously initiated affection, did not come for comfort when hurt, and seemed to "look through" people as if they were not there.

Paco's mother also reported that he was very unresponsive to his surroundings, and the family feared he might be deaf. Yet his unresponsiveness to auditory stimulation was inconsistent. For example, he often failed to respond to his name or other sounds but invariably responded to the sound of the ice cream truck on the street. A subsequent hearing evaluation indicated Paco's hearing was well within normal limits.

One of the most serious concerns of the family was the total absence of language. Paco had never spoken, had minimal receptive language, and displayed no interest in communicating with others in any way.

Paco's self-stimulatory behaviors included humming, rocking from foot to foot, rocking on hands and knees, gazing at lights, gazing at his outstretched hand, and spinning the wheels on toy cars. He spent much of his time engaged in this type of activity. Attempts to stop this behavior or denying his wants often led to severe tantrums. He would scream, stomp, throw himself on the floor, and slap himself in the face repeatedly and with force. Paco was always fussy and his mother described him as having a very "short fuse." Tantrums were frequent and could be long lasting.

Paco engaged in several ritualistic behaviors that are often characteristic of autism. He frequently demanded to hold two cylindrical objects — one in each hand. These were typically pens, pencils, straws, or Tinker Toy dowels. In fact, a common behavioral pattern (observed also during the initial evaluation) was for Paco to stand, feet wide apart, rocking rhythmically from foot to foot, with a cylindrical object in each hand. As with the self-stimulation, attempts to get him to relinquish these items were often met with fussing and tantrums.

Paco's family felt certain that he was not mentally retarded because he showed skills inconsistent with mental retardation. He loved music and could hum melodies heard just once; he was fascinated by mechanical apparatus, and was skillful in their use. Perhaps most convincing of all was Paco's extraordinary deviousness in manipulating those around him.

Behavioral Assessment

Identifying Problem Behaviors

The first step in conducting a behavioral assessment was to obtain information regarding Paco's behavioral excesses and deficits. This was accomplished in several ways. First, Paco's prior psychological evaluations and medical records were reviewed. Second, during the initial interview and continued contacts, his parents provided in-depth information about Paco's behaviors. Third, direct observations were also conducted using a structured videotaped assessment procedure. This served to assess Paco's behavior in a free-play situation. It consisted of placing him in a large, toy-filled room with his mother, with an adult who was unfamiliar to him, and with a trained therapist, one at a time. At first, the adult did not initiate any interactions with Paco but was responsive to his initiations. The adult then left the room where Paco remained to assess his awareness of the adult's presence. The adult then reentered the room and actively interacted with Paco by initiating verbal interactions, giving simple commands, and inviting him to play with some of the toys. In this way, the extent to which Paco participated in social interactions was determined. Paco was also videotaped at home eating dinner with his family. Appropriate and inappropriate behaviors in that environment were similarly assessed.

Defining the Problem Behaviors

A second important step was to utilize the obtained information in developing operational definitions of Paco's behaviors as well as to identify the variables that set the occasion for those behaviors (Schreibman & Koegel, 1981). Previous records and parental reports revealed that Paco's behavioral *excesses* included tantrums, self-stimulation, and noncompliance. Tantrums consisted of prolonged episodes of crying and screaming and were quite severe. Such episodes were typically precipitated by even minimal demands and removal of, or refusal of access to, various desired objects or activities. Self-stimulation involved rocking back and forth while seated or rocking from foot to foot while standing, usually with a stick or other cylindrical object in each hand. Rocking was usually accompanied by humming and grunting sounds and appeared to be Paco's dominant topography of behavior since he would continue to engage in it for extended lengths of time. Paco exhibited noncompliant behavior in the form of failing to follow simple requests or commands. When demands were made of him, he would run away and often have a tantrum.

Paco was also markedly *deficient* in the use of expressive language, self-care skills (dressing and feeding), social skills (appropriate visual and physical contact with people), and attending behavior (paying attention to, or showing interest in, toys and appropriate activities).

Occurrence percentages of appropriate and inappropriate behaviors were obtained from the structured videotape assessment. Appropriate behaviors measured were exploratory play with toys, appropriate play with toys, appropriate or in-context verbalizations, and social nonverbal behavior (responding to the presence of the adult with compliance, cooperation, or affection or initiating those behaviors with the adult). Inappropriate behaviors measured were tantrums, self-stimulation, psychotic verbalizations (out-of-context or unintelligible speech), and noncooperation in the presence of opportunities to comply. As can be seen in Figure 20.1, Paco exhibited a high percentage of inappropriate behaviors and very few of those considered to be appropriate.

Standardized Measures

Several standardized measures were also administered in order to determine Paco's level of intellectual, social, and skill functioning. The Bayley Scales of Infant Development measure motor and mental development status in children aged 2 to 30 months. Administration of these scales revealed that Paco's mental age was 1–3 and his intelligence quotient was 57. The Vineland Social Maturity Scale assesses both a social quotient and a level of social maturity in years with reference to population norms. On this measure, Paco obtained a social age of 1.3 years and a social quotient of 62. The social quotient is calculated by dividing the social age by the life age and multiplying by 100. The normative average on this test is 100. The Assessment of Children's Language Comprehension (ACLC) was also administered. This instrument assesses levels of receptive language difficulty in children aged 3 to 7 years by having them identify pic-

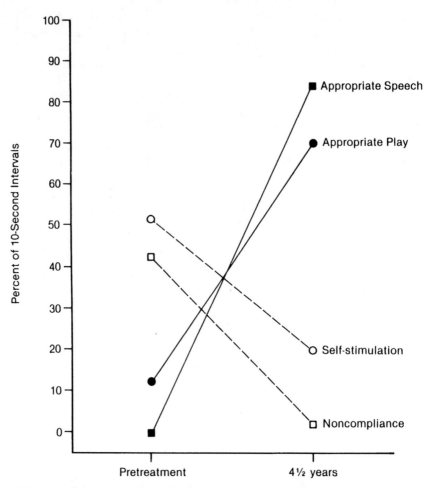

Figure 20.1.   Percent of 10-second intervals in structured observation in which
Paco exhibited appropriate play, appropriate speech, self-stimulation, and noncompliance; measured before treatment and
after 4½ years of treatment.

torial representations of increasingly complex stimuli (critical elements) and is norm referenced. Paco was untestable on this measure.

Finally, the Autism Program Training Curriculum was completed by Paco's mother and a trained therapist. This training curriculum
is designed to assess children's typical behaviors and performance
in the areas of learning readiness, fine and gross motor skills, expressive and receptive language skills, conceptual abilities, socialization,

and self-help skills. Behaviors are rated as to whether they occur often, sometimes, or never. Prior to treatment, Paco was deficient in most skill areas.

Selection of Treatment

The information obtained during the assessment phase was evaluated and served to guide the development of Paco's treatment program. Paco's behavior excesses were sure to severely impede his acquisition of appropriate behaviors. His tantrums and self-stimulatory behaviors had to be controlled in order to increase his attention to the therapists and learning tasks.

It was then necessary to increase Paco's compliance so that academic tasks could be introduced. Once this was accomplished, the simplest items from the training curriculum were targeted. Some of these included nonverbal imitation, verbal imitation of simple sounds and words, and receptive identification of colors, shapes, and objects. Nonverbal imitation was an important skill to establish so that imitation could later be used as a prompt in teaching many other behaviors (e.g., dressing, bathing, labeling). Verbal imitation of simple sounds and words was critical because it is a precursor to more advanced expressive language. Receptive labeling would help Paco become familiar with his environment and aid in the learning of concepts.

More complex tasks included learning use of pronouns, rote counting, order and causation concepts, gender identification, and sequencing. These were tasks that would be useful for Paco in his school environment as well as in his overall intellectual functioning.

Course of Treatment

First Year of Treatment

During the first three months of Paco's treatment, the majority of each clinic session (90 minutes, three times a week) was focused on reducing tantrum behaviors. We hypothesized that the tantrums served as a means to escape the educational activity. Thus, termination of the educational activity would have served to negatively reinforce the tantrum. Therefore, the first procedure used to decrease these behaviors was extinction. The therapist ignored all tantrum behaviors and continued to deliver commands to Paco (e.g., "look at me," "do this") as would occur in a regular therapy session. This procedure was coupled with differential food reinforcement for quiet behaviors. After continuous monitoring of tantrums for several weeks, it was apparent that this procedure was not effective. We next tried delivering verbal punishers (e.g., therapist saying "no crying" or "stop crying" in a loud voice) coupled with the extinction and differential reinforcement procedures described above. Tantrum behaviors still continued to occur for up to half of each therapy session and prevented treatment progress. Consequently, parental consent for the use of physical aversive procedures was obtained. A slap to the thigh or arm was administered for crying, and differential reinforcement for quiet behavior was continued. The program was effective and within a short period of time crying came under verbal control. A slap to the thigh was still given for self-injurious behaviors and physical aggression toward the therapist.

Once the tantrum behaviors were under control, work began on remediating some of Paco's behavioral deficits. The training followed a discrete trial format by which consecutive learning trials were presented. Each trial is comprised of the therapist presenting a question or command (S^D), the child's response (R), and the therapist's presenting an appropriate consequence (e.g., S^{R+}). (For a more complete description of this procedure, please see Schreibman and Koegel, 1981.)

The first behavioral deficit addressed was Paco's failure to establish eye contact. Eye contact was established using a discrete trial format and prompting procedures. That is, the therapist prompted the response by holding a small piece of candy in front of his or her eyes and giving the S^D "Paco, look at me." When the child looked at the candy, the therapist responded with the verbal consequence "good looking" and gave Paco the piece of candy. The visual prompt was gradually faded until Paco looked at the therapist in response to the S^D "look at me." Paco acquired this behavior within a few weeks. However, spontaneous eye contact always remained intermittently problematic and sometimes required additional work.

The next phase of treatment focused on nonverbal imitation. A manual prompt fading procedure was used to teach Paco to touch the table when the therapist gave the S^D "do this" and simultaneously touched the table. Once the manual prompt was successfully withdrawn, Paco was taught to imitate another behavior such as clapping hands. The procedure was repeated until Paco would imitate novel behaviors without prompts. Generalized nonverbal imitation skills were acquired within a few weeks of the first imitative behaviors.

We then began to focus on vocal imitation. There were some sounds that Paco frequently repeated as part of his self-stimulatory repertoire. These included "ah-ah-ah," "ee-ee-ee," and "ba-ba-ba." The first step in teaching vocal imitation was to bring one of these high-frequency sounds under imitative control. This was accomplished by first reinforcing that sound (e.g., ee) with a small bit of food each time it occurred. When Paco was voicing the sound several times per minute, the therapist would reinforce only those responses occurring within five seconds of the therapist's S^D "ee." A shaping procedure was used so that Paco's response was as close as possible to the original S^D. A second sound was added using the same procedure and then Paco was taught to discriminate between the two sounds and respond accordingly. Each time Paco acquired a sound, a new sound or combination of sounds was introduced. Paco was very slow to respond to vocal imitation training; the first few sounds took several months to bring under imitative control.

During this same period of time, Paco was building a receptive vocabulary. Receptive labeling skills were taught using a trial-and-error alternating two-choice discrimination paradigm. For example, two objects (e.g., boat and horse) were placed on a small table in front of Paco and the therapist alternately asked for one or the other object. Paco learned the first discrimination in approximately one month but acquired new labels relatively quickly. As is often the case, there was a "saving effect" across tasks in which initial behaviors were slow to be mastered but additional ones were mastered much more readily.

After one year of treatment, Paco had learned the receptive labels for approximately 10 objects and could imitate a few sounds but no words. The behavioral excesses, crying, screaming, hitting, and biting still continued although far less frequently or intensely than they had in the previous year.

The Second and Third Years of Treatment

Parent Training. It was equally important to work with Paco's mother so that she could teach him new skills, deal effectively with his behavior problems, and help to ensure that treatment gains would be maintained in the home environment. This was accomplished during approximately 25 hours of parent training that occurred concurrently with Paco's clinic treatment sessions. (During Paco's first year of treatment, however, parent training sessions were not conducted because of his participation in a research project designed to compare the effects of clinic treatment only with parent training only.)

When parent training was initiated, Paco's mother was asked to read a manual on behavioral management techniques (Baker, Brightman, Heifetz, & Murphy, 1976) and a manual describing the specifics of teaching autistic children (Koegel & Schreibman, 1982). Parent training sessions consisted of discussing the reading material and reviewing a parent training videotape. Paco's mother also did considerable amounts of reading on her own.

She then began to observe trained therapists working with Paco during clinic treatment sessions. First with the help of the therapists and then on her own, she also worked with Paco in the clinic. Continual feedback was given to her during those sessions. Concurrently, she began to develop home treatment programs with the help of the clinic parent trainers. Two such programs were increasing Paco's eye contact and teaching language skills. Programs similar to those in use at the clinic were implemented for the behaviors at home.

Behavioral Deficits: Language Training.   The receptive labeling program continued until Paco was learning several new labels each day. He seemed to enjoy learning new labels and would "ask" the names of unfamiliar objects by pointing to them and making some sort of a vocalization. We also began training expressive language skills. For example, the therapist held up a piece of food and said, "What do you want?" Paco then received reinforcement for making the sound "ee" (for "eat"). The expressive labels for several objects were taught using a similar procedure. Paco's articulation was very poor, and at this stage of treatment only his regular therapists and family members could understand what he was saying.

At approximately 1½ years into treatment, Paco spontaneously made his first sentence. This occurred at a birthday party in the clinic for one of the other children. Paco went over to one of the therapists who was eating some birthday cake and said "ee foo" (i.e., eat food). Of course, Paco was given some of the cake and he repeated "ee foo" until the therapist's cake was gone. This event seemed to be a turning point for Paco, and he rapidly learned to ask for desired objects in three word sentences such as "I want cookie" and "I want peanut." Despite his increased use of language, Paco's articulation was still very poor and a large portion of his clinic time was spent on articulation training using shaping and prompting procedures. Other expressive language skills taught included answering simple questions such as "What is your name?" and "How old are you?" For responding to questions to which he had no answer, he was taught to say, "I don't know." Language training for receptive skills included shapes, colors, prepositions, and following two- and three-part commands.

Behavioral Excesses. Paco was still displaying his compulsive attachment to long cylindrical objects, usually sticks or Tinker Toy dowels. This attachment was so pervasive that he carried these objects, one in each hand, at all times during the day and would scream incessantly if the objects were removed. Simply taking the objects from him was not effective in reducing the compulsive behavior nor was it effective in reducing the length of tantrums resulting from the removal of the objects. A fading procedure was implemented which consisted of gradually reducing the size of the objects (by cutting off the ends) to very small pieces and eventually they were faded altogether. Although Paco would still pick up sticks and other cylindrical objects, the procedure was effective in reducing the compulsive aspects of the behavior. Paco's mother was also able to greatly reduce his self-stimulatory rocking by physically stopping the behavior and firmly saying "No rocking."

Paco's tantrums at home occurred several times per week and consisted of crying, screaming, jumping up and down, and shouting "no." The original procedure used by his mother for decreasing tantrums was to send Paco to time-out in his bedroom. This procedure was subsequently changed to time-out sitting on a kitchen chair because Paco was urinating and defecating in the bedroom. The new time-out procedure was effective and was adopted as a procedure for decreasing many of Paco's inappropriate behaviors. However, time-out was not effective for self-injurious behavior and a slap to the thigh or arm was still necessary to control this behavior.

Interestingly, as Paco's repertoire of behavioral skills became more elaborate, he incorporated these newly acquired skills, such as language and toileting, into methods for manipulating his environment. A prominent example of this occurred after Paco had been toilet trained at school. He apparently enjoyed this activity and asked to "go potty" frequently. If he was not allowed to go, he would threaten to "pee pants." This threat usually resulted in Paco being taken to the bathroom – thus serving as an escape from work. The program used to decrease this behavior during clinic sessions was simply to "call his bluff." That is, his threats were ignored and escape was not forthcoming. We predicted that this would be effective since not only was the behavior not negatively reinforced (i.e., escape) but we knew that Paco became upset whenever anything wet or sticky touched his body. As predicted, the procedure was immediately effective. The treatment program implemented by Paco's mother involved initially letting Paco go to the toilet once every 15 minutes and gradually increasing this time interval. Other requests to go to the toilet were ignored. During the early stages of the program, Paco would also urinate on his bedroom floor. Paco's mother employed a restitution procedure in which Paco cleaned the floor where he had urinated. Appropriate toileting at appropriate times was achieved shortly thereafter.

Paco's mother also gained extensive control over several of Paco's manipulative behaviors. She accomplished this by stating the contingencies to Paco and, if he failed to comply, removing a preferred toy. This was done consistently until Paco learned his attempts to manipulate would fail, and he discontinued these behaviors.

Fourth and Fifth Years of Treatment

Behavioral Deficit: Language Skills. The language program during this period focused on teaching receptive and expressive skills for the correct use of pronouns (e.g., your/my, his/her); counting from 1 to 30; recognizing and naming upper- and lowercase letters of the alphabet and the numbers from 1 to 30; the concepts of before, after, why, when, first, and last; and organizing two and three picture cards depicting a sequence of events. Paco was also taught to recite his address and phone number and to use the concepts in the calendar (i.e., days of the week and months of the year). Paco's speech became much more spontaneous than it had been in the previous year. He asked for things he wanted and answered questions using novel phrases and sentences other than the rote answers he had been taught. This spontaneity and creativity in language was particularly encouraging.

Behavioral Deficit: Self-care Skills. As part of the training program, Paco's mother devised programs using shaping and chaining to teach Paco to dress himself, make his bed, comb his hair, brush his teeth, and take a bath. At this point, only minimal assistance from the therapists was required.

Behavioral Excesses. Problems in this area included Paco running away from his mother when they were out in public (e.g., at the grocery store), walking up to strangers and grabbing them, and stepping on people's feet. Paco's mother spanked Paco whenever the first two behaviors occurred. At the same time, she recorded their frequency of occurrence. When Paco stepped on someone's feet, his mother would step on his feet or ask the "victim" to do so. These consequences were effective in that Paco's mother's records showed a rapid decline in the behaviors until, finally, they completely ceased to occur.

Paco's tantrum behavior was relatively infrequent by then. Instead, Paco used his language skills to try to get out of work situations. His responses to requests to work included, "No, it's hard," "Do I have to work all day and all night?," "I can't," "I don't have to," and so on. Although in this area Paco's behavior was quite normal, he still engaged in some bizarre behavioral excesses. His interest in cylindrical objects was now expressed by frequently talking about pipes, hoses, knives, saws, and hatchets. Unless the conversation was directed to other topics by an adult, Paco often spoke of nothing else. In addition, he would occasionally mimic the action of saws, knives, and hatchets by rubbing his hand back and forth in a sawlike fashion over his arm or other part of his body. This behavior was occasioned when he was physically hurt (e.g., fell down). Such rubbing frequently escalated into self-injurious behavior wherein he would leave marks on his body or sometimes draw blood. To remedy this, Paco's mother instituted a token economy in which he earned pennies for engaging in appropriate behaviors such as completing his household chores and complying with parental requests. Pennies were taken away contingent upon any of the target behaviors (self-injury; talking about hoses, hatchets, etc.; noncompliance). Paco could spend his pennies during a weekly trip to the store. If he had lost the money, he was unable to purchase anything. His mother then reiterated the contingencies to him. Within a matter of a few weeks, the target behaviors ceased to occur and the token economy became unnecessary.

While Paco's mother continues to have intermittent contacts with the therapists, she has become quite proficient at designing and implementing behavior management programs on her own. We feel that her participation has contributed significantly to Paco's treatment gains and will continue to play a major role in his future development.

Termination and Follow-up

Because of the nature and severity of the autistic syndrome, it is typically considered a life-span disorder. As such, one rarely comes to a termination point in treatment. Rather, as the child progresses, the treatment targets change as old needs are met and new ones arise. Such is the case with Paco. After 4½ years of intensive treatment, we can look back on his progress to date and look ahead to the more advanced treatment targets we will need to address in the future.

We look first at progress as measured by observational and standardized assessments. Figure 20.1 presents the pretreatment-to-present changes in Paco's inappropriate and appropriate behaviors. As can be seen there has been a dramatic increase in targeted appropriate behaviors (e.g., speech and play) and decrease in inappropriate behaviors (e.g., self-stimulation and noncompliance). Similar changes were noted in the dinnertime home videotape measures. In addition, where the Bayley Scales placed him at an IQ of 57 at pretreatment, after 4½ years of treatment he achieved an IQ of 98 on the Leiter International Performance Scale. Paco's social quotient as measured by the Vineland Social Maturity Scale rose from a pretreatment low of 62 to a current level of 117. Importantly, on the ACLC Paco was untestable at pretreatment yet recently reached a ceiling on this language assessment.

We can also evaluate Paco's progress by looking at other generalized effects of treatment. For example, he has advanced from a very highly structured classroom for the severely handicapped to a current class for the communicatively handicapped which also involves mainstreaming in a normal classroom for 40% of the day. Other important changes in Paco's behavior include learning from observing others, greatly increased social awareness and responsiveness (e.g., "Why is she sad?" "Will you play with me?" "I love you, Mommy."), more contextually appropriate emotional responses, and increased tolerance for demands made upon him. His language is no longer as concrete and literal as it once was. He can understand stories, make up his own stories, and use metaphoric language (to a limited extent). He frequently seeks information by asking questions of others. For example, seeing a workman using a piece of machinery may trigger a string of questions such as "What is that machine?" "What is he doing?" "Will it hurt me?" A particularly positive change is Paco's increased attachment to others. An example is his appropriate response to loss of a significant person. One of the authors explained to Paco that she was moving away and thus would not be seeing him anymore. Since she had worked with him for three years, it proved to be an emotional moment for both. As one might expect of any normal child this age, Paco, obviously unhappy, withdrew and announced, "I don't like you anymore."

In many ways Paco seems like a normal six-year-old boy. However, as mentioned above, improvements are accompanied by the need to address new target behaviors. In this case, the new targets involve more subtle and sophisticated behaviors. Specifically, Paco's speech, while contextually and semantically excellent, is dysprosic. His vocal articulation, rhythm, and intonation are still not normal, and a good deal of our present efforts are directed at improving his vocal production. Also, he still has difficulty interacting with peers in play and conversation. We are also addressing this need. Perhaps the most important target for Paco's treatment is enhancing the generalization of his treatment gains. While he learns readily, he also can discriminate when and if contingencies are present. If they are not, he may revert to some of his noncompliant behaviors. We are now instituting programs to ensure that treatment gains generalize to new environments and people.

Overall Evaluation

Everyone involved in Paco's treatment has reason to be pleased. We initiated treatment with a noncompliant, tantrumous, totally nonverbal little boy of two and now have a more cooperative, conversational, near-normal six-year-old. While Paco's progress is impressive, it needs to be put into perspective.

First, it should be noted that this child has probably progressed further than many nonverbal autistic children. The reasons for his progress (independent of clinic efforts) probably include: (1) early age at start of treatment; (2) relatively mild self-stimulation; (3) intense parent involvement in treatment; and (4) lack of mental retardation.

Second, Paco's progress is also the result of thousands of intensive treatment hours. Particularly in the early stages of treatment, progress was slow. Between the clinic, his mother, and the school, he was in an almost total treatment environment. It is unlikely that such improvement would have been achieved without this investment of time and effort.

Third, he still has a way to go before he is completely "normal," and vigilance in monitoring his behavior will be necessary for years to come. There probably will be subtle behavioral problems that will need to be addressed in the future. We hope that these will be mild and anticipate that because of a motivated and trained mother, they can be dealt with appropriately.

Given the gains achieved so far and the direction of current treatment, the acquisition of increasingly subtle and complex behaviors is anticipated. We foresee a very favorable prognosis in this case.

References

Baker, B. L., Brightman, A. J., Heiftez, L. J., & Murphy, D. M. (1976). *Behavior problems*. Chicago: Research Press.

Koegel, R. L., & Schreibman, L. (1982). *How to teach autistic and other severely handicapped children*. Lawrence, KS: H & H Enterprises.

Schreibman, L., & Koegel, R. L. (1981). A guideline for planning behavior modification programs for autistic children. In S. M. Turner & H. E. Adams (Eds.), *Handbook of clinical behavior therapy* (pp. 500–526). New York: Wiley.

21

Anorexia Nervosa

Francis C. Harris

Description of Anorexia Nervosa

The Diagnostic and Statistical Manual of the American Psychiatric Association (*DSM-III*) (American Psychiatric Association, 1980) outlines the primary features of anorexia as (1) loss of 25% of original body weight (adjusted for growth if under the age of 18), (2) distorted body image, (3) intense fear of becoming obese, (4) refusal to maintain normal body weight, and (5) no known physical illness that would account for the weight loss.

Anorexia occurs predominantly in females (85–95%), during adolescence or young adulthood. Although precise statistics regarding the incidence of anorexia are not available due to inconsistent diagnostic criteria and inadequate records, there are data suggesting that the prevalence of the disorder is increasing. Although methodologically adequate investigations regarding the prevalence of anorexia are lacking, conservative estimates suggest one in every 250 females develops the disorder, with girls 12–18 years of age at particular risk. Psychological and social characteristics which have been associated with anorexia include an intense fear of eating in the presence of others, idiosyncratic and monotonous diets (particularly prevalent is the avoidance of carbohydrates and fats), preoccupation with food, binging, vomiting, laxative abuse, hyperactivity, stealing, and lying. Recent attempts to identify subtypes of anorexia have focused on consummatory patterns, dividing anorexia into "restricters" or "abstainers," those who control weight by rigorous caloric restriction, and "bulimics," those whose weight loss is a function of vomiting and/or laxative and diuretic abuse. A related disorder is bulimia, in which binging and purging is used to maintain a *normal* weight.

Case Identification and Presenting Complaint

Marcia Morrison was a 16-year-old white high school junior who lived in an upper-middle-class suburban neighborhood with her mother, father, 14-year-old sister, and 9-year-old brother. Mr. Morrison was a business executive and Mrs. Morrison was a homemaker. Marcia had been an above average student throughout elementary and high schools, engaged in a variety of extracurricular activities, and enjoyed several close social relationships with female and male peers. She dated periodically but had not been sexually active.

Upon presentation Marcia was 5 feet 2 inches tall and weighed 91 lb. She had been binging and vomiting one or two times per day for three months. She often consumed more than 5,000 calories during binges which consisted almost solely of foods high in fat and carbohydrate. Virtually all of her intake was achieved during binges. She refused to eat unless she could be sure that she would be able to consume a quantity of food great enough to enable her to induce vomiting easily. Thus, even though she was consuming huge quantities of food she was, in fact, starving herself. She had been amenorrheic for five months. Marcia and her parents described a marked change in her mood and behavior pattern during the few months prior to presentation. Specifically, she withdrew from extracurricular activities and casual social contacts and spent most of her time alone in her room. She became extremely "irritable" at home, engaging in almost daily disputes with parents and/or siblings, and refused to eat or sit with the family at mealtimes.

History

Marcia had been somewhat overweight throughout early childhood and preadolescence. She gained weight rapidly after puberty and by age 15 she weighed 165 lb. and was 5 feet 1 inch tall. She reported becoming very upset over her overweight condition and resolved to lose weight. She began a course of dieting after reading several articles and books in the popular literature. After approximately three months of dieting, she had lost only four pounds and became even more upset with her failure. She had read about the use of vomiting as a weight control method and after an especially large meal one evening Marcia, feeling very uncomfortable and guilty over overeating once again, induced vomiting. She experienced immediate relief and, as is often the case, believed she had discovered the "perfect solution" which would enable her to eat whatever she wanted without gaining weight. For the next several months she relied on binging and vomiting, rather than a systematic reduction in her intake, to lose weight. Unfortunately, this method was quite effective, and her weight decreased approximately 70 lb. in less than nine months.

Assessment

The Beck Depression Inventory (BDI) is a 21-item self-report instrument that assesses the presence and severity of various behaviors and feelings commonly associated with depression. A score of greater than 20 is considered "depressed." Since depressive features are seen quite often in eating disorder patients, it is almost always advisable to conduct such an assessment. Prior to treatment Marcia scored 32 on the BDI.

The Eating Attitudes Test (EAT) also was administered. The EAT is a 40-item, forced-choice, self-report questionnaire that quantifies features commonly associated with anorexia nervosa. A higher score is indicative of a more severe eating disturbance, with a score above 30 in the "anorexic range." Upon presentation Marcia's total EAT score was 64.

A physical examination revealed no significant abnormalities other than amenorrhea.

Marcia had been a very compliant and sensitive child who had presented no major problems. Mr. and Mrs. Morrison were very close with their children and were actively involved in many of their activities in and outside the home.

Marcia reported that until one year prior to presentation she had experienced no prolonged periods of dysphoria nor was she particularly concerned about her overweight condition. As she entered her 16th year two significant changes occurred. First, she began to feel uncomfortable with her new opportunities to be independent from her parents. She did not believe that any of her friends were experiencing such feelings and became concerned that she was somehow "different." Second, Marcia began to experience the discomfort typically associated with adolescents' preoccupation with body image. Unfortunately, her obesity exacerbated these feelings such that she began to spend "hours at a time" simply worrying over her plight. After she began to vomit to achieve weight loss Marcia reported beginning to "use" binging and vomiting to reduce feelings of anxiety and depression. As she put it, "I didn't have time to be nervous or upset because I had to concentrate too hard on losing weight." The primary issues in this case were conceptualized after six hours of interviews with the patient and her parents and a review of a diary kept for two weeks by Marcia. The topics covered in the interviews and diary have been presented elsewhere (Harris, Hsu, & Phelps, 1983; Harris & Phelps, 1985).

The following composition by Marcia, written four weeks after presentation, is included to give the reader an understanding of Marcia's preoccupation with her weight and her perception of its importance in various areas of her life.

> There are a lot of good things about losing weight and trying to keep it off. I've finally gotten myself to a point where I've started to look like everyone else, the guys at school are treating me nice and every one [sic] is treating me like a normal person. I can walk through the mall or at a game without everyone laughing at me. Im [sic] still not as skinny as I think I should be, but things are getting better. I don't know how I can keep from getting fat again. Thats [sic] the bad part. I'd like to eat like everyone else, maybe not all the junk, but just the regular food. I can't though, because as soon as I eat something I gain weight. I can't do that. And I know thats [sic] what will happen if I eat and I'd never want that. The worst thing in the world is to be fat, its [sic] worse than being dead. Sometimes I get so hungry I just can't help it and I eat everything, then I get so upset and I hate myself and then I make myself throw up. Thats [sic] bad too, but it works and I have to if I don't want to get fat. Its [sic] kind of scary but I don't know what else to do. People are trying to push food at me all the time and I get so sick of it I want to die. Why can't they let me alone? Things are finally getting good and they're trying to ruin it and I won't let them make me fat again. I can't do it. My parents will do anything for me if I eat. I guess I kind of use this against them but I end up getting rid of the food and they're still happy. It seems to be the perfect solution, but something inside me tells me its [sic] wrong, but I can't help it. I just want to stay happy, lose my heavy legs and hips and have everyone off my back, but I don't know if this is possible. I'm trying, its [sic] really important to be thin and I don't want to be different. I just want to fit in with everybody else.

Selection of Treatment

Based upon the obtained assessment information, a three-component behavior therapy program was designed. The first component focused on the training of skills that would enable Marcia to manage her own eating behavior such that she would monitor carefully her intake, eat regular meals, and maintain a "normal" weight of 125 lb without binging and vomiting. The specifics of the self-management program, which include the use of self-instructions to minimize binging and vomiting, have been described elsewhere (Harris & Phelps, 1985; Stuart & Davis, 1972). The second component was a cognitive behavioral intervention designed to provide Marcia with a means to generate alternative self-statements to use whenever she experienced urges to binge and vomit. The steps in this process were (1) identification of the problem situation, (2) listing possible alternative activities, (3) evaluating the potential short- and long-term consequences of each alternative, and (4) selecting the "best" alternative under the circumstances. The third component, to which was devoted approximately one fourth of each session, consisted of an ongoing discussion of the "independence crisis" Marcia had been experiencing. These discussions were intended to provide a background for the more discrete aspects of the treatment program. The main theme of these discussions was to point out the relationship between Marcia's eating problems and the difficulties associated with her ongoing independence and emancipation from her parents.

Course of Treatment

Marcia was seen twice weekly during the first three weeks of treatment. During this period the intake self-management program was initiated, self-instructions were developed, and the dialogue regarding independence was started. By the end of the third week Marcia had gone eight consecutive days without binging and vomiting and her weight had increased from 91 to 100 lb. She had consumed approximately 1,100 calories per day. In addition, after several discussions it appeared that Marcia understood the relationship between her eating behavior and other stressful events she had been experiencing. Neither she nor her parents reported any changes in her social withdrawal and frequent disputes with her family. During the next six months, meetings were held weekly. Marcia's weight increased gradually to the target weight of 125 lb. She reported eight episodes of binging and vomiting during the six-month period. The circumstances of each of these episodes were reviewed, and it was clear that each one had been triggered by disputes with one of her parents. These disputes centered on issues such as curfew time and Marcia's choice of friends. These issues were discussed in the context of Marcia's ongoing struggle for independence.

During the subsequent nine months Marcia binged and vomited only five times and went as long as three months without an episode. Marcia and her parents reported gradual improvements in her "mood" and social life. However, during that period her weight increased to 160 lb., approximately 35 lb. above her "target weight."

At first Marcia was quite distressed over her weight gain but remained determined not to return to her binge–vomit pattern. The therapist became concerned that the weight gain would lead to a recurrence of Marcia's chaotic eating patterns. This seemed especially likely since being overweight appeared to be one of the factors contributing to the onset of the problem. However, since it appeared that Marcia was making considerable progress in all areas except the maintenance of a "normal" weight, and that prior to the onset of anorexia she had been generally well adjusted at a relatively high weight, the therapist suggested that the weight management program be discontinued. Following the termination of weight loss efforts Marcia was seen on a monthly basis for six months. During that period she maintained improvements she had made in terms of returning to her premorbid patterns of social interaction with peers and family members and had no episodes of binging and vomiting.

Follow-up

Marcia was seen for three-month and six-month follow-up visits. She reported no episodes of binging and vomiting during the follow-up period. She completed the BDI and EAT at the three-month follow-up and scored within the normal range (6 and 14, respectively) on both instruments. She continued to engage in frequent social activities with male and female peers during the follow-up period. Her weight remained in the 160–165 lb. range. Following is an excerpt from the three-month follow-up interview.

Therapist: How have things been going at home in the last few weeks?

Patient: Not as bad as it used to be. It's still not wonderful, but it's not constant screaming at each other all the time.

Therapist: What do you think has made it different?

Patient: I don't know. My mother's not constantly watching me. A few months ago I'd walk upstairs and she'd follow me just to see what I was doing. I'd be sitting in my room reading a book or something and she would walk past the door to make sure what I was doing. She was driving me crazy.

Therapist: Why do you think she's not doing that now?

Patient: I don't know. She seems like she trusts me a little more. She lets me do more.

Therapist: Is that good?

Patient: Yeah.

Therapist: Something just came over her?

Patient: I don't know. She's just different.

Therapist: Is there anything that you have done that could be responsible?

Patient: She said that as long as I'm not giving her any reason to think I'm doing something stupid she's not gonna bother me.

Therapist: How would you characterize yourself? How would you compare yourself now to when you were right in the middle of your binging and vomiting?

Patient: Lots of people, just recently, have said to me "You're finally yourself." This is me, not somebody else that they didn't even know.

Therapist: Who said that to you?

Patient: A lot of my friends said: "We'd say stuff to each other but we could never talk to you and you were just someone that we didn't even know and we couldn't talk to you. We didn't know what you were doing."

Therapist: So it's different. They're telling you. How about from your point of view? How does it compare to when you were really into it?

Patient: It's really different. I didn't do anything. I mean I didn't talk to anybody, I didn't go out and do anything. Now it's all different.

Therapist: How about the way you feel about yourself?

Patient: I'd still like to be thinner but I'm not going to kill myself over it.

Therapist: How about your moods? Are they any different now?

Patient: Before I always felt like saying "Get away from me, I
don't want anybody near me" and I couldn't stand anybody looking at me or watching me. People can't understand when I say
that I'm finally me. That sounds really stupid but it's true. And
I don't know what . . . I mean, when I think of some of the stuff
I used to do, I think "you had to be crazy." I mean, was that really
me?

Therapist: What kind of stuff?

Patient: I used to set my alarm all the time, like every two hours
and then I'd get up and I'd exercise like 2 o'clock to 4 o'clock and
I just would do that all the time. I never slept. And I wouldn't
eat. I would just go and exercise instead of eat and if I did eat
anything at all I'd go throw it up even more, which was stupid.

Therapist: Were any of the specific things that we did especially
helpful for you?

Patient: Yeah. When I wrote down what I was really eating I
thought, "that's nothing." It isn't anything. And I was sitting at
home, sitting there eating, and it was like this is tons of food, and
I'm going to gain 50 pounds from eating and it was really nothing. When I saw what it actually was, I didn't feel so bad. When
I saw on the paper, how many calories I was eating and how
much that I needed just to stay where I was; it wasn't anywhere
near it. It helped me. I didn't feel so bad then.

Therapist: How about the meal plan? Was that helpful to you?

Patient: Yeah, because before I'd either eat nothing or I'd eat
everything. I mean I'd just go and I would just eat everything.

Therapist: How is it different now?

Patient: If I write down what I'm going to eat then I'll get that.
Or if I have it there then I'll get that instead of just running and
getting anything. It's better that way.

Therapist: We talked a lot about independence and growing up.
Was any of that helpful for you?

Patient: I think it was weird. I mean, I was the only person who
didn't want to grow up and get out of here. I mean, I didn't want
to leave home. No matter how much I got yelled at or anything.
I think it was really strange. No one else felt like that. I felt like

I was the only one and I was afraid to say anything to anybody because everyone would think I was really strange or something.

Therapist: If you said what?

Patient: That I didn't want . . . you know, didn't want to grow up and don't want to, you know . . . be more independent.

Therapist: Was having problems with your eating one way to say that without really saying it?

Patient: Yeah, cause everybody treated me like I was still a little kid.

Therapist: How did that feel? Was it a way to get that attention without really having to ask for it like a little kid?

Patient: Yeah. Cause I could have anything I wanted then and they'd do anything for me.

Therapist: Yeah, so it's been a long time. But you're doing extremely well. We have to see how it works for the next few months. And especially since you're going away to school in two months. Are you anticipating any problems with that?

Patient: No. I don't completely want to go, but I'll get used to it. Before the whole idea really scared me, but I'm kind of looking forward to it now.

Overall Evaluation

This case study describes the cognitive behavioral treatment of anorexia in an adolescent female. The author found it to be especially instructive in that it highlights the importance of being *flexible* in the implementation of a treatment program. One of the initial treatment goals was to have the patient maintain a weight of 125–130 lb. This goal was dropped when it became clear that Marcia was able to refrain from binging and vomiting, remain free of self-deprecating thoughts associated with her eating patterns, and engage in a full and active social life at a higher weight.

References

American Psychiatric Association. (1980). *Diagnostic and statistical manual of mental disorders* (3rd ed.). Washington, DC: Author.
Harris, F. C., Hsu, L. K. G., & Phelps, C. F. (1983). Problems in adolescence:

Assessment and treatment of bulimia nervosa. In M. Hersen (Ed.), *Outpatient behavior therapy: A clinical guide*. New York: Grune & Stratton.

Harris, F. C., & Phelps, C. F. (1985). Anorexia nervosa. In M. Hersen, & A. S. Bellack (Eds.), *Handbook of clinical behavior therapy with adults*. New York: Plenum.

Stuart, R. B., & Davis, B. (1972). *Slim chance in a fat world: Behavioral control of obesity*. Champaign, IL: Research Press.

22

Tantrums

John C. Piacentini
Elizabeth A. Schaughency
Benjamin B. Lahey

Description of Tantrums

In general, tantrums can be characterized as a constellation of noxious behaviors such as screaming, yelling, crying, kicking, biting, scratching, and hitting that most commonly develop between the ages of 18 and 36 months. These outbursts can range in severity from mild yelling or crying to severe and potentially harmful attacks. Tantrums can be particularly upsetting to inexperienced parents and pose an important challenge to parental control and often set the stage for coercive interchanges and conflict.

In operant terms, tantrums may be viewed as behavior that is reinforced either through negative reinforcement (termination of a demand or restriction on the child) or positive reinforcement (adult attention). Tantrums are salient events that are very likely to bring about some adult reaction that may be reinforcing. Inconsistent response to these outbursts may not only lead to intensification of the tantrums, but may also increase resistance to extinction. Moreover, because it is these behaviors that are reinforced, rather than more appropriate coping strategies, the child may fail to develop the adaptive behaviors necessary to comply with adult requests and adequately deal with frustration.

Case Identification

Cindy was an attractive four-year-and-four-month-old Caucasian female who had no siblings. She was normal in height and weight for her age and had no serious health problems. At the time of the initial assessment, Cindy resided in an apartment with her mother, Ms. C., and had just begun her second year of preschool. At that time, Ms. C. had been divorced from Cindy's father for over two years and was employed as secretary for a local physician. Cindy has had only infrequent and irregular contact with her father since the divorce. Ms. C., a 23-year-old high school graduate, reported a long history of alcohol and drug abuse as a teenager. She reported a rather turbulent adolescence, and described herself during that time as a constant "partier" who cared little for school or her future. She reported, however, that she had totally abstained from drugs and alcohol for several years and regularly attends meetings of Alcoholics Anonymous. In general, Ms. C. seemed to be well adjusted, but to be somewhat displeased with her life in general. Specifically, she voiced concerns about the relative lack of direction in her life; she appeared to have no clear goals for the future. There were no major physical health problems in either family. According to Ms. C., Cindy's father and his parents drink heavily, and the maternal grandmother was described as chronically dysthmic.

Presenting Complaints

Cindy was brought to the University of Georgia Psychology Clinic by her mother because of concerns about temper tantrums, problems at bedtime (refusal to sleep alone), and the mother's overall difficulties in behavior management. Cindy's tantrums were characterized by lying on the floor, flailing her arms and legs, screaming, yelling, and crying. These tantrums would usually last several minutes, and Ms. C. reported that the frequency of tantrums was approximately one per day. Ms. C. reported being inconsistent in her response to these outbursts, with ignoring Cindy and giving in to Cindy's demands being the two most common consequences. Ms. C. reported that more intense tantrums would occur about once a month. These outbursts usually would take place when Ms. C. and Cindy were alone in the car. In addition to the behaviors described above, Cindy would also scratch, bite, and attempt to choke her mother. Typical maternal responses to these more severe tantrums included physical and/or verbal punishment (i.e., hitting or screaming at the child), but on some occasions the mother complied with Cindy's demands.

Cindy's tantrums were most likely to be displayed under the following circumstances: (1) when Ms. C. attempted to set limits on Cindy's behavior; (2) when Ms. C. made a request for compliance from Cindy; and (3) when Ms. C. failed to comply with Cindy's demands. She described bedtime and leaving Cindy with a babysitter as especially difficult times. In addition, Ms. C. reported that Cindy becomes very upset when she sees her father. Her teacher did not report behavioral problems nor did she observe tantrums in the preschool setting.

History

Cindy was the product of an unplanned pregnancy that led to her mother's marriage at age 18 to her former husband. Ms. C.'s pregnancy with Cindy was normal and ended in an uneventful Caeserian delivery. Her mother described Cindy as having a relatively "easy" infant temperament and as reaching developmental milestones within normal limits. Specifically, Cindy sat at 6 months, stood alone at 12 months, and began speaking in single words at around 14 months.

Ms. C. first recalls problems with Cindy at about one year of age when Cindy began to "whine" a great deal. In addition, Cindy would appear anxious, become very "clingy" and cry for no apparent reason. Ms. C. responded to these and other problematic behaviors by nursing Cindy when she appeared to be unhappy. Ms. C. reported that this usually pacified the child. She continued nursing Cindy until she was 22 months old; after this time, Ms. C. used physical affection, such as hugging, stroking, and kissing in order to stop Cindy's whining and tantrums. It seemed clear that these responses to Cindy's whining and clinging reinforced this class of behavior.

Mother–child interaction patterns have also been characterized by the mother as giving in to Cindy's demands, especially when she behaved in ways that were aversive to the mother. Ms. C. reported usually backing down from a request or giving in to a demand of Cindy's in response to tantruming by the child. An example of this was Cindy's demand to sleep with her mother. Although Ms. C. had repeatedly tried to have Cindy sleep in her own room, her refusal to comply and accompanying tantrums resulted in being allowed to sleep with her mother every night.

Ms. C. reported that she and Cindy had occasionally seen a therapist at the local community mental health center over a one-year period prior to contacting the Psychology Clinic. She said that she had initially contacted the mental health center for help in dealing with Cindy's maladaptive behavior, but that they had assessed the child and reported that there seemed to be nothing wrong with her.

Course of Treatment

Following assessment, a session was devoted to explaining the rationale for the proposed treatment to Ms. C. and introduction of treatment. The goals in providing the client with the case formulation were: (1) to introduce Ms. C. to behavioral principles as they related to the development and maintenance of Cindy's tantrums, and (2) to provide the basis for parent training in childrearing methods. Because of the mother's role in the acquisition and maintenance of Cindy's tantrums, care was taken not to "blame" Ms. C. for the problem. Rather, she was told that her responses to Cindy's responses were the usual and understandable responses of a loving parent. However, it was made explicit that her well-intentioned responses were inadvertently teaching Cindy to behave badly.

The introduction to treatment followed the case formulation sequentially and logically. During the latter part of the first treatment session, Ms. C. was taught the use of time-out and extinction to eliminate noncompliance and tantrums. Although didactic in nature, the therapist individualized the presentation by referring to specific instances of Cindy's noncompliance and tantruming. Specifically, Ms. C. was instructed to use the following rules of discipline:

1. When Ms. C. had made an appropriate request of Cindy, the mother would, within reason, *never* change or remove the request as a result of Cindy's noncompliance or tantruming. As an example, Ms. C. was told, "When we were talking to you and Cindy at the playground, I remember that you told Cindy that it was time to leave and she pitched a little fit. You had seemed pretty sure that you wanted to leave, but you hesitated when she became upset and said that she could stay a few minutes more. That was a loving, generous thing to do in one sense, but it had the effect of *teaching* Cindy that she can get her way if she throws a tantrum. In effect, you're telling her we'll do what mom wants if you behave nicely, and what Cindy wants if you behave badly. One thing that we need to do in order to teach

Cindy not to throw tantrums is to show her that they no longer will cause you to give in. From now on, you must *never* give in to her just because she has a temper tantrum. If you have made an appropriate request of her, *never* let a tantrum make you back down. Now, no parent is perfect; we all catch ourselves making mistakes from time to time, but try to come as close as possible to never giving in to a temper tantrum."

2. Ms. C. was instructed to explain to Cindy that evening that Cindy would be sleeping in her own bed from now on. Ms. C. was told to take Cindy to bed, tuck her in, and leave the room promptly. Ms. C. was to ignore all requests to leave the room, except for the first request to use the bathroom, and was not to go to Cindy's room again until morning unless she had reason to believe that some unusual circumstance posed a danger to Cindy. In particular, tantruming was to be ignored. If Cindy left the room at any time during the night, the mother was to tell her firmly, but not harshly, to return to her room. If Cindy did not go to her room, her mother was to take her to bed without any further comment and promptly leave the room. This procedure was to be repeated as frequently as necessary. Support was provided to Ms. C., as she anticipated the difficulties involved in the early stages of implementing this procedure. In particular, it was (a) admitted that it would require a great deal of effort, loss of sleep, and patience, but that (b) it would quickly make life more pleasant for both mother and child.

3. Ms. C. was told to use time-out to punish tantrums that involved any form of verbal or physical aggression. Specifically, she was told to send Cindy to her room for five minutes after every instance of aggression. If Cindy left the room before the time was up, she was to be returned with only a brief comment and the five-minute interval was to be started again. Tantruming in her room during time out was to be ignored, but Cindy was not to be allowed out of her room until the tantruming had ceased for approximately one minute.

Again, Ms. C. anticipated the difficulty of implementing this procedure with considerable negative emotion. Support was again provided, but it was also emphasized that use of time-out provides an opportunity for the child to learn that the parent is now in control. Ms. C. was specifically told: "You're right. You're going to go through hell getting her to stay in time-out. But when you stop and think about it, it's an excellent time to teach Cindy that mom is now the boss. You will be creating a confrontation that you will be fully prepared to win. If you follow the rules we've laid out, you'll easily win and she will have learned an important lesson about who is the boss."

Tantrums that occurred in the car were to be ignored if they were not aggressive or were to be consequated with time-out if they were aggressive. Time-out could be delayed until they reached home or could be implemented by pulling off the road and ignoring Cindy for five minutes (while physically fending off aggression), but was not to be terminated until the tantrum had ceased for one minute.

4. Ms. C. was instructed to positively reinforce Cindy for compliance with praise, hugs, pats on the head, and the like.

In the following session, Ms. C. reported immediate success in all areas except bedtime management, saying she was unable to ignore Cindy's demands to sleep with her. At this point, the importance of not giving in to Cindy's coercive demands was reemphasized, and the therapist provided Ms. C. with a technique for explaining the new bedtime rule using hand puppets.

Ms. C. was told to make hand puppets at home from small paper bags and let Cindy use crayons to color one to look like herself and one to look like her mother. Ms. C. was told to explain the new bedtime rules to Cindy again and then to use the puppets to enact the new rules. She was told to initially use both puppets herself and have the mother puppet put the Cindy puppet to bed. The Cindy puppet was to whine, beg, complain, and get out of bed, and the mother puppet was to implement the rules calmly and firmly. Next, the mother was to repeat the puppet enactment two times, first with Cindy using the Cindy puppet and then with Cindy using the mother puppet. Ms. C. later reported that Cindy cooperated well with this procedure and seemed to understand this enactment.

Termination

In the next session, Ms. C. stated that implementation of the new discipline methods had been successful in dealing with Cindy's bedtime behavior. In addition, Ms. C. reported continued success with the other child-management techniques described above. Therefore, treatment was terminated at this time contingent upon continued success. In the remainder of the session, general parental management techniques were discussed again in an attempt to provide her with the skills to intervene with problematic behaviors that might arise in the future. Before closing the session, the therapist cautioned Ms. C. that Cindy might test the limits to see if her mother was going to stick to her new discipline strategies. The session was ended with the instruction that Ms. C. should recontact the Psychology Clinic if the improvements were not sustained.

Follow-up

At the six-month telephone contact, Ms. C. reported that she and Cindy were experiencing no current difficulties. She noted that, as predicted, Cindy seemed to backslide a little following termination. She said she remembered the therapist's prediction that this might occur and his admonition that by remaining consistent such testing of the limits would soon dissipate. Keeping this in mind, then, she continued to utilize the parent management strategies provided and Cindy's behavior again improved. The one-year follow-up revealed no further difficulties.

Overall Evaluation

Cindy was a four-year-old Caucasian female initially referred to the Psychology Clinic because of maternal concern over her temper tantrums, refusal to sleep alone, and the mother's general difficulties in behavior management. Cindy's behavior problems seemed to be limited to the home, as assessment conducted in the school setting and an earlier mental health evaluation revealed no school difficulties. It was assumed that Cindy had developed a coercive pattern of influencing her mother through tantrum behavior. These behaviors were seen to have been developed and maintained through both positive and negative reinforcement (i.e., they were positively reinforced by maternal attention and negatively reinforced through the removal of maternal demands).

Parent training was provided to Ms. C. in three sessions over a period of four weeks. She quickly learned to extinguish Cindy's coercive behavior or to punish it using time-out. She also learned to positively reinforce the child's compliant behavior. Six-month and one-year follow-ups revealed continued appropriate behavior on the part of mother and daughter, and long-term prognosis appeared favorable.

23

Oppositional Behavior

Alan M. Gross

Description of Oppositional Behavior

A common problem encountered by behavior therapists specializing in the treatment of children and adolescents is oppositional behavior. The essential features of oppositional disorder include disobedience and negativistic and provocative opposition to authority figures (APA, 1980). Such opposition generally is manifested in the form of temper tantrums, violations of minor rules, procrastination, and/or passive resistance to authority. The primary recipient of the youngster's oppositional attitude is his or her parents and teachers. Although this problem may occur as early as age three, it most commonly begins during late childhood or adolescence.

Oppositional children sometimes are inappropriately referred to as conduct disordered, because temper tantrums, rule violations, and oppositional behavior are common to both diagnostic categories (Gross, 1983). However, unlike conduct disordered youngsters, the behavior of an oppositional child does not result in the violation of the basic rights of others or the breaking of major societal norms. While oppositional children may be disobedient and argumentative, their behavior generally does not include persistent lying, truancy, theft, aggression, or vandalism.

Presenting Complaints

The assessment and treatment of an oppositional child is illustrated with the following clinical case history. Art was an 11-year-old boy who lived with his mother and stepfather in a large Southeastern city. Parents reported that in the past six months Art had become a tremendous behavior problem. His mother (Mrs. S.) stated that he was doing very poorly in school. He also was very difficult to manage at home. She reported that he had a terribly negative attitude. Whenever he was asked to do any task he virtually always refused. Overall, he was reported to be disobedient and noncompliant.

His negative attitude also was becoming a source of concern at school. Mrs. S. noted that his teacher had complained that it was difficult to work with Art because of his opposition to all authority figures. She told Mrs. S. that he simply refused to do what he was told. This included his assignments.

History

Art, the son of a stockbroker and a nurse, was an only child. According to his mother, he reached all the developmental milestones at the appropriate ages. Mrs. S. reported that prior to the present difficulties Art had been a model son. He had always done well in school and appeared to be well liked by his peers.

Mrs. S. reported that she and her first husband were divorced when Art was nine. Following the divorce she noted that Art went through a period in which he displayed a dramatic increase in dependent and attention-seeking behavior. He attempted to spend a great deal of time with her and sought out her attention for tasks that previously went unnoticed. He did not, however, exhibit any problems in school or with his friends at this time. Art was an active boy who played on a youth soccer team and a Little League baseball team. During the period following the divorce, Art continued his participation in these activities. Mrs. S. reported that throughout the pre- and post-divorce period she made an effort to continue to spend time doing things with Art that they always had done. These activities included swimming, playing table games, and talking about the day's events. Mrs. S. further stated that Art's display of attention-seeking behavior dropped out approximately three months following the divorce.

Since the divorce Art has seen his father regularly. He spends alternate weekends with him as well as living with him during summers. Mrs. S. indicated that Art gets along fairly well with his father. However, she would not characterize their relationship as one in which father and son did many traditional activities (e.g., sports) together. During their marriage Art frequently expressed a desire for his father to spend more time playing with him.

Eighteen months following the divorce Mrs. S. remarried. Mr. S. was a very successful and busy lawyer. Mr. and Mrs. S. bought a new house in the same school district, so that when they moved in together Art would not have to change schools and lose touch with many of his friends. Mr. S. reported that he liked Art very much and enjoyed doing things with him. However, the demands of his law practice left him with little time to divide between Art and his wife.

Since the marriage Mr. and Mrs. S. had noticed a drastic change in Art's attitude and behavior. Both he and Mrs. S. felt that Art had become immensely argumentative and hostile. Mr. S. stated that it appeared as if Art went out of his way to break household rules. He had become very disobedient, and even the simplest request seemed to result in an automatic refusal. Mr. S. acknowledged that Art's behavior could be much worse: "He doesn't lie or get in trouble with the police." However, his constant display of provocative behavior, violation of minor household rules (e.g., curfew), and his noncompliance to requests had made it extremely unpleasant to interact with Art. Moreover, there was a constant state of tension in the house. Both Mr. and Mrs. S. had a strong commitment to solve these family problems.

Assessment

The assessment process was implemented at the initial interview. During this session the clinician met first with Art's parents. He attempted to obtain a general description of the presenting problem and relevant historical data. Developmental information also was requested. Further, the therapist had Mr. and Mrs. S. describe in detail an example of a recent problematic interaction with Art. This was done in order to begin to identify potential antecedent and consequent stimuli that might have been contributing to their difficulties. A brief segment of this portion of the initial interview follows.

T: Please describe in detail a recent difficulty you had with Art.

Mr. S.:   The day before yesterday was garbage collection day. Before I left the house in the morning I asked Art to please take the garbage can out to the street before he left for school. He didn't even reply. He just sat there and ignored me.

T: What did you do then?

Mr. S.:   I repeated myself in a more forceful voice and asked him if he heard what I said. He continued to ignore me.

T: Then what occurred?

Mr. S.:   I lost my temper and began to yell at him, which didn't seem to bother him in the least. It was getting late so I told him I would deal with him later. Then I took the garbage out to the street myself.

T: Did you speak to Art about the episode later when you returned from work?

Mr. S.:   No.

Following the meeting with Art's parents, the therapist met alone with the boy. In this interview he attempted to assess the youth's knowledge of why he was brought to the clinic, as well as identify potential rewarding stimuli for use during treatment. The youngster reported that things were "okay" at home. However, he did feel that his parents "hassled" him all the time and that he would like them to leave him alone. Further questioning from the therapist revealed that Art also perceived that he was receiving similar treatment from his teachers.

The first interview was concluded with the therapist presenting a brief summary of his assessment observations. He also requested permission to speak with Art's teacher in order to determine what problems Art was displaying in school. Last, in order to gather further information regarding the antecedents and consequents of the family's problem interactions, Mr. and Mrs. S. were asked to record in detail two examples of family arguments that occurred during the week prior to the next session. This procedure was performed throughout the course of treatment in order to assess progress, as well as to provide data upon which adjustments in treatment could be made.

The therapist interviewed Art's teacher in a telephone conversation. She reported that Art was falling behind in school. His recent failures, however, were not due to his inability to do his schoolwork, but rather his unwillingness to complete assignments. She stated that he was a fairly bright boy who did extremely well when he put some effort into his work. In the past few months Art had become very noncompliant. He did not pay attention in class and did not listen when he was told to do something. She stated that he frequently ignored her when she spoke to him. Displays of disobedience and passive resistance to authority figures characterized his interactions with most of the school staff. His teacher also noted that he seemed to be well liked by his peers and that he did not appear to have any difficulties socially.

When Mr. and Mrs. S. returned to the therapist's office for the following week's session, homework data revealed a pattern in their interactions with Art. That is, Art's noncompliance and negative attitude resulted in a great deal of one-to-one time with his parents. The consequences of noncompliance also included escape from an unpleasant or aversive task. For example, when Art was asked to perform a household chore and he refused, his parents generally presented him with a short lecture about his behavior. Following such discussion, which generally did not produce the desired response from Art, his parents often performed the task. As such, noncompliance was not punished, but was inadvertently reinforced. A similar pattern, in which Art's inappropriate behavior did not result in immediate aversive consequences, characterized his interactions with his teachers at school.

Art's parents also were very inconsistent in their use of punishment. Although they would impose a punishment for inappropriate behavior, they rarely followed through with the contingency. For example, if Art was grounded for exhibiting noncompliant behavior and was not supposed to leave the house after school, after a few hours at home his mother frequently would give him a lecture about "being good" and then allow him to go out and play with his neighborhood friends. Parental reports also suggested that displays of appropriate behavior usually went unnoticed.

Selection of Treatment

Results of the assessment indicated that Art's parents were inadvertently rewarding their son's inappropriate responding. Moreover, their attempts to use punishment to elicit good behavior from Art were failing. These failures were due to inconsistent and inaccurate applications of the procedure. Therapy consisted of training Mr. and Mrs. S. in behavior management techniques. After being taught to observe their own as well as Art's behavior, they were instructed on how to develop clearly defined response contingencies. Instruction regarding use of reinforcement, punishment, and extinction techniques also was provided. It was hoped that by teaching Mr. and Mrs. S. to reward Art's appropriate behavior and punish or extinguish his inappropriate responses that his behavior would improve, and that he would learn more socially acceptable methods of obtaining attention from his parents. It also was expected that getting Mr. and Mrs. S. to stop yelling at Art would greatly improve the nature of their relationship with him.

A second major component of treatment consisted of prompting Mr. S. to increase the amount of time he spent with Art. Assessment revealed that he had been alone with Art very little since the marriage. Onset of Art's oppositional behavior, which coincided with the marriage, resulted in a dramatic increase in tension between Art and his stepfather. Art's mother stated that when Art and his stepfather went off and did something by themselves, Art seemed to really enjoy it. However, at present frequency of these interactions was extremely low. Research has shown that children who experience the divorce of their parents often display behavior problems during the post-divorce adjustment period. The remarriage of a divorced parent is considered to be a major part of this adjustment period (Hetherington, 1979). Gross (1982) has suggested that increasing the amount of quality one-to-one time with children undergoing this experience may reduce inappropriate behavior. As such, increasing the frequency of individual play time between Art and his stepfather was included as a goal of treatment.

Course of Treatment

The first session of treatment (session 2) began with the therapist explaining to Art's parents the relationship between their son's inappropriate behavior and their own reactions to his responding. This was done in order to begin to educate them as to the relationship between behavior and its consequences. This lesson also served to introduce them to the principles and procedures of reinforcement, punishment, and extinction. A segment of this interview follows:

T: An illustration of reinforcement can be seen in the way you frequently respond to Art when he does not follow your instructions.

Mr. S.: What is that?

T: Let's take the example we talked about earlier. Your wife asked Art to take his clean clothes up from the laundry room and put them away. Art didn't pay any attention to this request. Your wife began to holler at him and they started arguing. According to your report it wasn't long before you joined in and began lecturing him. Your wife said she became so frustrated with all of this that she finally took the clothes up to his room herself.

Mrs. S.: That's true. It is just so hard to get him to do things sometimes that it is easier to do them myself.

T: I understand that. But if we take a closer look at this interaction we see that the consequence of his disobedience is a large amount of individual attention from the two of you. Some of this attention may appear to be aversive to you and me, such as yelling and scolding, but nevertheless it is attention. When he is being a good boy he does not get this much direct attention. A second consequence of his noncompliance is that he avoids having to perform what he considers to be an aversive task. He has learned that after you finish yelling at him you will do his work. So his noncompliance appears to result in receiving reinforcement in the form of attention and avoidance of an unpleasant event.

Following discussion of the relationship between behavior and its consequences the therapist began training Mr. and Mrs. S. in specific parenting skills. These included teaching them to use direct commands, to state response reinforcer relationships clearly, and to deliver rewards for appropriate responding.

In order to assist Art's parents in learning to develop these skills, the Premack Principle was explained. Below is an account of that portion of the interview.

T: As I just explained it is very important when you tell Art to do something that you give him a chance to display the response, and that you clearly convey to him the consequences that are associated with compliance and disobedience. One way to make it a bit easier to think of rewarding and punishing consequences when you are issuing a command is to use the Premack Principle. It states that you can increase the rate of a low-probability behavior by making access to a high-probability response contingent on the occurrence of the low-priority behavior. For example, most children would rather eat dessert than their vegetables. The Premack Principle suggests that you could prompt a child to eat his vegetables by simply stating that he must do this in order to get dessert.

Mrs. S.: That seems easy enough.

Mr. S.: So, for example, if he was watching television and I wanted him to feed the dog I should tell him that if he doesn't feed that dog right now he can't continue watching TV.

T: That's pretty much it. I would encourage you to present the request in a more positive manner. You might state it something like this, "I want you to feed the dog please. Why don't you do it at the next commercial? After you feed him you can continue to watch TV. However, if you don't feed him you can't watch television." I also suggest that you praise Art generously for complying with your request.

The therapist concluded this session with a homework assignment designed to provide the parents with an opportunity to attempt to implement the procedures discussed. They discussed two situations that were problematic and created a number of possible contingency statements that they might use in those situations. They were instructed to attempt to practice these new parenting skills whenever it was appropriate, and in particular in these two specific situations. They also were requested to record these interactions so that they could be discussed in the following session.

The results of Mr. and Mrs. S.'s attempts to use contingency statements and reward Art's appropriate behavior were the major focus of the third treatment session. They reported that in the instances in which they used this technique it proved to be fairly successful. Both parents indicated that they had a difficult time remembering to praise Art for his good behavior. They also noted that it was not always easy to think of rewards to use when they were trying to make a contingency statement. However, they did report that it seemed to be getting a little easier as the week went by. Suggestions were made regarding ideas to help them remember to notice and praise their son's appropriate responding. Additional problematic situations also were discussed and possible ways to apply contingency management strategies were presented. In order to assist Mr. and Mrs. S. in developing these skills, role-plays were enacted. This strategy also allowed the therapist to provide Art's parents with constructive feedback regarding use of the procedures. The session was concluded with the therapist requesting that they continue to use these methods over the course of the following week and to record an instance when the procedure was successful and one when it was not. Mr. S. also was asked to write out a brief list of activities that he felt both he and Art would enjoy doing together.

Mr. and Mrs. S. returned to the fourth session and reported that things had been going much better at home. They were finding it fairly easy to use contingency statements when making requests of Art and this procedure seemed to be working very well. They reported that there still were difficulties, but that there was a dramatic decrease in the amount of arguing and yelling that was going on at home. They also noted that Art seemed to be responding very positively to receiving praise and attention for his good behavior. Reduction in family conflict surrounding Art's behavior also seemed to be having a very positive effect on Art's attitude. Mr. and Mrs. S. reported that he seemed to be more friendly toward them, and there no longer seemed to be the same degree of tension in the house.

Following the portion of the session in which the therapist provided Art's parents with specific feedback regarding their applications of the behavior management skills, the clinician prompted Mr. S. to talk about his feelings about spending more individual time with Art. Mr. S. stated that before he married Art's mother he really enjoyed doing things with Art. However, following the marriage he found that his work load at the office increased and he had less free time. He felt that getting married was a change for everyone. In adjusting to living as a family he inadvertently began to spend the few moments he had away from work primarily with his wife. When Art began to be so difficult at home, he found himself even less inclined to try and do things with him. The therapist explained that it was very important for him to develop a good relationship with Art. He further informed Mr. S. that joining Art in activities that he knew Art and he both enjoyed was a good strategy for achieving this goal. At the previous session Mr. S. had been asked to list some activities that met these criteria. After talking about these events the therapist asked Mr. S. to engage in one of them with Art during the week following the session. As in the previous treatment sessions, they also were asked to record two applications of their newly acquired contingency management skills.

Similar to the previous treatment sessions, the fifth meeting began with a review of the week's events. Art's parents were happy to report that things were continuing to improve at home. Art was considerably less disobedient. They also noticed an increase in family interactions. Art was no longer immediately going to his room as soon as he entered the house, but often stopped to share some information about his day. Mr. S. reported that he and Art went fishing Saturday afternoon, and the two of them had a really good time despite their failure to bring home enough fish for a family dinner.

Art's parents were praised for their good work. Further discussion of how Mr. S. could continue to develop his relationship with his stepson also occurred. Mr. S. agreed to arrange for another outing with Art for the following week. Moreover, possible methods for increasing his daily interactions with Art also were discussed. Having demonstrated a fairly good grasp of the procedures taught thus far in treatment, the therapist shifted the focus of the session to assess

Art's situation at school. His parents reported that as far as they knew Art's change in behavior had not carried over to his classwork. Their discussion with his teacher the previous week revealed that he still was not completing assignments. Negotiation and contracting training was suggested as the best method for dealing with Art's academic problems. Mr. and Mrs. S. were given a brief lecture on this procedure and instructed to bring Art to the next session.

The therapist met alone with Art at the beginning of the next session. They discussed Art's feelings about what was going on at home and at school and he reported that he was pleased with his situation at home. When informed that his parents were very concerned about his schoolwork, he stated that it was true he hadn't been doing many of his assignments and that every time he and his parents tried to talk about it they ended up fighting. The therapist explained that kids and their parents frequently fought about rather than solved these kinds of problems. It was further explained that the purpose of having them all in the office today was to teach them a set of skills that generally was helpful in these situations. Art was then given instruction in negotiation and contracting skills. After role-playing a few practice examples, Art's parents were asked to join the session and attempt to negotiate a contract regarding Art's academic performance. The transcript of that portion of the session follows:

T: Mrs. S., why don't you tell us what it is that you want from Art concerning his school work.

Mrs. S.: Really, all I want is for him to start doing as well as we know he can.

T: What exactly do you mean?

Mrs. S.: I want him to do the assignments his teacher requests and to do them carefully and accurately.

Art: I hate doing all that work. Some of the stuff is so boring.

Mr. S.: Don't you think that a lot of what I have to do at work is boring? I still have to do it.

T: Yes, I suppose that is true. However, there are very clear tangible rewards you get in return for your effort. It is difficult for an 11-year-old to appreciate the value of drawing maps or writing book reports. Art, do you think that you deserve some privileges for working hard at school?

Art: Yeah, I guess so.

Mrs. S.: I think we would be willing to reward you for doing better in school. You could stay up a half-hour later or I would be willing to play any game with you for a half-hour every day you brought home a good report from your teacher.

Mr. S.: That sounds fair to me.

T: What do you think of that compromise? One of those privileges in return for a good teacher's report.

Art: Can I have a choice of which I want each night?

Mrs. S.: That would be fine.

T: A good way to know how Art does each day at school is to have his teacher fill out a very brief check sheet. He can have his teacher fill it out at the end of each school day. As I stated earlier, the check sheet has to be very specific so that everyone knows what is expected of each other. What exactly is it that you want his teacher to report on?

Mrs. S.: I want it really to simply tell us whether he did all his daily assignments and whether they were completed satisfactorily.

T: Is that all right with you Art?

Art: Sure.

After completing the contract, it was written out and everyone was given a copy. Art and his family were instructed to begin this program the following day. Mr. and Mrs. S. also were encouraged to continue to use the skills they had been working on during the preceding weeks.

The primary focus of the next couple of sessions was to help Art's parents perfect their newly acquired behavior management skills. As time passed and Art appeared to be responding very favorably to the academic contract, his family was given assistance in making minor adjustments in the contract, as they became necessary. A significant portion of these sessions also consisted of instructing Mr. and Mrs. S. regarding how to apply these techniques in novel situations. Last, Mr. S.'s progress in developing a better relationship with Art was monitored.

Termination

The termination phase of treatment was conducted over two sessions. In the first of these, the therapist discussed methods of programming maintenance of behavior change. He explained that over time it would become less and less necessary to maintain written contracts such as the one they developed for Art's academic work. They were told that creating a contract was an excellent method of generating an increase in the rate of behavior. Once the response was occurring at the desired frequency, however, they could slowly fade the extremely formal aspects of the agreement, or they might find it necessary to create a new agreement. They then discussed ways that this could be achieved. An example of that aspect of the session is provided below.

> *T*: One possible way to slowly fade out a written contract is to make the minor adjustments you desire and restate it verbally. For example, you could emphasize how well Art had been doing and that it didn't seem necessary to continue making him get his paper signed everyday. You also could tell him that he could continue to have his privileges as long as he continued to do well on his assignments. He also would need to know that you would be checking on how he is doing from time to time.
>
> *Mr. S.*: That sounds relatively easy.

Art's family continued to discuss this topic over the remainder of the session. They were instructed to attempt to implement it and return the following week with their son.

In the final session the therapist first met alone with Mr. and Mrs. S. His questioning revealed that things were continuing to go well for them at home. They reported that there had been no serious problems with Art during the past week, and they felt very confident that things were going to continue that way. When questioned about whether they were successful at renegotiating Art's academic contract, it was noted that they had agreed to stop having Art have his teacher send home daily notes. Instead, they were going to get weekly reports from her. Art would continue to have free access to his chosen privileges in return for good reports. They also mentioned that they planned to gradually fade out formal regular teacher reports if Art continued doing well. Mr. S. also indicated that he and Art had been spending some time together on a regular basis and that he planned to continue doing this.

When Art met alone with the therapist he said that things were much better at home. He felt that he was being treated very fairly. He also was enjoying his time alone with his stepfather. The therapist praised Art for his hard work during the course of therapy. He also prompted him to remember that he could apply his negotiating and contracting skills with his parents in areas besides school. He noted that this was a great way to develop a plan to earn new privileges. Art was informed that this was to be the last treatment session and asked if he had any further problems that he wanted to discuss. Art reported no additional concerns.

The entire family met with the therapist to conclude the session. Once again everyone was praised by the therapist for his or her hard work. They were encouraged to continue to use their new skills. They also were told that if further difficulties arose, or if they had some questions about how to handle a particular situation, they should feel free to call the therapist. Last, the therapist indicated that he would call them in a few weeks just to see how progress was being maintained.

Follow-up

Four weeks following the final therapy session the therapist contacted Mr. and Mrs. S. via the telephone. At this time he enquired whether they were experiencing any difficulties with Art. They reported that things were continuing to go well. They had successfully renegotiated their academic contract and had developed a new contract regarding behaviors that Art could perform in order to earn an allowance. Art had spent a week living with his father during a recent school vacation. Although they feared that there might be some behavioral difficulties upon his return home, this did not turn out to be the case. Mr. and Mrs. S. interpreted this as an indication that Art and his stepfather appeared to be well on their way to developing a very good relationship.

Overall Evaluation

The case described is a relatively straightforward treatment program. A young boy was brought to the clinic by his parents because of his oppositional behavior at home and at school. An assessment consisting of interviews was performed and target behaviors were identified. A parent training program was implemented and the youth, and his parents also were taught negotiation and contracting skills. Data collected by the child's parents throughout treatment revealed a large increase in appropriate behavior and a similar decrease in inappropriate responding. More important, these changes were maintained at the follow-up. Attempts to improve the child and his stepfather's relationship also proved successful. Overall, the youngster and his family responded to treatment very positively. This case study highlights a set of assessment and treatment procedures that may prove successful in the treatment of oppositional children.

References

American Psychiatric Association. (1980). *Diagnostic and statistical manual of mental disorders* (3rd ed.). Washington, DC: Author.

Gross, A. M. (1982). Acting out in children of divorce: An argument for behavioral contrast. *Child and Family Behavior Therapy, 4,* 87–89.

Gross, A. M. (1983). Conduct disorders. In M. Hersen (Ed.). *Outpatient behavior therapy.* New York: Grune & Stratton.

Hetherington, E. M. (1979). Divorce: A child's perspective. *American Psychologist, 34,* 851–858.

24

Conduct Disorder

Ronald A. Mann

Description of the Disorder

There is some disagreement as to the validity of a specific diagnostic category, conduct disorder. Nevertheless, for the purpose of this chapter a conduct disorder may be defined as a pattern of continuous repetitions of behaviors engaged in by children or adolescents considered socially unacceptable by members of their family or by members of the community within which that family resides. Thus, such unacceptable behaviors may occur within the home, the school, other environs of the community, or combinations of these. Examples of behaviors identified with conduct disorders include school truancies, persistent lying, stealing, substance abuse, tantrums, and refusal to do classwork or homework. Other examples include disobedience to authority figures, insulting remarks directed at peers or adults, and physical aggression. Typically, youngsters identified as having conduct disorders exhibit various combinations of these behaviors.

It should be noted that so-called conduct disorders can overlap or be associated with other serious problems, such as depression, alcoholism, suicide attempts, a deficit of social skills, communication handicaps, and criminal activities such as dealing in drugs.

Case Identification

The patient, Michael D., was a 15-year-old male. He and his younger brother, John, age 13, were both adopted before either was two months of age. Michael had been tested one year before coming to therapy with the WISC-R and had a full-scale IQ of 109. He and his family were referred for treatment by a school psychologist because of declining low school grades and frequent truancies. The referral was made after a number of meetings with Michael's parents and his teachers resulted in little change in his behavior. Michael had yearly physical examinations and had no known medical problems.

Presenting Complaints

The initial evaluation meeting was with Michael's parents. This was the first time that professional help had been sought. Michael had a two-year history of family conflict which was getting progressively worse. His school grades had dropped markedly over the last year. This was associated with frequent school truancies, refusing to do homework, and lying. The mother also reported that recently she had found a marijuana cigarette in Michael's bedroom while cleaning. Michael had claimed that a friend had left the marijuana in his room. Nevertheless, both of Michael's parents expressed emphatic opposition to the use of any drugs or alcohol, if, in fact, Michael was using these. In addition, both parents were concerned about Michael's persistent teasing of his younger brother who himself was performing quite well in school. Finally, the parents reported that when angry, Michael would frequently shout or yell insults and obscenities at family members.

History

Michael's parents could not have children of their own. His father was an electronics engineer and his mother a housewife. According to his parents, Michael had done relatively well in school receiving some grades of A but mainly B and C grades throughout elementary and junior high school years. During the last year, his grades began declining with his most recent report card indicating one F grade and the rest D grades. The low grades were associated with an intensification of conflict in the form of an increase in Michael's use of yelling, arguing, and directing insults at family members. Prior to the escalating problems, Michael had always been "very outspoken but rarely insulting to others."

Michael's father admitted to "sinking to Michael's level" by also yelling and calling him names during "some" of their "disagreements." Most of these arguments centered around incomplete homework assignments and poor test grades "after repeated discussions had failed to produce results." In addition, Michael's father expressed deep concern over the "type of friends that Michael chose to associate with" and felt that "these friends were influencing Michael adversely."

On numerous occasions, Michael's mother admitted to either criticizing Michael or discussing with him "the reasons why" she felt his behavior was inappropriate, especially as it related to the teasing of his younger brother. These discussions were inconsistently followed by punishments such as going to bed early, sometimes enforced by Michael's father when he returned home from work. Michael's mother had also characterized Michael as "a manipulator," stating, "he can really be charming when he has to be." Thus, she admitted that there were times when she had reduced a punishing consequence.

Both parents agreed that they had been inconsistent with respect to using penalties or praise as consequences. Further, they often disagreed with one another on what types of consequences to use. The mother admitted that she and her husband often had arguments between themselves with regard to the use of appropriate parenting techniques. In addition, the father stated that he was now developing resentment toward Michael "because of the stress he was causing in the home." Finally, both parents found it difficult to praise Michael because of their lingering anger "even when he does do things right."

An initial evaluation meeting with Michael was conducted with his parents absent. Michael confirmed that there was a relatively long history of arguments with his parents concerning homework, the required time to be home, and selection of friends. However, Michael was quick to point out that his friends "don't get me to do anything that I don't want to do." Michael did admit that he had used marijuana with friends on some of the occasions that he had been truant from school. Still, he insisted he had never bought any and had used it on only two or three occasions. He also stated that he did not like marijuana and no longer was using it. On the other hand, Michael admitted drinking beer infrequently at parties, stating that "this was normal" for his peer group. He insisted, "I never have more than two beers at any one time." Michael agreed that his parents' descriptions of many of the problems were relatively accurate. However, he felt that they were "at least partially to blame." He did not agree at all that his parents "should have the right to pick my friends."

Michael indicated that he was bothered by the fact that his parents were "too critical" and often each parent inconsistently changed the penalties when he did something wrong. Further, he felt both parents were "nags" and "yelled too much." In addition, they would lecture him using their own experiences of "when they were young" to establish the validity of their arguments. Michael's comment was that he "could care less how it was when they were kids. Things are different now." Finally, Michael emphasized that he rarely was noticed by his parents when he did do chores or studied.

Assessment

As part of a standardized evaluation format, the patient's parents were seen alone. During this initial phase of evaluation, a history of the current problems was taken. The parents then were asked to identify the patient's problem behaviors, deficits, assets, and potential reinforcers (i.e., frequently engaged-in activities, hobbies, allowance, etc.). These were delineated using behaviorally objective terms. For example, if the parents used terms such as "poor attitude," "was always angry," or "was insulting," they were helped by the therapist to describe objectively the specific behaviors that cued the use of those terms. They were also asked to specify the conditions under which those problems occurred. Finally, it was agreed upon both by the parents and by the patient that when their son was seen in session alone, the therapist would adhere to the principle of confidentiality, with one exception. Anything that the patient stated that was considered a danger to either himself or others would not be kept secret from his parents.

During the subsequent session, the patient was seen alone. First, he was asked to ascertain from his point of view if he agreed with the identified problem behaviors, assets, deficits, and reinforcers specified by his parents. Second, the patient was asked to identify areas in which he felt his parents needed to make changes in their behaviors and to identify their assets and deficits.

Thus, two groups of lists were generated, one from the parents and one from the patient. Both the patient and his parents were then seen together during the same session. With all parties participating, the lists were used initially to help evaluate the issues of conflict between family members and to assess one another's recognition of the other's assets. Finally and most important, these lists would later help the therapist to design an individually tailored contingency contract. Such a contract would serve as a major therapeutic intervention by guiding the parents in the use of relevant contingencies.

After basic agreement was established on major items of the lists, a consent for release of information from the patient's school was signed by patient and parents. Thus, copies of requested school records could be obtained. These included psychological testing results, attendance records including truancies and excused absences, and cumulative grade reports.

The records obtained on Michael confirmed both the parent-reported truancies and the negative trend in his grades. Thus, the presenting problems and history described by the parents and confirmed by the patient as well as the school reports served as a sort of baseline. That is, this information could be used later as a reference from which to make comparisons during and after treatment.

Finally, in addition to obtaining the above information on this patient, arrangements were made with the psychologist at Michael's school to have Michael bring home weekly progress reports every Friday. These reports would be signed by Michael's teachers and specify his daily attendance for the week and his daily record of homework completion in each of his classes. This information would allow school performance requirements to be incorporated into a contingency contract. Thus, the data from the weekly progress reports would be used to determine some of the reinforcing and punishing consequences which would be specified in that contingency contract. Such consequences would be delivered by Michael's parents.

Selection of Treatment

As is common with most children and adolescents diagnosed as having a conduct disorder, there is an inconsistent use of consequences by parents. Frequently, the parents disagree with one another, quarrel, and individually use different consequences. This was surely the case with Michael's parents. His parents admitted that on many occasions the selection of a consequence was determined, in part, by their mood or state of emotions. Thus, rarely were there specific consequences assigned to specific behaviors. In addition, positive consequences such as praise or compliments for adaptive behaviors were lacking. In fact, Michael's parents had stated: "Why should we praise him for doing homework or chores? Those are his responsibilities."

As the conflicts between Michael and his parents progressed, most of the consequences they used became more punitive. It was pointed out to the parents that punitive consequences often produce immediate short-term results, which serve to reinforce the parent's use of them. Further, positive consequences take time and repetition to produce results, and so their use often is not reinforcing to parents.

Thus, there sometimes is found in dysfunctional families a natural drift toward an increasing use of punitive consequences with and accompanying decrease in the use of reinforcing consequences. As part of treatment, Michael's parents were taught how to use praise and compliments for adaptive behaviors normally taken for granted. Still, it was clear that Michael's parents lacked an understanding of basic behavioral parenting techniques and an educational format alone would not be enough to rectify the problems.

In order to establish a consistent and predictable set of consequences for Michael's behaviors which could be administered by his parents, a number of treatment goals would have to be met. First, the parents were taught the basic principles of reinforcement and contingency management. This was integrated into all subsequent therapy sessions and was prerequisite to being able to implement a contingency contract. Second, they were introduced to the concept of *parental traps*. Third, and most important, a contingency contract was developed. Finally, ongoing weekly therapy sessions were conducted to correct current or new problems and to evaluate the effectiveness of treatment procedures.

Basic Principles

Michael's parents were taught basic principles of reinforcement and punishment using their own reported experiences as examples. In addition, the importance of considering variables that facilitate the effectiveness of consequences were presented using everyday illustrations. These included concepts such as the magnitude, duration, repetition, and immediacy of consequences. Further, the parents were instructed in the use of extinction procedures. That is, they were taught how to identify maladaptive behaviors that could be ignored such as nagging. Finally, they were instructed on the importance of shaping. Thus, this parent education format was designed to help the parents make sound contingency management decisions ultimately independent of the therapist.

Parental Traps

Parental traps are commonly engaged-in patterns of behavior that parents often use in response to inappropriate behaviors of their children. These behavior patterns typically serve to reinforce, albeit inadvertently, the same inappropriate behaviors that the parents are attempting to eliminate. For example, arguing with Michael served to reinforce his argumentativeness, and Michael's parents when arguing between themselves or with Michael acted as role models for this behavior. Nagging and repetitive requests by Michael's parents taught Michael that consequences rarely occurred if he did not comply. Further, on those occasions when consequences did occur, it was only after additional cues followed the requests, such as yelling or threatening. Thus, when Michael finally complied, his parents were reinforced for a chain of behaviors which included nagging, becoming agitated, yelling, and using threats to cue his behavior. It was also pointed out to Michael's parents that their displays of being upset may have acted to reinforce Michael's delays and noncompliance, especially when he was angry at them.

Other parental traps were explored with Michael's parents to help them eliminate these problems. For example, Michael's parents often would have philosophical or insight-oriented discussions with him immediately after he had engaged in some inappropriate behavior such as teasing his younger brother. They would take time to explain to Michael why such behavior was inappropriate and inform him that later he would be punished by having to go to bed early. At times, Michael was punished by being required to go to bed early immediately after completion of chores or homework. Thus, potential reinforcers such as parental attention and discussion followed inappropriate behaviors (i.e., teasing) and potential punishers followed appropriate behaviors such as chores or homework. Michael's parents were instructed as to the importance of timing consequences correctly based on earlier discussions of reinforcement principles. These discussions on parental traps helped Michael's parents discover and correct some of the parenting mistakes that they had been making prior to seeking professional help.

Contingency Contract

The most important phase of treatment consisted of designing and implementing an individually tailored contingency contract. The use of contingency contracting has been described and demonstrated to be an effective technique to modify behavior problems other than conduct disorders (Mann, 1972, 1976). A contingency contract is an explicit statement of contingencies. That is, it is a set of rules. As such, it specifies objectively a number of behaviors whose occurrence will produce specified consequences, in this case to be delivered by parents.

In order to be effective, such a contract requires two major considerations: First, it requires that the behaviors to be changed or maintained occur in a measurable or observable manner. Second, it requires that the therapist or parent discover and gain systematic control over relevant consequences.

After reviewing the two lists previously generated by Michael and his parents (i.e., lists of problem behaviors, assets, deficits, and reinforcers), and meeting with them to discuss as well as negotiate what their respective needs would be, a contingency contract was designed. Some of the items were negotiable, such as Michael's allowance and what time he was expected home on weekend evenings. Other items were not open to negotiation, such as missing school or using drugs. It was made clear that these types of behaviors would produce punishing consequences.

During a review of the finished contract, it was made very clear to Michael that almost all of the privileges that he had previously taken for granted would now have to be earned. These would include the use of TV, telephone, radio or stereo, going out with friends, and receiving spending money. In addition, his parents were told that the contract required them to present either reinforcing or punishing consequences based on Michael's behavior and not on their emotions. Still, Michael was less enthusiastic than his parents with the finished contract. However, he did express satisfaction with some of the specified reinforcers which had not been available before therapy. These included the opportunity both to earn a higher allowance and to come home later in the evenings.

The following is a copy of the completed contingency contract administered by Michael's parents:

It is understood that the full purpose and intent of this contract is that Michael D. be responsible for his own behavior. Thus, he agrees that his performance will determine any rewards or penalties which are specified in the following clauses of this contractual agreement.

1. Michael's parents agree to pay Michael an allowance of $8.00 per week contingent on his completing the following chores to his parent's specifications: (A number of chores with objective criteria were listed.) It is understood by Michael and his parents that neither credit will be advanced nor money loaned and allowance will be paid once per week after completion of chores.

2. Michael agrees to deposit with his parents a minimum of 50% of all money he earns both from his allowance and from any employment. This money will be deposited in a special bank account in his parents' name and collect interest for him at current rates. It is understood that

the deposited money may be used by Michael's parents for purposes of paying penalties if Michael violates contract rules.

3. It is understood that Michael may request his parents to withdraw for him a sum of money to purchase any item that is legal. Before this request will be honored, two conditions must be met: (A) Michael's behavior must have been appropriate for four consecutive weeks without violating any major clauses of this contract. (B) After withdrawal of the money, there must remain in the special bank account a balance equal to at least $15.00. In addition, after completing four consecutive weeks without major violations, Michael will receive his full allowance and full paycheck from any employment. On the other hand, should a major violation occur again, Michael will be required to deposit 50% of all earned money into the special bank account for four consecutive weeks. Major violations include truancy, lying, and drug or alcohol use.

4. Michael agrees to complete all homework assignments daily to his parents' approval prior to watching TV, listening to radio or stereo, using the phone, going out, or engaging in any pleasurable activities.

5. It is understood that Michael will bring his weekly progress report home from school every Friday. The report will specify daily attendance in all classes and homework assignments completed for the week, and will be signed by teachers from each of his classes. Perfect attendance and all homework completed will result in Michael receiving full weekend privileges. This will include staying out with friends until 11:00 P.M. on Friday and Saturday nights pending that Michael's parents can verify an approved destination. Failure to bring home the weekly progress report for any reason will result in being restricted to the home for the entire weekend.

6. Michael agrees not to be truant from any of his classes. Any violation will result in immediate loss of all money in the special bank account and restriction to the house without privileges for one full week.

7. Michael's parents agree to reward Michael with $20.00 for every grade of A he receives, $15.00 for every B, and $5.00 for C grades. On the other hand, Michael agrees to pay his parents $10.00 for grades of D and $15.00 for any F grades. In addition, Michael will be required to attend summer school for classes in which he receives F grades.

8. Michael agrees not to lie to either parent. Any violation will result in a $5.00 fine and two days restricted to the house without privileges.

9. Michael agrees not to direct obscenities or insulting remarks at family members. Any violation results in the loss of one half-hour of TV time and 50 cents for each obscenity or insulting remark.

10. Michael agrees not to tease his younger brother. Each infraction results in a fine of $1.00 and loss of TV privileges for the evening.

11. Michael agrees never to use or have in his possession any drugs including marijuana, alcohol, or other intoxicating substances. Further, he agrees not to have in his possession any paraphernalia associated with

drugs. It is understood that the smell of marijuana or alcohol on clothing or breath will be considered the same as using drugs. Any violation of this clause will result in immediate loss of all money in the special bank account and restriction to the house for two weeks.

12. Michael agrees not to associate with anyone who is in the process of using drugs including marijuana or alcohol or who already is intoxicated. Any violation will result in a $20.00 fine and five days restricted to the house.

13. Michael's parents agree that if Michael does not have any major violations of this contract for six consecutive weeks, they will celebrate by taking Michael and one friend to a movie and restaurant of his choice, all expenses paid.

I, Michael D., have read fully the above contract and understand and agree to the terms set forth in all of the clauses specifying the behavioral requirements and their consequences. Further, I understand that the conditions of this contract are binding on my parents as well as on myself. Finally, it is understood by all parties to this contract that should any revisions be considered necessary, such revisions shall be made only under the direct supervision of the therapist.

The contract was then signed by Michael, his parents, and the therapist as a witness. The contract was dated and copies presented to each family member.

Weekly Therapy Sessions

Each week the therapist met first with the patient's parents. Weekly progress reports from school were reviewed as well as the patient's progress in the home. Use of contract contingencies were carefully scrutinized by the therapist, with appropriate feedback and education given to the parents as was needed. Next, the patient was seen alone to ascertain from his point of view what progress both he and his parents had made. He was also questioned about the accuracy of his parent's use of contract consequences. Finally, both the patient and his parents were seen together during the latter part of each session to resolve any discrepancies in contract implementation, if any, or to help correct issues of conflict.

During these sessions, both the patient and his parents were encouraged to use compliments and praise for many of their behaviors that typically had been taken for granted. Often the therapist would serve as a role model to illustrate the use of praise, compliments, and assertive skills.

Course of Treatment

Michael and his parents were seen for therapy during eight weekly one-hour sessions. This was followed by three more sessions spaced two weeks apart. The first two sessions were used to obtain a history, evaluate behaviorally the family dynamics, and identify the family's behavior problems, assets, and deficits. The next two sessions were used to educate the parents as well as to negotiate, develop, and complete the contingency contract. The remaining sessions were used to educate Michael and his parents, correct current and new problems, and evaluate the effectiveness of treatment variables.

After initiation of the contingency contract, Michael's parents reported significant improvement in his behaviors. He was attending school regularly and completing homework assignments with relative consistency. This, of course, was confirmed by the weekly progress reports which the parents were instructed to bring to these sessions. In addition, both Michael and his parents stated that there was far less arguing between themselves. Michael stressed that his parents no longer were "nagging" him and were "lecturing and criticizing" him far less. Further, Michael's parents reported that name-calling had diminished to near zero and Michael had reduced the frequency of teasing of his brother. The parents did indicate, however, that Michael was punished for these behaviors on several occasions prior to the "good results."

The parents reported that on three occasions Michael had not completed his chores. They were proud to add that they did not nag him. Michael simply did not receive his full allowance. Further, if Michael nagged them for money, his parents refused, gave him the reasons, and referred him to the contract while ignoring further nagging if it did occur.

Finally, Michael's parents brought to the final session a number of quizzes that had been returned to Michael. He had been receiving B and C grades in his classes. Michael's mother expressed that she felt "more adequate and in control again." Further, Michael's father indicated that he no longer had any resentment toward his son. Both parents pointed out that since they had started using the contract, Michael was displaying more signs of affection toward them. Finally, Michael reported that he felt better about himself and admitted that he always "knew the contract was fair."

Termination

Termination of weekly therapy sessions was faded to having sessions every other week. This was initiated by the therapist with the agreement of Michael's parents after it was clear that Michael had attended school with no truancies for four consecutive weeks and minimal family conflicts.

An additional six weeks passed with Michael and his parents coming to therapy sessions three more times. During those six weeks, Michael had continued to attend school without truancies, completed most homework assignments, and demonstrated grade improvements in class quizzes. Although there had been some minor rule violations such as infrequent teasing of his brother, Michael's parents had expressed confidence that they were dealing with the problems adequately. Thus, they had initiated termination of therapy with the understanding that should any difficult problems occur, they would schedule appointments for further therapy sessions. The therapist agreed and therapy in the office but hopefully not in the home was terminated.

Follow-up

Follow-up consisted of phone calls near the end of the semester. These were made both to the school psychologist and to Michael's parents. The school psychologist had sent evaluation forms to each of Michael's teachers. All had reported that Michael was doing well and had no unexcused absences. Further, at the time of the evaluation, Michael was receiving a grade of C or better in all of his classes. Michael's parents reported that there still was infrequent teasing by Michael of his younger brother but insisted that there were no other serious problems that could not be handled by them.

Overall Evaluation

The use of contingency contracting and parent education to treat this conduct disorder was considered an effective method. The effectiveness of such a contract was based on a number of assumptions. First, positive changes in the patient's behavior would, in fact, reinforce the parents to use the specified consequences systematically. Second, the consequences chosen for the patient's behavior were relevant. Third, the behaviors to be changed were observable. Finally, the consequences could be presented systematically.

It should be pointed out that there was a major disadvantage to the use of this type of contract. Namely, not all of the behaviors specified could be observed or monitored reliably. For example, it was never established that Michael ceased using beer or marijuana even though he had insisted that he had. Illicit behaviors typically are not engaged in openly. Still, the contract did specify his parents' position on this issue as well as the consequences that would occur if Michael was caught using drugs.

On the other hand, the contract did serve a large number of important functions. First, it forced Michael's parents to attend to adaptive, not only inappropriate, behaviors. Second, it helped reduce tension in the home by minimizing arguments between Michael's parents with respect to what types of consequences to use with Michael's behaviors. The contract also reduced conflicts between Michael and his parents. That is, Michael's parents had been taught to administer specified penalties dispassionately in a calm, matter-of-fact manner. On the other hand, all reinforcing consequences were to be presented paired with praise, compliments, and as much passion as honesty would allow. Finally, the contract made explicit to Michael his parents' expectations with minimal ambiguities as well as a set of consistent consequences. Thus, the contract was a guarantee to Michael that his needs would be realized if he met his responsibilities in the home and in school. This would be the case even if his parents were upset or irritable. In summary, the major function of the contract was to control the parents' behavior in a systematic fashion in order to modify the patient's behavior.

References

Mann, R. A. (1972). The behavior-therapeutic use of contingency contracting to control an adult behavior problem: Weight control. *Journal of Applied Behavior Analysis, 4,* 99–109.

Mann, R. A. (1976). The use of contingency contracting to facilitate durability of behavior change: Weight-loss maintenance. *Addictive Behaviors, 1,* 245–249.

25

Learning Disability

Mary Margaret Kerr

Description of the Disorder

The child under study in this case illustrates what is known as a *specific learning disability*; in this case, dysgraphia, or dysfunction in the area of writing. This case was selected as the focus of this chapter because it highlights the importance of extended (and often tedious!) norm-referenced and criteria-referenced* assessments in the diagnosis and treatment of learning disabilities. Furthermore, this case typifies a pattern seen in many learning disabled children who present at clinical settings: with their parents, they often have participated in multiple diagnostic procedures that served merely to confirm the initial diagnosis of learning disability without providing valuable treatment plans.

While learning disabilities are not the major focus of most behavior therapy clinics, frustrated parents often seek out specialized clinics in an attempt to answer long-standing educational questions. The disorder described in this chapter is one of several types of specific learning disabilities seen each year in mental health clinics. The

The author thanks Jamey Joy Pentek for her assistance in preparing this chapter.

*Criterion-referenced assessments assess a learner's performance against criteria established for the satisfactory mastery of a given skill or skills. Two examples of criterion-referenced assessments are Red Cross swimming tests and informal teacher-designed arithmetic tests. These measures differ, then, from norm-referenced assessments, in which one's performance is judged against the scores (or norms) of others' performance of the same task.

generally accepted definition of learning disabilities, set forth in Public Law 94-142, The Education for All Handicapped Children Act, is:

> . . . a disorder in one or more of the basic psychological processes involved in understanding or in using language, spoken or written, which may manifest itself in an imperfect ability to listen, think, speak, read, write, spell, or to do mathematical calculations. The term includes such conditions as perceptual handicaps, brain injury, minimal brain dysfunction, dyslexia, and developmental aphasia. The term does not include children who have learning problems which are primarily the result of visual, hearing or motor handicaps, of mental retardation, of emotional disturbance or of environmental, cultural, or economic disadvantage.

Case Identification and Presenting Complaints

Sam was a 12-year-old boy living with his natural parents. His parents referred him to our Center because of their concerns about his academic difficulties, particularly in the areas of handwriting and math. On the other hand, patients with behavioral problems often present with serious academic difficulties that may be described as learning disabilities.

History

Sam's birth and health history were unremarkable, and there appeared to be no speech, language, or hearing problems. All developmental milestones had been attained within normal limits.

During the parent interview, Sam's parents expressed their concern about his academic difficulties. Although his grades were average, they felt that he just "does not try hard enough." They indicated that their major concern revolved around a determination of Sam's academic potential. From this evaluation they hoped to gain a better understanding of Sam's educational needs.

In making the initial referral, Sam's mother spoke of prolonged difficulties in penmanship, extending back to his first year in school. At the time of referral, Sam's math test performance was slipping, although he appeared to grasp mathematical concepts with ease. His social studies teacher reported poor test performance, also.

The apparent precipitating event in this referral was a recent decision by the school to enroll Sam in its summer remedial program, where penmanship exercises would be emphasized. This chain of events is common. Many parents take unprecedented action when faced with school placement changes. The clinician in these instances must be wary of parents "shopping" for unrealistic or unattainable counteroffers to a school's proposal.

When asked to estimate Sam's potential, both parents cited anecdotes to support their view of Sam as a bright child. His advantaged and stimulating background gave them further rationale for their views. Both parents held graduate degrees. As their only child, Sam had enjoyed travel and other educational experiences since he was a young child.

Assessment

Prior to administering any tests, a psychoeducational evaluation team (composed of a school psychologist, reading specialist, math specialist, and the author) reviewed and discussed the extensive performance and test record forwarded by Sam's school. Previous tests included a Peabody Individual Achievement Test (PIAT), the Stanford Diagnostic Mathematics Test (SDMT), and the Wechsler Intelligence Scale for Children – Revised (WISC-R).

The Peabody Individual Achievement Test revealed at or above grade level performance for Sam in all areas (reading, math, spelling, and general information). The Stanford Math Test similarly revealed no major problems.

Following the school record review, Sam was administered the (1) Test of Written Language (TOWL) and (2) Criterion-Referenced Assessment of Cursive Writing. Both tests were administered individually in offices of the Center on an individual basis. The following sections detail the results of these two assessments, interpreted in the context of previous testing and teacher reports.

Intellectual Factors

Because Sam recently had been administered the Wechsler Intelligence Scale for Children – Revised (WISC-R), he was not given any individual test of cognitive skills. The recent psychological evaluation indicated "Superior" verbal abilities and a relative weakness ("Low Average") in items of perceptual motor functioning. A significant discrepancy between verbal and performance skills was observed (31 scale points). (A discrepancy of this magnitude is observed in less than 2% of children from families so advantaged.)

Test of Written Language (TOWL)

Sam was tested on five out of six of the subtests on the TOWL. (The spelling subtest was omitted as he had been tested earlier in that area.) The Test of Written Language (TOWL) was designed to tap six aspects of children's written expression: vocabulary, thematic maturity, handwriting, spelling, word usage, and style. To assess handwriting and thematic maturity, the student is given several stimulus pictures and told to write a theme about them. The examiner follows prescribed criteria for evaluating this writing sample. Spelling is evaluated by scoring a list of words spelled by the student. Word usage is examined through a subtest that requires the student to fill in the word missing in an incomplete sentence. Finally, on the style subtest, students correctly punctuate and capitalize sentences by rewriting them.

Sam scored significantly above average on the following TOWL subtests: vocabulary, thematic maturity, word usage, and style. On the handwriting subtest he scored significantly below average. His raw scores, percentiles, and standard scores are presented below:

Subtest	Raw Scores	Percentile	Standard Scores*
Vocabulary	39	99	17
Thematic Maturity	17	99	20
Word Usage	24	95	15
Style	17	91	14
Handwriting	4	25	8

As the scores indicate, Sam performed well in all areas of written language, with the exception of handwriting.

Sam also was asked to write a short composition on the topic of his choice. He selected a mature subject and wrote a very clear essay. Occasionally Sam made the error of not capitalizing the first word in a sentence. Spelling errors in his compositions included the words *restaurant, item, colored, servant, Nigeria, surrounded, millionaire,*

---

*Standard scores are derived scores that transform raw scores so that they have the same mean and standard deviation. Here the scores range from 1 (lowest) to 20 (highest).

and *machines*. These errors are not uncommon for a student in the sixth grade.

Both essays (TOWL and free-choice writing sample) were comprehensive, imaginative, and amusing. Sam, a very clever writer, presented himself as a young man who took the test seriously. He easily established rapport with the examiner and worked diligently for the hour and a half testing period. The only area targeted for concern was handwriting.

Penmanship Evaluation

Sam was administered a criterion-referenced assessment of handwriting, following the guidelines by Haring, Lovitt, Eaton, and Hansen (1978) and Starlin (1982). This assessment concentrated on cursive rather than printing, given Sam's age and grade placement. (Sam also told this examiner that he found printing much more difficult than cursive, a finding not uncommon among students experiencing handwriting problems.) To assess handwriting prerequisites, Sam was asked to copy shapes upon which cursive (and manuscript) forms are based and to name all of the cursive letters. Following this initial assessment, he wrote all letters as follows: (1) uppercase letters, with a model, (2) uppercase letters, without a model, (3) lowercase letters, with a model, (4) lowercase letters, without a model, (5) upper- and lowercase letters in context (words and sentences), with a model, and (6) upper- and lowercase letters in context, without a model.

All of these probes were timed, to determine Sam's *rate* of handwriting. In addition, each writing sample was scored for legibility according to the system prescribed by Haring et al. (1978). Reliability of scoring was established by having both Sam and a second examiner also evaluate his writing samples. (See Kerr & Lambert, 1982, for a discussion of self-evaluation and reliability in writing.) Finally, in each probe Sam was invited to use one of a wide choice of writing instruments (pencils, markers, and pens).

Results of this assessment suggested that Sam had *significant* problems in handwriting. While Sam successfully completed the prerequisite activities, he encountered and reported difficulty in cursive writing samples, both with and without models. While Sam's writing generally *appeared* legible, an analysis of individual letters and connections* reflected malformations including: (1) uppercase letters: A B F H K L M N P R T X Z, (2) lowercase letters: a b d k r s v y z,

---

*"Connections" are the written links between two cursive letters. Connections do not appear in printed (manuscript) writing.

(3) connections: r w n v y g a, and (4) digits: 4, 9, 3, 5. These problems are illustrated in Figure 25.1.

While these letters and connections may appear to be formed acceptably, Sam's strokes in forming them were awkward and inefficient. Fortunately, he was able, once he was made aware of this issue, to self-report "letters that don't feel right," and to ask for "faster ways" to form the letters and connections.

Sam's major problem in handwriting was his *rate*. Repeated probes indicated that Sam wrote at an average rate of 36 correct letters per minute. When he was asked to write as neatly as he could, his rate dropped to 25 letters per minute. By contrast, Groff (1961) cited 50 correct letters per minute as the normal rate for students in Sam's grade. Freedman (1954) suggested 72 letters per minute, and Starlin (1982) recently suggested a rate of 100 letters per minute as the criterion for fluency, regardless of age or grade.

Because Sam wrote more slowly than would be expected for his age and yet had superior verbal aptitude, he encountered frustration in completing written assignments, particularly when work was to be done within a prescribed time period. Teachers, too, commented on their exasperation with this student who contributed significantly to class discussions but failed to exhibit the same level of sophistication and analysis on tests. (Recall that social studies tests had just become a problem when Sam was referred.)

Sam's difficulty in forming certain letters and connections reflected the perceptual-motor weakness mentioned by other examiners. One could only speculate about the cause of this problem, but it appeared to be long-standing. The mathematics problems reported by Sam's teachers did not exhibit themselves on either of the standardized tests given previously (PIAT, SDMT). The reason for this apparent discrepancy rested in the response requirements of the two formal measures; neither required much handwriting because they are administered in a multiple-choice format.

Selection of Treatment

As a result of the extremely fine-grained analysis of Sam's penmanship difficulties, the selection of a treatment plan was obvious: to provide a treatment that would directly affect Sam's rate and legibility of cursive writing. Two possibilities existed. One was a treatment program focusing on a "process model." Under this model, Sam would engage in exercises akin to penmanship, such as copying and figure

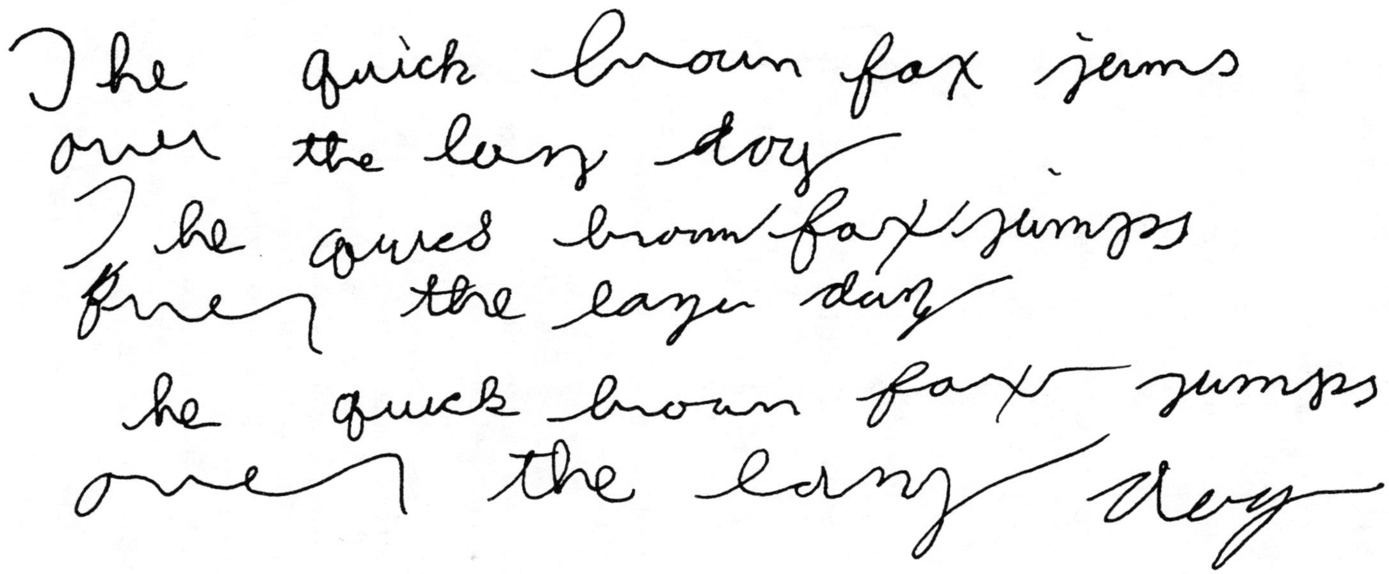

Figure 25.1. Handwriting sample.

drawing. (In fact, Sam's mother had proposed a studio art class for this exact purpose.)

In Sam's case, the second treatment option was chosen: to enroll in a "direct instruction model" of penmanship remediation, in which he would spend most of his time forming actual cursive letters and connections with time limits. Sam's age and grade in school played a major role in this decision, since the increasingly advanced demands of his curriculum required as fast an effective remediation program as possible. The direct instruction model of penmanship was viewed to have better empirical validation than the process model (see Kerr & Lambert, 1982).

Course of Treatment

Sam began an intensive (i.e., 30 minutes daily) remediation program focusing on speed, and on accuracy of problem letters, digits, and connections. Materials for this program, developed at the Center, were mailed to Sam on a biweekly basis. In addition, the following suggestions were offered:

1. Sam should be allowed to use any reasonable writing instrument of his choice. (He seemed to write better with instruments of a large circumference.)

2. Sam should have more time than the other students to express himself fully on written assignments. (His school was to be informed of the situation, so that necessary arrangements could be made.)

3. Sam's math assignments in the future should be in *both* timed and untimed formats, since his problems in this area probably reflected his handwriting difficulty.

4. Sam should be encouraged to report on problems he encounters in writing specific letters, because self-evaluation information is essential to the ongoing assessment and treatment of his problem.

5. Sam should be reassured about his general excellent learning abilities. High standards in *nonwritten* academic tasks (e.g., reading) and in "student responsibilities" (e.g., meeting due dates, finishing projects) should be held up to remind him of his general competence in these nonproblem areas.

6. Whenever appropriate, handwritten tasks should be replaced with an alternative means of communication (e.g., taping notes rather than writing them, phone calls in lieu of letters)

or reduced (e.g., postcards instead of letters), to prevent Sam from experiencing inordinate frustration.

7. Sam's pediatrician should be consulted regarding the possible benefits of muscle-strengthening exercises.

Because examiners and teachers had commented on Sam's poor organization of work materials, suggestions for studying were made. (The author noticed a tendency on Sam's part to hurry through tasks, possibly to compensate for the slowness with which he completed them.) Sam also exhibited poor proofreading skills. The following were suggestions for general study habits:

1. Sam's teachers should be consulted for advice on study habits to emphasize at home.
2. Sam should be trained to proofread his work, looking especially for spelling, punctuation, and arithmetic errors.
3. Sam may have had few opportunities to practice proofreading, if he had used all allotted time to write down his ideas and answers. Therefore, he should be given the opportunity to proofread his own work and should be strongly reinforced for doing so.

Periodic "timings" of Sam's handwriting served as progress measures. A "timing" refers to the sampling of a behavior – in this instance, the number of properly (and improperly) formed letters, digits, and connections produced per minute. Sam was taught to time himself informally, using a digital stopwatch. For formal measures of progress, his clinician or teacher conducted three-minute timings.

It should be noted that studies of penmanship remediation emphasize the importance of conducting reliability checks, or comparisons of two persons' evaluations of a writing sample. Sam often served as his own reliability checker, while the clinician and teacher regularly compared their evaluations for reliability.

Sam's progress was reflected by an increase (to the level of grade-peers) in his correct handwriting rate. After four months, he was able to produce 65 correct letters per minute.

Termination and Follow-up

Sam was released from his remediation program once his penmanship improved to the grade-peer level. Five timings, conducted across two weeks, confirmed the stability of his newly acquired fluency. For purposes of tapping a broad range of writing tasks, the timings included all 26 letters, the digits, and connections, both in and out of context.

Overall Evaluation

Sam, a specifically learning disabled child, responded successfully to the treatment outlined by a psychoeducational assessment team evaluating his poor penmanship. Previous attempts to isolate the source of Sam's academic difficulties had overlooked the pervasive and critical role of handwriting in other academic subjects, including mathematics. Misguided remediation efforts, exclusively on improving *accuracy* of handwriting, had failed to treat the essential problem of *rate*.

This case illustrates several key points in the identification and treatment of any learning problem. First, a *multidisciplinary* team of specialists often combs through previous test reports, school files, and parent interview information finding new clues about the apparent difficulty. This task is best shared, with each specialist independently reviewing the chart prior to any case discussions. Second, we know that children frequently offer some of the most useful information about their difficulties. Careful interviewing and interactive assessment procedures allow this information to surface. Third, systematic assessment, begun in the evaluation phase, should be continued throughout treatment. Teaching this to the child and his parents may help overcome their previous frustration with apparently conflicting test results — results that often accrue because of diverse response demands and test formats. Finally, the clinician confronted with a possible learning disability must have patience and a flexible schedule. The assessment described above required nearly 24 clinician hours, with several case conferences called throughout to discuss and compare findings.

References

Freedman, F. (1954). Teaching handwriting. *What Research Says to Teachers, 4,* 1–33.

Groff, P. (1961). New speeds in handwriting. *Elementary English, 38,* 564–565.

Haring, N. G., Lovitt, T. C., Eaton, M. D., & Hansen, C. L. (1978). *The fourth R: Research in the classroom.* Columbus, OH: Charles E. Merrill.

Kerr, M. M., & Lambert, D. L. (1982). Behavior modification of children's written language. In M. Hersen, R. M. Eisler, & P. M. Miller (Eds.), *Progress in behavior modification.* New York: Academic Press.

Starlin, C. (1982). Reading and writing: Iowa Monograph. Des Moines: Iowa State Department of Public Instruction.

26

Self-Abuse

Trevor F. Stokes
Pamela G. Osnes

Description of the Disorder

The three clients described were diagnosed as displaying behavior consistent with the pervasive developmental disorder *Infantile Autism* (299. 0x, *DSM-III*). They displayed problems in their responsiveness during interactions with other people and in their communication skills. Onset of these problems was usually noted at a very young age, although some diagnoses were made without clear evidence of an early onset. Tantruming, ritualistic, self-stimulatory, and self-abusive behaviors were also evident. Mental retardation, either mild (317.0) or severe (318.2) was also diagnosed, which reflected deficits in intelligence and adaptive behavior. One client was diagnosed with Tourette's disorder (307.23), a stereotyped movement disorder which includes multiple vocal tics.

Case Identification

Consultative services were requested of the authors by the director of a short-term residential facility for the assessment and treatment of children who were autistic, retarded, and developmentally delayed and who displayed various behavior problems. This report summarizes the consultation concerning three children whose major presenting problem was frequent self-abuse. The agency had a progressive and sophisticated program that based its treatment on the principles of behavior therapy. The goal of the program was to provide training so that clients could be placed in the least restrictive appropriate environment.

Robert

The first client, Robert, was a nine-year-old autistic boy who had been removed from his home at the age of three because of neglect. He now lived with foster parents who were in their 50s. Records indicated that a first-grade teacher was the first to report self-abuse, which occurred from the beginning of her contact with Robert. She felt that self-abuse started excessively when demands were placed on Robert. Robert had been in a special school program but difficulties had occurred because of his unmanageable self-abuse. He had been at the current facility for eight months, and it was expected that he would return to the special school program in five months after an effective behavior management program had been developed.

Steven

The second client, Steven, was a 17-year-old autistic boy who also was diagnosed as mildly mentally retarded and for Tourette's disorder. Steven lived with his parents in a small rural town. He attended a school for the deaf and blind prior to his current placement. He had congenital cataracts as an infant, which were removed when he was a few months old. Currently, Steven is almost blind, having only light perception in one eye. A self-inflicted eye injury resulted in loss of the other eye. Aggressive, destructive, and self-abusive behavior were prohibitive to further enrollment at his previous school. If the current placement was successful, Steven would transfer again to his previous school.

Brian

The third client, Brian, was a 13-year-old autistic boy who was also diagnosed as severely mentally retarded. Brian also had a history of seizures. Consultation with Brian's classroom teacher was requested because she had expressed difficulty in controlling his self-abuse.

Brian's records showed that problems had occurred since he was two
and a half years old, when speech was delayed and he showed signs
of hyperactivity.

Presenting Complaints

All three cases presented problems with self-abusive behavior that
had proven to be difficult to manage. Consultation in assessment,
treatment planning, and staff training in behavior management techniques was requested.

Robert was referred primarily because of excessive head banging with either arm to the forehead. He rarely hit his head against
walls or floors, although he hit the walls with his hand. Behavior problems also reported by staff were self-stimulation, tantruming, language and communication deficits, noncompliance with instructions,
inattention to task, and not sitting in a chair for any period of time.

Steven was referred because of self-abusive, aggressive, and destructive behaviors. Self-abusive behavior consisted primarily of head
banging, back hitting, and hand biting. Aggression included biting
and kicking, which usually occurred during tantrums. Destructive
behavior consisted of kicking walls and windows, banging doors, and
butting windows and walls with his head. Besides the physical injury
to Steven, this activity resulted in extensive and costly physical
damage to facilities. Bizarre verbalizations and swearing were also
presented.

Brian was referred because of self-abusive behavior in the classroom which included hits to the forehead and chin with his hand. In
addition, his off-task, out-of-seat behavior prohibited skill acquisition.
Aggressive behavior was also noted.

History

Robert had been in many special programs since an early age. For
six months prior to consultation, he had worn a brace on his right
arm that did not allow bending at the elbow and thereby prevented
him from striking his head. His other hand was tied with a cord and
held at the waist. Robert wore a neck and back brace for scoliosis (a
side twist of the spine). He received Thorazine (chlorpromazine hydrochloride) 10 mg q.i.d. and Haldol (haloperidol) 4 mg q.i.d. Although
he once was able to feed himself, he now was fed by staff members.

It was reported that whenever the restraining arm brace was removed, Robert would commence head banging.

Steven had a long history of abusive and aggressive behaviors. This had resulted in numerous placements and in permanent physical injury to himself. He was capable of many independent behaviors including dressing, eating, and conversation. Steven received Valium (diazepam) and chloral hydrate during the day and as an aid to sleeping.

Brian had a five-year history of self-abusive behavior, including head and ear banging. Behavior modification techniques had been somewhat successful in previous special programs. Physical restraint and time-out were noted in his records as having been used for self-abuse. Mechanical restraint had not been recommended. Brian was receiving four medications: Mellaril (thioridazine hydrochloride) 25 mg b.i.d., Tranxene (clorazepate dipotassium) 15 mg t.i.d., Serentil (mesoridazine besylate) 100 mg/day, and Ritalin (methylphenidate hydrochloride) 20 mg b.i.d.

Assessment

In each case, the assessment and functional analysis of the child's behavior involved development of a precise and objective description of the behaviors and their controlling environments. The goal of this assessment was to analyze the functional relationship between events antecedent to the behavior, the behavior which was the clinical target, and the consequences which followed the occurrence of the behavior. The assessment also included an analysis of the client's behavioral excesses, deficits, and assets. In addition, it included a survey of the client's functional environment to provide an overview of consequences that might give clues as to which consequences could be used to reinforce or punish behaviors targeted for treatment (Stokes, in press).

Robert

Initial direct observation of Robert revealed the following behavior problems: hits by the fist to the forehead, chin, and temple, weaving of the head, hand and wrist flapping, finger flicking, table tapping, lying on the floor, mouthing objects, whining, grunting, grimacing, leaving his chair and the room during demand situations, and jumping in place while out-of-seat. The staff described potential reinforcers in the initial survey as milk, Coke, juices, pudding, M&Ms, apples, swimming, swinging, and music.

Robert then was observed directly by the consultants in order to assess possible differences in self-stimulatory and self-abusive problem behaviors with the restraints in place and without them. A simple instructional task, a pegboard, was used. During a 10-minute evaluation with restraints on, Robert had no head bangs, 2 head weaves per minute, 6 finger taps on table per minute, 15 finger flicks per minute, and left his seat once per minute. With restraints off for 10 minutes, Robert hit his head 41 times per minute, engaged in 2 head weaves per minute, 5 finger taps on table per minute, 6 finger flicks per minute, and left his seat once every 5 minutes. Clearly, restraint was an effective procedure in controlling self-abuse, but it was not an acceptable procedure to be used over time because of its restrictive nature.

Attention then turned to the demand situations in the child's classroom and in other areas at the facility. Robert currently was receiving management and training continuously by one staff member. His individual educational plan (I.E.P.) was in need of expansion to include a larger number of skill-development areas. Compliance with instructions was deficient. Speech and self-help skills (e.g., use of utensils at mealtime) also needed to be improved. In consultation with Robert's teacher and other staff, a comprehensive list of goals was developed. These goals included behaviors to be both increased and decreased. Behaviors to be increased included compliance with instructions, eye contact with staff, periods of time without head banging or self-stimulation, periods of quiet, independent self-help behaviors (feeding self, opening doors, dressing, toileting), academic task completion, and verbalizations. Behaviors to be decreased included head banging, head weaving, self-stimulation (mouthing hand and objects, table tapping, wrist and finger flicking), jumping in place, ankle bending, rocking side to side, whining, and crying.

Observation of Robert suggested that access to the arm-brace restraint may have been functioning as a reinforcer for head banging. That is, it was observed that when restraints were removed, head banging increased and at the same time Robert would try to reach out and grab the restraints. In addition, even though it was possible to head bang while in restraints, there was a clear increase in head banging without restraints. Furthermore, it was observed that when staff members moved to get the restraints to put them back on Robert, his rate of head banging dramatically decreased. Therefore the consultants tested a procedure in which Robert gained access to the restraints by exhibiting short periods of time without head banging.

Effects were not immediate, but after a few sessions, this manipulation resulted in a decrease in the rate of self-abuse. In addition, the function of praise, physical contact and affection, and liquids (water, juice) were tested to see whether they could be used to increase such behaviors as sitting in seat and establishing eye contact with an adult.

It was also noted that Robert's crying and whining often was followed by instructions from staff members to discontinue those behaviors or followed by questions asking him what he wanted. It was hypothesized that such attention might be functioning as a reinforcer for whining and crying.

Steven

Initial direct observation of Steven revealed the following behavior problems: head hitting, back hitting, hand biting, head weaving, eye rubbing, finger flicking, wrist flapping, rocking, table pounding, and masturbation. In addition, there were repetitive head jerking (tics), various sounds and grunts, and coprolalia (utterance of obscenities). The staff described potential reinforcers as water and soft drinks, peanut butter cups, walks outside, music, attention, praise, conversation, applause, headshakes, pats on the back, and tickling.

When the consultants worked with Steven, some self-abusive and self-stimulatory behavior were displayed: In a period of five minutes, there were no head hits, three hand bites per minute, two back hits per minute, three eye, hand, or face touches per minute, five finger flicks per minute, three episodes of body rocking per minute, three episodes of body rocking per minute, one occurrence of rubbing the genitals, eight head weaves per minute, and two "Agh" sounds per minute. Aggression did not occur. It was decided to test the effect of attention on Steven's behavior. It had been observed that staff members provided a great deal of attention following both appropriate and inappropriate behaviors. Therefore, a DRO contingency was implemented during a spelling task. The word to be spelled was not presented unless Steven had been quiet and had not engaged in self-abusive or self-stimulatory behavior for two seconds. Within five minutes, this requirement was increased to five seconds. Steven began sitting appropriately for longer periods of time. He had protested at first, saying "Where are you? Say something," but after an initial brief burst, his behavior came under the control of the contingency. It was also noted in observations that Steven worked to be "in control." Frequently it seemed that he was able to coerce and scare people into doing what he wanted. For example, at one point he demanded that an academic task be ended after about 15 minutes. The consultant then required another 5 minutes of work before ending the task requirements. This ensured that tasks did not end immediately following Steven's demands.

It was also observed that staff members refrained from touching Steven except when they needed to restrain him during self-abusive behavior. The consultants worked with Steven to test his reaction to affectionate touch. He enjoyed handshakes, a pat on the back, and an arm around his shoulders. Usually, these were preceded by a comment so that Steven would not be surprised by suddenly feeling the touch. The affectionate touch seemed to be a positive consequence for Steven. The effect of using tape recorded music was also tested, with positive results.

Further observation of staff and Steven showed that both self-abusive and aggressive behavior occurred in two situations: when staff members did not comply with his demands, and when Steven attempted to escape from a demand situation. In both cases, he engaged in behaviors likely to prove aversive to staff (i.e., self-abuse and aggression). The staff likely were maintaining these behaviors by allowing Steven to obtain what he wanted or to escape from their demands.

Brian

Initial direct observation of Brian revealed the following behavior problems: head hitting, chin hitting, standing up and moving from his desk, and looking around the room for long periods of time while seated at his desk. A hands-held-down restraint for 10 seconds was used whenever Brian hit his head, and popcorn and free time were given contingent upon task completion. Brian had been placed at the end of the room by himself because of the severity of his problem behaviors. Observation of the interactions with the teacher showed that Brian hit his head more frequently when the teacher was at the other end of the room with other children. Whenever Brian hit himself, the teacher needed to move five meters across the room to restrain him. Then he went back to his task for a few seconds. The teacher provided some attention and praise and returned to work with the other children. Brian would work for a further 5 to 20 seconds and then hit himself again three to six times. The teacher promptly returned to restrain him. If the teacher did not notice the head hitting or was not prompt in returning to restrain Brian, hitting increased in both frequency and intensity. Occasionally, Brian would wander around the classroom or go to the door and leave the room, requiring the teacher to pursue him and bring him back to his desk. He usually would be reprimanded while being returned to his desk. Sometimes Brian would stand up at his desk. He would be told to sit down. If the teacher did not attend to him when he stood up, Brian would hit himself on the head.

Selection of Treatment

Robert

For Robert, restraint, which had been introduced as a procedure to control self-abuse, had apparently developed a reinforcing function (Favell, McGimsey, & Jones, 1978). The restraints could not be removed, however, without the possibility of serious physical harm. Therefore, a treatment was developed that used one minute of the arm-brace restraint as a consequence for periods of time gone without self-abuse and self-stimulatory behavior. At the same time physical restraint for five seconds followed each occurrence of self-abuse. This was a differential reinforcement of other behaviors procedure (DRO). In order to provide a range of positive consequences for the absence of self-abuse, attention in the form of talking, praise, and physical affection were also given. When Robert hit his head or exhibited self-stimulatory behaviors, both arms were held down at his sides for five seconds (Foxx & Azrin, 1973). No verbalization accompanied the restraint or release from restraint, and the staff member looked away from Robert while holding his arms down. Following head weaving, the staff member held Robert's head for five seconds with two hands while looking away and not talking. In a similar manner, jumping and rocking were followed by five seconds of restraint by holding Robert down from behind with two hands on his shoulders. Ankle bending was restrained by holding Robert down at the ankles, with the staff member behind Robert being careful not to let him fall over.

Use of the arm-brace restraints as a reinforcer for the absence of self-abuse and self-stimulation was used according to a changing criterion. The initial requirement was determined to be 10 seconds, which was the length of time that Robert occasionally went without head banging and self-stimulation. As improvements were noted in Robert's behavior, this criterion was increased in length. At the beginning of treatment, the mechanical restraints were removed only during meals and individual academic sessions. These times were expanding as the treatment progressed.

Whining and crying were ignored, which was consistent with the observation that attention may have been maintaining the behaviors.

In addition to these procedures, positive consequences were systematically introduced following the performance of targeted behaviors. That is, attention, praise, affection, physical contact, and drinks of water, milk, and juice were given for compliance with instructions, task completion, periods of time without head banging and self-stimulation, and independent self-help behaviors.

The academic program was expanded to include in-seat work with visual motor tasks, such as a sorting box with shapes, identification and matching of colors, and puzzles. An important target was for Robert to complete tasks independently at his desk without constant supervision and attention from the teacher. The consequences for task completion included access to a positive activity such as a period of play. Individual activities also included verbalization/communication training, and an instructional compliance program involving gross motor activities such as playing with a ball. Self-help activities targeted included walking independently without a staff member holding Robert's hand, opening and closing doors, turning lights on and off, toileting, dressing, and eating and cleaning up after meals.

Steven

For Steven the primary treatment involved the use of attention, affection, and other positive consequences as reinforcers for periods of time without self-abuse, self-stimulation, or aggression and to reinforce increased on-task behavior in academic settings. In addition, staff were trained not to give in to his attempts to control his environment by being self-abusive or aggressive (Carr, Newsom, & Binkoff, 1980). If a demand or instruction was given, the staff were asked to always require compliance or provide follow-through guidance in order to ensure compliance. Steven's complaints and demands were ignored. If self-abuse, self-stimulation, or aggression occurred during a free-time activity, the activity ended at that time. If these behaviors occurred during demand situations (e.g., in classroom), they were ignored and the activity continued. Restraint of arms was not used because bodily injury was not likely to occur and because it meant that Steven had successfully entrapped physical contact with a staff member. Of course, if attention was reinforcing abusive and aggressive behavior, ignoring would be an extinction condition, and an extinction burst of these behaviors might occur. Therefore, the effects of the procedure needed to be carefully monitored and changes made if the problem behaviors escalated in frequency or severity to levels in which tissue damage was likely.

Another goal of treatment for Steven was to increase performance during academic periods. Positive consequences (i.e., praise, affection, soft drinks, and crackers) were given contingent upon periods of appropriate on-task work without self-abuse, self-stimulation, or aggression. He also earned a break from work to play in the adjacent gym or to listen to music. Breaks of three minutes were earned, for example, following 10 minutes of good work. If self-abuse, self-stimulation, or aggression occurred during the break, Steven was immediately returned to the classroom and given another task.

Brian

For Brian the treatment involved the manipulation of the teacher's attention and activity consequences so that there was a consistent positive consequence following on-task behavior and the absence of self-abuse. Restraint was still used contingently upon head banging, although the type of restraint was modified slightly. Apparently, Brian had been successfully controlling the teacher's attention through his self-abuse. He would work for only brief periods of time before self-abuse in order to recruit the teacher's proximity and attention. Instead of holding his arms down at his side while standing in front of Brian, the teacher began to hold his arm down across his stomach, with the teacher standing or kneeling behind him so as to minimize physical contact and eye contact.

In addition, the placement of desks was reorganized so that Brian was close to the other children and the teacher would not need to move far to restrain him following head banging. Furthermore, after a period of on-task behavior (e.g., five minutes or the completion of a task), Brian was allowed to leave his desk to play in the other part of the room for a few minutes. If Brian hit his head during this time, he was immediately returned to work and given another task.

Course of Treatment

Robert

For Robert the staff members kept records on the number of head bangs during sample 15-minute observations. In addition, the total time spent out of the arm-brace restraint was monitored. The goal of treatment was to see a decrease in the rate of head banging while at the same time increasing the time Robert spent out of restraints.

During the initial assessments, Robert was head banging 30–60 times per minute. After the beginning of treatment, this reduced to 5 to 15 times per minute. However, after this initial decrease in three weeks, there was an increase in both self-abusive and self-stimulatory behavior. The staff suggested that more "aversive" consequences be built into the program. The consultants encouraged the treatment managers to persist because the program had been working. Monitoring of the fidelity of treatment implementation and ensuring that positive consequences were enthusiastically presented following the absence of self-abuse and self-stimulation were regarded as more critical areas for attention. The positive program of treatment was not changed, and within two weeks the rates of self-abuse and self-stimulation were decreasing again. The rate of head banging reduced to one or two per minute while the time without restraints was increased to many hours.

The feedback given to staff members during the course of Robert's treatment included the following: Keep a list of positive consequences that may function as reinforcers of Robert's behavior. Stick to the program when using restraint—don't try to intervene with every inappropriate behavior that may occur. Resist the temptation to respond to approximations of head hitting. Devote attention to what Robert is doing well rather than acting according to the prediction of what he may do wrong. Increase rather than decrease demand situations. Decrease the latency between inappropriate behavior and physical restraint as well as between appropriate behavior and positive consequences.

Because of the intensive nature of this program, one-to-one management occurred at the beginning of the treatment. It was essential, however, that this ratio be changed so that Robert did not always have a staff member available. Thus, more children were included in activities with Robert and multiple staff members in multiple settings were used in the program of treatment. Training of many staff members to implement these procedures was itself a comprehensive program.

Steven

For Steven the staff members monitored self-abusive behaviors. These decreased from an average of 394 per day in the first five days of the program to an average of 48 per day for the five days at the end of one month of treatment. Self-abusive behavior included head and back hitting and eye poking. Aggression (hitting, biting, kicking, spitting, punching, and throwing objects) decreased from 231 per day in the first five days of the program to an average of 3 per day for the five days at the end of one month of treatment.

Feedback given to staff members during the course of Steven's treatment included the following: Because of his blindness, Steven should always be told who is present. Do not try to coax him into being calm. Provide positive attention enthusiastically. Vary the content of praise – do not say the same thing every time. Talk to Steven as a young adult; do not treat him as a retarded person with nothing to say. Give him choices when there is a choice; otherwise provide a clear instruction. Do not deliver praise and affection for working too soon after Steven stops engaging in self-stimulation. Attend positively to Steven's compliance with instructions. Do not attend to answers to questions when they have been given five seconds or more following the question. During academic work, provide positive consequences both for correct answers and for on-task behaviors.

The intensive supervision of Steven was decreased while he continued to show improvements. For example, no one staff member worked exclusively with Steven, even if he/she had been hired to implement Steven's program. Staff members in the classroom and at mealtimes, for example, attended to the programs of other children as well as to Steven.

Brian

For Brian the teacher monitored head banging during two sample 15-minute periods per day. Frequency of head banging reduced dramatically from a rate of 16 times per minute to one per five minutes within three weeks. He also showed improved on-task performance at his desk.

Feedback given to the teacher during the course of treatment included the following: Use differential attention by praising other children when Brian is off-task. Praise Brian from across the room rather than walking over to him every time. Occasionally pair a question or instruction with praise of Brian's behavior. Develop a diversity of positive consequences and activities to follow appropriate work. If Brian gets out of his seat return him briskly without talking to him. Make a discrimination in voice tone between neutral instructions and positive, enthusiastic praise. Do not repeat instructions. Follow through with guidance following noncompliance.

The teacher also asked for advice concerning the medications that Brian was receiving. Because the consultants were not qualified to make judgment about them, the teacher was encouraged to seek advice from the child's physician because the length of time on some medications may have been inappropriate and a review of all medications may not have been conducted recently. The child's father, who was a physician, subsequently took the child off all of his medications and reviewed the case with the child's pediatrician.

Termination

Robert's program continued successfully for four months prior to his return to his previous school placement. A teacher from that school visited this agency to observe the conduct of Robert's program, and a staff member from this agency visited the school after Robert's transfer to assist the teachers in their implementation of treatment procedures.

Steven's program continued successfully for two months. His parents were trained to use the effective procedures. It was observed near the end of Steven's stay in the facility that he sat outside on a bench talking with his father without occurrences of self-abuse, self-stimulation, or aggression. The parents effectively used differential attention procedures. They were extremely happy with the outcome. Staff from the facility visited the deaf and blind school. They continued working directly with Steven in that setting, and then reduced their contact and feedback as the staff continued to implement the procedures effectively.

Brian's program continued successfully for three months. The parents continued to enjoy the increased time that Brian was able to spend at home.

Follow-up

The consultants visited the special school attended by Robert two months after his transfer. Unfortunately, because Robert was presenting some problems, the staff had decided to return him to the arm-brace restraint for much of his day. A 10-minute observation of

Robert when he was out of restraint during lunch showed that he engaged in head banging eight times a minute. This rate would have been higher except that the teacher prevented many attempted hits by using physical restraint. The interaction between Robert and the teacher could generally be characterized as the teacher's providing noncontingent attention and preventive physical restraint. In discussion concerning Robert, the staff noted that they wanted to make the restraint more aversive. The consultants described the successful program again and urged the school staff to follow it.

The consultants' last contact with Steven was following his successful transfer back to the school for deaf and blind children. Reports of Steven's progress continue to be positive. At the school for the deaf and blind he is described as a model student.

The teacher reported that Brian continues to do very well in his program four months after the conclusion of consultation.

Overall Evaluation

All three clients improved significantly while in the residential program, although generalization and maintenance of changes was notable with only two clients. A thorough analysis of operating functional contingencies proved essential to the development and implementation of the individual treatment strategies. The programs described were intensive, thus requiring additional procedures to make them approximate typical conditions. Programming generalization during transitions and parent training in addition to the training of residential staff was also essential (Stokes & Osnes, in press).

Accountability of programs was emphasized within the facility, both in terms of written individual plans of treatment and in systematic continuous collection of program data to allow analysis of program effectiveness. The cooperation and involvement of the voluntary institutional human rights committee was also critical. It should also be noted that the advocacy of parents, staff, and groups supporting programs for children with developmental disabilities was important in these cases. The three clients were sent to this special program because of pressure from the children's advocates.

References

Carr, E. G., Newsom, C. D., & Binkoff, J. A. (1980). Escape as a factor in the aggressive behavior of two retarded children. *Journal of Applied Behavior Analysis, 13,* 101–117.

Favell, J. E., McGimsey, J. F., & Jones, M. L. (1978). The use of physical restraint in the treatment of self-injury and as positive reinforcement. *Journal of Applied Behavior Analysis, 11,* 225–241.

Foxx, R. M., & Azrin, N. H. (1973). The elimination of autistic self-stimulatory behavior by overcorrection. *Journal of Applied Behavior Analysis, 6,* 1–14.

Stokes, T. F. (in press). Contingency management. In A. S. Bellack & M. Hersen (Eds.), *Dictionary of behavior therapy techniques.* New York: Pergamon Press.

Stokes, T. F., & Osnes, P. G. (in press). Programming the generalization of children's social behavior. In P. S. Strain, M. J. Guralnick, & H. Walker (Eds.), *Children's social behavior: Development, assessment and modification.* New York: Wiley.

Index